# A SHORTER HISTORY OF ROME

# A SHORTER
# HISTORY OF ROME

BY

M. CARY

*Author of 'A History of Rome'*

AND

JOHN WILSON

LONDON

MACMILLAN & CO LTD

NEW YORK · ST MARTIN'S PRESS

1965

*First Edition 1963*
*Reprinted 1965*




MACMILLAN AND COMPANY LIMITED
*St Martin's Street London WC2*
*also Bombay Calcutta Madras Melbourne*

THE MACMILLAN COMPANY OF CANADA LIMITED
*70 Bond Street Toronto 2*

ST MARTIN'S PRESS INC
*175 Fifth Avenue New York 10010 NY*




PRINTED IN GREAT BRITAIN

# PREFACE

ANYONE who undertakes an abbreviated adaptation of so well-known and so comprehensive a work as the late Professor Cary's *History of Rome* cannot avoid feeling, if he takes his job seriously, that he is in some sense a trespasser and a mangler of masterpieces. It is rather like trying to reduce a French château into a block of modern flats. My first concern, therefore, must be to apologise to those people — and there must be many — to whom Professor Cary's original work has for long been the Authorised Version, as it were, of Roman history.

I feel, however, that I can justifiably plead necessity : the necessity arising from the needs of a modern, less leisured and more competitive age, and in particular from the vastly increased numbers of students who are now studying Roman history as a part-time subject or at an elementary level, whether for examination purposes or not. For these students in particular a less spacious version is essential. They need, above all, the basic facts set out in a clear, logical and coherent manner. Roman history is notoriously complex, and I have tried to arrange the material in such a way that any reader will be able to distinguish, analyse and master the facts relating to different periods and subjects without difficulty, whilst at the same time attempting to preserve something of the wide scope and comprehensiveness of the original work.

This has not been easy : and though judicious rearrangement has enabled nearly all the essential facts in the original to reappear in this adaptation, it has been impossible to support or enlarge on many points to the extent that I would have wished. There may thus be much which is open to doubt or scholarly criticism : and in answer to this I can only plead shortage of space. It is my hope, however, that its merits as an educational textbook may go some way towards making up for its deficiencies as a work of scholarship.

I should like to express my thanks to Mr. C. E. Stevens of Magdalen College, Oxford, for teaching me practically everything I know about Roman history : to Messrs. Macmillan for constant help and guidance in producing the book : to Dr. H. H. Scullard for assistance on many important points : and above all to the Trustees of the Cary Estate for allowing the work to go forward.

JOHN WILSON

# CONTENTS

|  |  | PAGE |
|---|---|---|
| PREFACE | | v |

### CHAPTER I

## THE GEOGRAPHICAL BACKGROUND

| (A) | The Mediterranean | 1 |
| (B) | Italy | 1 |
| (C) | Latium | 5 |
| (D) | Rome | 7 |

### CHAPTER II

## ITALY BEFORE THE RISE OF ROME

| (A) | Early Peoples of Italy | 9 |
| (B) | The Greeks | 11 |
| (C) | The Etruscans | 12 |
| (D) | The Origins of Rome | 16 |

### CHAPTER III

## ROME IN THE PERIOD OF THE KINGS

| (A) | The Seven Kings | 20 |
| (B) | Economic Conditions | 23 |
| (C) | Social and Political Conditions | 24 |
| (D) | The Army | 28 |

### CHAPTER IV

## THE CONQUEST OF ITALY

### Part 1: *500–350 B.C.*

| (A) | Rome and Latium | 29 |
| (B) | Sabines, Aequi and Volsci | 31 |

PAGE

(c) The Etruscans ... 32
(d) The Gauls ... 33

### Part 2 : *350–264 B.C.*

(A) The First Samnite War ... 34
(B) The Second Samnite War ... 36
(c) The Third Samnite War ... 39
(d) The War with Tarentum ... 41

### Part 3 : *War, Politics and Economics*

(A) Military Growth ... 44
(B) The Political Organisation of Italy ... 47
(c) Economic Conditions ... 50

### CHAPTER V

### POLITICS OF THE EARLY REPUBLIC

(A) The First Republican Constitution ... 53
(B) The Plebeians ... 54
(c) Legislation ... 57
    1. The Twelve Tables ... 57
    2. Economic Legislation ... 58
(d) New Assemblies ... 59
    1. The Comitia Centuriata ... 59
    2. The Comitia Tributa ... 62
(E) Plebeians in the Magistracies and the Senate ... 63
(F) Changes in the Magistrates ... 64

### CHAPTER VI

### CONQUEST OF THE WEST

### Part 1 : *The First Punic War*

(A) Carthage ... 67
(B) The Affair of Messana ... 71
(c) War in Sicily ... 72

PAGE

(D)  The Invasion of Africa                                   73
(E)  Later Operations in Sicily                               74
(F)  The Capture of Sardinia and Corsica                      75

### Part 2 : *The Second Punic War*

(A)  The Carthaginian Conquests in Spain                      75
(B)  The Affair of Saguntum                                   76
(C)  Hannibal's Invasion of Italy                             77
(D)  The Roman Effort after Cannae                            79
(E)  End of the War in Italy                                  80
(F)  The War in Sicily                                        81
(G)  The Scipios in Spain                                     81
(H)  The War in Africa                                        83

### Part 3 : *Italy, Spain and Gaul*

(A)  Italy                                                    84
        1.  The Last Gallic Invasion                          84
        2.  South Italy                                       85
        3.  North Italy                                       88
        4.  Liguria                                           88
        5.  Istria                                            89
(B)  Spain                                                    89
(C)  Gaul                                                     92

### Part 4 : *The Third Punic War*

(A)  Rome, Carthage and Numidia                               93
(B)  The War                                                  95

CHAPTER VII

# CONQUEST OF THE EAST

### Part 1 : *Greece*

(A)  Early Contacts between Rome and Greece                   97
(B)  The First Macedonian War                                 98
(C)  Pergamum, Rhodes and Rome                                98
(D)  The Second Macedonian War                                99

PAGE

(E)  Antiochus III and the Aetolians            101
(F)  The Third Macedonian War                  102
(G)  The Fourth Macedonian War                 103
(H)  Rome and the Greek Cities                 104

## Part 2 : *Asia*

(A)  The War against Antiochus                 105
(B)  Rome and the East from 188 to 129 B.C.    108
        1. Pergamum                            109
        2. The Seleucids                       109
        3. Egypt                               109

### CHAPTER VIII

# ROMAN GOVERNMENT DOWN TO 133 B.C.

## Part 1 : *Provincial Government*

(A)  The Dependent Kings and Cities            111
(B)  Political Status                          112
(C)  The Provincial Governors                  113
(D)  Finance and Economics                     114
(E)  The Defects of Roman Rule                 116
(F)  Attempts at Reform                        117

## Part 2 : *Roman Politics and Economics*

(A)  The Assemblies                            119
(B)  The Nobles                                120
(C)  The Magistracies                          123
(D)  Reforms in the Legal System              124
(E)  Finance                                   125
(F)  Italy                                     125
(G)  The Army                                  126
(H)  Economic Conditions                       127
        1. Agriculture                         127
        2. Slave-labour                        128
        3. Industry and Trade                  130

CHAPTER IX

133–90 B.C.

## Part 1 : *Politics at Rome*

PAGE
(A)  133–132 B.C. : Tiberius Gracchus                     133
(B)  132–123 B.C.                                          136
(C)  123–122 B.C. : Caius Gracchus                        139
(D)  122–103 B.C.                                          142
(E)  103–99 B.C. : Saturninus and Marius                  144
(F)  99–90 B.C. : Livius Drusus                           146

## Part 2 : *Foreign Wars*

(A)  The War against Jugurtha                             148
(B)  The Invasion of the Northmen                         150
(C)  Marius' Army Reforms                                 152
(D)  The Slave War in Sicily                              153

CHAPTER X

90–60 B.C.

## Part 1 : *Rome and Italy*

(A)  The Italian War                                      154
(B)  Sulla and his Enemies in Rome                        157
        1. Marius                                         157
        2. Cinna and Carbo                                159
(C)  Sulla's Rule in Rome                                 161
(D)  Lepidus                                              165
(E)  The Slave War in Italy                               165
(F)  Pompey, Crassus and Caesar                           166
        1. 73–66 B.C.                                     166
        2. 66–63 B.C.                                     170
        3. 62–60 B.C.                                     172

Part 2 : *Foreign Wars*                          PAGE

(A) Mithridates and Tigranes                        175
    1. 90–80 B.C.                              175
    2. 80–63 B.C.                              177
(B) Sertorius                                       180
(C) The Pirates                                     181
(D) Pompey's Settlement of the East                 182


CHAPTER XI

60–44 B.C.

Part 1 : *Caesar in Gaul*

(A) Background History                              185
(B) 58–56 B.C.                                      187
(C) 55–49 B.C.                                      188

Part 2 : *Politics at Rome to 49 B.C.*

(A) 58–57 B.C.                                      191
(B) 56–52 B.C.                                      192
(C) 51–49 B.C.                                      195

Part 3 : *The Civil War*

(A) 49–48 B.C.                                      196
    1. Italy and Spain                        196
    2. Dyrrachium and Pharsalus               198
(B) 47–45 B.C.                                      199
    1. Egypt and the East                     199
    2. Thapsus and Munda                      200

Part 4 : *Caesar in Power*

(A) Reforms and Reconstruction                      201
    1. Rome and Italy                         201
    2. The Provinces                          202
(B) Political Powers and Death                      204

### CHAPTER XII
### 44–31 B.C.

#### Part 1 : *The Death of the Republic*

|  |  | PAGE |
|---|---|---|
| (A) | The Rule of Antony | 207 |
| (B) | The Second Triumvirate | 210 |

#### Part 2 : *The Victory of Octavian*

| (A) | 42–40 B.C. | 213 |
|---|---|---|
| (B) | 40–36 B.C. | 214 |
|  | 1. The War with Sextus Pompeius | 214 |
|  | 2. Antony in the East | 215 |
| (C) | 36–30 B.C. | 216 |

#### Part 3 : *Economic Conditions by the End of the Republic*

| (A) | Agriculture | 218 |
|---|---|---|
| (B) | Industry and Trade | 220 |

### CHAPTER XIII
### AUGUSTUS

| (A) | Augustus and Caesar | 224 |
|---|---|---|
| (B) | Constitutional Settlement | 226 |
| (C) | The Civil Service | 230 |
| (D) | Rome and Italy | 232 |
| (E) | Moral, Social and Religious Laws | 233 |
| (F) | Frontiers of the Empire | 235 |
|  | 1. Africa and the Red Sea | 238 |
|  | 2. Asia Minor and the Euphrates | 238 |
|  | 3. Western Europe | 239 |
|  | 4. The Danube | 241 |
| (G) | Military Reforms | 243 |
| (H) | Provincial Administration | 245 |

PAGE

(I) Finance                                                   247

(J) The Succession                                            248


CHAPTER XIV

THE EMPIRE A.D. 14–68: CONSOLIDATION

(A) The Emperors                                             250

    1. Tiberius (A.D. 14–37)                          250

    2. Caligula (A.D. 37–41)                         252

    3. Claudius (A.D. 41–54)                         253

    4. Nero (A.D. 54–68)                             255

(B) The Constitution                                         257

(C) Frontiers of the Empire                                 258

    1. Africa                                        259

    2. Judaea                                        259

    3. Armenia and Parthia                           260

    4. The Danube                                    262

    5. Germany                                       263

    6. The Conquest of Britain                       264

(D) Provincial Administration                               265

(E) Finance                                                 267

(F) Economic Conditions                                     268

    1. Agriculture                                   268

    2. Industry and Trade                            269


CHAPTER XV

THE EMPIRE A.D. 68–180: STABILITY

Part 1: *A.D. 68–96*

(A) Civil War A.D. 68–69                                    275

    1. Summer 68 to January 69                       275

    2. January to July 69                            276

    3. July 69 to Summer 70                          278

# CONTENTS

(B) The Emperors                                    280
    1. Vespasian (A.D. 70–79)                    280
    2. Titus (A.D. 79–81)                         281
    3. Domitian (A.D. 81–96)                      281
    4. The Opposition                             281
(C) The Constitution                                282
(D) Rome and Italy                                  283
(E) Finance                                         284
(F) The Provinces                                   284
    1. The Jewish War                             285
    2. Britain                                    285
    3. Germany                                    285
    4. The Danube                                 287
    5. The East                                   288

### Part 2: *A.D. 96–180*

(A) The Emperors                                    288
    1. Nerva (A.D. 96–98)                         288
    2. Trajan (A.D. 98–117)                       289
    3. Hadrian (A.D. 117–138)                     289
    4. Antoninus (A.D. 138–161)                   290
    5. Aurelius (A.D. 161–180)                    290
(B) The Constitution                                291
(C) Finance                                         293
(D) The Provinces                                   295
    1. Africa                                     297
    2. Armenia and Parthia                        297
    3. Judaea                                     299
    4. Dacia                                      302
    5. The Marcomannic Wars                       303
    6. Britain                                    303
(E) The Army                                        305

### Part 3: *Economic Conditions from A.D. 68 to 180*

(A) Agriculture                                     307
(B) Industry and Trade                              309

CHAPTER XVI

# THE EMPIRE A.D. 180 ONWARDS: DECLINE

## Part 1: *A.D. 180–234*

|   |   | PAGE |
|---|---|------|
| (A) | Commodus (A.D. 180–192) | 315 |
| (B) | Civil War (A.D. 193–197) | 316 |
| (C) | Severus (A.D. 193–211) | 316 |
|   | 1. Military Policy | 317 |
|   | 2. Internal Administration | 319 |
| (D) | Caracalla (A.D. 211–217) | 321 |
| (E) | Macrinus (A.D. 217–218) | 322 |
| (F) | Elagabalus (A.D. 218–222) | 322 |
| (G) | Alexander Severus (A.D. 222–235) | 323 |

## Part 2: *A.D. 234 onwards*

| (A) | Civil War (A.D. 234–285) | 324 |
|---|---|------|
|   | 1. A.D. 234–253 | 324 |
|   | 2. A.D. 253–267: Valerian and Gallienus | 325 |
|   | 3. A.D. 267–275: Claudius and Aurelian | 328 |
|   | 4. A.D. 275–285 | 329 |
| (B) | Diocletian (A.D. 285–305) | 330 |
| (C) | A.D. 305 onwards | 332 |
| (D) | Frontier Defence | 337 |
| (E) | The Constitution | 340 |
| (F) | Finance | 342 |
| (G) | Economics | 343 |

CHAPTER XVII

PAGE

ROME IN RETROSPECT 346

APPENDIX A : Religion 355

APPENDIX B : The City of Rome 367

LISTS

(A) Chronological Table 373
(B) Legions and Provinces 385
(C) The Roman Emperors, from Augustus
to Constantine 388

INDEX 391

# ILLUSTRATIONS

| | PAGE |
|---|---|
| Bronze She-Wolf, probably of the Sixth Century B.C. | 23 |
| The *Fasces* | 26 |
| Silver Coin of the Second Punic War | 76 |
| Bust of Cicero | 169 |
| Coin. Struck by Caesar in 49 B.C. | 197 |
| Coin. Struck by M. Brutus | 206 |
| Coin. Of Augustus | 224 |
| Statue of Augustus in the Vatican | 231 |
| The *Ara Pacis* | 234 |
| Coin. Head of Livia | 250 |
| Coins. Head of Drusus | 251 |
| Head of the Elder Agrippina | 251 |
| Coin. Head of Claudius | 253 |
| Coin. Head of Nero and reverse | 255 |
| The Roman Theatre at Arausio (Orange) | 270 |
| The Peristyle of the House of the Vettii at Pompeii | 272 |
| The Pont du Gard, near Nîmes | 273 |
| Coins. Head of Galba | 276 |
| Head of Vitellius | 276 |
| Coins. Head of Domitian | 280 |
| Head of Vespasian | 280 |
| Head of Titus and reverse | 280 |
| The 'Saalburg' | 286 |
| Coins. Head of Trajan and reverse | 289 |
| Head of Hadrian | 289 |
| Bust of Hadrian | 290 |
| The 'Praetorium' of the Camp at Lambaesis | 297 |

PAGE

Trajan's Column — Soldiers building a bridge 300

Trajan's Column — The final Roman victory 301

A Roman Camp (Housesteads) 306

Gallic 'Terra Sigillata' 308

'Castor' pottery 308

The Aqueduct at Segovia 310

The Corbridge Lion 311

The Roman Villa at Chedworth 312

The Roman Bridge at Alcantara 313

Coin. Head of Septimius Severus 317

Coin. Head of Caracalla 321

Coin. Head of Gallienus 326

Coins. Head of Claudius Gothicus 328

Head of Aurelian 328

Coin. Head of Probus 329

Coin. Head of Diocletian 330

Coin. Head of Constantius and reverse 331

Baths of Diocletian 332

The Wall of Aurelian 338

## ACKNOWLEDGMENTS

THE publishers wish to thank the following, who have given permission for the photographs to be reproduced on the pages quoted.

Anderson, p. 338
British Museum, pp. 290, 332
Brogi, pp. 230, 234
The Curator, Colchester
and Essex Museum, p. 308

Gibson & Son, Hexham, p. 311
Radio Times Hulton
Picture Library, pp. 272, 273
Señor Ruiz, Madrid, p. 313
Stoedtner, pp. 270, 286, 301

## MAPS AND PLANS

| | PAGE |
|---|---|
| Italy : Physical Features | 2 |
| Latium | 6 |
| Rome in the Regal Period | 7 |
| Expansion of Roman Power | 30 |
| Italy : General (throw-out) | 46 |
| Central Italy | 52 |
| The First Punic War | 68-69 |
| The Western Mediterranean and the Third Punic War | 86-87 |
| Greece and Asia Minor at the beginning of the Second Century B.C. | 96 |
| Republican Rome | 134 |
| Italy 90–60 B.C. | 154 |
| Greece and Asia Minor in the First Century B.C. | 174 |
| Roman Gaul in 59 B.C. | 184 |
| Roman Empire 44 B.C. | 222-223 |
| Roman Empire under Augustus, Trajan and Hadrian | 236-237 |
| The Eastern Frontier | 261 |
| The German Frontier | 263 |
| Roman Britain | 304 |
| The Later Roman Empire | 334-335 |
| Imperial Rome | 344 |

### CHAPTER I

# THE GEOGRAPHICAL BACKGROUND

## (A) *The Mediterranean*

ROMAN history is the record of a nation that extended its boundaries from a small territory in the valley of the Italian river Tiber to include all the lands that border on the Mediterranean Sea. The countries round the Mediterranean Sea form a natural geographic unit. They are, on the whole, alike in their climate and vegetation, and travel from one to another is relatively easy. They are also cut off, in a greater or lesser degree, from the hinterland countries ; travel between the Mediterranean area and the three adjacent continents is hindered by an almost continuous barrier of mountains and deserts. Only sometimes does a river valley, or a low mountain pass, provide a convenient route to the interior. But the Mediterranean Sea connects rather than separates the lands which surround it. The Romans, who called it 'Mare Nostrum' ('Our own sea'), regarded it as a necessary link in their empire. In short, the natural features of the area make it easy for the Mediterranean countries to be grouped into a unified state : so that the Roman empire followed the natural lines of development.

## (B) *Italy*

In comparison with other Mediterranean countries Italy is on the whole a favoured land. Its climate conforms to the general Mediterranean type, but has several local variations. The winter of most of Italy is mild : but the region north of the Apennines, being cut off by these mountains from the warm sea winds, becomes frostbound like continental Europe. In the summer months the west coast is exposed to the occasional sirocco (a fierce westerly wind). But these

ITALY : PHYSICAL FEATURES

disadvantages are more than compensated by the comparative coolness and moistness of the Italian summer. At Rome or Florence the rainless season does not normally last more than a month.

The Apennine range, the backbone of Italy, does not rise to more than a moderate height : its tallest peak falls slightly short of 10,000 feet. Like most other Mediterranean mountains, the Apennines fill the rivers full in winter, and starve them in summer. On the other hand, the Alpine chains of mountains on the northern border make the short summer drought there almost harmless, for their perennial snow keeps the rivers comparatively well fed throughout the rainless season.

Italy possesses a larger expanse of rich soil than most Mediterranean lands. From the Alps the northern plain receives not only plenty of water, but a mass of fertilising matter which the rivers leave on the land during the winter floods. The eventual decline of cultivation of corn in Italy under the Romans was due to political causes rather than lack of good arable land : but the development of orchards and of ranching by the Roman landowners was in accordance with the country's natural line of growth. In particular, Italy has plenty of 'saltus', summer pastures in the highlands, as well as the winter grasslands in the plains. Taken as a whole, Italy has a smaller percentage of cultivable land than France or England : but it has fewer waste or semi-waste districts than most other Mediterranean countries.

Italy is not well supplied with minerals. But it possessed one important metal-bearing area on the northern coast of Tuscany, and in the adjacent island of Elba. The copper mines of the mainland and the large deposits of iron on Elba went a long way to supply ancient Italy with its two most essential metals.

Thanks to its natural advantages, Italy is, next to the Nile valley, the most densely populated of Mediterranean lands. At present it has nearly twice as many people as Spain, though its area is only half as large. In ancient times its abundance of man-power contributed in a large degree to its political superiority over its neighbours.

Italy is severely handicapped in its internal communications by its great length from north to south, and by the diagonal barrier of the Apennines, which hinders both the passage from coast to coast and the passage from the peninsula into the Po valley. Its rivers are mostly too rapid and variable for purposes of transport. The ease and swiftness of inland travel which the country came to enjoy under Roman rule was chiefly due to the construction of the Roman high-roads.

The Alpine ranges which mark off Italy from the European mainland are not so formidable an obstacle as their height might suggest. On the north-east frontier of Italy a gap in the Carnic Alps provides a route no more than 2500 feet high. In the Central and Western Alps the passes rise to 6000-8000 feet, yet on the outer side the river systems of the Rhine and Rhône give easy access to them. The Alps were repeatedly crossed by ancient armies, and where soldiers went, traders also were sure to find their way. Nevertheless, for many centuries of early Italian history the Alps remained an almost insurmountable barrier. Unlike the wandering tribes of the vast plains of Central Europe, the Italians could develop their own civilisation without interference.

The coast of Italy offers no such sheltered inlets as the neighbouring Greek peninsula. As is the case with all Mediterranean coast-lands, its river estuaries are positively dangerous to shipping, for the sea has no strong tides to scour them, so that their entrances are often blocked with banks of silt. Neither Po nor Tiber has ever been accessible to large vessels : under the emperors the port of Ostia at the Tiber mouth had to be refashioned at some distance from the river. Yet the coasts of the peninsula were frequented from early days by seafarers of other nations, and its people soon came under the influence of visitors from overseas. With the rise of the Roman empire Italy inevitably became the centre of Mediterranean navigation.

Lastly, Italy possesses one obvious geographical advantage. Its central position in the Mediterranean marks it out to be the natural seat of any Mediterranean empire. Once the ancient Italians had been united under Roman rule, their overseas conquests were made easier by the commanding position of their country within the circle of Mediterranean lands.

## (c) *Latium*

Latium, the cradle of Rome, consisted originally of the coastal plain from the mouth of the Tiber to the Circeian promontory, and its adjacent foot-hills. In the south its habitable zone was narrowed by the Pomptine marshes and by the Mons Lepinus, a spur from the Apennines extending toward the sea. On its northern and western border the lower valleys of the Tiber and of its tributary the Anio — the 'Roman Campagna' of the present day — formed a wider belt of open land. The centre of the region consisted of a group of volcanic hills, the principal of which, the Mons Albanus, rose to a little above 3000 feet.

The Latin hill country still possesses fine woodland ; in the early days of Roman history it was noted for its tall beech copses. On these pleasant uplands the villages of primitive Latium clustered most thickly. The remaining settlements were mostly built on the low but steep hills that jut out of the plains here and there.

Latium is cut off from the eastern face of Italy by an almost continuous ridge of high land. The only easy road across the Apennine range, by way of the Anio valley and the Lacus Fucinus, extended along the northern border of the Latin territory. Coastal communications with the bay of Naples were impeded by the Mons Lepinus and the Pomptine marshes. On the other hand, two low passes between the Alban mount and the Apennine foot-hills provided gateways into the valleys of the Trerus and the Liris, and so gave an easy approach from Latium into Campania. Between Latium and Etruria the Tiber formed a strong natural boundary. Though not the longest of Italian rivers, the Tiber is one of the most voluminous, and even at its lowest summer level it is not easy to ford, except at a few easily guarded points. On this side lay the most vital frontier of Latium: if the Alban hills formed the geographical heart of the country, the line of the Tiber was the natural seat of its political capital.

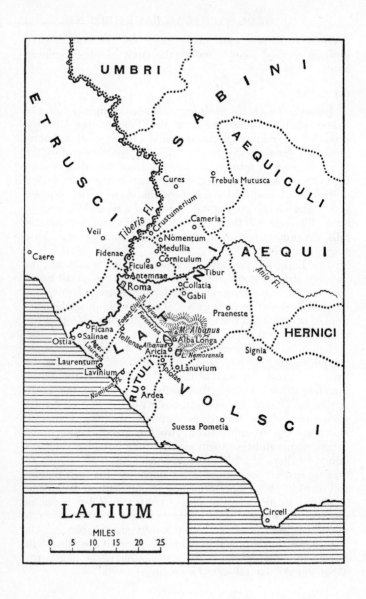

UMBRI

ETRUSCI

SABINI

AEQUICULI

Cures

Trebula Mutusca

*Tiberis Fl.*

Crustumerium

Cameria

Veii

Nomentum

Caere

Fidenae

Medullia

Corniculum

AEQUI

Ficulea

Tibur

*Anio Fl.*

Antemnae

Roma

Collatia

Gabii

Praeneste

*Fossa Cluilia*

Ficana

*Aqua Ferentina*

*M. Albanus*

HERNICI

Salinae

Tellenae

*Albanus*

Alba Longa

Ostia

*Ager Laurens*

Aricia

*L. Nemorensis*

Signia

Laurentum

Lanuvium

Lavinium

Pedum

*Numicius Fl.*

RUTULI

Ardea

VOLSCI

Suessa Pometia

LATIUM

MILES

0    5    10    15    20    25

Circeii

(D) *Rome*

Rome was situated on the borderland of Latium and Etruria, at a distance of fifteen miles from the Tiber estuary. At this point the combined activities of the Ciminian and Alban volcanoes threw up a ring of hillocks to a height of two to three hundred feet above sea level, and of a hundred feet or more

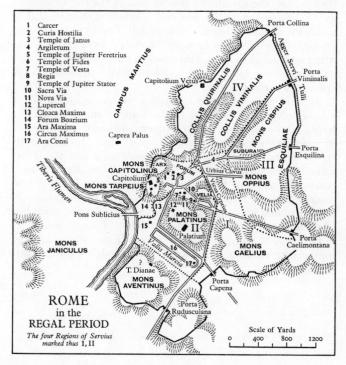

1  Carcer
2  Curia Hostilia
3  Temple of Janus
4  Argiletum
5  Temple of Jupiter Feretrius
6  Temple of Fides
7  Temple of Vesta
8  Regia
9  Temple of Jupiter Stator
10  Sacra Via
11  Nova Via
12  Lupercal
13  Cloaca Maxima
14  Forum Boarium
15  Ara Maxima
16  Circus Maximus
17  Ara Consi

ROME
in the
REGAL PERIOD

*The four Regions of Servius*
*marked thus I, II*

Scale of Yards
0      400      800      1200

above the surrounding plain. The western arc of the ring consisted of two isolated ridges on the right bank of the Tiber, the Janiculan and the Vatican. The eastern arc, on the left bank, formed a continuous stretch of high ground, from which four spurs, the Quirinal, Viminal, Esquiline and Caelian, projected into the river valley. Within the circle three inner hills, the Capitoline, Palatine and Aventine, guarded the passage of the Tiber. Of the central hills the Capitoline, which was the smallest in extent, stood detached on every side. The Palatine was separated by a deep-cut valley from its southern neighbour, the Aventine, and from the Quirinal on the north; on the north-eastern side it was connected with the Esquiline by a land-bridge, the so-called Velia. Through the rim of volcanic soil the Tiber cut itself a new bed. Avoiding the Quirinal by a sudden westward bend, the river left a wide piece of open ground, the site of the Campus Martius; by a return curve it approached close to the three inner hills, and in this reach its channel was bisected by an island which made it easy to cross by a ford or bridge.

In this position Rome enjoyed a unique combination of natural advantages. A city of the Latin plain, it stood in a fertile territory which, under proper cultivation, was capable of maintaining a large population for its size. Its hills partly raised it above the reach of the floods to which the Tiber valley is peculiarly exposed. In the Tiber Rome had a potential avenue of foreign commerce. At the same time it commanded the most convenient passage of the stream in its lower reaches, and thus held a key position on the main line of travel along the western face of Italy. Finally, Rome lay in the heart of Italy, at equal distances from its northern and southern extremities. In a word, it was Italy's natural centre of communications.

### CHAPTER II

# ITALY BEFORE THE RISE OF ROME

## (A) *Early Peoples of Italy*

THE earliest traces of human life in Italy date to sometime before 10,000 B.C., but the first people of whom we have any definite knowledge were a Stone Age folk, who shaped and polished stone tools, made a rough sort of pottery, and could weave clothes. These are known as 'Ligurians', because some people of this race still lived in Liguria in classical Roman times and were known to the Romans. About 2500 B.C. this people learnt the use of copper, which slowly began to replace stone as the usual material for tools and weapons.

Between about 2000 and 1500 B.C. various foreign peoples invaded Italy and occupied it. They brought with them greater knowledge of the use of copper and bronze, and improved methods of agriculture. By about 1000 B.C. the use of soft metals and intensive cultivation of the land was common throughout all Italy, except for one or two remote mountain areas. The last wave of invaders was part of a larger movement of the Aryan or Indo-European peoples towards the south, peoples who at this time also entered Greece and Asia Minor. They brought with them a common basic language, also known as Indo-European, from which Greek, Latin and other European languages are derived.

Soon before 1000 B.C. Indo-European invaders of Greece, in the course of their journey towards the south, displaced various peoples living in Illyria, who came to settle in Italy. Among these we can identify the Venetians on the north-east coast, and the Iapygians further south.

About 1000 B.C. the use of iron began to be adopted, though for several centuries bronze was the most commonly-used metal.

By 1000 B.C. the ingredients of the future Italian nation were assembled within the country. At this stage the general culture of the Italic peoples gave little promise of their eventual leadership among the nations. Their material civilisation had not advanced, save in a few districts, beyond that of a self-contained agricultural people ; they were unacquainted with writing ; their craftsmanship was competent, but their art was crude, and their social organisation primitive.

The Italic peoples mostly lived in open villages (*vici*), to which an *oppidum* or fortress (usually a hill-top with a rough fence) might be attached as a temporary place of refuge. But these villages have left scarcely any trace of a governing authority. The chief administrative unit was rather the *pagus*, a territory comparable in size to our smaller English counties. Each *pagus* possessed a council to which all freemen from its *vici* were admitted, but its magistrates and councillors were drawn from a class of larger landowners. For purposes of common warfare groups of *pagi* might join into larger units (whose collective names, 'Sabini', 'Umbri', 'Lucani', etc., were most commonly used by Greek and Roman writers, and are therefore most familiar to us) ; but these associations were merely temporary.

The eventual union of the Italic folks into one state was made easier by the early fusion of their various racial elements, and by their common use of the Indo-European language. A first step toward political union was taken in the formation of a rough code of international usage. The distinctive feature of this code was that it required at least a formal justification for making war upon neighbours, and prescribed a recognised procedure in which claims for compensation had to be made previous to the declaration of war.

Yet the dawn of Roman history saw the Italic populations still in disconnected and potentially hostile groups. Their Indo-European tongue was split into a variety of dialects. Among the Italic idioms two main branches, the 'Umbrian' of the northern and the 'Oscan' of the southern Apennine districts, bore a fairly close resemblance ; but the 'Latin' dialect of central Italy was sharply distinguished from either. There was no common literature like that of the Homeric

poems among the early Greeks. Neither were the early
Italians brought into closer contact by community of religious
worship. The Italic gods were very different from one
another, and offered little opportunity for meeting at common
religious festivals.

Lastly, though the Italic peoples as a whole were funda-
mentally law-abiding, and did not exalt warfare into a national
industry, they were none the less drawn into frequent conflicts.
Disputes about frontiers easily gave rise to hostilities, and
there was a permanent feud between the lowlanders, who had
settled peacefully in the coastal plains, and the highlanders,
who descended from their mountain homes to rob and plunder.

### (B) *The Greeks*

By about 1000 B.C. the Italic peoples had laid the foundations
of a settled and ordered life, but their civilisation lagged behind
that of the older cities in the Nearer East. The next stages in
the development of Italy were the result of increased contact
with peoples from the eastern Mediterranean.

Occasional visits by mariners from the Greek lands before
2000 B.C. were made to the south of Italy. After 1200 B.C.
the prehistoric civilisation of Greece broke down under the
stress of the Indo-European invasions, and the visits of traders
were stopped for several centuries. In the meantime the
exploration of the western Mediterranean was completed by
the Phoenicians, who established colonies in North Africa, in
Sicily and in Spain, and paid trading visits to the coasts on
Tuscany. In the sixth century the trade of the Phoenicians
with Italy came into the hands of their colonists at Carthage
who cultivated friendly relations with Tuscany. But the
Phoenicians left very little trace of their visits to Italy, and
they had no enduring influence upon its early civilisation.

A much closer and more fruitful contact was established
between the Italic peoples and the Hellenic or (as the Romans
came to call it) the Greek nation, which had been formed in
the Aegean area after the Indo-European invasions. Stray
finds of Greek pottery on the coasts of Apulia, of Campania
and of Tuscany show that the Aegean seafarers resumed intercourse with Italy about 800 B.C. In the eighth, seventh and

B

sixth centuries the Greeks made one chain of settlements in Sicily, and another on the southern and western coasts of Italy from Tarentum to the bay of Naples. From this base-line Greek traders carried their characteristic merchandise, bronze-ware and pottery, to central and northern Italy. One stream of traffic moved from Tarentum up the Adriatic coast, extending northward as far as Hadria (near the Po estuary), and inland as far as the Apennines. Another proceeded from Cumae, the oldest permanent settlement of Greeks on Italian soil, to Latium and Tuscany, and spread itself like a flood over the Tuscan inland. Between 800 and 500 B.C. Italy became one of the chief markets for the Greek export trade.

But the influence of the Greek merchant and colonist went further than the mere exchange of goods. Greek settlers introduced into Italy the cultivation of the vine and the olive, which had hitherto existed there in the wild state only. Having acquired from the Phoenicians an alphabetic system of writing, the Greeks adapted it to the needs of Indo-European tongues, and they made a gift of this improved script to the Italic peoples, all of whom, directly or indirectly, took over their letter-signs from Cumae or some other Greek colony. The bronzes and pottery which the Greeks spread over Italy, the sculpture and architecture with which they decorated their cities, provided the natives with art-patterns which here and there found skilful imitators. The Greeks also gave the future conquerors of the world their first lessons in scientific war-craft, in the fortification of towns with stone walls and the fighting of set battles by the shock-tactics of armoured spearmen.

Nevertheless, the Greeks accomplished far less in Italy than they might have achieved, had they applied their superior civilisation in a systematic manner. They quarrelled amongst themselves and frittered away their opportunities in warfare between their several cities, or in civil strife within each town wall. Under these conditions they scarcely advanced their power beyond their original area of settlement.

## (c) *The Etruscans*

The name of 'Etruscans' was given by the Romans to their neighbours in the district now known as Tuscany. They were

a city-dwelling people who established their towns in commanding situations and fortified them with ring-walls of stone.
The interior of their cities was laid out on a regular plan ;
two intersecting main roads formed the central cross, and the
principal streets were paved and drained.   The wealthier
inhabitants dwelt in timber houses, with a central courtyard,
on to which suites of apartments in one or two storeys opened.
The dwellings of the gods were built on a plan resembling
that of Greek temples.   In Etruscan cemeteries the more
elaborate tombs were laid out with furniture which vividly
illustrates the luxury and artistic taste of the Etruscan nobility.
Their chief contents were fine Greek vases of every type.
The metal ware of bronze and gold was mostly of native work-
manship.    Among this were toilet-cases and mirrors with
decorations which plainly betrayed Greek influence ;  the gold
ornaments were less dependent on foreign models, and in
craftsmanship equalled the finest Greek work.   The frescoes
in the Etruscan rock-tombs were poor imitations of Greek
painting, and they did little sculptured work in stone.   On the
other hand, their realistic portrait-statues in terra-cotta will
bear comparison with the best Greek sculpture of the sixth
century.   The numerous tomb-inscriptions indicate that the
Etruscans had adopted alphabetic writing from the Greeks
before 600 B.C.

The wealth of which the Etruscan cemeteries have offered
such dazzling proof was derived in part from the copper and
iron mines of northern Tuscany, and in part from the intensive
cultivation of the rich soil in the southern district.

The advanced character of Etruscan civilisation was likewise
shown in its elaborately organised religion.   The principal
deities were the patron gods of crafts, and the protecting gods
of cities.   Their ritual was of such complexity as to require
special classes of experts to preserve and expound the traditional lore.   Special ceremonies were observed at the foundation of cities :  Etruscan towns were encompassed not only
with walls of stone, but with spiritual or symbolic ring-fences
(*pomeria*), which were marked out by ploughing a furrow outside the line of fortifications.   On all important occasions an
elaborate ritual of divination, based on the observation of

lightning, or on the inspection of animal entrails, was practised by trained interpreters (*haruspices*). But the most distinctive feature of the Etruscan religion was its gloomy and cruel character, which differentiated it sharply from most of the Greek and Italic cults. This is illustrated by numerous scenes in Etruscan tomb-paintings, which depict the torments of the dead at the hands of the demons of the underworld. For the appeasement of their divine fiends the Etruscans offered up human sacrifices ; a common method of dispatching the victims was to set them to kill each other off in duels, which later served as the models for the gladiatorial contests in Rome.

The social and political organisation of the Etruscans was rigidly aristocratic. A few lords owned the best part of the land, which was probably cultivated for them by serf or slave labour, and held the government of the cities securely in their hands. Executive power was originally held by the city-kings, who were apparently appointed by election from a small circle of noble families ; in the sixth or fifth century the kings were generally replaced by annual magistrates. The kings or other high officials were attended with great pomp. They wore robes of purple and rode on chariots of ivory, and they were escorted by retainers carrying bundles of rods and axes, a symbol of their right to punish and to take life. In the Etruscan armies the lords and their attendants constituted a special fighting force which wore heavy defensive armour of Greek type and fought on horseback. The general body of infantry was partly recruited mercenaries and subject peoples from beyond the borders of Tuscany.

The origin of the peculiar Etruscan civilisation is the most vexed question of early Italian history. It is beyond dispute that the Etruscans owed much to Greek influence. Yet many Etruscan institutions were not derived from that quarter. Were the Etruscans native Italics, or were they immigrants, like the Greeks? The controversy on this question is almost as old as the Etruscans themselves, and it remains alive to this day.

A final decision on the Etruscan problem will hardly be possible until the discovery of a bilingual text solves the riddle of the Etruscan language, or further excavations provide the

missing archaeological links.  Provisionally, however, it may
be assumed that the population of Tuscany as a whole was
descended from the Villanovans or earlier inhabitants, but that
a gradual infiltration of immigrants from western Asia Minor
(attracted, perhaps, by the mineral resources of Tuscany) took
place between about 1000 and 800 B.C., and that these newcomers eventually became a ruling class in the Etruscan cities.
On this theory, Etruscan civilisation was a mixture of the Italic
culture and of the cultures of Greece and Asia Minor.

In the eighth and seventh centuries B.C. Tuscany became
the seat of a group of city-states with ample material resources
and a strict political organisation, and possessed of armies
which might crush as well as rout an enemy.  After 650 B.C.
the Etruscans crossed the Tiber, broke into Latium and
occupied part of Campania, where they founded the important
city of Capua and a group of lesser towns.  A century later
they passed beyond the Apennines and established a base for
further conquest at Felsina (near Bologna).  From this point
they took possession of the Adriatic coast between Hadria
and Pisaurum (where Ravenna proclaims its Etruscan origin by
its name), and beyond the river Po as far as Mantua and
the lakeland.

The Etruscans did not penetrate far into Venetia or into the
upper valley of the Po ;  they made little impression upon the
peoples of the central and southern Apennines ;  they failed to
dislodge the Greeks from Cumae or any other point on the
southern coast.  Yet in acquiring the western sea-front of Italy
from the Arno to the bay of Naples, and the greater part of
the Po valley, they had gained all the richest portions of the
country, and they ruled over a territory far exceeding that of
any Greek or Italian city.  At the same time they gained
control of the seas on either side of Italy.  Their control of
the western sea was shown by the name of 'mare Etruscum'
or 'Tyrrenum' (from the Greek name for the Etruscans),
which it kept throughout antiquity.  The wider range of the
Etruscan conquests enabled them to exercise a more extensive
and enduring political influence than the Greek.  The
Etruscans not only founded cities of their own on conquered
territory, but they set the example of urban civilisation.

Another lasting result of the Etruscan rule in Italy was the spreading of the Etruscan alphabet to Umbria and Latium.

But the Etruscans had overrun Italy rather than secured it with a firm hold. Moreover, they failed to preserve unity among themselves. For all their rigid organisation, the governing aristocracies of the cities could not prevent armed risings of the unprivileged serfs or artisans. Neither could the several cities achieve any durable harmony among themselves. Although there existed a formal federation of the original twelve towns in Tuscany, and a union among the twelve later foundations in northern Italy, these associations were more concerned with religious ceremonial than with common political action. The Etruscan conquests, therefore, were not the product of a concerted drive across Italy, but the isolated results of haphazard thrusts by individual cities or private war-bands, and no effective organisation was formed to defend these gains.

After 500 B.C. the political destiny of Italy passed out of Etruscan hands. The centre of political power and culture moved across the Tiber to Latium and Rome.

## (D) *The Origins of Rome*

The origins of Rome became a subject of speculation even before the city had given clear signs of its future importance, and an endless variety of foundation-legends was composed in its honour. The starting-point of the native tradition was the creation of a founder 'Romulus' out of the name of the city. Romulus was fitted out with a twin-brother Remus. The story grew up that, as an unwanted child, he was cast forth into the Tiber, but was saved for Rome by Providence, which directed the river to swirl him ashore, and a wolf to suckle him. Romulus, grown to manhood, founded a settlement on the Palatine, and provided wives for his settlers by raping the women of a neighbouring Sabine community on the Quirinal. The tale of Romulus in its native version had come into existence not later than the fourth century B.C. ; and the fact that in 296 a bronze statue of a wolf suckling human twins was set up in the Forum shows that by then the main outlines of the legend were familiarly known at Rome.

The principal Greek contribution to the foundation-story of Rome was the introduction of the Trojan warrior Aeneas into it.  Greek legend had busied itself with Aeneas since the seventh century, when the Sicilian poet Stesichorus traced the Trojan hero's wanderings to his native isle, and either he or (more probably) a somewhat later writer had made him the founder of the Campanian city of Capua.

By 300 B.C. the story of a Trojan landing in Latium had been accepted in native tradition, for relics of Trojan origin were exhibited in the temple of Venus at Lavinium.  At the end of the third century the process of bringing the Roman and Greek versions into harmony was carried further.  A distinctive novelty was the interpolation of a line of kings at Alba Longa between Aeneas and Romulus.  Early Roman writers assigned various dates to the birth of Rome : 900, 748 and 728 B.C.  In the first century B.C. the date 753, proposed by the scholar Varro, became generally accepted.  In the Augustan age final shape was given to the legend by Virgil and Livy.  Virgil's chief personal contribution to the legend was the episode of Aeneas and Dido.

In common with all other places exposed to the action of the Latin and Etruscan volcanoes, the territory of Rome was not permanently occupied until the first millennium B.C.

Communities grew up in turn upon the Palatine, Esquiline and Quirinal hills.  These communities were at first quite distinct ; indeed the marshland of the Forum interposed an effective physical barrier between the Palatine and Quirinal groups.  Evidence of the coalition of the villages into a city may be seen in a festival known as the ' Septimontium ' (' Seven Mountains '), whose celebration was still kept up in the days of the emperors.

A more definite stage in the formation of the city is indicated by another religious institution, the *pomerium* or ritual furrow round the urban area.  This spiritual boundary, which Rome possessed in common with the Etruscans, was originally drawn so as to include the Palatine, the spurs of the Esquiline and Quirinal, and probably also the Capitoline hill.  Since the *pomerium* of an ancient Italian city usually followed a line immediately outside a ring-wall, probably the area comprised within the *pomerium* was at some time enclosed within a common line of defences. Since the district within the *pomerium* was nearly coextensive with the four urban 'tribes' or city wards of the republican period, the area enclosed by it has received the name of the 'City of the Four Regions'. This took place shortly before 600 B.C.

In the process of unification which created this city the principal step was the coalescence of the Palatine and Quirinal villages across the Forum, for this involved the draining of the Forum marshes. The fusion of the three hill communities on the Palatine, Quirinal and Esquiline, and the annexation of the Capitoline as a common citadel, may be regarded as the decisive moment in the birth of Rome. With an area of some 450 acres within its ring-wall, Rome was from the outset a considerable city according to ancient standards.

The population of Rome was mainly of Latin stock, but the original settlers were reinforced by later comers from the central Apennine regions, to whom the valley of the Anio offered an easy avenue into the Tiber basin. A small Sabine element in the vocabulary of the Romans points to the same conclusion.

Did the Etruscans have any connexion with the foundation of Rome ? The date at which the City of the Four Regions was created was not long after the Etruscan occupation of Praeneste. It is a plausible theory that towards the end of the seventh century the Etruscans forced the crossing of the Tiber opposite the hills of Rome and fortified the area of the four regions as a bridgehead for a further advance into Latium. But if Rome was founded as an Etruscan city, it was Etruscan in this sense only, that an Etruscan ruling class formed a city out of a Latin subject population. The lack of Etruscan remains within the city, and the almost complete absence of Etruscan elements in the language of the Romans, preclude the belief that Rome ever contained a considerable Etruscan population, and it is hardly credible that the foundation-story of Rome could have assumed the shape which it received if the founder had been an Etruscan. We may therefore conclude that the Etruscans had no direct share in the making of the city. Yet to this extent they may have contributed to its foundation, that it was the fear of an Etruscan attack that induced the inhabitants of the separate hills (aided perhaps by colonists from other Latin communities) to unite their villages into a fortified city. Such large enterprises as the draining of the Forum marshes and the fortification of the four regions point to some compelling necessity, such as defence against an Etruscan peril. In this case Rome, the greatest builder of fortresses in ancient times, began its own career as a military bulwark against foreign invasion.

If we compare the ancient legends about the foundation of Rome with the results of modern research, we shall find that the Greek stories of an immigration from overseas into Latium before 1000 B.C. have no foundation. On the other hand, Roman tradition contained some historical truth. The dates assigned by Roman authors to the foundation of the city imply at least a knowledge of the most striking fact about the birth of Rome, that it did not date back to a distant past. The derivation of Rome from Alba Longa and the tale of an inter-marriage with Sabines reflect, however hazily, the fact that it was essentially a Latin city with a mixture of central Apennine folk ; and the location of Romulus' abode on the Palatine accords with the fact that here, in all probability, the first village settlement was made. But Roman tradition had no recollection of the stages by which the villages were united into a city; and if it missed this point, it naturally remained ignorant of the lesser details.

### CHAPTER III

# ROME IN THE PERIOD OF THE KINGS

## (A) The Seven Kings

AT the time when the city of Rome was founded, the usual form of government among those Italian communities which had formed city-states was monarchical. City-kings reigned in Etruria and in the larger towns of Latium. The Roman tradition was in agreement about the names and sequence of their own monarchs : Romulus, Numa Pompilius, Tullus Hostilius, Ancus Marcius, Tarquinius Priscus, Servius Tullius, Tarquinius Superbus. The only variation in the catalogue was the occasional insertion of one Titus Tatius as a colleague of Romulus, but this intruder never obtained a secure place on the list.

Among the traditional kings Romulus was a mere personification of the city whose name he assumed. Titus Tatius was similarly invented to explain the name of one of the original Roman tribes ('*tribus*'), the 'Tities'. On the other hand, the actual existence of a family bearing the name of Tarquinius is shown by tomb inscriptions at the Etruscan cities of Vulci and Caere ; at Vulci the name of Tanaquil, the queen of Tarquinius Priscus, has also been found. In view of these discoveries, the historical character of the Tarquins who ruled at Rome can hardly be denied. The names of Pompilius, Hostilius, Marcius and Tullius recur in the list of consuls belonging to the first fifty years of the republic, and may equally be accepted as historical. There is no need to assume that any names of actual rulers dropped out of memory. Granted that the city of Rome was founded in the second half of the seventh century, the duration of the monarchy extended over a little more than a century. To fill this gap, a series of six kings is sufficient. We may therefore retain the list of Roman kings after Romulus and Titus Tatius. But if the traditional names of the Roman kings may be accepted as historical, the events which the tradition fitted into each reign deserve so little belief that any attempt to give a separate account of each reign would be misleading.

Roman tradition represented all of the kings, save Numa Pompilius, as engaged in frequent and almost monotonously successful warfare. It is quite certain that many of the conquests with which the kings were credited were nothing but anticipations of victories gained in the republican period. The only extensions of Roman territory which may safely be attributed to them lay in the narrow region of northern Latium. The conquest and destruction of Alba Longa may be dated to this period, and we may also accept the tradition that the kings incorporated their lesser neighbours in the Tiber valley from Ostia to Fidenae and Nomentum, so as to control a reach of some thirty miles from the coast to the northern frontier of Latium.

In annexing the entire lower valley of the Tiber, a well-populated territory of some three hundred square miles, the Romans acquired a man-power far exceeding that of any other Latin town. But the kings of Rome never exercised any general dominion over Latium, and at the end of the period of monarchy there was as yet no sure indication that Rome would some day advance its frontiers far beyond the Tiber basin.

In the line of the seven kings the two who bore the name of Tarquin were believed by the Romans to have been newcomers from the city of Tarquinii in central Etruria. This belief may have been no more than a guess from the name of the town. But the Etruscan origin of the Tarquins can scarcely be denied, and a period of Etruscan rule in Rome is further indicated by the influence of Etruria on Roman institutions, as seen in the formalism of the Roman state-religion, in the external attributes of the Roman kings, perhaps also in their real power. These facts seem to point to a conquest of Rome by Tarquinii or Caere. But Roman tradition declared that the elder Tarquin won his way to the throne by his wealth and ability rather than by force of arms, and although this story

has all the appearance of a patriotic fiction, it is confirmed by
the extreme scarcity of Etruscan remains at Rome, which can
hardly be explained as a mere accident.

The Etruscan rule was interrupted by the reign of Servius
Tullius, whose name clearly proclaims his Latin nationality.
From his character in Roman tradition, where he appears as
the most popular of Roman monarchs, we may infer that he
led a temporary reaction against the alien rulers. The alien
origin of the second Tarquin was no doubt also a reason why
this king was the last. In the belief of the Romans their
monarchy was ended in 509 by a bloodless but forcible revolution, and the hatred which for many centuries to come attached
to the very name of *rex* in Rome is clear proof that the
monarchy ended by becoming deeply unpopular. The second
Tarquin made himself odious by tyrannical practices, and was
expelled by a conspiracy of nobles under the leadership of
L. Iunius (afterwards surnamed Brutus). At the same time
the rising against Tarquin was probably more than a protest
against personal misrule. It can hardly be pure accident that
it synchronised with a rebellion on the part of the Latin towns
of Antium, Aricia and Tusculum against Etruscan rule. The
'expulsion' of the Tarquins may therefore be regarded as an
episode in the collapse of the Etruscan dominion in Italy.

The last Tarquin was caught by surprise and fled from the
city without a struggle, but he presently came back with reinforcements from the neighbouring towns of Tuscany. Of the
conflicts which the republic had to sustain in defence of its
liberty the most memorable was waged against an Etruscan
chieftain 'Porsenna'. The cherished Roman legends of the
heroism of a Horatius, a Mucius Scaevola and a Cloelia in this
war could not wholly obliterate a rival tradition, that Porsenna
actually subdued Rome and endeavoured to keep it subject,
as the Philistines sought to keep down the Israelites, by pro-
hibiting the use of iron weapons among the vanquished.
Almost certainly Rome fell back for a moment into servitude.
But Porsenna's stay in Rome was brief. His speedy retreat
from the city is to be explained by the defeat of his forces in a
battle near the Alban lake, in which his son Arruns attempted
to recover the rebel Latin cities of Antium, Aricia and Tus-

culum, but suffered a decisive reverse at the hands of a Greek auxiliary force from Cumae. After this episode Rome definitely shook off Etruscan rule. But its control over the Tiber valley was weakened by the loss of Fidenae, which at this time fell into the hands of the neighbouring Etruscan city of Veii.

## (B) *Economic Conditions*

The original territory of Rome did not extend over more than some sixty square miles. An appreciable part of Rome's

BRONZE SHE-WOLF, PROBABLY OF THE SIXTH CENTURY B.C.

earliest wealth lay in its flocks and herds. But until the Roman conquests extended into the Apennines, the lack of suitable summer pasture must have prevented large-scale sheep or cattle farming. Vineyards were not yet common in Central Italy, and the olive had probably not been introduced into the neighbourhood of Rome. The greater part of the cultivable land was under the plough or hoe, and the chief crop was a species of wheat, which was hardy and prolific. The yield of the Roman land was high according to the

standards of the day, and supported a relatively large population. While the pasture-land remained for the most part undivided, it is probable that from the beginning of Roman
history the arable land was divided between many owners.
The buildings of the city were for the most part of sun-dried
clay or wood. A new ring-wall, which advanced the line of
fortifications to the brow of the Viminal hill and enclosed no
less than 700 acres, was built by one of the later kings ; tradition assigns this work to Servius Tullius. But part at least of
Servius' wall, perhaps even the whole of it, was made of earth.
The production of pottery increased, and a solitary but splendid
example of bronze-founding in early Rome (the Wolf of the
Capitol) still stands in modern Rome near the site at which it
was originally set up. The flourishing character of industries
is indicated by a tradition which attributed to King Numa the
constitution of nine gilds, viz. of flute-players, goldsmiths,
carpenters, dyers, leather-workers, tanners, smiths, potters
and general craft-workers.

Roman tradition was silent about trade in the regal period.
Instead of money the Romans used cattle or lumps of copper
weighed in the balance. But evidence of overseas commerce
in the sixth century survives in the considerable finds of Greek
pottery on the site of the city. Presumably these foreign goods
were paid for in salt from the Tiber mouth, timber from the
upper valleys of the Tiber and Anio, and slaves acquired in
war. With the growth of Roman trade we may connect the
beginning of a new settlement on the Aventine, under which
the first river wharves were built, and the institution of a fair
at the sanctuary of Diana on that hill, where merchants from
other Latin towns could meet traders from overseas.

## (c) *Social and Political Conditions*

The social structure of early Rome was that of a free community with an inner circle of aristocratic families. In the
city the artisans and traders were their own masters, and the
slave population was limited to a few debtors. In the countryside the peasantry were not tied to the soil, and they were
usually the owners of a small plot of land. But the *plebs*
('common people') or mass of the people in city and country

gradually became distinct from the privileged class of the *patricii* ('patricians' or 'aristocrats'). A limited number of families, in whose hands the larger estates were held, had gradually acquired a hold over the peasants among whom the subdivision of land had been carried so far that they were driven to labour in the service of their wealthier neighbours. This economic bond was reinforced by a social bond between the patrician and his 'client'. The patron gave economic support to the client and assisted him in obtaining his rights against others. In return the client gave his labour, military aid and occasional contributions of money, like those of a medieval peasant to his overlord. These mutual obligations, though not enforceable by law, were sanctioned by custom and religion and were handed on from generation to generation, so that for many centuries the relation between patrician and client remained one of the strongest links in Roman society.

The patriarchal organisation which was common to all peoples of Indo-European stock was maintained at Rome longer than elsewhere. The *pater familias* ('father of the household'), having acquired his wife by simple arrangement with the bride's father, had complete disciplinary control over her, over his sons, of whatever age, and over his unmarried daughters. For many centuries his omnipotence within the family circle was unrestrained by law. Roman husbands might put their wives to death, and fathers might sell their children into slavery, without committing a crime.

The social organisation of Rome was dominated by the *gentes* ('family groups' or 'clans'), as was usual in Italic peoples. These groups long remained a powerful force among the ruling families of Rome; but they never formed part of the machinery of government. For political purposes the citizen body was grouped into thirty *curiae* and (originally) three *tribus*, the so-called Tities, Ramnes and Luceres. The *curiae* probably originated in prehistoric times as groups of *gentes* associated for common defence, but after incorporation in the newly-founded city they became local units. The members of each *curia* met occasionally to witness adoptions and testaments and to decide disputed cases of legitimacy. Thus the *curiae* controlled admission to the citizen body.

The *tribus* may have been newly created at the foundation of the city. As Roman territory expanded their number increased from time to time.

Most of the power was held by the Senate or Council of Elders, an assembly made up from families of patrician rank. This council was merely an advisory body, whose pronouncements had no legal binding force. But its opinion inevitably gained in weight from the personal importance of its members. Moreover, at the death of a king his sovereignty passed back into its hands. At the end of each reign the Senate appointed

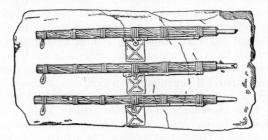

THE *FASCES*

out of its own number an ' interrex ' or viceroy to conduct the election of a new monarch, and it made the actual choice of the next ruler.

The Meeting of the Curiae (*Comitia Curiata*) constituted the original Roman council. The chief function of this assembly was to confirm the senate's choice of a new king. The Comitia Curiata might also confirm a sentence of death upon a citizen, or pledge its loyalty in a war or other political crisis. But it could not meet, save by the king's wish ; it had no power, or only a restricted opportunity, of discussion. The Comitia Curiata made the people's voice audible, but not necessarily effective.

The monarchy at Rome was a trust rather than a family possession. It was not exercised by dynastic right, but was conferred by Senate and people without regard to family claims. The royal *imperium* or right of command was unlimited in range, and could be enforced by capital punishment.

The power of the kings was reflected in their outward insignia. Like the rulers of the Etruscan cities, they were clad in purple, rode in an ivory chariot (*sella curulis*), and were attended by lictors bearing the *fasces* (bundles of rods and axes), the visible symbols of their imperium. On their return from a successful war they rode at the head of their army in a 'triumphal' procession to the Capitol.

As executive head of the state, the king had three areas of power:

(i) *Religious.*—The king was responsible for the maintenance of religion, though he delegated much of his work to special priests (*flamines*) whom he chose from the patrician class, and the tending of the eternal fire of Vesta to six daughters of leading families, who gave thirty years of their life to this never-ending task and lived in maiden seclusion for the term of their office. The king maintained the duty of preserving and expounding the general law of state ritual (*ius divinum*) to a college of five priests (*pontifices*), and the interpretation of omens to a board of three interpreters (*augures*). These delegates of the king were nominated by him out of the patrician families, but they had few regular duties and could only express their opinion at the king's special request.

(ii) *Military.*—He made treaties, decided on questions of peace and war, levied troops and money, and took the field as *imperator* (commander-in-chief).

(iii) *Judicial.*—The king made and declared the law. The rules of civic intercourse, however, were regulated by custom rather than by statute, and it is probable that the royal laws were mainly confined to the sphere of religious ritual. The king's power was restricted by the authority of the *pater familias* over his household; and his interference in the disputes between private citizens was limited to the appointment of arbiters. On the other hand the Roman king, as guardian of public security, freely exercised large powers of penal justice. His criminal jurisdiction extended particularly to two fundamental offences against the community, treason and murder. Such 'capital' cases, involving exile or death (sometimes by hurling from the Tarpeian Rock, a cliff of the Capitol), he delegated to specially appointed judges. The efficacy of the king's criminal justice is shown by the total absence of the blood feud in early Rome. The practice of private war, which proved so difficult to eradicate in the cities of early Greece and in medieval Europe, had been abolished at the very beginning of Roman history.

In comparison with other ancient communities at a similar stage of development, Rome in this period possessed a strong and active government. The chief feature of its early constitution lay in the exercise of *imperium* by the king, which gave him not only full powers of military discipline in the field of war, but an unlimited right to enforce his will in time of peace. Later, the *imperium* was limited and made less arbitrary, but the drastic right to use force which the Roman community gave to its executive officers was one of the clearest expressions of that practical turn of mind which made them realise that political discipline is prior, in fact if not on paper, to political liberty.

## (D) *The Army*

The normal *legio* (a body of conscripted soldiers) was a force of 3300 men, to which each of the three tribes contributed a thousand foot-soldiers and a hundred horsemen. This made no severe demands upon the available man-power of the Roman community, but was composed solely of the nobles and their attendants, and of the more well-to-do peasantry who could provide themselves with body-armour. The infantry was equipped for combat at close quarters in Greek fashion. Its defensive armour consisted of a helmet, a breast-plate and a shield ; its offensive weapons were a heavy javelin (*pilum*) or a thrusting-spear, and a short sword. But the armament of the foot-soldiers was by no means uniform, and their training as yet was not rigorous ; the enforcement of regular conscription on a universal basis and the standardisation of equipment were introduced at a later date. The only officers were the tribal commanders of foot and horse (*tribuni militum, tribuni celerum*). An army of this composition was well suited for the border-warfare of ancient city-states, but was unfitted for systematic conquest.

### CHAPTER IV

# THE CONQUEST OF ITALY

## Part 1 : *500–350 B.C.*

### (A) *Rome and Latium*

IN Latium the war alliance which had been formed against the Etruscans was consolidated into a more permanent league. Eight of the Latin cities — Ardea, Aricia, Cora, Lanuvium, Lavinium, Pometia, Tibur and Tusculum — joined together in a political union. From this association the Romans were excluded, and their claims to leadership in Latium were denied. The Romans and Latins fought at Lake Regillus (near Tusculum) in 496. The result of the battle was probably doubtful, for Latium remained divided into two warring sections.

By their quarrels the Latins brought upon themselves persistent attacks by the peoples of the central Apennines. In the fifth century the Tiber valley was continually exposed to their invasions. These invasions, which were an even graver menace to the neighbouring Latin towns than to Rome, compelled the Latin League to ally with the Romans. About 493 a treaty was entered into by the Romans on the one hand, and the collective Latin federation on the other. A common army of defence was formed, to which each party pledged itself to contribute an equal number. Whichever side summoned the other's aid took command of the combined forces.

The Latin League refrained from an open break with the Romans after 390, but it could not prevent individual Latin towns making war. About 360 the city of Tibur joined Praeneste (which had always stood out of the League) and the Hernici in a campaign against the Romans. Their defeat was followed by a fresh settlement of Latin affairs, in which

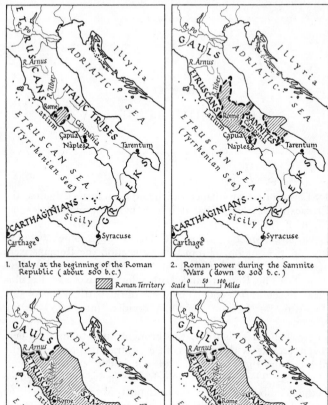

1. Italy at the beginning of the Roman Republic (about 500 B.C.)

2. Roman power during the Samnite Wars (down to 300 B.C.)

///// Roman Territory    Scale  0  50  100  Miles

3. Roman power after the Samnite Wars (290 B.C.)

4. Roman power after the war with Pyrrhus (275 B.C.)

## EXPANSION OF ROMAN POWER

the Romans imposed a new treaty upon the League, so as to convert their former allies into dependents. In the re-organised League (into which Praeneste was now obliged to enter) the Romans permanently assumed military control, and the two annual praetors who replaced the previous federal dictator were the subordinates of the Roman consuls.

## (B) *Sabines, Aequi and Volsci*

The edge of the Sabine attack on Latium was blunted at the outset by a wise concession on the part of the Romans, who won over a Sabine chieftain named Attus Clausus with a gift of land between Tiber and Anio. By this diplomatic act they eased the pressure of invasion from the north-eastern side and acquired a new *gens*, which played a leading part in their history under the Latinised name of Claudius. About 460 another Sabine chief, Appius Herdonius, stole in by night into Rome and occupied the citadel on the Capitol. But his band, left without reinforcements, was driven to surrender after a short siege.

A more persistent pressure was maintained by the southern neighbours of the Sabines, the Aequi. Passing at will through the territory of Praeneste (which stood aloof from the Latin League), these invaders established themselves on Mount Algidus, between the basins of the Anio and the Trerus, and fortified it. The chief incident in the Aequian wars was a campaign in which a Roman force, sent to dislodge the garrison of Mt. Algidus, was caught in a trap, but was extricated by a relief force under L. Quinctius Cincinnatus (*c.* 460).

But the most formidable enemies of the Romans and Latins were the Volscians. From the valley of the Liris this tribe moved across the Mons Lepinus to the edge of the coastal plain of Latium. From this position they more than once obtained possession of Antium and other towns, and occupied the adjacent hillside towns as far north as Velitrae. Roman tradition retained a vivid recollection of a Volscian invasion, led by a traitorous Roman noble, Cn. Marcius Coriolanus, by which the city itself was threatened. The Volscians at some time in the early fifth century pushed their advance as far as the Alban mount.

In the second half of the fifth century the Roman armies at last turned the tide of the border wars. About 430 the Aequi were definitely dispossessed of Mt. Algidus.

In 389 the Romans brought their attacks to a dead stop in a single campaign. They threw back the Volsci, who had resumed their raids and carried them as far as Lanuvium, in a series of campaigns which ended about 380.

## (c) *The Etruscans*

After the battle near the Alban Lake the Etruscans definitely retired beyond the Tiber, retaining nothing on the left bank save the bridgehead at Fidenae, where the city of Veii maintained a garrison. About 480 the Romans, apparently without support from their Latin allies, made an attempt to recover this last corner of Latium. But they sustained a heavy reverse. Half a century after this disaster the reformed Roman army renewed the attack upon Fidenae. In a pitched battle the Roman commander A. Cornelius Cossus slew with his own hand Tolumnius, king of the Veians (*c.* 425).

For some twenty years the Romans remained content with this prize. But about 405 they entered upon a war which aimed at nothing less than the capture of Veii. This struggle, which marked the first definite step in Rome's career of world conquest, was remembered in Roman tradition as a turning-point in the military history of the city. The siege of Veii strained Rome's resources to the utmost. The besieged town was not inferior in size to Rome, and its situation on a steep rock, with a moat of running water on three sides, rendered it almost impregnable, but the Roman general M. Furius Camillus carried Veii by assault in 396. Thus Veii was struck off the roll of Etruscan cities, while Rome was enriched with a large haul of loot, and acquired a fertile region which nearly doubled the total extent of its territory. A considerable portion of the conquered land was allotted to the poorer citizens.

After 390 the Romans consolidated their gains. They defeated an attempt by Falerii and Tarquinii to recover the territory of their former ally, Veii, and made secure a new frontier line along the transverse ridge of the Ciminian mountains.

In 359 the city of Tarquinii resumed hostilities, and three years later all the towns of the Etruscan League for the first time made common cause against Rome. With all the forces of Latium at their disposal, the Romans beat off the combined Etruscan assault. In 353 they detached their former friend Caere by a grant of favourable terms ; two years later they overran the land of Falerii and Tarquinii, and compelled these cities to accept a forty years' truce.

## (D) *The Gauls*

In 391 a miscellaneous host of Celtic invaders (whom the Romans knew as 'Gauls'), under a chieftain named Brennus, broke into Etruria and drew near to the town of Clusium. The threatened city appealed to the Romans, who had recently captured Veii while the Etruscan League looked on. The Senate sent envoys to warn off the invaders, but this remonstrance was accepted by the Gauls as a challenge. In the following year a reinforced army of Celts made a pounce upon Rome and arrived within ten miles of the city before it was brought to battle. On the banks of the Allia, a small tributary of the Tiber, the Romans met the Gauls with their full force, and with troops from the neighbouring Latin cities, so that their total forces were probably not inferior to those of the enemy. The 'disaster of the Allia' long survived in the memory of the Romans as the black day of their early history. The Roman line was crumpled up, and although part of the defeated army escaped, the road to Rome now lay open.

Had the victors pressed on in pursuit, they would in all probability have carried everything before them. A brief delay on their part enabled the city folk to improvise a last refuge on the steep height of the Capitol ; but no attempt was made to man the town walls. The Gauls occupied the city without opposition. The Capitol was held under blockade for seven months, during which it received no assistance from Veii or the Latin cities, and the garrison was eventually driven by famine to a capitulation, which it obtained on easy terms. The besiegers, who were more intent on plunder than on conquest, accepted a ransom of gold and went as suddenly as they had come.

Later the Gauls continued to make occasional attacks on peninsular Italy, but they mostly kept clear of Roman territory. In 360 a sudden attack on the Alban hill-country so unnerved the Romans that they tamely retired behind their new fortifications and there waited for the invaders to withdraw. In 349 they prevented a further attack by quickly calling up the other Latins, and a second failure of nerve—this time on the part of the Gauls, who retired suddenly—ended the campaign without a battle. Meanwhile the Gauls completed their occupation of northern Italy, and in 331 the Senones, who had headed the invasions into central Italy, made their peace with Rome.

## Part 2 : *350–264 B.C.*

By 350 B.C. the Romans had acquired enough territory to satisfy their immediate economic needs. But there were always opportunities for extending Roman power in Italy, and the Romans usually took them. They then became simultaneously involved in conflicts with many different races and states, so that their relationship with the Latin League and the Etruscan cities became part of a wider and more complex picture, and cannot be dealt with separately.

Towards 350 B.C. the Romans began to face a new enemy in the Oscan peoples. These were divided into three groups :

(1) The Samnites, a race of shepherds and peasants who lived in the southern Apennines.

(2) The settlers of Lucania, whose way of life was similar to the Samnites'.

(3) The settlers of Campania, who had acquired an urban civilisation. The Campanian towns, of which the chief was Capua, were the centre of industry in Italy during the fourth century.

### (A) *The First Samnite War*

The first meeting between the Oscans and the Romans was friendly. In 354 the Samnites offered the Romans a treaty which they accepted. But in 343 the Romans entered upon a contest with them, in the course of which the stakes were raised to nothing less than supremacy over southern Italy. Their change was caused by a rival offer of alliance from the Capuans. Despite their recent treaty, the Romans opened hostilities against the Samnites.

In the same year a large Roman force helped the Capuans in driving the Samnites out of Campania. But the gains of the season were endangered in 342 by a mutiny among the Roman troops, who had not yet acquired the habit of prolonged service in distant fields. It was fortunate for the Romans that at this point the Samnites had to attend to their southern neighbour, the city of Tarentum, and so consented to the renewal of the previous treaty with Rome (341). But in coming to terms with the Samnites the Romans threw over their more recent allies in Campania. The Campanians now made an alliance with a group of other Latin cities, who gave them support in beating back the raiders. On the other hand a call by the Samnites for Roman assistance against Tarentum was left unanswered. This had the further effect of bringing to a head a gathering quarrel with the Latins. Under the terms imposed upon them in 358 the Latins had been called upon to supply troops for wars (such as the Etruscan campaigns of 358–351 and the recent operations in Campania) in a Roman rather than a collective Latin interest. In 358 they had seen the Romans take for themselves land recovered from the Volscians, and on this occasion the land distributions to Roman citizens were not balanced by the establishment of new colonies for the Latins. The attitude of the Romans towards the Latins was shown in two treaties which they made with Carthage, possibly in 348 and 343. In return for a promise not to invade the trading-grounds of Carthage they required the Carthaginians not to obtain a permanent foothold in Latium, and not to molest the towns which accepted Roman supremacy ; but they left them free to make slave hauls at the cost of the independent Latin cities. Finally the fiasco of the First Samnite War encouraged the Latins to send an ultimatum to Rome, in which they demanded a restoration of the previous equality between themselves and Rome (340).

Upon refusal of these terms the Latins confirmed their alliance with the Campanians and made a league with their old enemies, the Volsci. But the Romans had by now restored order within their own ranks, and they received loyal support from the Samnites, who stood by the treaty of 341. While their adversaries were still collecting their forces, the Roman armies joined with the Samnite forces and defeated the Latins and Campanians. The Romans followed up this success with an offer of favourable terms to the Campanians, so as to break up the enemy coalition (340). Having detached the Campanians, they proceeded in the next two campaigns to defeat the Latins in detail, and they finally took from the Volscians the seaboard town of Antium, which had frequently changed hands in the previous border wars.

The settlement dictated by the Romans in 338 finally established their supremacy in central Italy. The federation which had held the Latins together since the end of the Etruscan dominion was broken up, and each city was obliged to enter into a separate convention with Rome. Ten of the Latin towns, including the cities of Gabii, Praeneste and Tibur, retained their independence, but were bound to furnish troops to Rome whenever required. Tusculum, Aricia and three other cities were incorporated into the Roman state. The policy was also applied in a modified form to Capua, Cumae and some lesser towns in Campania and on its out-skirts, which consented to accept the duties of Roman citizen-ship and the obligation to serve in the Roman armies, in return for the military protection which Rome now guaranteed to them.

## (B) *The Second Samnite War*

After the campaign of 340 the Romans did not take the Samnites into any further consideration. They ignored them in the settlement of 338, which had the effect of binding all the peoples of the western plain together against those of the mountains. In 334 they secured Capua against further Samnite raids by posting a colony at Cales on the border of the Campanian lowland. In 328 they established a colony at Fregellae. In 334 the Romans gave offence to the Samnites by entering into a treaty with the Tarentines. This led to open hostilities in 327, when the Samnites, having regained a free hand by concluding a peace with Tarentum, renewed their thrusts towards the west. In this year they took advantage of internal strife in the small Greek town of Neapolis (Naples) to introduce a garrison into it. In answer to a protest from Capua, the Romans put Neapolis under siege and eventually stole it from the Samnites with an offer of favourable terms. The scene was now laid for the first serious trial of strength between the two chief military powers of Italy.

In the opening campaigns of the war operations on the western front soon reached a state of deadlock. The Samnites could not pass the Roman outposts in the valleys of the Liris and Volturnus, and the Romans would not dare to follow these streams upward into the heart of the mountains. In 325 a move was begun by a Roman force which crossed the central Apennines by way of the Lacus Fucinus and showed Roman arms for the first time on the Adriatic coast. On this expedition the Romans won over the Marsi and Paeligni in the central Apennine massif, and reduced by force the Vestini on the Adriatic seaboard, so as to prepare for a final advance into Apulia. But before this operation could be completed, a frontal attack attempted in a moment of impatience brought the whole Roman offensive to a standstill. In 321 a Roman and allied force of 20,000 men set out from Capua with the apparent intention of finding a short cut through the Apennines to Apulia. At the 'Caudine Forks' it was trapped in a valley between two mountain passes and forced to surrender. The price was a treaty by which the Samnites got possession of Fregellae and other Roman outposts.

To the Romans, however, the Caudine peace was merely a pause for reorganisation. In the next five years they made provision for the increase of the ordinary infantry from two to four legions of 4200 men each, and the trebling of the mounted forces, which were now raised from six to eighteen centuries. With an equal number of soldiers from the allied states, the total Roman field army in a normal campaign was henceforth fixed at 35,000–40,000 men.

In 315 the Romans broke their treaty and resumed their attempts to take the Samnites in the rear by way of Apulia. Their plans were crossed at the outset by an enemy flying column which made a dash from Fregellae to the coast, so as to cut the Roman lines of communication with Capua. A reserve force was sent from Rome under Q. Fabius Rullianus to recover the coastal road to Campania, but was caught in the pass of Lautulae (near Tarracina) and suffered a defeat scarcely less complete than that of the Caudine Forks. For a while the loyalty of the Campanians, who had held firm in 321, was shaken, and Capua actually changed sides. But before revolt could spread further the Romans, drawing heavily upon their man-power, made good their casualties and recovered the lost ground. In 314 they drove the Samnites from Tarracina and received a hasty surrender from Capua ; in the next two years they recovered the line of the Liris and strengthened it with additional outposts at Interamna and Casinum. At the same time they secured a permanent foothold in Apulia by capturing the Samnite stronghold at Luceria and establishing a colony on its site (314). Finally, they took in hand the construction of the most famous of their highroads, the Via Appia, which provided an all-weather line of communications from Rome to Tarracina and Capua (312).

The Samnites now seemed well held on every side except the south. But in 311, the date at which Rome's armistice with Tarquinii and Falerii lapsed, they persuaded the Etruscans to mobilise against Rome, and in the next year they detached Rome's new allies in the central Apennines, the Marsi and Paeligni, as well as their old friends the Hernici. But the Romans, all the time retaining their hold on Campania and Apulia, systematically reduced the rebels and fought the Etruscans to a standstill (311–304). The way at last was open for an invasion of the southern Apennine highlands in full force, when the Samnites, now dangerously isolated, sued for peace. The Romans, rather than prolong the strain of a twenty years' struggle, left the Samnites in enjoyment of their full independence and contented themselves with their existing gains. The Romans could enter upon the next Samnite War with the dice heavily loaded in their favour. In the recent war they had definitely detached the Campanian Oscans from their kinsmen, they had made secure the western seaboard as far as Naples, and they had ringed in the Samnites on three sides.

In the interval between the Second and the Third Samnite Wars the Romans consolidated their gains by making or renewing alliances with the lesser tribes on the northern fringe of Samnium — the Marsi, Paeligni, Marrucini, Frentani and Vestini — and by establishing colonies at Alba Fucens and Carseoli, so as to control the main passage through the central Apennines.

The Second Samnite War incidentally brought about an extension of Roman ascendancy in Etruria. In 310 Fabius Rullianus redeemed his previous defeat at Lautulae by a brilliantly daring march through the dense forest of the Ciminian mountains, by which he outflanked an advancing Etruscan army and drew it into central Tuscany. A defeat in a set battle broke up the Etruscan League. In the next two years one city after another made separate terms with the Romans, and the Etruscan League followed suit. Though the Romans were content for the present to conclude alliances with the Tuscan cities on a footing of equality, they had in effect reduced the whole country to a condition of dependence.

The added prestige which these victories conferred upon the Romans also brought them into relations with the Umbrians. The Romans made treaties with the Picentine people and with several Umbrian cities. In order to prepare a passage to the Adriatic through Umbrian territory a colony was planted at Narnia, near the confluence of the Tiber and the Nar (299).

## (c) *The Third Samnite War*

The Samnites now offered an alliance to their Lucanian kinsmen. But the Lucanians refused these overtures, and when the Samnites used force they asked for Roman intervention (298). The Lucanian appeal came from a quarter in which the Romans as yet had shown no interest, but it offered them the opportunity of completing the encirclement of the Samnites and was therefore accepted. A relief expedition under L. Scipio Barbatus drove the Samnites out of Lucania.

In the Third Samnite War the Romans at once carried operations into enemy territory. But their new obligations to the Lucanians had compelled them to extend their lines to such a perilous length that in 296 the Samnites succeeded in a break-through at two points. The main Samnite army under Gellius Egnatius slipped past the Roman outposts at Alba Fucens and Carseoli and advanced across the Sabine and Umbrian country as far as the land of the Senones, collecting troops from the peoples on its route of march. This sudden coalition was further strengthened by the appearance of troops from several of the Etruscan cities. In the following year a crushing defeat sustained by Scipio made the Romans aware of their danger. Calling the older men and the ex-slaves to arms for garrison service, they put together a field force of full 40,000 men under their tried veteran, Fabius Rullianus, and a new leader named Decius Mus, who brought the enemy to battle at Sentinum in northern Umbria. In this encounter more troops were engaged than in any previous action on Italian soil, and the fate of all Italy appeared to depend on its issue. The Roman forces all but gave way before an un-expected onslaught of Gallic chariots ; but Decius rallied his wing at the price of his own life, and Fabius carried the day with a final charge by the Campanian horsemen. With the destruction of the Samnite forces and the death of their leader, the hostile coalition fell to pieces. In the same year Fabius received the surrender of the Umbrian rebels and forced the Senones to come to terms by overrunning their territory. In 294 the Etruscan cities made their peace with Rome.

After the failure of Egnatius' grand scheme for the union of all Rome's enemies the Samnites were left exposed to invasion by Roman armies from several quarters. Though they beat off more than one attack, they could not prevent two of the new plebeian leaders, L. Papirius Cursor (293) and M'. Curius Dentatus (290) from harrying their territory from end to end. In 290 they applied for peace, and were fortunate to receive much the same terms as after the previous war. But they were now cut off on every side by a network of alliances which Rome had industriously spun round them. On the Lucanian border the Romans established a colony of unusually strong numbers at Venusia ; for the purpose of shutting off the Samnites securely from their recent allies in the north they annexed the territory of the Sabines.

The results of the Third Samnite War were for a moment

endangered by a sudden return of the Senones, whom the campaign of Sentinum had checked but not crushed. In 284 the Gauls renewed their invasions of Etruria by laying siege to Arretium. On the defeat of a Roman relief force several Etruscan cities renounced their allegiance, and the unrest spread momentarily to Samnium and Lucania. But the blaze that threatened was promptly stifled by Curius Dentatus, who led a Roman force directly into the invaders own territory and defeated them in a battle which left them at his mercy. The neighbouring Boii attempted to draw off the Romans by another invasion of Etruria (283). Gathering Etruscan troops on their way, the Boii arrived within some fifty miles of Rome, but were held fast and defeated near Lake Vadimo by P. Cornelius Dolabella, and a second invasion in the following year also failed. They sued for peace, and obtained it on easy terms. Their Etruscan allies carried on the struggle for a few more years, but eventually capitulated. The only extension of territory with which the Romans rewarded themselves at this stage was at the expense of their former friend Caere, which was annexed in 273. The reason for this lucky escape of the Etruscans and Boii was that the Romans had in the meantime been called upon to face another war.

## (D) *The War with Tarentum*

Before the third century the Romans had hardly yet entered into relations with the Greek cities of the southern coast. To most of these the Roman power in south Italy was welcome as giving them some guarantee of security against the Oscans. But to the Tarentines it appeared as dangerous.

At the time of the First Samnite War the Tarentines took into their service a Spartan king named Archidamus, who eventually died in a battle against the Lucanians, but for a time kept these enemies in play and put even the Samnite people on their guard. In 334, the year in which Alexander the Great started out on his eastern campaigns, they engaged his brother-in-law, King Alexander of Epirus, who was bent on similar adventures in the west. In a few rapid campaigns Alexander beat off Lucanian and Samnite raiders from the territory of the Greek cities, and he obtained the neutrality of the Romans by an agreement which pledged them not to come to the assistance of their Samnite allies. But the Tarentines, suspecting the growth of Alexander's ambitions, presently withdrew their support and left him to be defeated and slain by the Lucanians. During the Second Samnite War the passage of the Roman armies into Apulia began to cause concern to the Tarentines. The rebuff with which the Romans met a Tarentine proposal for peace, and their establishment of Venusia after the Third Samnite War definitely made enemies of the Tarentines.

The ill-feeling at Tarentum against Rome was brought to a head in 282. In that year the Romans sent a force at the request of the Greek city of Thurii on the Gulf of Otranto to relieve it from the attacks of the Lucanians, including a small fleet. This expedition was resented by the Tarentines as breaking the agreement with Alexander of Epirus, by which the Romans had agreed not to send their ships into the Gulf. Without waiting for explanations, the infuriated Tarentines' army and fleet sank several of the Roman ships, and drove the relief force away from Thurii. With an Etruscan and Gallic campaign still on their hands, the Romans could do nothing. But the Tarentines rejected their request for compensations, for they had in the meantime secured the services of another Epirote king, whose army was considered more than a match for that of Rome.

King Pyrrhus of Epirus was the last of the race of Greek military adventurers. He sought a new outlet for his energies in the west and hastened to the aid of the Tarentines with a force of 25,000 men. Pyrrhus was accounted the best general of his day and his entry into the field put the Romans to a severe test, and their victory over him was remembered with particular pride.

The Romans brought him to battle at Heraclea, on the Gulf of Otranto, with a force of only 20,000 men (280). In this action the Roman legions successfully withstood the highly trained but clumsy spearmen of Pyrrhus' heavy infantry. But the cavalry was thrown into disorder by his corps of elephants — for untrained horses could not be brought to face these unfamiliar beasts — so that Pyrrhus' horsemen were enabled to take the Roman infantry in flank and put it to rout. The king's victory was sufficiently decisive to enlist on his side the other Greek cities and to win over the Lucanians and Samnites. Pyrrhus marched through Campania and Latium and penetrated within fifty miles of Rome. But in these regions he won no fresh allies, and he was obliged to fall back upon south Italy.

In 279 Pyrrhus advanced into Apulia with a force of 40,000 or 50,000 men, where he was met by a reinforced Roman army of equal strength. At the battle of Asculum, Pyrrhus' elephants again won a victory after a hard-fought action, but the Romans made good their retreat to their fortified camp, and the winners' casualties were almost as heavy as those of the vanquished.

The victories of the Epirote king merely served to convince him that the war against Rome could only be won by endurance, and that his reserves might not outlast those of the enemy. After the battle of Heraclea he had conducted negotiations about the ransom of prisoners, and the gestures of friendliness which his agent Cineas had made on his behalf at Rome had been met by the Senate with courtesy. The king made a formal offer of peace, on the condition that the Romans should abandon all southern Italy — a proposal which the Senate rejected. After Asculum Pyrrhus made new offers, in which he demanded nothing more than freedom for the Greeks. On these terms Cineas and the Roman negotiator Fabricius came to an agreement, but the Senate refused to ratify them. This attitude was inspired by the visit of an envoy from the Carthaginians, who suspected that Pyrrhus might be planning an attack upon them, and accordingly made an offer of naval and financial aid to the Romans. Pyrrhus, however, broke off his unhopeful Italian campaign and sought a more promising field of adventure in Sicily.

In the three years of Pyrrhus' absence the Romans beat his Oscan allies out of the field and pressed the Samnites so hard that in 275 they sent him an urgent call for help. The king hastened back to Italy. He laid a plan to surprise and destroy a Roman consular army under the veteran Curius Dentatus near Beneventum ; but Curius held him fast until the other consul was able to come up, and in so doing he won the entire

C

war. Checkmated by the superior Roman forces, Pyrrhus slipped back to Epirus. He posted a garrison in Tarentum, but left his Oscan allies defenceless, and if he ever had thoughts of returning to Italy with a second Greek force he soon forgot them. Shortly before his death in 272 the king recalled the remnant of his troops from Tarentum, and to secure a safe retreat the garrison made over the town to the Romans. In the same year the Roman field armies completed the conquest of the Samnites, Lucanians and Bruttians.

By the settlement of 272 Tarentum and the other Greek cities had Roman garrisons thrust upon them ; but in losing their independence they obtained security against a renewal of the Oscan invasions. The Samnites, Lucanians and Bruttians lost a good deal of territory. The Romans planted colonies at Paestum (on the Lucanian coast), at Aesernia and Beneventum (in the heart of the Samnite country). At the same time they broke up the Samnite confederacy. In the ensuing years some further colonies, including Ariminum, were founded on the Adriatic coast as a defence against the Gauls. By 264 Roman supremacy was recognised in every corner of peninsular Italy.

In 273 King Ptolemy II of Egypt entered into a treaty with Rome. This agreement, it is true, was a mere gesture of diplomatic courtesy and did not commit anybody to anything. But it implied that the Roman republic was now gaining recognition as one of the 'Great Powers' and might soon play a leading part in Mediterranean politics.

## Part 3 : *War, Politics and Economics*

### (A) *Military Growth*

About 450 the Roman army underwent a thorough-going reconstruction. The ill-assorted infantry was replaced by a more compact corps of the Greek type, whose value had been demonstrated at the battle of the Alban Lake, and more uniformity of equipment was introduced into it, for only on this condition could shock tactics by massed foot-soldiers achieve their full effect.

About 430 the Romans provided that in a special military emergency, if the crisis called for complete unity of command, either consul might at short notice nominate a dictator, who would in turn nominate a *magister equitum* ('master of horse') as his chief subordinate. The officer thus appointed had the joint powers of the two consuls and in effect became the absolute ruler of the Roman state, but he was required to 'abdicate' as soon as the crisis was over, or at the latest after six months.

The extension of military conscription to all except the poorest of the peasantry entailed the provision of pay for service in the field. The funds required for this purpose were partly raised by sales of booty, but in part out of the accumulated money in the treasury. The distribution of pay to the troops on campaign also necessitated additional paymasters. In 421, accordingly, the number of the quaestors was raised to four, of whom two (*quaestores consulis*) followed the consuls or other high commanders into the field and administered the military funds; the remaining couple (*quaestores urbani*) kept control of the central treasury in Rome.

After the Gallic invasion a further reform of the Roman field forces was carried out. The battle of the Allia had shown that a column of foot-soldiers armed in Greek fashion with spears might be successfully rushed by a mobile enemy, and that a formation of spearmen, once broken, could not cope with swordsmen. The heavy infantry was therefore provided with a screen of slingers and javelin-throwers. In the main body of the legions the men of the front ranks (*principes*) were rearmed with two *pila* (javelins) and a sword apiece. The middle and rear ranks (*hastati* and *triarii*) for the time being retained their thrusting spears, but eventually the *hastati* were re-equipped on the pattern of the *principes*. The centuries composing each of the three divisions were constituted into separate tactical units or 'maniples' (*manipuli*) with special officers (*centuriones*). On the field of battle the maniples of each division were drawn up with intervals between them; in the course of the action the maniples of the second division would be pushed up into the gaps between the maniples of the *principes*, and the maniples of the *triarii* would, if necessary, reinforce the first two divisions in the same manner. Henceforth the Roman legion combined compactness with elasticity in a remarkable degree. It could fight in loose order or serried ranks, as occasion might require, and the independence of the maniples ensured that if the legion as a whole lost its unity, it could rally round the intact maniples. The superiority of this more mobile formation over the Greek phalanx was decisively proved in Rome's later wars in the eastern Mediterranean.

The Roman army which conquered Italy was no more than a city-state army, whose strength lay in the heavy infantry of the legions. The horsemen had become little more than scouts and flank-guards; the light infantry were incapable of independent manœuvring; the commanders were not sufficiently trained. The war against Pyrrhus revealed that the Roman legions were not yet on a level with armies trained up to the best Greek standards. But in comparison with the other Italian states the Roman forces had several decisive advantages. The man-power supplied by the largest city of Italy and a densely populated suburban area was fully used; and the citizen troops were reinforced from the allied states. The Roman reserves were therefore sufficient to repair even such disasters as those of Lautulae and of Heraclea. But Rome's battalions, besides being the biggest of all Italy, were also the best. Most of their enemies regarded warfare half in the nature of a sport; the Romans looked upon it as a business operation, requiring careful preparation and methodical execution. They submitted themselves to a more rigorous drill and a stricter discipline than their neighbours. In the field the *imperium* of the commander was unrestricted, and offences such as breaking the ranks in battle or sleeping on sentry duty were punished with the death penalty; misconduct by entire units was occasionally punished by the method of 'decimation', which meant the execution of every tenth man (drawn by lot). Also the Romans studied the results of their past operations, and were ready to learn from an enemy, even from a beaten one. Thus the equipment of the legions became the best balanced of all armaments carried by ancient infantry, and their manipular formations was equal to any emergency in a straightforward infantry battle. Three further instruments of victory were created, the military road, the field camp and the colony. The Via Appia and the Via Latina provided two lines of communication with Capua, and became the first strands in a network which eventually covered the whole of Italy. The original Appian and Latin Ways were all-weather routes, which enabled the Romans to throw their forces at any season into Campania or the Samnite borderland. While the roads improved the mobility of the Roman troops, the marching camps which they had to construct at the end of every day in the open field increased their security. The value of these was demonstrated after the battle of Asculum, when the pre-pared camp behind the defeated Roman army preserved it from destruction by Pyrrhus' pursuing cavalry. Lastly, the *coloniae* consolidated the ground won in battle and prepared for a further advance. These settlements usually consisted of some 4500 to 6000 men, who were in most cases provided by Rome and the Latin cities (*coloniae Latinae*), but in some instances mainly by Rome (*coloniae Romanae*). While the colonies gave more land to the Roman and Latin peasants, their primary purpose was to guard strategic points such as river crossings (Fregellae, Interamna), the exits of mountain passes (Alba Fucentia, Ariminum), natural road-centres (Aesernia, Venusia), or convenient landing-places on the coast (Antium, Sena Gallica). By the middle of the third century the network of Roman fortresses, which at that time numbered some twenty-five or thirty, still showed gaps here and there, but it was spread over the whole of peninsular Italy.

## (B) *The Political Organisation of Italy*

In their political settlement of Italy the Romans did not keep to any hard-and-fast scheme of treatment, but treated each case on its own merits. After the Roman conquest the Italians were divided into two broad classes : (1) those who had been incorporated into the Roman state, which included the peoples of Latium, of Campania and southern Etruria, and of the Sabine country with a population of about one million inhabitants in the third century ; (2) those who were bound to Rome by the looser tie of a treaty including the more outlying communities in northern Etruria and Umbria, in the Apennine highlands and in the south of Italy. The *socii*, as the communities bound by treaty were called, numbered about two million people.

There was considerable variety in the status of the individual communities. Among the annexed peoples the Latins obtained the full franchise. The Campanians, Etruscans and Sabines received the 'private' rights of Roman citizenship, which included security of person and property under the protection of the Roman law. But in the view of their farther distance from Rome, and of their unfamiliarity with the Latin tongue, they were not yet regarded as competent to have the 'public' rights, and were therefore denied the privilege of a vote in the Roman Comitia and of holding Roman magistracies.

Among the *socii* the more backward peoples of the central and southern Apennines, where urban centres of population were still rare, entered into collective treaties with Rome which bound the entire tribe (of Marsi, Paeligni, Hirpini, etc.). But wherever city life had developed, the Romans made a separate agreement with each individual town. The total number of treaties made by the Romans with the *socii* rose to over 120.

Some of the *socii* went under the name of '*nomen Latinum*'. This 'Latin denomination' consisted of a few of the original Latin communities and of the so-called 'Latin colonies', which consisted of settlers from Rome and the lesser Latin towns in every region of Italy. Since most of the cities of Latium had been incorporated into the Roman state, the word 'Latin' became a purely legal term, and had no necessary connexion with Latium. In contrast with the remainder of the *socii*, the 'Latins' were granted *commercium* (the right of conducting private suits in Roman courts on the same terms as Roman citizens), and *conubium* (the right of intermarriage, so that a Latin woman might become the lawful wife of a Roman citizen and her sons would inherit Roman franchise). In addition, individual Latins passing through Rome might exercise a vote in the Tribal Assembly, and if they came to reside permanently in the capital they might obtain the full Roman franchise.

All Italians, of whatever category, were made liable to

military service on Rome's behalf. The new citizens of the incorporated states were enrolled on the census lists and drafted into the Roman legions. The *socii* were bound to supply military aid (or, as in the case of the Greek seaboard towns, transport vessels and cruisers). In practice, one-half of the infantry in a Roman field force of the third century consisted of allied troops, grouped in special *cohortes* or battalions under a Roman *praefectus*; the greater number of the cavalry was drawn from the allied states.

All Italians on the census lists were subjected to all Roman taxes. For the enforcement of the Roman state's demands in men and money, four additional quaestors (*quaestores Italici*) were stationed at various points in the annexed territory. For the hearing of the more important lawsuits, both civil and criminal, in the more distant of the incorporated states, the praetor at Rome nominated a number of *praefecti* or deputy-judges, who visited some of the outlying districts.

The *socii* retained their full rights of local self-government, and their constitutions were left untouched: indeed the Romans had little reason to interfere with the local administrations, for most of the Italian states were ruled by landowning aristocracies whose interests were naturally bound up with those of the Roman governing class. The use of the local dialects and the observance of the traditional religion were not discouraged in any way. The *socii* paid no taxes to Rome; they were not placed under the regular supervision of Roman officials; and they were not called upon to accommodate Roman garrisons, except as a special war measure in rare cases.

On first impression the Roman organisation of Italy would appear to be unjust. The dependants of Rome were bound to render military aids, yet none of them, save a few Latin communities which had received the full Roman franchise, had a voice in determining peace and war.

But, in return for military service, they shared the fruits of the Roman victories. All alike received their quota of the booty; and the Roman supremacy gave the Italians such security as they had never yet possessed, and could never have realised except under Roman leadership. It guaranteed them against Gallic invasions from the north, against wars within Italy and against internal revolutions.

Again, provided that they discharged the few obligations which the Roman laid upon them, the Italians were left free. They were not subjected to jealous supervision or to financial exploitation. Lastly, the Italians could look forward to an eventual admission into Roman citizenship. Under these conditions the Roman settlement found general acceptance in Italy, and Roman rule became firmly established.

### (c) *Economic Conditions*

The Romans were so much absorbed in their career of conquest in the fourth century that their city lagged behind several of its dependent towns in point of wealth. Such economic progress as Italy experienced in this age was due to the Greeks in the south of the peninsula. An improved breed of wheat (*frumentum*), which they introduced from overseas, now gradually displaced the native Italic *far*, and baked bread began to supplant the customary dish of porridge. The use of silver or bronze coinage, which became common among the Greeks of Sicily and Italy after 550, spread in the fifth century to Etruria ; but it was not until about 300 that any considerable number of Italic communities set up their own mints. Among individual Greek cities Tarentum became the chief trading-place of the peninsula. North of the Tiber the Etruscans kept their metal and pottery industry. Their armourers and ironworkers found good markets in Italy, and chiefly in Rome itself. In the fourth century the potters of Campania and Apulia imitated the fine painted vases of Greece ; at the same time Capua grew into a centre of bronze manufacture.

In the fifth and fourth centuries the citizen community of Rome was almost wholly engaged in agriculture. The ruling families derived their wealth from the land ; distinguished senators were not too proud to reside on their estates and supervise the farm-work in person, or even to put their own hands to the plough. Imports into Rome were restricted to articles of necessity, such as grain in seasons of shortage. The lack of Roman interest in foreign commerce is plainly shown by the terms of the fourth-century treaties with Carthage, in which the integrity of the Latin coast is jealously safeguarded against foreign occupation, but the claims of Carthage to set up a trading monopoly in the western Mediterranean are allowed. The seaboard colonies of Ostia and Antium were intended to protect the coast-lands against military attack rather than to open up an overseas trade.

The slowness of Rome's economic development is also shown in the history of its coinage. Its first mintage of bronze was probably not issued until about 300, and the earliest silver coins not long before the Pyrrhic War. Possibly the first Roman silver pieces were coined in the interest of traders, or for the benefit of Roman soldiers on service in southern Italy, where money had long been the ordinary medium of exchange.

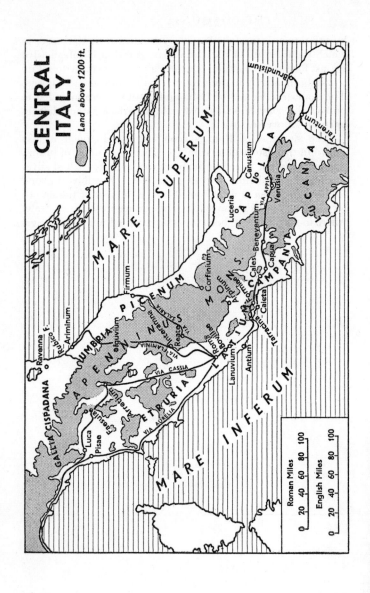

CENTRAL ITALY

Land above 1200 ft.

MARE SUPERUM

MARE INFERUM

GALLIA CISPADANA

Ravenna
Rubico F.
Ariminum

UMBRIA

APENNINUS

Iguvium

ETRURIA

Arretium
Faesulae
Clusium
Luca
Pisae

VIA CASSIA

VIA AURELIA

PICENUM

Firmum

VIA FLAMINIA

Interamna
Reate

VIA SALARIA

Corfinium

MONS

Roma
Lanuvium
Antium

LATIUM

Terracina
Caieta

VIA APPIA

APULIA

Luceria
Canusium
Venusia

Cales Beneventum
Minturnae
CAMPANIA
Capua

Brundisium

Tarentum

LUCANIA

Roman Miles
0  20  40  60  80  100

English Miles
0  20  40  60  80  100

### CHAPTER V

# POLITICS OF THE EARLY REPUBLIC

## (A) *The First Republican Constitution*

THE revolution which ended the monarchy at Rome was achieved by the nobles and for the nobles. The Roman republic was therefore at first an aristocracy. About 500 B.C. the patrician *gentes*, which at that time numbered about fifty, contained less than one-tenth of the free population. But their wealth and power gave them unchallenged authority. The patricians did not dispute the ultimate sovereignty of the people ; by the new constitution the commons met from time to time in the Comitia Curiata to ratify important acts of state. But the decisions of the Comitia were made subject to the approval of the Senate. The Comitia Curiata was further tied by the bonds of clientship which attached many of its members to the patrician families and stopped them voting against the wishes of their patrons.

The powers of the kings passed virtually intact into the hands of two magistrates, who at first carried the name of praetors ('headmen'), but at a later date adopted the title of consuls ('colleagues'). The two consuls held office for one year only, and as each had equal authority and the same range of functions as his partner, each possessed in fact an unlimited power of veto over the other. To this extent the sovereignty of the consuls was less complete than that of the kings. But in actual practice the head magistrates usually shared out their duties amicably, or at least refrained from mutual interference ; therefore while their power lasted it was in effect monarchical. The kings' successors retained (most significantly) the twelve lictors and the *fasces*. They continued to exercise the king's personal command in war, and the importance of their military duties increased as the range of Roman warfare grew wider.

They assumed the same disciplinary power over the citizens, but delegated some of it to officers of lower rank, the *quaestores*. The quaestors also retained custody of the *aerarium*.

In religious matters alone the consuls did not inherit the functions of the king. The major part of these was made over to the Pontifex Maximus, who nominated the Flamines and the Vestal Virgins.

The royal powers were jealously conserved within the narrow circle of the aristocracy. The choice of the head magistrates was probably made at first by the outgoing pair, who nominated their successors with the agreement of the Senate, subject to a formal ratification by the Comitia Curiata, which was invited to confer the *imperium* upon the consuls, as it had formerly upon the kings. Under this system the consular office remained securely in the hands of the noble families. Among the patrician *gentes* a small inner ring, who secured most consular places, was formed at the very outset of the republican period, for the chief magistracy fell again and again into the hands of men carrying the name of Aemilius, Cornelius, Fabius and (after 450) Claudius. But alongside these names the lists of the early consuls contain many others which are seldom or never repeated. The aristocratic ideal of sharing out power equally within the privileged circle was fairly well realised under the early republic.

But their chief source of patrician power was the Senate. Under the republican constitution the Senate could not meet except at the pleasure of a magistrate, nor discuss any business beyond that which he laid before it. Yet in actual practice the consuls were dependent on the Senate, because of the brevity of their term of office. The Senate no doubt controlled the head magistrates, and influenced their choice of successors. But while it gained in authority, it became more rigidly aristocratic.

## (B) *The Plebeians*

Under patrician rule the Roman republic maintained an uphill fight against hostile neighbours, with eventual success. But it suffered under economic hardships which brought political disorder.

In the first half of the fifth century the extension of the Roman frontiers was brought to a standstill, and the productivity of the land was reduced by frequent enemy attacks. To avert a famine, the republican government was repeatedly compelled to make special purchases of grain in Etruria, Campania or Sicily. The expulsion of the Tarquins and the interruption of communications with Etruria caused a decline of overseas trade (much of which had probably reached Rome by way of the Etruscan town of Caere).

Under these conditions even the patricians were reduced to a life of severe simplicity, and a single bad season might plunge the peasants into debt. But in early Rome rates of interest were high, and the penalties for inability to pay were merciless. Failure to repay meant losing one's land, or even one's liberty. Many no doubt obtained loans under more humane conditions by attaching themselves to a patron; some succeeded in paying off their liability by personal service. But it was a not uncommon fate for Roman freemen to end their days as serfs or to be sold to an Etruscan or Greek slave-dealer. Another grievance of the commons lay in the general severity of punishments inflicted upon public offenders, and in the powers to convict people which the consular *imperium* (whether exercised in person or by the quaestors) carried with it.

Out of these grievances arose the 'Conflict of the Orders', a class struggle between the patricians and plebeians which lasted over two centuries. The most distinctive feature of the Conflict is that the plebeians entered it as an organised body. Their methods were not those of mob violence, but of collective bargaining and preconcerted resistance.

In the earliest wars of the republic the patricians carried the brunt of the fighting. But the continual hostilities of the period necessitated a heavier call upon the man-power of the state. In order to get more troops a new organisation of the Roman territory was carried through at some date before the middle of the fifth century. The three original tribes of the Ramnes, Tities and Luceres were replaced by a new division into four 'urban' and sixteen 'rustic' tribes, which covered the whole of the private land in the Roman state.

In assuming the burden of regular military duty the

plebeians became more conscious of their own value to the
state, and acquired habits of discipline and co-operation which
enabled them to assert their rights more effectively. The
leadership which they required in their political warfare was
supplied by the richer landowners who stood outside the
privileged circle and were not qualified for the consulship, but
might hold commands as *tribuni militum*. As self-appointed
*tribuni plebis* they became the spokesmen of the plebeians. In
the last resort the tribunes of the *plebs* would organise a strike
against military service.

The publication of the Twelve Tables in 451 (see page 57)
disappointed the plebeians. The reply of the plebeians was a
'secession' to the Aventine, in which the aggrieved peasants
went to seek the support of the small middle-class trading
community there. At the Aventine convention the assembled
plebeians completed their organisation by making themselves
into a new corporation, a state within the state. The controlling body within this opposition-state was a general parliament of the plebeians grouped according to the tribes in which
they were enrolled (*Concilium Plebis Tributum*). The executive
consisted of two officials called *aediles* and ten tribunes, who
were to be annually elected by the Concilium. The tribunes
undertook to represent the community before the consuls and
Senate, and to protect individual plebeians against a harsh use
of the consular *imperium*. They soon acquired a higher status
within the plebeian organisation than the *aediles*.

To this the patricians made no immediate answer. Yet in
refraining from active opposition, they virtually conceded the
right of holding plebeian parliaments — which before long
were transferred without protest from the Aventine to the
Forum — and acknowledged the *ius auxilii* ('right of giving
help') of the tribunes, which these eventually developed into
a general power of veto.

After the Gallic invasion of 390 the economic distress again
became acute. The devastations of the Gauls had damaged
heavily the smaller landowners. In the next thirty years,
during which the Romans made good past losses rather than
gained fresh ground, the distribution of new land almost came
to a standstill. Neither did industry or trade give the plebeians

any relief, for throughout the fourth century these remained at a low ebb. At the same time the burden of conscription grew more oppressive. It is no accident that the severest political conflicts of the fourth and early third centuries usually took place soon after the more difficult wars of the period. But the demand for economic remedies was now reinforced with a claim for political reforms. This was due to the rising ambitions of the more well-to-do plebeians. These men, having already been admitted to the higher commands in the Roman army, had confidence in their own powers, and now aimed to abolish aristocratic privilege.

On the other hand the patricians, with equally firm leaders and a docile group of clients to vote as directed, fought every position inch by inch. But the final success of the *plebs* was virtually assured through the growing difficulties in the numbers of either party. The patricians had suffered a progressive decline in their numerical strength. This decrease was partly due to their losses on the field of battle, of which they had always borne their full share ; but its principal cause was the self-imposed ban on intermarriage with plebeians. Of the fifty-three patrician *gentes* whose names are recorded in the history of the fifth century only twenty-nine reappear in the fourth century. By 300 the ratio of nobles to commons must have fallen to less than one in twenty.

Moreover several noble families were induced by ambition, to show favour towards the plebeians. The Fabii, the foremost *gens* of the early republic, befriended several of the plebeian champions and helped them to high military commands ; the Aemilii, the Valerii and the Claudii (who rose into prominence towards the end of the fourth century) supported a policy of yielding to the plebeians.

## (c) *Legislation*

1. *The Twelve Tables.*—Since the first object of the plebeians was fuller security of person and property, they tried to get a written code of laws. In 451 the patricians eventually appointed a commission of ten men to reduce the existing law, both public and private, into definite and permanent shape.

The code of the 'Twelve Tables' covered both public and

private life.  In private law it regulated the rights and duties attaching to the family and to individual property, and the limits of defence of those rights.  In public affairs it defined offences against the community, and it laid down a few fundamental rules of the constitution.  In the matter of family law it permitted, under certain conditions, the freeing of wives and children from the rule of the *pater familias*.  It conceded the right of association for purposes of trade, and safeguarded the community against abuses of personal liberty.  Above all, it set a ban on the taking of life except by sentence of a competent court.

The constitutional laws contained in the Twelve Tables affirmed the right of appeal from any sentence and any court to the popular assembly, and in particular they gave the final decision in a case of death or exile to the Comitia Curiata.  In 447 the appointment of the quaestors, who usually dealt with capital charges and introduced them to the Comitia, was transferred to this assembly.

The code of the Twelve Tables was never repealed ; indeed some of its statutes remained in force to the end of Roman history.  In course of time Romans learnt to take a sentimental pride in it, and with reason.  Taken as a whole, it was the law of an orderly but progressive community.  To the oppressed plebeians it gave the general security of written rules.

Yet the Tables left a number of points unsettled.  They did not curtail the *imperium* of the consuls.  Above all, they did not cure the economic distress.  In the interests of the debtor they provided that execution of a court order against him should be delayed for thirty days ; they required the creditor to give him adequate food and not to overload him with chains ; and they laid down a further interval during which the prisoner was to be given the opportunity of raising the amount of his ransom before he was sold into permanent slavery.  But they provided no remedy for the conditions which plunged men into debt.  Finally, they placed a legal ban upon intermarriage between the two orders.

2. *Economic Legislation.*—In the economic field the plebeians made frequent vain attempts to remedy distress by legislation

in the Concilium Plebis. In 357 they fixed the maximum rate of interest at 10 per cent ; in 347 they lowered it to 5 per cent ; in 342 they prohibited it altogether. Another measure, the Lex Poetelia of 326, compelled creditors to accept any property which debtors might offer in payment, and required under all circumstances a judgment by a court of law to authorise enslavement.

A further act, which was carried in 367 by the tribunes C. Licinius Stolo and L. Sextius, was directed against the taking over of public pastures by the larger flock-masters. The law was a step in the right direction in that it liberated land for the impoverished peasants, which was the only lasting solution of the agrarian problem. Before 360 the total amount of land available for this purpose was small, and the legislation of 367 could have been little help. But after that date large tracts of territory were acquired in the newly-conquered parts of central and southern Italy. In regions where Roman colonies were needed the patricians of their own accord gave territory to the colonists ; in other districts the plebeian leaders demanded the distribution of land in individual allotments. On this latter principle the Pomptine level was re-peopled with Roman peasants in 358, and in 318 a large tract in the country of the Volscians and in northern Campania (the *ager Falernus*) was disposed of in the same way. It has been reckoned that between 343 and 264 some 60,000 new holdings were created by colonisation and allotment. Of these some were reserved for Latins, but it is safe to assume that not less than 40,000 Roman families benefited. In this manner the Roman conquests, which to a large degree were the cause of the economic crisis, brought their own remedy with them.

(D) *New Assemblies*

1. *The Comitia Centuriata.*—In order to make the fullest use of the state's available man-power a census or National Service Register was instituted about 450, on which all land-owners except the poorest were inscribed in five 'classes' or conscription-groups, according to their wealth and the standard of equipment to which they could conform. Each *classis* was also subdivided into a varying number of *centuriae* or companies

of one hundred men apiece. The Roman army was divided
into two corps (to which the name of *legiones* was now transferred), each about 4000 strong. The preparation of the new
register was given to a number of 'censors', and new censors
were appointed from time to time (usually at intervals of five
years) to keep the list up to date. The censors would summon
all those liable for service to an inspection parade, which was
held in military array on the Campus Martius, the assembly
ground of the Roman army. At this assembly the citizens
were marshalled in their appropriate 'centuries', and it received
the name of *Comitia Centuriata*.

The new Comitia became a political parliament. It took
upon itself the duty of appointing the censors, and the consuls
who led it into battle. By 427 it had further claimed and won
a final voice in the declaration of war. Before long the Comitia
Centuriata as a political body became distinct from the censors'
parade. The political rights once obtained by the men on the
military roll could not in fairness be withdrawn from them
after they had passed the age limit (forty-six years) for field
service. The *seniores* were accordingly permitted to retain
their vote, and for this purpose were grouped in separate
'centuries'. The centuriate assembly acquired an *esprit de
corps* which rendered it more self-reliant and independent than
the Comitia Curiata. The Comitia Curiata eventually lost
what little importance it had ever possessed ; soon after 400
its meetings were reduced to a mere formality.

In the fourth century the Comitia Centuriata extended its
power so as to become a legislative body and a high court of
law. Before 350 it had replaced the Comitia Curiata as a court
of appeal, and it took special charge of all cases involving the
loss of *caput* or citizen status, i.e. death or exile. A new
statute, introduced by the consul, M. Valerius, in 300, reaffirmed the right of appeal from all criminal courts in such a
way as to leave the patricians no loophole of escape.

The electoral power of the Comitia Centuriata received a
slight extension in 366. In order to leave the consuls a freer
hand a new official, for whom the name of 'praetor' was
revived, was annually appointed. Though the praetor might
act as a delegate of the consuls in any capacity, his primary

duty was to supervise civil law. The election was naturally entrusted to the assembly that appointed the consuls. The electoral acts of the Comitia Centuriata remained subject to the Senate's approval until 338.

Before the end of the fourth century the Centuriate Assembly received a more definite organisation. The voters were still grouped into five property classes, but in the re-arranged Comitia the number of centuries, which had previously risen with the increase of the citizen body, was fixed at a permanent total of 193, so that a political *centuria* henceforth contained an indefinite and constantly increasing number of individual voters. At the same time the rating of the voter's property, which had previously been made in land, was reckoned in money, so that the landless citizens (as yet only a few) were enrolled on the same terms as landowners. The following scheme illustrates the new organisation :

| Property Class | Number of Centuries |
|---|---|
| *Equites* (cavalry class) | 18 |
| Class 1 | 80 |
| Class 2 | 20 |
| Class 3 | 20 |
| Class 4 | 20 |
| Class 5 | 30 |
| Others | 5 |
| | Total 193 |

The remarkably high proportion of centuries of the first class might suggest that the reorganisation of the Comitia was a device whose real object was to deliver the assembly into the hands of a wealthy minority. But an arrangement by which a small group of voters could have controlled the entire Comitia would have been such an obvious device, that it could never have been tolerated by the plebeians at a time when they had become fully conscious of their political power. In all probability the centuries of the first class were not the preserve of the patricians — these were for the most part enrolled in the Equites — but of the more prosperous Romans, whose sympathies did not ordinarily go with the nobility. The only privilege accorded to wealth was that the several classes voted in succession and that a *centuria praerogativa* ('first-voting century') of the Equites recorded its vote in advance of all others.

2. *The Comitia Tributa.*—The plebeians' principal gain in the fourth and third centuries lay in the recognition of their Concilium Plebis as a legally constituted parliament of equal authority with the centuriate assembly. Grouped into tribal divisions which were no less convenient than the centuries for taking a popular vote, the Concilium Plebis had always more rules for itself which it enforced by the tribunes. Presently it began to pass resolutions of wider scope, which the tribunes endeavoured to make binding upon the entire people. All such rules and resolutions were called 'plebiscita'.

This claim was not admitted at first by the patricians. But in 366 they entrusted the election of the quaestors and of a new pair of magistrates, the curule aediles, to a tribal assembly of their own creation, the Comitia Tributa, and soon after this date they began to use it (under the presidency of a consul or praetor) as an alternative to the centuriate assembly. This assembly always remained legally distinct from the Concilium Plebis. Yet the composition of the two tribal assemblies was the same, and once the Comitia Tributa had been instituted, recognition could no longer be withheld from the Concilium Plebis. In 339 the patricians agreed to a law carried by the dictator Q. Publilius Philo in the Centuriate Assembly, that *plebiscita* should be binding on the whole community, subject to the consent of the Senate. Later the Senate's right of veto on plebiscites was abolished, and the Concilium Plebis became the principal assembly for legislative purposes.

Within the Tribal Assembly (for the Comitia Tributa and the Concilium Plebis may be treated as one) all the landless citizens were included in the four urban tribes. Since the number of the city tribes was not increased with the growth of the town, whereas the number of the rustic tribes was, their individual votes eventually counted for less. But so long as the proportion of landless citizens remained small, this was of slight importance.

The Comitia of the third century played an effective and

essential part in the government. With a membership of several thousands, they were unfitted to discuss public questions in detail. Therefore they never claimed the initiative in bringing forward new measures, but left it to the appropriate magistrate to summon them at his discretion ; and although a certain amount of free debate took place in the informal *contiones* (assemblies) which preceded the formal assembly for registering votes, speech-making was in fact almost confined to the persons of high political standing. But in the third century the membership of the Comitia was still drawn for the most part from the peasants of the neighbouring countryside, who had sufficient economic independence and adequate knowledge of the general outlines of current politics to give an intelligent personal vote.

(E) *Plebeians in the Magistracies and the Senate*

About 370 the tribunes Licinius and Sextius brought forward a resolution in the Concilium Plebis, that one of the two consulships should be thrown open to plebeians. This demand was resisted by the patricians. But in 367 the presiding officer at the elections accepted the candidature of Sextius, who proceeded to hold the first plebeian consulship in 366. From 341 the plebeians regularly obtained possession of one of the consulships.

In 366 they gained entry to the new magistracy of the curule aediles. At the same time, the curule aediles came to an understanding with the plebeian aediles, so that henceforth the four aediles formed in fact a united magistracy. But a far more important prize was won by the plebeians in 356, when a distinguished soldier of their order, C. Marcius Rutilus, was nominated to a dictatorship. In 351 the same plebeian leader was elected to a censorship ; in 357 Q. Publilius Philo, who had already held a dictatorship in 339, held the first plebeian praetorship. Finally, in 300 the tribunes Q. and Cn. Ogulnius carried a measure which raised the number of the pontifices and augures from four to nine each, and laid down that the additional members of either board should be plebeians.

The admission of plebeians to the Senate could be at the most a rare exception, so long as the lists of the House were made up by patrician magistrates. This power, which had originally been in the hands of the consuls, was transferred to the censors (probably in 366, after the opening of the consulate to the plebeians). But in 351 the censorship in turn was thrown open to the *plebs*, and at some later date the choice of new senators came to be made in the first instance from ex-magistrates. Strangely enough, the tribunate was not included among the qualifying magistracies until late in the second century. But as plebeians came to hold the other offices, their representation in the Senate became progressively stronger.

Promotions of plebeians to the consulship came by fits and starts rather than in a steady flow. In the next hundred years only some ten plebeian *gentes* definitely established themselves among the ruling houses at Rome. New elements which penetrated into the governing circles at Rome were derived not only from the leading plebeian families of the capital, but from the ruling houses of the neighbouring Latin and Italian towns. Under the electoral system of the third century the magistracy became fairly representative of the best talent in the Roman state. Furthermore, since a magistracy now conferred almost automatically a seat in the Senate, this body in turn became a reservoir of political ability, and the great majority of its members had received a training in executive responsibility.

## (F) *Changes in the Magistrates*

The rapid growth of the Roman state had entailed an increase in the number of the magistrates and a new division of functions among them. This was carried out in the years 367–366. Henceforth the general framework was complete, and the various offices gradually arranged themselves in a definite ladder. The foundations of a political career would be laid in a term of military service, usually lasting from the seventeenth to the twenty-seventh year, and ending with a military tribunate. After that a would-be politician could try for a quaestorship, with an aedileship or, alternatively, a tribuneship of the *plebs* to follow. If he proceeded to a higher magistracy, he might qualify for a consulate by a previous term of office as praetor ; after 227, when the number of the praetorships was increased, this office became a necessary preliminary to the consulship. The censorship and dictatorship were kept for men of consular rank. The same office might be held for more than one term, and men of high ambition made a point of holding as many consulships as they could obtain. About 330 a law was passed which laid down an interval of ten years between holding the same office twice, but during the major wars of the fourth and third centuries this measure was often suspended by the Senate, in order to establish some continuity in the higher commands.

The consulate was tending to become an exclusively military office. The ever-growing scale of military operations gave it a peculiar glamour. A successful Roman general could look forward to being greeted as *imperator* by his troops on the field of battle, to a triumphal procession on his return to the city, and to a large share in the booty. Within the circle of the ruling families the distinction of the individual families came to be reckoned by the number of consulates which their members had gained.

The praetor had a narrow range of duties, for his powers were concerned with civil law only. A more important function of the praetor was that of publishing *edicta* or general ordinances, in which he laid down principles for the handling of cases on which law or common custom gave no clear ruling. In addition, he acted as a general deputy of the consuls, assembling the Senate in their absence, and sometimes even following them into the battlefield.

In the fourth and third centuries the censorship attained a position of peculiar authority. In distributing the citizens into their appropriate property classes, the censors took into consideration other qualifications than those of property, and could degrade into a lower class persons whom they could convict of bad citizenship in any form. A further function of the censors was the duty of drawing up the list of the Senate. Though restricted in the choice of new members, they retained the right of not replacing on the roll former members whom they considered unworthy, so that their disciplinary power extended to the ruling families of Rome. But the exercise of these arbitrary powers could only remain tolerable so long as the censors themselves were men of high character. The censors' office therefore came to be reserved for men who had reached the top of the ladder of power (known as the '*cursus honorum*', or 'course of honours').

Another increasingly important function of the censors lay in finance. They took into their hands the arrangements for the collection of indirect taxes, and they hired out the contracts for public works undertaken at the state's expense, such as the construction of the great military roads.

But the most remarkable rise in status among Roman offices was that of the *tribuni plebis*. It never became a magistracy in the strict sense, for the tribunes always lacked the right to wear a purple-edged toga, and to be attended by lictors. Yet, however, the tribunes had by 300 attained a power without parallel among ancient states. In the last resort their position depended on their opportunities of obstruction. By enlargement of their original *ius auxilii* on behalf of oppressed plebeians, the tribunes of the fifth and fourth centuries had brought the actions of all the magistrates, the resolutions of the Senate and the bills submitted to the various popular assemblies within the scope of their veto. Indeed they had established an unquestioned right to exercise this veto at will.

In practice power could only have been secured by restraint in its use, and readiness to compromise on the part of the patricians. Eventually an arrangement was made, by which the tribunes were transformed from leaders of opposition into instruments of government. Though they might not have a seat in the Senate, the tribunes received the right of putting motions to the House ; by 216 they were even authorised to summon it and preside over it. Without losing their ultimate power of using their veto at will, the tribunes placed it at the general disposal of the Senate. Without sacrificing their rights of carrying laws in the Tribal Assembly, they usually consulted the Senate beforehand.

CHAPTER VI

# CONQUEST OF THE WEST

## Part 1: *The First Punic War*

### (A) *Carthage*

AFTER the conquest of peninsular Italy the Romans possessed
as much land as they could cultivate effectively. Their interest
in overseas trade, which to them was an accidental result of
conquest, had scarcely yet been awakened. Yet they had
hardly completed the conquest of the Italian peninsula than
they launched out into an endless succession of overseas
adventures.

Rome's first antagonist outside of Italy was the city of
Carthage. Founded about 800 by Phoenicians from Tyre, in
a commanding position at a meeting-point of Mediterranean
trade routes, Carthage was marked out by nature to be a centre
of commerce.

At the time of their first clash with the Romans the Carthaginian (or, as the Romans called it, the 'Punic') empire
consisted of the coastlands of North Africa, of southern Spain,
of Sardinia and Corsica, and of western Sicily. Their city was
the largest and richest in the western Mediterranean. Its
wealth was not derived from agriculture. But Punic commerce
acquired a virtual monopoly in the western Mediterranean and
the Atlantic. In the fifth century Punic explorers opened up a
lucrative traffic in Cornish tin, and in gold and ivory from
West Africa. Additional money came to Carthage from the
contributions levied upon the other Phoenician cities in the
western Mediterranean, and from the rents imposed upon
the Libyans of the Punic hinterland.

The chief weakness of Carthage, from both a political and
a military point of view, lay in its dependence upon slave

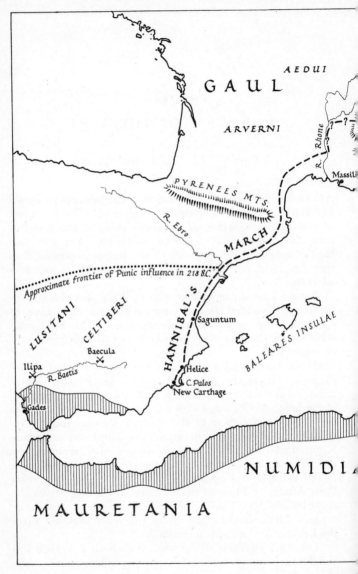

GAUL

AEDUI

ARVERNI

Rhone

R. Rhone

Massili

PYRENEES MTS.

R. Ebro

MARCH

Approximate frontier of Punic influence in 218 B.C.

HANNIBAL'S

LUSITANI

CELTIBERI

Baecula ✕

Ilipa ✕

R. Baetis

Saguntum ●

BALEARES INSULAE

Helice ●

C. Palos

New Carthage

Gades ●

NUMIDIA

MAURETANIA

VENETI

Aquileia

ILLYRIA

Mediolanum

INSUBRES

Placentia

LIGURIA

Parma   Mutina

BOII

Lucca

R. Arno

Faesulae

Arretium

Cortona

Ariminum

R. Metaurus

Sena Gallica

UMBRIA

Pharos

Issa

Scodra

Lissus

ETRURIA

L. Trasimene

Sabines

SAMNIUM

Rome

CORSICA

CAMPANIA

Naples

Capua

Nola

R. Aufidus

Cannae

Canusium

APULIA

Tarentum

EPIRUS

LUCANIA

SARDINIA

BRUTTIUM

Croton

Corcyra

M. Ercte

Panormus

Drepana

Aegates Is.

Motya

Mylae

Rhegium

Messana

Himera

HIEROS

KINGDOM

Syracuse

C. Farina

Lilybaeum

Utica

Carthage

Agrigentum

Ecnomus

R. Bagradas

Zama

✕   Site of battle

Area of Punic Empire in 264 B.C.

Scale   0   100   200 Miles

ᴾUNIC WAR

labour, and in the consequent lack of a solid, loyal body of middle- and lower-class citizens who would be prepared to support their country to the bitter end. However, their economic resources allowed the Carthaginians to build up a force which proved a match for all comers until they met the Romans. The war fleet, on which the citizens themselves served, was equipped and navigated by expert seamen ; in the third century it had definitely taken the control of the western seas from Syracuse and Tarentum. The foreign-service armies of Carthage contained hardly any citizen troops, but were a mixture of conscripts from Africa, of auxiliary troops hired from the chief of the free native states of Numidia, and of mercenaries from all corners of the western Mediterranean. Such mixed collections of men were naturally not easy to control, and they had performed poorly in the warfare against the Greek cities of Sicily. But the command of these forces was held by officers who made a special profession of war, and so gained a wider experience than the Roman consuls, who changed every year.

The Carthaginian government was an oligarchy of wealthy merchants. The organs of administration were a senate with an inner council of thirty leading nobles, and a high court of one hundred judges, also drawn from the ruling families. The aristocracy kept a jealous eye on its professional generals, and took ample precautions against attempts at military revolutions.

In its foreign relations the Punic government was prepared, if necessary, to defend its interests by force of arms, but avoided war where peaceful methods availed, and it never fought without some definite gain in view. In Africa it annexed no more than a portion of Tunisia and Tripoli, in all some 20,000 square miles. In its relations with the Italian states (where its trade was not extensive) it relied upon diplomacy to remove in advance the causes of a possible clash. In the sixth century it had come to amicable terms with the Etruscan seaboard towns. In the fourth century, as soon as the Romans acquired an extensive coastline in Latium, it offered them two successive treaties, and in 279 a military alliance against Pyrrhus.

But the Romans suspected that the Carthaginians might

seek to control the Italian coasts in the same manner as they dominated the coasts of Spain and Sicily. In each of their three treaties they had insisted that the Carthaginians must not take any permanent foothold on Italian soil. Between 350 and 270 they had established a chain of coastguard colonies, composed of Romans without any mixture of Latins, from Etruria to Campania. In 311 they had a flotilla of cruisers to patrol the Italian coast, and in 267 they had specially entrusted the new *quaestores Italici* with the supervision of naval defences. Nevertheless as late as 264 a clash between Rome and Carthage seemed a remote possibility.

## (B) *The Affair of Messana*

The city of Messana stood in a commanding position in Sicily on the straits between Sicily and Italy. Since 289 it had been in the hands of a corps of discharged Campanian mercenaries, who went by the name of 'Mamertines' (sons of Mars). In 264 it was besieged by Hiero, the ruler of other Sicilian states. The Mamertines accepted an offer of help from a Punic fleet, whose admiral induced Hiero to call off his attack. But as soon as they were rid of Hiero, they at once tried to get rid of the Carthaginians, and offered themselves as allies to the Romans.

In the Senate opinions were so evenly balanced that it referred the matter to the Comitia without any positive recommendation. The voters in the popular assembly showed equal hesitation at first, but were eventually won over to action by the presiding consuls, who told the commons that an expedition to Sicily might bring in large 'benefits', i.e. military reputations for the commanders and booty for the troops. The Comitia, it is true, at first went no further than to order a relief expedition to Messana, and the Roman detachment which was sent to carry out these instructions fulfilled them without any shedding of blood, for the Punic commander lost his nerve at the unexpected appearance of the Romans and tamely withdrew from the city, which the Romans garrisoned. But the Carthaginian government sent an expeditionary force to recover the lost prize, and succeeded in bringing Hiero back, this time against the Romans. On the other hand the Senate reinforced the small garrison with a consular army. Thus the scuffle round Messana drew on the Romans and Carthaginians into formal war : a war in which the Romans were certainly the aggressors.

## (c) *War in Sicily*

Before the Roman reinforcements could reach Messana, the city had been placed under siege by two separate forces from Carthage and from Syracuse. On his arrival the consul Appius Claudius split up these allies, who withdrew their troops in different directions. In 263 a strong Roman army under the consul Manius Valerius invaded Hiero's territory and besieged Syracuse. Against the immensely strong fortifications of the city, Valerius' attack was bound to fail. But the consul had a diplomatic success in detaching Hiero from his alliance with Carthage. Hiero was admitted to an alliance on equal terms with Rome.

With Messana in their hands and the king of Syracuse on their side, the Romans had completely cut off the Carthaginians from the Straits. Nevertheless the Punic government made a second and greater attempt to make good its losses. It prepared to throw a new army of more than 50,000 men across to Sicily, using as its base the Greek city of Agrigentum on the south coast. To stop this, the Romans in 262 advanced across the whole breadth of the island and put Agrigentum under siege. After a hard-fought campaign, they stormed and sacked the city. The capture of Agrigentum was a turning-point in the First Punic War. Henceforth the Romans frankly allowed their policy to be dictated by military ambitions, and in this spirit they set themselves new war objects which in 264 had been far from their minds.

The decision of the Romans to conquer the whole of Sicily cost them twenty years of further warfare. The campaign of 261 made them realise that they badly needed a fleet. At this time the Carthaginian fleet consisted of some 120 quinqueremes (galleys propelled by fifty or more large oars), and containing a crew of 120 marines. Against these the Romans had nothing but a few cruisers. They now built a fleet of quinqueremes slightly outnumbering that of Carthage. The challenge which they threw out to the more practised Punic navy was not quite so rash as might appear at first sight. In ancient naval warfare the advantage of superior manœuvring was severely limited by the lack of efficient artillery: the final decision could only be won by ramming or boarding. Every ancient sea-fight therefore tended to become a land-battle, in which the marines rather than the rowers settled the fight.

In 260 the completed Roman battle-fleet, some 150 strong, met a Punic squadron of equal numbers off the north coast of Sicily near Mylae. The Carthaginians rushed in upon them, only to find themselves held fast by grappling-irons and involved in a hand-to-hand fight. In the end they broke away with a loss of fifty vessels. The battle of Mylae gave them the command of the Sicilian waters for several years to come, for the Punic government made no immediate attempt to recover its naval power. On the other hand the Romans wasted their victory by indecisive warfare against the Carthaginian colonies in Corsica and Sardinia (259). In the meantime the Roman land forces in Sicily had taken all the towns in the centre of the island, but had not come within reach of the three main Punic strongholds at Panormus, Drepana and Lilybaeum.

## (D) *The Invasion of Africa*

In 256–255 the Romans prepared to deliver a fatal blow to Carthage. The consuls Atilius Regulus and Manlius Vulso set out for Africa in 256 with a fleet raised to 230 galleys. Near Cape Ecnomus, off the south coast of Sicily, they met an equal number of the Carthaginian ships, and after some difficulty defeated them.

The battle of Ecnomus gave the Romans an unopposed landing in Africa. Here Atilius Regulus, who had a mere 15,000 men, gained such rapid successes that he advanced his winter quarters within one day's march of Carthage. The campaign of 256 had virtually won Sicily for the Romans, for the Carthaginians entered into peace negotiations with Regulus. But by laying down conditions such as only an utterly defenceless enemy could have accepted, he goaded the Carthaginians into a last-minute defence. With the assistance of a Spartan named Xanthippus they equipped and drilled their home-defence force according to the best Greek methods, and in the spring of 255 they fought Regulus in the valley of the Bagradas. In this action Xanthippus pinned down the Roman centre with his infantry and elephants, and encircled both their wings with his horsemen. The invading army was virtually destroyed, and their commander was taken prisoner. A counter-attack which the Carthaginians made with their fleet was less fortunate, for in a battle off Cape Hermaeum against the Roman navy they sustained losses which crippled their sea-power for the next five years. But the victorious Roman fleet, on the way home, was caught in a storm, in which more than 250 vessels (including some hundred Carthaginian prizes) were sunk.

## (E) *Later Operations in Sicily*

At the end of 255 the Romans had grasped the importance of sea-power so firmly that by another effort they replaced all the lost ships. The reconstructed fleet, however, instead of being used to convoy fresh expeditions to Africa, was directed to co-operate with the army in Sicily for an attack upon the remaining Carthaginian fortresses. In 254 the city of Panormus was taken. In 250 a Carthaginian commander attempted to recover Panormus, but was heavily defeated and lost the whole of his elephant corps.

In 249 the consul Claudius Pulcher, who was stationed with 120 ships off Lilybaeum, made a dash into the port of Drepana, where the new enemy ships were being concentrated ; but the Punic commander, Adherbal, sailed out of the harbour and drove ashore Claudius' ships as they doubled back in pursuit, capturing most of them. A few days later the other division of the Roman fleet, under the consul Iunius Pullus, was destroyed by a gale. After this the Carthaginians negotiated with the Romans about peace. Yet the Romans refused.

From 248 to 242 the Carthaginians had leisure to prepare a decisive counter-attack upon the exhausted Romans. In 247 they gave the chief command in Sicily to a young officer named Hamilcar Barca. Hamilcar made several raids upon the Italian coast, which obliged the Romans to establish some more protective colonies. In Sicily Hamilcar seized in succession two natural strongholds, Mt. Hercte near Panormus, and Mt. Eryx by Drepana, from which he conducted a successful guerrilla warfare against the Romans. But by 242 the Romans recovered the initiative. The Senate equipped 200 new galleys to complete the siege of Drepana and Lilybaeum. The Carthaginians hurried out a relief fleet of poor quality. Against this the Roman admiral, Lutatius Catulus, fought the last action of the war off Drepana, gaining a victory as complete as it was easy. With Lilybaeum and Drepana now past all hope of rescue, and the way open for a new invasion of Africa by the Romans, the Punic government accepted peace. It gave up all claims to Sicily and undertook to pay a substantial fine.

## (F) *The Capture of Sardinia and Corsica*

The peace of 241 was tested in the very next year, when the mercenaries whom Hamilcar had brought back to Africa broke into open mutiny over a quarrel about their wages. The Carthaginians were besieged, and they could not have escaped without reinforcements of fresh mercenary troops from overseas, for which they were dependent upon Roman goodwill. In the first instance the Romans helped them. But in 238 Hamilcar was given the chief command and completely restored Carthaginian sovereignty, and this caused a change of attitude in Rome. In the same year an offer from the Punic mercenaries in Sardinia was accepted by the Romans, who sent a force to occupy the Carthaginian stations on the south-western coast. The Romans met a protest from Carthage with a declaration of war. For the moment the Carthaginians had to submit to the Roman conditions of peace, which required them not only to abandon their claims upon Sardinia, but to surrender Corsica and to pay an additional fine.

## Part 2 : *The Second Punic War*

### (A) *The Carthaginian Conquests in Spain*

While the Romans were advancing their frontiers from Apennines to Alps, the Carthaginians were making an

D

unexpected recovery from their recent disasters. After the suppression of the revolts in Africa, Hamilcar was able to extend the Punic rule in Spain, by way of compensation for the territory lost to the Romans. The interest of the Carthaginians in the Iberian peninsula had hitherto been confined to trade. Hamilcar gave a new turn to his state's policy. In the remaining nine years of his life he laid the foundations of a Punic empire, which his son-in-law Hasdrubal and his son Hannibal extended to the Ebro and the Sierra de Toledo.

The chief object with which Hamilcar and his successors launched out on a new policy in Spain was to find fresh money to make up for the recent war losses. Since their conquests

Silver Coin of the Second Punic War

included the richest parts of the peninsula, the finances of Carthage were soon restored to prosperity. But the other purpose of the Punic general was to secure the man-power of the peninsula for the service of Carthage. Under their own leaders Spanish soldiers were undisciplined, but under Carthaginian commanders they were capable of being trained into excellent infantry. Hamilcar and his successors raised troops by conscription and by voluntary enlistment, and built up a larger and better land army than Carthage had yet possessed. In creating this new force Hamilcar was preparing for a second war with Rome.

### (B) *The Affair of Saguntum*

On the death of Hasdrubal in 221 the command in Spain came to Hamilcar's son Hannibal. Although he was only in his twenty-fifth year, Hannibal had already won the complete confidence of the troops. At the end of the following year he picked a quarrel with Saguntum and made preparations to put the town under siege. At the request of the Saguntines, Roman envoys visited Hannibal in his winter-quarters to tell him to keep his hands off. But Hannibal merely refused and the Punic government upheld the action of its general. The Senate allowed Hannibal to capture and enslave the town (autumn 219). But early the next year news of fresh preparations by Hannibal convinced the Senate that he was planning some major campaign beyond the Ebro. It now sent to Carthage a demand for the surrender of Hannibal. When the Punic government stood firm the Roman envoy replied with an immediate declaration of war (March 218).

## (c) *Hannibal's Invasion of Italy*

The Senate prepared an army and fleet to strike directly at Carthage, and a lesser force to hold Hannibal in Spain. But Hannibal staked his fortunes on an invasion of Italy — an audacious plan, but the only one that appeared to him to offer final success. His expeditionary force probably numbered less than 50,000 men; but long years of warfare in Spain had given them unity and experience, and Hannibal had won their loyalty completely.

While the Romans were collecting their forces, Hannibal crossed the Rhône a little distance above the Delta. At the mouth of the Druentia he was seen by patrols of the Roman force on the way to Spain, but he gave his opponents the slip in order to reach Italy, if possible, with an intact army. In crossing the Alps (most probably by one of the passes of the Mont Cenis or the Mont Genèvre) he had to fight his way to the summit against the resistance of the mountain tribes, and on the descent he suffered heavy losses on ice and fresh snow. On his arrival in the Po valley he had 26,000 men left, yet with these he conquered northern Italy in a two months' campaign. On the bank of the Ticinus he fought his first action with the consul P. Cornelius Scipio, and showed plainly the superiority of his light African horsemen over the poor Italian cavalry. Scipio abandoned the Transpadane plain and fell back upon the Apennine foot-hills near Placentia. In this position he was joined by his colleague, Sempronius Longus. The combined

Roman forces now crossed the swollen River Trebia and attacked Hannibal. As soon as they had become closely engaged, they were taken in flank and rear by hidden Carthaginian forces. With their retreat cut off by the river, the Romans saved little more than 10,000 men out of a force of some 40,000. After this disaster the Romans withdrew all their forces from northern Italy, except the garrisons of the colonies, and the Gauls flocked to join Hannibal.

In 217 the Romans posted one consular army at Ariminum to hold the line of the Via Flaminia, and a force of some 25,000 men under C. Flaminius at Arretium to cover Etruria. Hannibal stole through an unguarded Apennine pass, and slipped round the defence at Arretium which followed him to Lake Trasimene in central Etruria. As his pursuers passed between the lake and the adjacent mountains he attacked them in flank and rear, so that most of the Roman army perished in the pass or in the lake.

The victory of Lake Trasimene gave the invaders an open road to Rome, yet the city could now no longer be captured by sudden attack as in 390, and it could not be put under siege so long as the besiegers lacked a base of supplies. But no nearby town of Central Italy threw open its gates to the Carthaginians. Hannibal therefore tried to raise rebellion in southern Italy. But among the southern Italians he met with no support, and he was shadowed by a new Roman army under a veteran campaigner named Q. Fabius Maximus, who had been appointed dictator. Fabius obstinately refused to risk a pitched battle. Yet by his mere presence Fabius heartened the allies of Rome to keep their gates closed against the invaders.

But in 216 the Romans played into the enemy's hands. They raised their field army to not less than 50,000 men and transferred its command from Fabius to the two consuls, L. Aemilius Paullus and M. Terentius Varro, neither of whom had previous experience of Hannibal's tactics. Against this force Hannibal had no more than 40,000 men, yet he offered battle on a bare plain near the Apulian town of Cannae. In this open position the Romans could deepen their infantry column so as to increase the weight of its impact upon Hannibal's front. Hannibal, on the other hand, starved his centre of troops and told it to fall back before the enemy's charge. While the retreat of the Punic centre drew on the enemy infantry, the light troops on the Carthaginian wings took it in flank, and the cavalry closed in on the rear of the Roman centre. At a cost of barely 6000 men Hannibal virtually annihilated the Roman forces within this ring of steel.

## (D) *The Roman Effort after Cannae*

Having lost 100,000 men in the recent battles, the Romans were further weakened by rebellion in south Italy. Except the Roman and Latin colonies and the Greek cities of the coast, practically the whole of southern Italy was lost to Rome. The most serious blow was the revolt of Capua, which was won over to the Carthaginian side by the prospect of taking Rome's place as the first town of Italy. Since Capua at this time was the chief industrial centre in the country, its alliance with Hannibal gave him an excellent base of supply.

The Romans never forgave the Carthaginians their victory ; yet in the actual crisis they kept their nerve. By the lead which it now gave, the Senate justified its power in Rome, and the Roman people proved itself worthy of its supremacy in Italy. The Roman people were prepared to make sacrifices. It answered the call to service so readily that before the end of 216 the losses of citizen troops at Cannae had been more than made good, and in the next five years the number of Roman legions was raised to an unprecedented total. At the same time the rate of tribute was doubled ; the wealthier families contributed slaves for service in the army or fleet, and advanced money or supplies ; and the troops did not ask for back pay. But the coinage had to be devalued ; and the troops on service overseas had to be left unpaid. Yet not a voice was raised in favour of peace.

After Cannae the conduct of affairs was left in the hands of the Senate, who reserved the chief commands for men of tried merit.

The example set by the Romans was not lost on their remaining allies, who contributed their increased quotas of troops and made no attempt to bargain with Rome for higher

privileges.  Cannae gave Hannibal a secure foothold in south
Italy and long immunity from attack ; but it failed to give
him numerical superiority.  From the southern Italians he
received no strength, and so long as central Italy remained
solid in its loyalty to Rome he was cut off from his Gallic
allies, and Carthaginian help.  Moreover Hannibal never
obtained a further chance of another great battle, for Fabius
and his officers refused to engage in any but minor actions
with limited risks, and contented themselves in general with
guerilla operations.

## (E) *End of the War in Italy*

Hannibal captured the city of Tarentum by treason (212).
But this gain was outweighed by the loss of Capua in the
following year.  While Hannibal's main force was near
Tarentum, the consul Q. Fulvius Flaccus besieged Capua
with a ring of trenches which Hannibal was unable to break
through on his return from Tarentum.  Capua was starved
into surrender.  This was followed in 209 by the recovery of
Tarentum, and the Roman armies began to close in upon the
Punic forces in Lucania and Bruttium.

Hannibal's only remaining chance in Italy now depended
on his receiving a large reinforcement from outside.  In 207
this hope appeared likely for a moment to be fulfilled.  His
brother Hasdrubal arrived in north Italy with an intact force.
Hannibal prepared to join hands with his brother at some
point in central Italy.

The consul C. Claudius Nero, who held the chief command in southern Italy, slipped away to join his colleague
Livius on the northern front.  Hasdrubal, who had been
advancing along the Adriatic coast, was eventually cornered
and brought to battle against the superior forces of the two
consuls on the banks of the river Metaurus.  In this action
Nero stole round the rear of Livius' lines with a strong force,
which he threw upon the enemy's right flank.  The Punic
army collapsed and Hasdrubal himself fell fighting.

After this the Senate allowed Hannibal to retire into the
mountains of Bruttium, and there to maintain himself for four
further years.

(F) *The War in Sicily*

In Sicily King Hiero of Syracuse entered the war as an ally of the Romans. But after his death in 215 the Carthaginians had a strong following in Syracuse. At the news that a Roman army under Claudius Marcellus had captured and sacked Leontini, the Syracusans massacred Roman supporters and made an alliance with Carthage (213).

Marcellus at once put Syracuse under siege by land and sea. But the Roman assault was baffled at every point. In the meantime the Punic government, with Hannibal's consent, had equipped a force of some 30,000 men, which established a base at Agrigentum. One Sicilian town after another came into alliance with Carthage, so that in the winter of 213–212 Marcellus was more besieged than besieging. But the Roman general never relaxed his hold ; and in a night surprise he eventually captured the outer defences of Syracuse. Reinforcements from Carthage hurried to the relief of the city ; but the Punic army was destroyed by fever, and a squadron of 130 galleys — the largest Carthaginian fleet of the Second Punic War — dared not fight a Roman force of 100 vessels. The city was finally given to the Romans by a traitor (211). In 210 Agrigentum was handed back to the Romans by mutinous Carthaginian auxiliaries, and the rest of the island soon gave in.

Sardinia and Corsica played a minor part in the military operations. In 215 a fresh revolt in Sardinia encouraged the Carthaginians to send a small force to recover the island. But the Romans, who looked to Sardinia for supplies of corn, which they could no longer obtain from Italy or Sicily, sent sufficient troops to make a quick end of the rebellion and of the Punic expedition.

(G) *The Scipios in Spain*

Although the Romans had failed to hold Hannibal in Spain, they still wished to extend the war into that country. P. Cornelius Scipio, on discovering that he was too late to prevent Hannibal from reaching Italy, returned in person to organise the defence of the Po valley, but sent his army on to Spain under the command of his brother Cnaeus. Cnaeus at once applied himself to the conquest of the eastern coast. A success of Cnaeus over a small Punic force near Tarraco encouraged the Senate to increase the Roman forces in the peninsula and to send back Publius. In 215 they had to sustain an attack from Hannibal's brother Hasdrubal, who had returned to Spain with troops from Africa. But in a battle near Dertosa the Romans won an orthodox victory by a quick and clean break through the Carthaginian centre, which Hasdrubal had left weak in order to entrap his adversaries, as at Cannae. The Carthaginian government, however, reinforced Hasdrubal on such a scale that in 211 he could resume the offensive. The Scipios were caught far from their base in the face of hopeless odds. They were cut off and perished with the greater part of their armies.

Although the career of the Scipios ended in disaster, their campaigns in Spain helped the Roman victory in the Second Punic War. During the most critical years they had not only prevented the passage of reinforcements to Hannibal, but had diverted to Spain African troops, which might have had a decisive influence on the war if they had found their way to Italy after Cannae. They had also undermined the loyalty of the Spaniards to the Carthaginians. In actual fact, the Carthaginian commanders merely retrieved their recent losses in the peninsula. In 211 and 210 they recovered the lost ground to the south of the Ebro but went no further.

In 210 the Senate sent a new army to Spain, and gave its command to an ex-aedile of twenty-five, the son of the P. Scipio who had fallen in 211. The younger P. Scipio had a mystic belief in his privilege of direct personal communion with the gods, the power of conveying his supreme confidence in himself to others, a keen sense for practical details and readiness to learn from his enemies.

In 209 Scipio made a sudden march along the eastern coast and pounced upon New Carthage before its garrison was ready for him. By this stroke he got for himself a secure base for an advance. But he did not seek to engage the Carthaginians in pitched battles until he had re-armed his troops with the long finely-made Spanish swords, and had exercised them in manœuvres. In 208 he began his advance across southern Spain and brought Hasdrubal to battle near Baecula and beat him. Hasdrubal then left to help his brother in Italy, and thereby gave Spain into the hands of the Romans. His successor, Hasdrubal, the son of Gisgo, had hardly any experienced troops left to oppose Scipio's highly trained force. In 207 he avoided battle and left Scipio to carry on a war of sieges. In 206 he risked a set fight. At the battle of Ilipa Scipio completely destroyed the enemy flanks, and he pursued the defeated army with such vigour that the Carthaginians were left without any field forces in Spain. Before the end of the year Scipio led his army to Gades and received its surrender. At the end of 206 Spain had been finally lost to Carthage.

## (H) *The War in Africa*

On Scipio's return to Rome in 205 he asked to carry the war into Carthaginian territory. His demand was refused at first by the Senate, but the people were on Scipio's side, and the Senate eventually allowed him to take over two legions in Sicily, together with any volunteers whom he might collect.

In 205 the new force went no further than Sicily. In 204 Scipio landed on African soil near Utica, but found the Carthaginians ready for him. They had raised a new army and the most powerful of the Numidian rulers, Syphax, had finally joined the Punic side. Scipio had won over a chief named Massinissa, who possessed some cavalry.

In 204 Scipio was held by the forces of Syphax and the Carthaginians, but extricated himself by a surprise attack. Syphax and the Carthaginians repaired their losses and offered an open battle in the valley of the Bagradas. In this engagement Scipio's manœuvres succeeded so well that the Punic centre was cut down to the last man, and Syphax was so weakened that a Roman force was able to expel him from his capital at Cirta and install Massinissa as joint king of Greater and Lesser Numidia (203).

The Carthaginians sued for peace. The terms imposed by Scipio, which included a heavy fine, were accepted at Carthage and by the Senate and Comitia at Rome. But on the return of Hannibal, who brought back some 15,000 seasoned veterans from Italy, the Carthaginians renewed the war.

In the summer of 202 the rival leaders met near Zama
Regia. Each army numbered from 35,000 to 40,000 men.
Hannibal had collected a large elephant corps, but his infantry
was poor, and the loss of Numidia left him weak in cavalry.
Scipio's forces were well trained, and his Italian cavalry had
been reinforced by Massinissa. Hannibal opened battle with
a mass attack by the elephants, which failed. After this the
two infantry forces clashed, but neither gained any advantage.
In the meantime, however, Scipio's cavalry had driven off the
Punic cavalry, and now turned in upon Hannibal's rear. The
battle of Zama thus ended like Cannae, but with the Carthaginians inside the circle of iron. The Punic army suffered
such utter destruction that Hannibal, who was among the few
survivors, insisted upon a quick peace. Scipio accorded the
same general terms as in 203, but doubled the fine, cut down
the Punic fleet to ten ships, and deprived Carthage of the right
of waging further war without Rome's consent. Massinissa
was rewarded for his services by a gift of all African land 'held
by him or his forefathers'. These terms were accepted on
both sides in 201.

## Part 3: *Italy, Spain and Gaul*

### (A) *Italy*

1. *The Last Gallic Invasion.*—After their encounters with
the Romans in the early part of the third century, the Gauls of
northern Italy showed a tendency to settle down to a more
peaceful mode of life. But in 225 a general coalition of Gallic
tribes, assisted by mercenaries from Transalpine Gaul, collected a force, estimated at 70,000 men, to overrun the peninsula. The Romans, however, with all central and southern
Italy to draw upon, rapidly mobilised a force of not less than
130,000 defenders. The invaders succeeded in breaking
into Etruria by an unguarded pass in the western Apennines and made their way as far as Clusium. But converg-
ing Roman armies presently shepherded them towards the
Tuscan coast, and another force cut off their retreat. At
Telamon, a point on the coast of central Etruria, the Gauls

made a last stand, fighting back to back against the Romans closing in upon them from two sides; but failing to break through — for the Romans by now had learnt to disarrange the first terrible charge of the enemy by concentrated javelin fire, and then to outfence them at close quarters — they were cut down almost to the last man.

The alarm caused by the attack of the Gauls persuaded the Romans to conquer northern Italy. In doing this they committed themselves to overrunning and colonising a territory nearly as large as the peninsula. Yet the Roman armies accomplished their task in three sweeping campaigns, during which they made short work of some isolated and irresolute attempts at defence by the separate Gallic tribes. In 224 they subdued Cispadane Gaul; in 223 a general named C. Flaminius crossed the Po, and won a victory over the Insubres. By 220 the Romans had conquered all the Gallic tribes except the Taurini of Piedmont and a few others. In the same year they established colonies at Placentia and Cremona to control the passages of the Po; and Flaminius, now promoted to a censorship, made arrangements for the construction of Rome's Great North Road (the so-called Via Flaminia) as far as Ariminum. About this time a parallel road, the Via Aurelia, was built along the coast of Tuscany to Pisae, and naval stations were established at Luna and Genua.

2. *South Italy.*—In peninsular Italy the recovery of the districts which had gone over to Hannibal after the Second Punic War was all but completed before his departure. Those regions of Lucania and Bruttium, which Hannibal had retained to the last, made an immediate surrender after his return to Africa. Capua lost its self-government, and the Bruttians were left for an indefinite period without any treaty rights, and with only such independence as Rome chose. Tarentum was allowed to renew its treaty with Rome, and in general the political status of the southern Italians was not disturbed. But the rebel communities were punished by drastic reductions of territory. One-half of the Bruttian peninsula and the whole of the domain of Capua were converted into Roman *ager publicus* (public land). The area thus acquired was far too vast for complete repopulation with Romans or Latins;

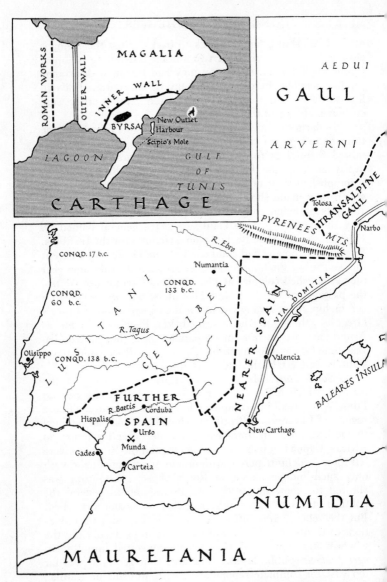

THE WESTERN MEDITERRANEAN

NORICUM
× Noreia

ILLYRIA

CISALPINE
Vercellae ×
R. Athesis
R. Po
GAUL

ALLOBROGES

R. Rhone

Genoa

× Arausio
Arles  Aquae
Sextiae
Massilia

CORSICA

Rome
Fregellae

Puteoli  Naples

Tarentum

SARDINIA

Enna  Former
Kingdom
of
Hiero

Acragas
(Agrigentum)

Utica

Carthage

Cirta

ZamaRegia

CARTHAGINIAN FRONTIER IN 150 B.C.

CARTHAGINIAN FRONTIER IN 201

× Site of battle

Scale  0    100    200 Miles

Capsa

TRIPOLI

AND THE THIRD PUNIC WAR

but a chain of colonies was founded in 194–192 along the south-west coast from the mouth of the Volturnus to the Straits of Messina. Of these settlements the only one that attained importance was Puteoli between Cumae and Neapolis, which eventually became the principal port of southern Italy.

3. *North Italy.*—In northern Italy the Second Punic War was followed by ten further years of fighting. During that war the Cisalpine Gauls had given so little support to the Carthaginians that a force of two legions was enough to hold them down. At the conclusion of peace, however, they feared that Rome would punish them and took the offensive. In 200 the Insubres, Cenomani and Boii attacked the river fortresses of Placentia and Cremona, and took and destroyed Placentia. Here their progress ended ; but in the next two years they held their own against the inadequate Roman troops sent to round them up. In 197 two consular armies arrived. While one division crossed the Apennines near Genua and made a drive down the Po valley, the other advanced beyond that river and defeated the Cenomani and Insubres on the banks of the Mincio. A second victory, gained in 196 near Lake Como by M. Claudius Marcellus, forced the Insubres and Cenomani to ask for peace. These two tribes were left in possession of their land, but they were probably bound by their treaties to render occasional military aids to Rome. In 191 the Boii were finally defeated by P. Cornelius Scipio Nasica. They were required to surrender one-half of their territory. The dispossessed Boii drifted away to the Danube regions.

Of the territory taken from the Boii a large part was reserved for colonial settlement. Placentia and Cremona received fresh drafts of settlers and three new colonies were founded at Bononia (189), at Mutina and Parma (183). But most of the surrendered land was disposed of in individual allotments. The Roman settlements in northern Italy were connected with several new military roads.

4. *Liguria.*—The Romans were slow to set foot on the territory of Liguria (the Italian Riviera and its hinterland). But in 187 the consul C. Flaminius added to the Via Flaminia

a trans-Apennine route from the Arno valley to Bononia. It was probably on this occasion that the future city of Florentia (from which point the new route started) was founded as a roadside post of Roman settlers. From 186 to 180 the Senate regularly commissioned two consular armies to reduce the native strongholds and to secure the Roman lines of communications. In these campaigns, conducted with heavy infantry in unfamiliar country against light-footed enemies, the Roman forces were often defeated. But in 181 L. Aemilius Paullus forced the tribe of the Ingauni into submission ; in 180 two proconsuls subdued the Apuani.

5. *Istria.*—At the other end of northern Italy the Romans were friendly with the Illyrian tribe of the Veneti. But occasional attacks by mountain peoples determined them to establish a large colony on the site of Aquileia, from which the passes through the Julian and Carnic Alps could be watched. This also served to watch the Istri. In 178 the consul A. Manlius Vulso, who had been sent to frighten a confederacy of Istrian tribes, went beyond his instructions in making an attack upon them. Two campaigns were enough for the final conquest of the Istrian peninsula. No further colonies were founded in this region, but private Roman settlers gradually converted it into an integral part of Italy.

## (B) *Spain*

The conquests made by the Romans in Spain during the Second Punic War were primarily intended to deprive the Carthagians of a base of attack upon Italy. An additional reason for retaining the recent Spanish conquests in Roman hands was the mineral wealth of the country, which had helped the Roman finances in the last stages of the war. In 197, therefore, the Senate converted Spain into two new provinces, Hispania Citerior and Hispania Ulterior ('Nearer' and 'Further Spain').

The Senate reduced the garrison of each province to a small corps of 8000 Italian auxiliaries. But it was not until 133 that Roman rule became firmly established.

In 197 hostilities began in the extreme south of Spain, where the tribe of the Turdetani rose in revolt and received the support of Malaca and other Phoenician towns. In the same year another rebellion broke out at the opposite end of the peninsula, between the Ebro and the Pyrenees. Between these the Celtiberians, whom the Turdetani hired as mercenaries, formed a connecting link. In 195 the Roman forces were increased to a total of some 50,000 men, and one of the consuls, M. Porcius Cato, was sent to take supreme command. This hard fighter stamped out the insurrection in the north, and he opened up a new line of communications between the two provinces by following the course of the river Salo (a tributary of the Ebro) towards the sources of the Tagus. In 194 the Turdetani were conclusively reduced to submission by the praetor Scipio Nasica. But the Celtiberians, whom Cato had vainly attempted to buy over or to bring to a set battle, carried on the war, and in the same year the Lusitanians joined in. In the next twelve years the only notable Roman success was the occupation of New Castile (the territory of the Carpetani and Oretani) (193–192), and its renewed subjection after a rebellion (185). Four years later the praetor Fulvius Flaccus gained a similar success over another army of Celtiberian invaders in New Castile. These actions prepared the way for a combined drive against the Celtiberians, which the propraetors Sp. Postumius and Tib. Sempronius Gracchus carried out in 179. The Celtiberians sued for peace and became tributary to Rome. Their submission was followed by a general settlement, which gave the Romans control of the whole peninsula except its Atlantic coast.

From 179 to 154 the Spaniards observed the terms of Gracchus' settlement; but Roman governors endangered it by acts of oppression, and the complaints addressed by the sufferers to the Senate had no effect. In the meantime, too, a new generation of Celtiberians and Lusitanians was growing up which wanted a new war. Thus another twenty-year round of campaigns was opened in 154, during which the two last-named tribes took it in turns to keep the Romans in play. An invasion of Further Spain by the Lusitanians in 154 was followed the next year by a Celtiberian rising. In 153–152 the consul Fulvius Nobilior attempted a direct invasion of Old Castile and forced his way as far as Numantia, where he lost a battle. His advance to the citadel of the Celtiberian land nevertheless achieved a moral effect, for his successor, the consul M. Claudius Marcellus, was able to conclude a fresh agreement with the Celtiberians. The policy of conciliation which Marcellus adopted in regard to the Spaniards was opposed by the Senate; but he successfully overrode his home government and gave Hispania Citerior eight years' respite from war (151–143).

The peace with the Celtiberians left the Roman governors free to concentrate against the Lusitanians. In their last struggle against Rome the Lusitanians were captained by a leader named Viriathus. From 146 to 141 Viriathus won an almost unbroken series of victories over five Roman commanders. His successes encouraged the Celtiberians to take the field once more (143), so that after ten years of fighting the Romans seemed as far off as ever from a settlement. In 141 Viriathus manœuvred the consul Fabius Maximus Servilianus into a position from which there was no escape, but he spared his opponent in return for a treaty, in which the freedom of the Lusitanians was acknowledged by the Romans. Fabius' agreement was ratified at Rome by Senate and Comitia. Nevertheless in 140 his successor, Servilius Caepio, persuaded the Senate to break it, in order to recommence war with the Lusitanians. In this new campaign Caepio took the opportunity to bribe Viriathus' agents to murder their chief in his sleep. Left without a capable leader, the Lusitanians shortly after made their submission (139).

In Hither Spain the Celtiberians were driven from the field in a rapid campaign by the consul Q. Caecilius Metellus, so that his successors had nothing left to do but to capture a few outstanding cities. Of these, however, Numantia defied the Romans for nine years. Its military population did not exceed 8000, but its position was one of great natural strength. The war dragged on until 134, when its conduct was entrusted to P. Cornelius Scipio Aemilianus. Scipio collected a force of 60,000 men, with which he systematically blockaded Numantia, until hunger drove the defenders to surrender (133). The inhabitants were sold by him into slavery, and the town was destroyed.

With the fall of Numantia the Spanish wars were brought to a close, though in 123 the Roman conquests were rounded off by the capture of the Balearic isles, which had become a haunt of pirates. These islands were placed under a 'praefectus' appointed by the governor of Hispania Citerior.

In Spain no systematic attempt was made to follow up the Roman conquest by colonisation. But in a few instances discharged soldiers were permitted to settle down near the scene of their campaigns. In 205 Scipio Africanus pensioned off some of his veterans with grants of land at Italica (near Seville), which was set up as a town of Italian pattern. In 171 a Latin colony was founded at Carteia (near Gibraltar). A mixed population of Roman veterans and of Lusitanian captives was settled at Valentia about 138, and the town of Corduba was probably composed of similar ingredients (152 B.C.). Round these centres the romanisation of southern and eastern Spain made an early start.

## (c) *Gaul*

During the Second Punic War Transalpine Gaul was only a land through which armies passed. In the early part of the second century the Romans were content to confide their overland communications with Spain to the safe keeping of their allies at Massilia. But in 154 the Massilians called for help against Ligurian raiders. The Senate sent an army under the consul Opimius to drive them off. For a further thirty years the Romans made no attempt to gain a foothold in Transalpine Gaul ; but in 125 a second call from the Massilians had the effect of drawing them on into new adventures.

In 124–122 the Ligurians of what is now the French Riviera were definitely reduced by C. Sextius Calvinus, who established a small settlement of Roman veterans at Aquae Sextiae (Aix) to protect Massilia. But this involved the Romans with another enemy, the Celtic tribe of the Allobroges, who lived in the Alpine foot-hills between the Isère and Rhône. In 121 the proconsul Cn. Domitius Ahenobarbus crushed the resistance of the Allobroges. This victory gave the Romans control of the whole left bank of the Rhône as far as Geneva, but brought the most powerful of the Celtic tribes the Arverni,

into the field against the Romans. The engagement which
finally decided the fate of Mediterranean France was fought
at the junction of the Rhône and the Isère, between an un-
wieldy army under the Arvernian king Bituitus and a much
smaller force under the consul Q. Fabius Maximus. This
battle ended in a Gallic disaster. The news reached Rome and
the pacification of southern France was completed by Domitius.
The districts conquered in the campaigns of 125–121 were
made into a new Roman province (within which Massilia remained an independent allied state). From the Rhône to the
Pyrenees Domitius built a road and on this route a colony
of Roman veterans was established at Narbo.

## Part 4 : *The Third Punic War*

### (A) *Rome, Carthage and Numidia*

Of all the problems which confronted the Romans after the
Second Punic War the question of their future relations to
Carthage was the simplest, and yet it was the least successfully
handled. By the terms of the peace of 201 Carthage was able
to resume its place as the mercantile capital of the western
Mediterranean. At the same time it obtained a rising revenue
from the African hinterland. The Punic administration was
improved by Hannibal, who used his influence with the
Carthaginian people to make the government accountable for
the money handled by it. Carthage, it is true, did not long
enjoy the benefit of Hannibal's honest statesmanship. His
political opponents took vengeance by accusing him before the
Roman Senate. On the arrival of the Romans, Hannibal at
once sought safety in flight, and the Punic aristocracy resumed
its former power (195). But the humble attitude of the
Carthaginian government to Rome gave plain proof that all
thought of revenge had passed out of its mind.

By the peace of 201 Rome's former ally Massinissa had
been made king over an undivided realm of Numidia. During
the next half-century he enlarged his dominion. With a
standing army of 50,000 men he reduced the border chieftains
to submission and gave Numidia security against raids from

the interior.   But his ultimate ambition was to form an empire including the modern territories of Algeria, Tunisia and Tripoli.   Under cover of the treaty of 201, which deprived the Carthaginians of the right of self-defence, he proceeded to conquer the states dependent on Carthage.   The Punic government sent protest after protest to the Senate, but achieved nothing.   In 150 at last the Carthaginians made open war upon Massinissa, but were defeated.

There had indeed always been in the Senate a party which wanted peace, and this group had the powerful support of the Scipios.   But the ghost of Hannibal still haunted Rome. Nurses told naughty children that Hannibal was coming to fetch them ;   politicians used the same name to throw the Senate into a thoroughly un-Roman panic.   The enemies of Carthage, moreover, were aided by the veteran M. Cato, an obstinate but impressive man, who said that the Carthaginians were not to be trusted and that they had broken the peace of 201.   He ended all his speeches in the Senate with the same words, ' Carthage must be destroyed '.   The Senate eventually yielded to Cato.   In 149 it obtained from the Comitia a formal declaration of war, and commissioned the consuls to fit out an expeditionary force.   The Carthaginians asked for peace.   On first demand they gave hostages and surrendered all their war-material (inclusive of two thousand catapults). But as successive instalments of the Roman blackmail were paid, the consuls made the terms of peace more difficult. Their final conditions required the Carthaginians to abandon their town and go to some inland site in Tunisia.   The threatened people turned from submission to defiance.   While the consuls were completing their unhurried war-preparations in Sicily, the whole population of Carthage worked feverishly at the defence of the city.   No help came from the neighbouring town of Utica or the other Phoenician settlements in Tunisia, all of which made an early peace with Rome ;  but a large force was conscribed (presumably by promises of high pay) among the Libyans of the hinterland.   But Massinissa did no more than look on, angry that the Romans had decided to destroy the city of Carthage which he had wanted for himself.

(B) *The War*

Thanks to the eleventh-hour effort of Carthage, the Third Punic War, instead of being a mere execution, lasted through four hard-fought campaigns. In 149–148 the Romans surrounded the city, but could make little headway against its massive fortifications and the determination of its defenders. Neither could they establish an effective blockade; indeed their own supply-columns were seriously hampered by the Punic guerrilla bands. In 147 the Senate and Comitia gave the command in Africa to P. Cornelius Scipio Aemilianus, a son by blood of Aemilius Paulus, and a grandson by adoption of Scipio Africanus. Pressing the attack against a garrison gradually overcome by hunger, he broke through the outer wall, and in a week of hard street-fighting made his way to the citadel, where the surviving inhabitants surrendered. They were sold into slavery; the city was razed to the ground. Roman aggression had triumphed once more.

The Romans would not let the territory of Carthage pass out of their hands. The remaining hinterland of the city was made into a Roman province under the name of 'Africa'. The Phoenician cities of the coast were rewarded for their desertion of Carthage with a guarantee of liberty; Utica inherited a large share of the trade of Carthage and became the capital of the Roman governor.

Three years before the fall of Carthage King Massinissa died at the age of ninety. After a temporary division between three of his sons, his realm was reunited under his eldest son Micipsa. This ruler had neither the opportunity nor the ambition to extend the Numidian boundaries further.

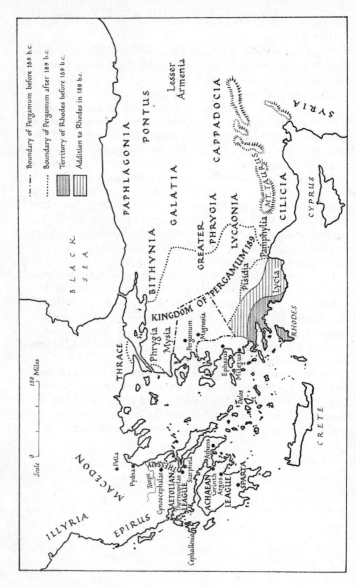

GREECE AND ASIA MINOR AT THE BEGINNING OF THE SECOND CENTURY B.C.

### CHAPTER VII

# CONQUEST OF THE EAST

## Part 1 : *Greece*

### (A) *Early Contacts between Rome and Greece*

THE Romans' chief enemies in the eastern Mediterranean were the Greeks. Between 800 and 500 B.C. the Greek people had occupied by colonisation the greater part of the Aegean coast and of the Black Sea coast. They could not combine their numerous city-states into a durable confederacy, and in the fourth century King Philip II of Macedon had conquered them. But by virtue of their superior culture the Greeks came to play the part of allies rather than of subjects to the Macedonians. It was in partnership with the Greeks that Philip's son Alexander overthrew the Persian empire (334–325); and it was the Greeks that reaped the chief fruits of Alexander's campaigns. But after the death of Alexander in 323 his empire was split up into a number of states, of which only three were at all comparable to the Roman republic of the third century. Of the three first-class powers in the 'Hellenistic' world (as the Greek world after Alexander is usually called), the dynasty of the Ptolemies ruled over Egypt, Cyrene, Cyprus, the greater part of Syria, and a chain of sea-ports in the Levantine and Aegean seas; their capital was established at Alexandria. The Seleucids, whose capital was at Antioch in northern Syria, held the eastern provinces of Alexander's empire and the southern half of Asia Minor. The Antigonids became kings of Macedonia, ruled Thessaly, and had some power over the rest of the Greek homeland.

After their victory over Pyrrhus, the Romans entered into alliance with Ptolemy II of Egypt. At the same time they became responsible for the protection of the Adriatic trade-routes, which had previously been under the care of the Tarentines. After the First Punic War, the scattered tribes of Illyria were united under rulers who organised piracy as a regular state industry. The Senate, however, took no action until 230, when it went so far as to protest to the reigning queen, Teuta. Teuta permitted the murder of one of the Roman envoys. In answer to this, the Senate sent the fleet which had won the First Punic War to sweep Teuta's subjects off the Adriatic. The Senate sent envoys to Athens and Corinth to report on the result (228), but this mission ended in nothing more than an exchange of courtesies.

## (B) *The First Macedonian War*

In 215 Philip V of Macedon made an alliance with Hannibal, hoping to gain a foothold in southern Italy, and perhaps to revive the schemes of King Pyrrhus for conquests in the west.

In 214 the admiral Valerius Laevinus disembarked a small Roman force at Apollonia on the Illyrian coast to keep Philip occupied; in 212 he negotiated alliances with the Aetolian League in Greece, which had a tradition of hostility against Macedon, and with Attalus I of Pergamum. This king was ruler over a small but prosperous territory in north-western Asia Minor. The bond thus formed between Rome and Pergamum was to have far-reaching consequences, but its immediate results were small. After a series of campaigns in the Greek homeland the First Macedonian War died. The Greeks made peace with Philip in 206; the Romans in 205. By his treaty with Rome the Macedonian king acquired a frontage on the Adriatic coastline between the rivers Aous and Apsus (the district of Atintania).

## (c) *Pergamum, Rhodes and Rome*

After the First Macedonian War Philip turned from the Adriatic to the East. In 203 he made a treaty with the Seleucid king, Antiochus III, who had invited him to attack the boy-king Ptolemy V of Egypt. With a newly created fleet the Macedonian king took several outposts of the Ptolemies in the Aegean area (202–201). But in this war he lost his popularity with the Greeks through the attacks of his admirals on Aegean shipping, and through his enslavement of the inhabitants of towns captured by him — a practice which the war-code of the Hellenistic Greeks no longer tolerated. Philip's barbarous methods of warfare made an enemy of the city-state of Rhodes, which had trading interests in the Aegean area and was always ready to use its war-fleet for the protection of its commerce. The Rhodians persuaded Attalus of Pergamum to fight once more against Philip. Attalus soon tried to enlarge the alliance against Philip by renewing his alliance with Rome.

In 200 the consul P. Sulpicius Galba, after some difficulty, got the Comitia Centuriata to declare war. The Romans delivered their message to Philip in the form of an ultimatum, which bade him pay a fine to Attalus and the Rhodians and required him to avoid any act of war against any Greek state. Philip refused.

(D) *The Second Macedonian War*

In view of the people's reluctance to declare war upon Philip, the Senate did not dare to conscribe many troops for service against him. The total number of Roman and Italian troops engaged in the Second Macedonian War was about 30,000, and most of these were new recruits, for the veterans of the Punic War escaped military duty in the east. The Senate made an attempt to form a general alliance of Greek states against Philip. But the only city to accept was Athens, which had little military power. In 199 the Aetolians resumed war against Macedon, and in 198–197 the Achaean League, under pressure from the Roman fleet, gave some slight assistance. Attalus and the Rhodians were content to leave the hard fighting to the Romans.

On the other hand, Philip was so unpopular in Greece that only a few of the lesser states took his side. The only substantial aid that he received was from Thessaly. From his partner Antiochus he derived no help at all. His total military forces were therefore merely equal to those of the Romans, and his fleet was hopelessly inferior. But the Macedonian army, man for man, was not inferior to the Roman legions.

In 200 the Romans accomplished little more than to establish a base at Apollonia. But their mere landing in Illyria was sufficient to put Philip on the defensive. In 199 the ex-consul Sulpicius planned a combined drive by land and sea against Philip. But the Roman and allied fleets, whose part it was to capture the coast towns of Macedon, accomplished next to nothing. The Roman legions forced a line of defence beyond Lyncestis, but lack of supplies compelled them to retreat to Illyria.

In 198 the Macedonian king, rightly guessing that the Romans might attempt to force the valley of the river Aous, in order to join with the Aetolians in Thessaly, moved forward to occupy a pass on this route not far from the Adriatic coast. Here he successfully held up a new Roman commander, the consul T. Quinctius Flamininus, for several weeks, until a traitor led the Romans round his position by a mountain track. Philip retreated to the pass of Tempe on the border between Macedon and Thessaly. Flamininus was thus able to occupy Thessaly and to make contact with the Aetolians ; but he did not dare to attack the difficult frontier line of Macedon in the face of Philip's forces.

After two campaigns it seemed as if the Romans might have to win the Macedonian war, as they had won the Punic wars, by sheer weight of numbers. But in 197 Philip decided on a pitched battle. Advancing across Thessaly with 25,000 men, he was making for the open ground in the valley of the Enipeus, when his scouts discovered Flamininus' army, moving in a parallel direction on the other side of the ridge of Cynoscephalae. The king won a race for the high ground, and sent one of his heavy infantry divisions down the hill against the Romans. The Macedonian 'phalanx', a weighty mass of men with spears about twenty feet in length, crashed into the left wing of the Romans and routed it. But Flamininus defeated the second Macedonian division, which was not yet closed up in battle formation. On the victorious Roman right wing a military tribune detached the maniples of the second and third lines in his legion and turned in with these upon the rear of the successful Macedonian division. By this move he finally won the day for Rome, for the tightly-packed phalanx on the Macedonian right wing could not swing round in time and went down helplessly before the swords of the legions.

The battle of Cynoscephalae gave the whole of Greece into the hands of the Romans. In 196 the Senate, to whom Flamininus referred Philip's request for peace, dictated a general settlement of Greek affairs and decided that the Greek cities should be free. It left the king in possession of Macedon, and imposed a moderate fine upon him; but it required him to surrender the whole of his fleet, and to withdraw all his garrisons and agents from the rest of Greece. The towns evacuated by him were partly given to the Achaean or Aetolian Leagues, but the cities of Thessaly became a number of small independent confederacies. In 194 Flamininus left Greece to its new freedom — under carefully chosen aristocracies — and withdrew all his troops to Italy.

## (E) *Antiochus III and the Aetolians*

In the Second Macedonian War the Aetolians alone of the Greeks had helped the Romans; but instead of being allowed to incorporate the whole of Thessaly into their League, they had been put off with a mere slice. They invited the king Antiochus III to set Greece free from the Roman rule. In 192 he landed at Demetrias (a city on the Gulf of Pagasae which the Aetolians had seized) with an advance guard of 10,000 men, and overran Thessaly. But the Greek cities did not support him, and the Aetolians soon regretted their alliance.

When Antiochus invaded Greece the Senate mobilised a force of over 20,000 men, which the consul M'. Acilius Glabrio embarked for Greece in 191. Glabrio made an unopposed march across Greece to Thessaly, from which Antiochus at once retreated to the pass of Thermopylae. Here the consul was held up for a while. But he managed to take Antiochus in the rear, and destroyed his army totally. After this Antiochus evacuated his remaining positions in Greece, leaving his Aetolian allies to make what terms they could.

The Aetolians' request for terms of peace in 191 was answered by Glabrio with a demand for unconditional surrender. But Glabrio's successor in 190, the consul L. Cornelius Scipio, granted an armistice to the Aetolians, so as to release the Roman troops for service against Antiochus ; and a second expeditionary force, which the consul M. Fulvius Nobilior brought from Italy in 189, was not put to use. But Fulvius made the League weaker by giving independence to its members.

(F) *The Third Macedonian War*

In 188 the Roman troops for a second time evacuated Greece, and seventeen further years passed before the next war. Philip's death in 179 put his eldest son Perseus on the throne. Unlike his father, Perseus was a cautious person. For some years diplomatic relations between him and Rome grew worse, till the Senate overcame its hesitation and forced a war upon him by the same methods as it had used against Philip in 200. On the grounds that the king had attacked some Balkan chieftains who were allied with Rome, it got the Comitia to declare war (171).

Lack of financial support from Perseus, and above all the memory of Cynoscephalae, held back most of the states from helping Macedon. In the event, Perseus received some ineffective help from a few cities of Boeotia, from Epirus and from an Illyrian chief named Genthius. The Romans for their part had offers of support from their old allies, Pergamum, Rhodes and the Achaean League. Thanks to the excellent internal administration of Philip and Perseus, Macedonia had made such a good recovery from the previous war that it could now put some 40,000 men into the field. The Romans slightly outnumbered Perseus and held complete control of the seas, but did not know how to derive advantage from their maritime superiority.

In 171 Perseus ventured into Thessaly and gained a victory in a cavalry action near Larissa against the vanguard of the Roman army under the consul P. Licinius Crassus. The king was so flustered by his success that he followed it up with offers of peace. The Romans rejected this and several later offers by Perseus, but were made helpless by bad discipline among the troops, by faulty co-operation on the part of the fleet, and by difficult country. Licinius never attempted an attack in force upon Perseus. While the consular armies were held in Thessaly, the king easily repelled a Roman force in Illyria ; but he missed his chance of an offensive in Greece. In 169 a consul named Q. Marcius Philippus successfully made a march of eleven days' duration across the densely wooded shoulder of Mt. Olympus, and by his mere appearance on Macedonian soil he so scared Perseus as to cause him to abandon the entire frontier line. Fortunately for the king, Marcius' army was too tired to advance any further.

In the fourth year of the war the Roman attack was at last driven home by the consul L. Aemilius Paullus, a veteran of the Spanish and Ligurian wars. With a better-disciplined army Paullus drew Perseus at last into a set battle at Pydna. The Greek phalanx, charging in one massive body of 20,000 men over level ground, flung back the Roman front. Yet the Roman line fell back in good order towards higher ground, while the phalanx, carried away by its own momentum, became disordered. Into the gaps thus formed, and round the flanks of the Macedonian column, the Romans thrust themselves maniple by maniple, and with their swords made short work of the disordered spearmen. The battles of Cynoscephalae and Pydna finally demonstrated the advantage which the elastic manipular formation possessed over the rigid Macedonian phalanx. The Macedonian cities surrendered at once to Paullus.

In 168 a second Roman force was sent to Illyria, where it captured Genthius. In the following year Paullus received orders to carry out a military execution against the people of Epirus. He simultaneously attacked all the towns and villages of the country and took 150,000 prisoners, who were sold off into slavery.

## (G) *The Fourth Macedonian War*

After the Third Macedonian War the Senate took Perseus and all the royal officials out of Greece. Left without any governing body, Macedonia was carved up into four separate republics. Restrictions were placed upon trade between the four sections and upon their trade with the rest of Greece. On the other hand, the Senate made no attempt to exploit the economic resources of the country. In Illyria, Genthius' kingdom was divided into three federal republics.

By these precautions Rome deprived the Macedonians of the power to harm their neighbours and to protect themselves. In 150 the armies of the republics were unable to deal with an adventurer named Andriscus, who by claiming to be a son of Perseus succeeded for a moment in reuniting Macedonia. In the 'Fourth Macedonian War', which Andriscus now started, the Romans made an even worse beginning than in the previous wars, for a small force sent in haste to hold Andriscus down met with a heavy defeat, and Thessaly was overrun by his army (149). But in 148 a stronger Roman force under Q. Caecilius Metellus expelled him from Macedonia and cornered him in Thrace.

The campaign against Andriscus produced an important change of Roman policy in regard to the Greek states. In 148 the Senate realised that to win military victories and still leave the Greek cities free was a bad policy and could bring no lasting peace to the Greek world. Rome therefore took over Macedonia. For the defence of the new province, into which Epirus and Thessaly were incorporated, alliances were made with several Thracian chiefs, and a highroad, the Via Egnatia, was built from Apollonia to Thessalonica.

In 155 a Roman force cleared the coast of lower Dalmatia; in 129 an expedition was directed from Aquileia against the more northerly tribes on the Carso. The entire Adriatic and Dalmatia were probably placed under the governor of Macedonia.

## (H) *Rome and the Greek Cities*

Among the feuds which disturbed Greece in the second century was a dispute between the Achaean League, which had extended its authority over all Peloponnesus in 192, and the city of Sparta, which wanted to keep its independence. This became a frequent subject for the Senate or Roman commissioners on tour in Greece to discuss but the decisions made from time to time by the Senate or its agents, failed to settle things permanently.

The commissioners also interfered in Greek home affairs.

After the Third Macedonian War they carried off one thousand of the leading citizens of Achaea to Italy. Despite protests from the Achaean League, the Senate detained the prisoners for fifteen years, and seven hundred eventually died. In 148 the Senate allowed the Spartans to leave the Achaean League. In the following year the Senate offered to reopen negotiations on the subject; but in the meantime the feeling against Rome had led to the appointment of a dictator named Critolaus at Corinth. In 146 Critolaus threw out a direct challenge to Roman authority by overrunning central Greece with an army, but he was easily routed by Caecilius Metellus, who came down upon him from Macedonia. Later in the year the consul L. Mummius, with reinforcements from Italy, destroyed a reserve force of Achaeans, which fought gallantly against hopeless odds in a final battle near Corinth.

After the Achaean war the Romans still left central Greece and Peloponnesus free. But they dissolved the Achaean League and authorised the governor of Macedonia to interfere, whenever necessary, to keep Greece at peace. In the other Greek towns they restored the rule of the wealthier classes; Corinth was destroyed and its inhabitants sold into slavery.


## Part 2 : *Asia*

### (A) *The War against Antiochus*

Rome's earliest enemy in Asia was the Seleucid king, Antiochus III. In the opening years of his reign this king had restored the power of his dynasty on the Asian continent; his victorious progress across Persia and Bactria to the frontiers of India (209–204) had earned him the title of 'Great' among the Greeks, and a reputation second only to that of Alexander. In 201–200 he had acquired southern Syria and Palestine; in 197 he had captured the southern coast of Asia Minor and the southern half of its western coast, where he made the city of Ephesus into a second capital. Antiochus was a diplomat as well as a soldier. He took care not to have more than one enemy at a time. His conquests in western Asia Minor scared the rulers of Pergamum. In 196, therefore, Eumenes II, who had recently succeeded Attalus I on the throne of Pergamum, decided to call the Romans to his assistance, as his father had called them against Philip.

The city-states of Smyrna and Lampsacus were being threatened by Antiochus and applied to the Senate for help. The Senate merely went so far as to refer the envoys of the two towns to Flamininus. The agents of Antiochus came to Corinth to see Flamininus, but he told the king to keep his hands off all the free Greek cities in Asia, ordered him to evacuate all Greek towns recently acquired by him from Ptolemy, and forbade him to set foot in Europe. These terms constituted as direct a challenge as the Roman ultimatum to Philip in 200. But Antiochus patiently argued his case at a conference with Flamininus' agents so effectively that the Roman commander in the next two years tamely allowed Antiochus to occupy the Gallipoli peninsula. In withdrawing his troops from Greece in 194 Flamininus showed that he did not fear a war with the Seleucid king in the near future.

In 195 the Romans were scared by the news that Hannibal had found his way to Antiochus' court at Ephesus. Hannibal was planning a fresh invasion of Italy with a Seleucid army. The Senate at once took steps to protect the coast of southern Italy with a chain of new colonies. But Antiochus had no desire for a fight to a finish with Rome. The cool reception which he offered to Hannibal stopped the Senate from any hasty diplomatic move against the king.

In 194 Antiochus sent an embassy to Rome to settle all outstanding points and negotiate a treaty of friendship. The Senate now hinted that it would be content with his withdrawal from Europe. Negotiations went on in 193 at Ephesus ; but the king's agents played their cards unskilfully, and the conference came to nothing. Next winter Antiochus prepared for an attack upon Europe. The Romans declared war.

The failure of Antiochus' expedition to Greece has already been described. At the end of 191 he evacuated European Greece and prepared to hold Asia Minor against the Roman counter-attack. His first line of defence was a navy of seventy battleships and a hundred cruisers. The Roman fleet of eighty battleships under C. Livius was sent to Aegean waters in the summer of 191 ; and Eumenes could produce some twenty-five additional ships. He had also to reckon with the navy of the Rhodians, who renewed their alliance with Rome, in order to secure the freedom of the Aegean Sea and the Dardanelles. His admiral Polyxenidas attacked the Romans and Pergamenes near Cape Corycus before the arrival of the Rhodians. He was beaten off with severe loss by the Romans, who successfully repeated the grappling and boarding tactics of the First Punic War.

In the winter of 191–190 Antiochus raised his fleet to ninety battleships. He also got Hannibal to equip another squadron in Phoenicia. In the following spring Polyxenidas heavily defeated the Rhodian fleet at Samos. But in a battle fought off Side (in southern Asia Minor) a second Rhodian fleet, under an admiral named Eudamus, defeated the Phoenician navy under Hannibal. The sea war was definitely decided by a battle off Myonnesus (near Cape Corycus). The battle of Myonnesus, the last notable victory of a Roman fleet over a foreign enemy, secured to the allies the command of the seas and prepared for the Roman army's passage into Asia.

While the naval campaign was being fought out, the Roman army was on a long march from Greece to the Dardanelles. It now stood under the orders of L. Scipio, the younger brother of Africanus and consul in 190 ; but the effective command was in the hands of Africanus himself. After a rapid journey through Macedonia it crossed the Straits unopposed, for after his naval defeats Antiochus had withdrawn all his troops into Asia Minor. Its numbers did not exceed 30,000 men. Antiochus had mobilised the entire army of his kingdom to the number of 72,000. At this point Antiochus offered to the Scipios to pay one-half of the Roman war expenses. But L. Scipio, on the advice of his brother, required the king to pay the entire costs of the Roman campaigns, and to evacuate not only the coast of Asia Minor, but all his possessions in the interior. This demand was plainly unacceptable to the king, and it was a cardinal point of Seleucid policy to maintain a seafront on the Aegean. Unable to get peace at a reasonable price, Antiochus offered a battle to the Romans on a piece of

E

open ground near Magnesia-ad-Sipylum.　Using his infantry
and elephants as a defensive wing to fix his opponents, he
staked his chances on a mass attack by his excellent Persian
horsemen, of whom he took command in person.　With this
force he put to rout the Roman left wing, but he let himself be
carried too far in the pursuit, and so lost touch with the rest
of his troops.　On the other wing the initiative was taken by
King Eumenes, who shared the effective command of the
Roman forces with the ex-consul Cn. Domitius Ahenobarbus
— for Scipio Africanus was prevented by illness from direct-
ing the battle.　Eumenes charged and confused the whole of
the opposite left wing.　The Seleucid centre, consisting of a
phalanx of 16,000 heavy infantry, stood its ground valiantly.
But the elephants of Antiochus were stampeded by the Roman
javelins and made gaps in the heavy infantry, into which the
Roman legionaries penetrated.　The entire Seleucid army was
scattered into fragments and destroyed.

Antiochus agreed to the peace terms previously offered by
the Scipios, and to surrendering his elephants and most of his
war-fleet.　He evacuated all his territory to the west of Mt.
Taurus and undertook to pay a fine of 15,000 talents — the
largest that Rome ever extracted from a beaten enemy.　In
188 the territories won in Asia Minor were shared out between
Eumenes and the Rhodians.　The latter received Lycia and
Caria (the south-western edge of Asia Minor, as far as the
river Maeander) ; the rest of Seleucid Asia Minor, together
with the Gallipoli peninsula, was given to Eumenes.　The
Romans pocketed Antiochus' fine, but none of the conquered
lands for themselves ; and in 188 they withdrew all their
troops from the eastern Mediterranean.

(B) *Rome and the East from 188 to 129 B.C.*

After the peace of 188 began a long series of diplomatic
moves between Rome and the eastern cities.　Eumenes of
Pergamum often asked the Senate for help, though he usually
got none : Flamininus demanded that Hannibal should be
surrendered by Antiochus, but the Carthaginian committed
suicide in 183, and the Senate set the cities of Lycia free from
the control of Rhodes in 177.　After the Third Macedonian

War more and more Greek cities sent emissaries to Rome, but the Senate did not act very sensibly in its relations to the Greek states. In 168 it crippled the trade of Rhodes, and in 167 began to plot against Eumenes.

1. *Pergamum.*—Eumenes died in 159, and in 133 the last king of Pergamum, Attalus III, bequeathed his kingdom to Rome in his will. Rome accepted it, but had to fight a son of Eumenes, Aristonicus, who started a rebellion. In 130 M. Perperna defeated Aristonicus, and in 129 the consul M'. Aquilius definitely took over the Kingdom of Pergamum as a Roman province under the name of 'Asia'.

2. *The Seleucids.*—By the peace of 188 the Romans had checked the power of the Seleucid kings. But a vigorous ruler named Antiochus IV invaded Egypt and laid siege to Alexandria (170–168). In spite of their treaty with Egypt, which they had renewed on its hundredth anniversary in 173, the Romans at first did nothing. But after the victory over King Perseus at Pydna the Senate intervened. Its envoy, C. Popilius Laenas, ordered Antiochus to call off his attack. Antiochus evacuated Egypt without delay. After the death of Antiochus IV the Senate sent three commissioners to administer the realm on behalf of his successor, who was only a boy (163). But when a rival claimant to the throne, Demetrius I, displaced Antiochus' son, it raised no objection and recognised his title. But again in 152 it encouraged another claimant to the Seleucid throne, Alexander Balas, to throw out Demetrius.

The Seleucid monarchy now passed into a period of chronic civil war and was reduced to the status of a third-class power. The Jews, who had been reduced to submission by Demetrius, now obtained their freedom. At the same time the last of the continental provinces of the Seleucids, Mesopotamia and Babylonia, were taken from them by the Parthians. After 150 the Senate paid no further attention to them.

3. *Egypt.*—At the time of Antiochus IV's invasion of Egypt two brothers, Ptolemy VI and VII, were rival claimants to the throne. Both made appeals to the Senate, but no definite help was given to either. Eventually the two brothers came to an understanding, by which Ptolemy VI retained

Egypt and Cyprus and the younger brother, Ptolemy VII, contented himself with Cyrene.

After the death of Ptolemy VI in 145 the Egyptian dominions were reunited under the surviving brother ; but a fierce dispute now broke out between him and his two successive queens, in the course of which he again lost and recovered his throne. In answer to the complaints which it received against the king, the Senate sent Scipio Aemilianus to investigate the state of Egypt (*c.* 135). But the report which Scipio made on his return to Rome was not sufficiently damaging to the king to stir the Senate into action.

### CHAPTER VIII

# ROMAN GOVERNMENT
# DOWN TO 133 B.C.

## Part 1 : *Provincial Government*

BY the middle of the second century B.C. every state in the Mediterranean, except Mauretania and a few Balkan states, was bound to Rome by some kind of political tie. The Romans had no ready-made plan for their control, but gradually worked out their rules of administration by trial and error ; and they never used a cut-and-dried system. But the main lines of their methods of government had been laid down before the end of the second century.

### (A) *The Dependent Kings and Cities*

The Romans had attached the Italians to Rome either by actually taking over their territory or by making alliances with them. For overseas countries in the second and third centuries B.C. they preferred to use the method of alliance. In some cases the position of a dependent state was limited in its armaments and political intercourse with other states. The terms imposed upon Carthage in 201 and upon the Aetolians in 189 were of this type. In other instances the Romans borrowed the common formulae of Greek cities, in which each partner agreed to give military aid to the other when called upon. The agreement made with the Jews in 161 and the treaties which bound the Romans to Egypt and to Massilia were on these lines. But these engagements usually ended by becoming dead letters, if indeed they had not been intended as such at the beginning. But since Rome had more power than the other Mediterranean states, alliances on an equal basis were bound in actual practice to become one-sided.

The commonest form of Roman treaty with states outside of Italy was of the type made with Massinissa, by which kings became *socii et amici* ('allies and friends') of the republic. These agreements did not bind the two states to render mutual aid, but left it to their choice to give active assistance or to remain benevolently neutral. In practice the Romans used the military resources of the client kings, but they avoided using Roman legions on behalf of their overseas allies. They requested the Numidian kings to provide troops in the Third Punic War. More often the allied kings made offers of help : Massinissa and Micipsa sent troops and elephants to assist the Romans in Spain. This vague relationship had the merit, from the Roman point of view, of securing the neutrality, if not the active assistance, of the allies, without committing the republic too deeply in return ; and to the allies the mere prestige of a treaty with Rome, though it might not have the backing of Rome's military power, was a big help.

## (B) *Political Status*

The system of alliances with *socii et amici* in the eastern Mediterranean remained in use for several centuries. In the western lands, on the other hand, their usual method was to incorporate conquered territory in the Roman state, and this method was later extended to the eastern states. The first Roman *provincia* was Sicily ; Sardinia and Corsica were joined together to make up a second province ; Spain was divided into a third and fourth. In all these cases the chief concern of the Romans was to keep safe regions taken by them from the Carthaginians. Military security was also the main reason for annexing Macedonia and the African territory of Carthage after the Third Punic War. Another motive for acquiring provinces, which became stronger in the later days of the republic, was the desire to make money from them. In the case of the Pergamene kingdom, Spain and Gallia Narbonensis, this motive played a large part.

The general outlines of the provincial constitutions were settled in a code known as the Lex Provinciae. The details of administration not covered by the Lex Provinciae were left to the successive governors of a province. A governor would publish an 'edict' containing the regulations which he intended to apply during his term of office. Like the praetor's edict at Rome, a provincial edict would set forth the principles according to which the governor proposed to administer law in his court; but it might contain other details, such as the restrictions imposed upon the local governments. In actual practice one governor usually took over part of his predecessor's code.

A few specially favoured communities, which had been bound to Rome by a previous alliance, neither paid tribute nor were brought under the jurisdiction of the Roman courts. These were called *civitates foederatae* ('states under treaty'). A larger number of communities, by a law of the Senate, paid no taxation and received a guarantee of self-government (*civitates liberae et immunes*) ('free and untaxed states'). The majority of the communities in any province possessed no legal guarantee of their status; but the Romans usually gave to the provincials a good deal of local self-government. Wherever municipal governments with a sufficiently long experience of administration were to be found, the Romans left local affairs in the hands of these; in the more backward districts they left them in the hands of tribal chieftains. They did not interfere in local politics without good cause, such as disloyalty, political chaos, or bad financial administration. On the other hand, the question of giving Roman citizenship to the provincials was not even considered in the third or second century. The enfranchisement of the Italians was not considered : still less that of states outside Italy.

## (c) *The Provincial Governors*

At first it was left to the consuls to nominate, on the Senate's advice, any two persons qualified to act as their deputies in Sicily and Sardinia. But from *c.* 228 to 225 the government of these two provinces was regularly given to two officers of the rank of praetor, who were elected annually, like the praetors at Rome, by the Comitia Centuriata; and in 197 two more praetors were chosen for Hither and Further Spain. After Macedonia and Africa became provinces, Rome developed the device of *prorogatio* (extension of command), which now turned into a permanent institution. After 146 it became customary to prolong the term of office of all the consuls and praetors, after a year spent in Rome, as governors of provinces with consular or praetorian rank (*pro consule, pro praetore*, 'proconsul' and 'propraetor', or literally 'in place of a consul' and 'in place of a praetor'). The Senate decided annually which provinces should be held next year by men of consular or praetorian rank. In times of emergency it might give particular provinces to individual magistrates; but ordinarily it was left to the consuls and praetors to select their several provinces by mutual arrangement or by drawing lots. The usual term of a provincial governor was of one year; but in an emergency his office might be prolonged to a second or even a third year.

The first duty of the governor was to defend his province against foreign enemies and civil war; but in normal times most of his work was jurisdiction. He would hear cases of treason and other serious crime; those in which a Roman citizen was involved; and disputes between people from different parts of the province. The governor's court was not permanently established in any one city, but moved about from district to district.

The only regular assistant of the governor was a quaestor, who dealt with taxes and finance generally. A governor also usually kept one or more *legati*, whom he appointed, subject to the Senate's approval, as his assistants.

(D) *Finance and Economics*

It was a fundamental point of difference between the provincials and the Italians that the former were not liable to the same degree to military service, but were subject to regular taxation. Conscription was applied to the more backward tribes who could make no payment to Rome in the form of taxes. In cases of emergency the governor might order a general conscription and the *civitates foederatae* were obliged by their treaties to give occasional military aid. But the Romans did not impose personal service on the provincials in the same manner as in Italy.

Taxation was not imposed by the Romans upon the *civitates foederatae*, nor upon the more favoured of the *civitates liberae*.

In their methods of taxation the Romans did not follow any set principle. The heaviest tax fell upon the owners of land. In most provinces the land tax was a fixed sum of silver. In Sicily and Sardinia the tax was paid in grain; in Asia it was a payment of money. An additional tax fell on each head of cattle. There was also a tax upon all goods entering or leaving a province, and a *tributum capitis* or income-tax was paid upon the profits of industries and professions.

For the business of gathering in these taxes the Roman governor's staff was too small. It was left in the hands of the local authorities, each of which was bound to pay to the Roman quaestor the lump sum at which it was assessed. The local governing bodies usually transferred the work of collection in detail to companies of private contractors, who paid in advance the agreed total of each tax and recovered the money, together with a profit, from the individual tax-payer. The Sicilian tax-collectors were mostly drawn from the native population, controlled by the municipal magistrates. In Asia the collection of the land-tax was transferred from the officials of the Pergamene kings to contractors at Rome, who paid the amount of the tax directly into the Roman treasury and got the money back in the province by means of their trained staffs of collectors. Because of the larger amount of capital at their disposal, the Roman tax companies were able to displace the native collectors in other provinces; but they never obtained a complete monopoly of this business.

The provincials also had to find billets, provisions, fuel and fodder for the governor's staff and his troops. The quantity was limited by Roman statutes or decisions of the Senate, and fair rates of payment were laid down for the grain delivered for the governor's use. Finally, in Sicily and Sardinia the Roman state reserved to itself the right of buying additional quantities of corn for the population of Rome or for the armies on foreign service. For this the provincials were repaid at full market rates.

Restrictions on commerce were imposed on particular provinces or for certain periods. In Sicily and Sardinia the Romans assured themselves of a plentiful supply of grain for their own uses by forbidding its exportation to other countries than Italy. But the Romans did not harm the economic activities of the provincials for the benefit of Italian traders.

In the western provinces, where coinage had been scarce before the Roman conquest, additional mints were opened by several towns of Sicily and Spain, but these mostly coined only copper pieces on the Roman standard. In the eastern Mediterranean many of the existing mints remained active, and no attempt was made by the Romans to impose a uniform standard upon them.

The provincials were not compelled to surrender land for allotment to Roman colonists. In countries where Roman troops on active service were stationed, Italian settlers were not considered necessary for military security. In southern and eastern Spain a few settlements of Italian veterans were authorised. On the territory of Carthage the Senate tolerated occupation by individual emigrants from Italy. In Gallia Narbonensis it consented to a colony at Narbo. In the eastern provinces not a single Roman colony was founded before the time of Caesar.

### (E) *The Defects of Roman Rule*

Roman rule in Italy gave general satisfaction; in the provinces it caused widespread discontent. The ultimate reason was that while the Italians rendered military aid to Rome, the provincials paid tribute. In the eyes of the Romans the provincials became a source of gain, and they could not prevent abuses of Roman power. They became victims of many forms of financial exploitation, for which Roman officials and private residents were both to blame.

Roman noblemen, who made it a point of honour to give public service at home without any reward, learnt to look upon their office in a province as a heaven-sent occasion for personal gain. Indeed, as public life in Rome grew more expensive, provincial governorships came to be regarded as necessary for recovering past expenses and providing for future costs. The lead which governors gave in extorting money was eagerly followed by their staff, who also had their careers in Rome to keep in mind. For a bribe, they would exempt the provincials from the burdensome obligation to provide billets for the troops and from the liability to furnish grain and means of transport. Bribery was also common in the administration of the law. The collection of compulsory contributions, supposed to be a voluntary expression of gratitude to the governor, was also an easy method of making money.

Roman citizens living abroad also took advantage of their nationality to make money. The most persistent were the Roman *publicani* (collectors of public taxes), who had an obvious interest in collecting more than their due. The *publicani* also used their funds to buy up grain at low prices after harvest in order to sell it at high rates in areas of shortage, or to lend money at high rates of interest. For the collection of their debts the Roman money-lenders could generally count on assistance from the governors, some of whom even put soldiers at their disposal.

The Romans paid themselves for keeping the peace and defending the frontiers of the provinces. But in most of the provinces the standing garrisons were cut down to the point of danger ; the governors often lacked experience in warfare under the local conditions, and their term of office was usually too short to provide them with the necessary training. Complaints by natives or by Romans were made, but so long as the protests were not carried beyond the province the governor could safely disregard them. Some governors imprisoned or killed their critics. Sometimes governors put to death Roman citizens, in defiance of a law (carried in 199 by the tribune P. Porcius Laeca), which affirmed their right of appeal outside Roman territory.

## (F) *Attempts at Reform*

The cause of the oppressed peoples was taken up by several of the military leaders who were patrons of the provinces pacified by them. The Spaniards could always count on a Sempronius Gracchus, the Allobroges of Gallia Narbonensis on Fabius Maximus and his descendants. The strongest champion of injured provincials in the second century was M. Cato. The Senate also showed some concern for the oppressed natives, and it saw the danger to Rome if Roman magistrates overseas were to form a habit of setting themselves above the law.

Individual champions of the provinces undertook prosecutions before the Popular Assembly against the worst offenders, and the Senate issued new regulations for the protection of the provincials. In 170 a more drastic procedure was adopted against an ex-praetor named Lucretius Gallus, who was prosecuted by the will of the Senate before the Tribal Assembly, which imposed a heavy fine upon him. In 149 the same Assembly acquitted a far worse offender, Sulpicius Galba, who had both plundered and massacred the Spaniards. Galba outmanœuvred his opponents by the device of exhibiting his family to the court in ragged clothes. This led to the transfer of cases of bad administration from the Popular Assembly to a special court. In 149 the tribune L. Calpurnius Piso carried a law by which prosecutions for extortion were made in a permanent court consisting entirely of senators, whose decision was placed beyond the reach of an appeal to the people and of a tribune's veto (*quaestio de rebus repetundis*, 'court of enquiry for recovering money'). Before 86 B.C. a second special court of the same type was set up to deal with cases of misuse of public money (*peculatus*).

The institution of the standing jury-courts marked an important stage in the history of Roman jurisdiction, but it failed to put a stop to extortion in the provinces. Prosecutions in a jury-court were difficult. There was no lack of Roman citizens to come forward as prosecutors — some acting out of public spirit, some from a desire of self-advertisement, others again in pursuit of a political feud — but the collection of evidence was liable to be impeded by a governor with a guilty conscience. Besides, the senatorial juries were biased in favour of defendants drawn from their own political class.

## Part 2 : *Roman Politics and Economics*

The expansion of the Roman empire in the third and second centuries B.C. was rapid and unforeseen. The Romans were slow to observe and control the reactions of their conquests upon their internal politics.  The political history of the later republic is largely a record of successive crises, which came because Rome did not adapt to a quickly changing environment.

## (A) *The Assemblies*

Until the middle of the third century the number of the tribes in the Comitia was increased from time to time, so as to keep pace with the extensions of Roman territory.  After 241, when their total was raised to thirty-five, no further increase in their number took place, and new citizens were henceforth distributed among the existing tribes.  At this period the constitution of the Tribal Assembly received its final shape.

At some time after the completion of the tribal organisation — between 241 and 179 — a change was made in the constitution of the Comitia Centuriata, which cut down the voting power of the higher classes.  The number of centuries in the first class was reduced from eighty to seventy, so that two centuries were assigned to each of the thirty-five tribes.

At the same time the eighteen centuries of Equites lost the privilege of providing the *centuria praerogativa*, which was transferred to the first property-class.  No change was made in the ratings of the several classes, except that the property qualification of the fifth class was reduced from 11,000 to 4000 asses.  But a devaluation of the *as*, which probably took place in the latter half of the second century, had the automatic effect of lowering the qualifications for every class.

With the expansion of Roman territory and the progress of Roman colonisation the number of country voters continued to rise.  But as the distance which separated them from the capital grew ever longer, their opportunities of actually voting became less frequent.  There was also a rapid growth of the urban population, from peasants, who had lost their land, and slaves who received their freedom and therewith Roman citizenship and a vote.  In the Tribal Assembly, it is true, the voting power of the freedmen was reduced by their confinement to the four 'urban' tribes, but in the Comitia Centuriata it had equal value with that of the free-born.

The urban voters of the second century were less independent than the sturdy peasants who had successfully resisted the patricians in the Conflict of the Orders. The ex-slaves were tied by the bond of clientship to their former masters, and the immigrant population in general was economically dependent on the wealthier classes. Also, politics at Rome became more and more complicated and difficult to understand. Thus it is not surprising that the urban voters became dependent on political 'bosses'.

The purchase of votes by candidates for office became so common in the second century that two laws *de ambitu* ('concerning bribery'), which were carried in 181 and 159, were not enforced. A collective system of bribery was introduced by the Senate, which took advantage of the frequent gifts of corn from Carthage and Numidia, to make free distributions of food to the urban proletariat, and sometimes of wine and oil also.

The ruling houses also influenced the people by keeping them amused with public entertainments. Before 220 the only regular public games in Rome were a one-day festival known as the *Ludi Romani*. In that year a second holiday, the *Ludi Plebeii*, was instituted. During the dark days of the Second Punic War the Senate appointed three further festivals, in order to keep up the spirits of the people, the *Ludi Apollinares* (212), *Megalenses* (204) and *Ceriales* (before 202). In 173 a sixth public entertainment, the *Ludi Florales*, was introduced. The duration of each of these festivities was later extended to five, seven or even fourteen days. In addition to the sums provided out of public funds, contributions were made out of their private pockets by the individual magistrates (praetors, curule and plebeian aediles) who presided over these festivals.

## (B) *The Nobles*

In the fourth and third centuries the admission of plebeians into the magistracy and the Senate had produced a slow but constant flow of new families into the governing class. By 179 more than half the Senate was composed of plebeians. In the third and second centuries the old hereditary aristocracy had been replaced by a new aristocracy of office, to which the name of *nobiles* came to be applied. Since admission to the ranks of the *nobiles* depended on election to the consulship, it always remained possible for a *novus homo* (a 'new man', i.e. a man of unknown family or low birth) to gain entrance into them, but in actual fact the 'nobility' became a closed caste. The ennobled plebeians had absorbed the exclusive spirit of the older families : they combined with the patricians to keep newcomers out of the higher magistracies. From 264 to 201 not more than eleven *novi homines* attained the consulship; between 200 and 134 the consulship virtually passed into the possession of some twenty-five families.

Thus the *nobiles* retained control of the Senate and the Senate was the instrument by which they directed Roman policy. The position of almost unchallenged authority which the Senate had attained in the Second Punic War was confirmed and extended in the second century. The consolidation of its power was an inevitable result of the overseas conquests. In questions of war and peace, of making treaties or new provinces, its word was law ; and it was the court before which foreign powers, provincial communities, and Italians pleaded. It gave provincial and military commands to individual magistrates. It had a tighter control over Roman finances, and by paying for games and festivals it kept the urban population under a due sense of obligation. By its power to vote supplies for provincial governors, to lengthen their commands or to cut them short, it gained additional holds on the magistracy.

In the second century the Roman constitution again became rigidly aristocratic. A nobility became an exclusive governing caste by controlling the elections, so as to monopolise the higher offices and acquire a commanding influence in the Senate. This class had to direct the foreign conquests and adapt the constitution to the needs of the Roman empire. For such a task, however, it was not well fitted. The nature of Romans was to advance by slow steps in politics and not to make any sudden or sweeping change. It was therefore only to be expected that the Romans of the second century became complacent about their constitution, and slow to realise the need of a better policy.

But in the governing circle competition for consulships and censorships was intense. Certain outstanding families — the Aemilii, the Claudii, the Cornelii Scipiones, the Fulvii and the Postumii — carried off for themselves more than a fair share of these prizes. Scipio Africanus worked for his friends, but there was an opposition group headed by M. Cato. The rivalries of these two were fought out not only at the elections but in the courts of law. Cato, himself the object of forty-four prosecutions in the course of his career, always tried to use the law against his enemies.

In 187 he persuaded two tribunes, each named Q. Petilius, to ask Lucius Scipio in the Senate about a sum of five hundred talents which he had used to pay a bonus to his soldiers. By way of reply, Africanus produced Lucius' account-book and tore out the entries, thus saying that his brother was not answerable. For the time being Cato let matters rest ; but in the year of his censorship (184) he made another attack, by getting another tribune to accuse Lucius before the Tribal Assembly. Lucius escaped, but Cato managed to drive his real enemy, Africanus, out of public life. Taking the attack upon his brother as a personal insult, Africanus retired from Rome and died in the following year.

Yet the feud between Cato and Scipio was a personal feud, and did not arise from differences in political belief, even though some of their opinions were slightly opposed to each other : for, at the most, a distinction might be drawn between their respective foreign policies. Scipio wanted a benevolent Roman protectorate in Greece, and Cato would have preferred to leave the Greeks severely alone. In domestic affairs both Cato and Scipio were extreme conservatives. Africanus, who had statues and dictatorships offered to him, treated the Popular Assembly with positive insolence, and he never began any constitutional reform. Similarly the preservation of the *mos maiorum* ('ancestral custom', i.e. traditional orthodox behaviour) was the very key-note of Cato's policy. He attacked phil-Hellenism, extortion in the provinces, and luxury in private life, because all of these were not in the Roman tradition. He never suggested any enlargement or improvement in the machinery of government.

The chief danger to the nobility did not arise from opponents in the political field, but from military leaders who were tempted by their power on foreign service to set themselves above the Senate's authority. A bad sign of disobedience was the frequency with which Roman generals started private wars without Senatorial warrant. In 189 Manlius Vulso exceeded his instructions in attacking the Galatians in Asia Minor, and campaigns were undertaken at various times in Liguria and Illyria by commanders acting on their own responsibility.

But for the time being Rome's prestige in the whole Mediterranean was high and the benefits of the Roman peace made up for the burdens of Roman imperialism. The stability of the Roman government had not yet been seriously threatened, and there still was plenty of time for the republic to set itself in order.

### (c) *The Magistracies*

In the second century the duties of the Roman government became far more complex. A permanent body of accountants and secretaries was attached to the treasury and to the bureaux of the chief magistrates. But this staff was recruited from ex-slaves and formed a class wholly distinct from the magistracy. Additional praetors and quaestors were appointed for the administration of the provinces, and after 150 proconsuls and propraetors were appointed for the same purpose. But no increase took place in the magistrates at Rome, and no attempt was made to prolong their terms of office. The Roman aristocracy clung obstinately to the ideal of unpaid half-time service by men born rather than trained to exercise authority. After the Second Punic War it brought back into operation the fourth-century law prescribing a ten years' interval between two successive consulships, and in 180 the Lex Villia Annalis arranged the magistracies in a definite order and spaced out the terms of office in such a manner that the age of thirty-three became the lowest at which a consulship might be held. At about 150, a law advanced the minimum age for the consulship to forty-two, and prohibited re-election to this office.

(D) *Reforms in the Legal System*

About 240 Rome's conquest of all Italy had increased the number of law-suits enough to render necessary the appointment of a second praetor, the *praetor peregrinus* ('foreign praetor'). The new praetor tried cases between foreigners; the original praetor, or *praetor urbanus* ('city praetor') (as he came to be called), took charge of cases between aliens and citizens. The cases in which aliens were parties were often of a kind for which the existing *ius civile* ('citizen law') in the Twelve Tables and in other codes were useless. In their courts, accordingly, the *ius civile* began to be overlaid with the *ius gentium* ('law of nations'), a composite code pieced together out of the laws and customs of surrounding states, and out of the praetors' own ideas of justice. In non-Roman law, moreover, the praetors were left free to use their own judgment in conducting the preliminary hearing and in giving instructions to the jury. The advantages of this became so clear that a Lex Aebutia, about 150, authorised its introduction into the court of the *praetor urbanus*.

In 199 the tribune P. Porcius Laeca gave the right of appeal to Romans in Italy and the provinces; in 195 the consul M. Porcius Cato exempted citizens from scourging; in 184 the consul L. Porcius Licinus safeguarded them from execution on military service. By 150 the infliction of the death penalty upon citizens had become obsolete, and the death sentence was, instead, changed into one of banishment.

In the first half of the second century the Concilium Plebis continued to act as a court in political cases, and several leading public men were brought before it by prosecuting tribunes. An important step was taken in 149 when the tribune L. Calpurnius Piso established the *quaestio perpetua de rebus repetundis*. In outward form this resembled the praetors' civil courts. It was presided over by a magistrate of praetorian rank, and the jury of senators who pronounced sentence were known as *iudices*, like the delegates of the *praetor urbanus*. But it eventually served as a pattern to other new courts for the trial of criminal offences. But the benefit of these reforms in criminal jurisdiction was confined to citizens. Aliens and slaves had to take their chance of a trial before the tribunes or aediles, and the Roman criminal courts might sentence a non-citizen to death after a very short hearing.

## (E) *Finance*

Since 264 the Romans' chief victims in war were states possessing large stocks of gold and silver ; the wealth collected by them was enormous. There was also a regular flow of tribute from the provinces, the Spanish mines, and rents from the public land. Thus the Roman government was able to issue plenty of silver coinage, which presently became the usual currency in the western Mediterranean ; and after 167 it had no further need of a land-tax in Italy.

But the expenditure of the republic also rose. From the Second Punic War the Roman treasury inherited a dead-weight of loans due for repayment. During the first half of the second century, moreover, the republic rarely had less than 100,000 men on active service ; for all of these it had to find provisions ; for the citizen troops, amounting to nearly half the total, it had to provide pay. These war expenses used up most of the additional income. From the income that was left over after meeting the costs of Roman armaments, large grants were made from time to time for the construction of military roads, for public works at Rome, and for the amusements of the citizens. By 157 the total reserve fund at Rome was only about 25,000,000 denarii (about £1,000,000).

## (F) *Italy*

During the Second Punic War the Italians had mostly been loyal to the republic, and in the second century they had provided more than half of the troops that won the Roman empire overseas. There had also been close contact of Romans and Italians on military service, and the Roman colonies on the Italian countryside. The cultural influence of Rome was extending far beyond the immediate environs of the city, and the time was undoubtedly ripe for the admission of the Italian allies to Roman citizenship, or to a more equal partnership with Rome.

In 188 three towns on the borderland of Latium and

Campania, Arpinum, Formiae and Fundi, received full Roman franchise in exchange for their previous *civitas sine suffragio*, and most of the other cities possessing the half-franchise received similar promotion not long after. Italian allies as well as citizens received shares in the individual allotments of land in Cisalpine Gaul, and they also shared in the colonisation of northern Italy.

But the Roman government did not really tackle the problem of Italian franchise. It had no desire to give citizen rights to large masses of men whose votes they would not be able to control. Still less was it prepared to share the magistracies at Rome with *novi homines* from the Italian towns. Therefore nothing was done at this stage to improve the status of the *socii Italici*. Indeed, about 187 a law was passed which actually withdrew the franchise from Latin immigrants to Rome, and twelve thousand Latins, already registered as Roman citizens under the previous regulations, were ordered to leave the city.

In the second century the number of soldiers demanded from the allies was frequently more than that of the citizens; yet their share in the spoils of victory was less. Since 177 their portion of the plunder was reduced to half of the citizens' allowance, and after 183 Latins were no longer invited to share in the foundation of colonies.

Both the Senate and individual Roman officials sometimes treated them badly. Money was extorted from them to pay for the games in Rome, and they had to give free entertainment to travelling Roman officials.

### (G) *The Army*

The Roman government did not seem to learn some of the most striking lessons of the Punic Wars. It cut down the navy, and after the Third Macedonian War it dispensed altogether with a regular fleet. It again neglected its cavalry and used only auxiliary horsemen from the allied kings or the provinces. The Roman forces were fortunate in not being called upon to meet an opponent of the calibre of Pyrrhus or Hannibal, and the Macedonian army was not well provided with horsemen. But if the legions escaped serious disaster in set battles, they repeatedly suffered defeats on difficult or unexplored ground, where inexperienced commanders often led them into ambushes.

But the worst feature of the warfare of the second century was the increasing reluctance of the Roman recruits to perform their duties. In the eastern campaigns the chance of rich plunder attracted large numbers of semi-professional soldiers : but Roman officers in Spain had difficulties in raising new troops. The example of evading duty was set by the nobles themselves, although they had to serve in ten campaigns before presenting themselves for election to a political office. Many managed to avoid enrolment in the cavalry troops, in which sons of senators were expected to spend at least five seasons, by getting an easier position on the general's staff. In 151 the consul L. Lucullus even had difficulty in finding volunteers to hold the junior commands in his Spanish campaign. In order to assist enrolment, the minimum property qualification for service was reduced from 11,000 to 4000 asses. Roman soldiers were not liable to the penalty of scourging and had the right to appeal to the Comitia against sentences of death. But this failed to satisfy the troops, and there were other more dangerous relaxations of discipline. In the early stages of the Third Macedonian War common soldiers received long leaves, or took them without asking, in order to trade behind the lines ; and pedlars and prostitutes were allowed to live close by the Roman camp.

The half-time army which had served well for warfare in Italy was unsuited for long campaigning in overseas countries. The protection or extension of the empire's frontiers urgently required a professional army.

(H) *Economic Conditions*

1. *Agriculture.*—The land taken after the Second Punic War and the campaigns in Cisalpine Gaul almost doubled the extent of Roman territory. In Cisalpine Gaul and southern Italy a lot of this land was distributed to Roman or allied settlers. These small peasants usually grew corn mainly for their own consumption, and thus had little to fear from the competition of exporters from overseas countries. But

military service abroad compelled many to neglect their farms. Many of them went to Rome, where food was cheap and amusements cost nothing. Soon after 177, the date at which the distribution of land was stopped, the number of farms declined steadily.

The big feature in the second century was the growth of large estates (*latifundia*), with areas exceeding one hundred acres and sometimes rising to over three hundred. The increase in the number of these *latifundia* was the result of the overseas conquests. Roman magistrates, who had made profits out of a war or a provincial governorship, and the rising class of tax-farmers and contractors purchased the land of the smaller peasants as these began to drift away from the country, and rented large tracts of the undistributed public land. They were to some extent restricted by a statute based on the Lex Licinia of 367 which set a limit of 300 acres to the amount of public land which any one person might occupy. But this act was never properly enforced.

The owners of the *latifundia* began to use scientific methods of farming by introducing rotation of crops, new deep-cutting ploughs, and the use of specially selected seed-corn. But the only market in Italy for grain was Rome, and Rome bought her corn from abroad. The corn crops on the *latifundia* were therefore largely replaced by plantations, which under scientific cultivation could be made to produce a far higher rate of profit. The richest land was converted into vineyards, the poorer into olive-groves. But the biggest development was in cattle-farming, which in southern Italy was organised on a large scale. The costs of looking after the herds were reduced to a minimum, while the wool and the hides, if not the meat, of the animals made good money. Ranching was therefore considered most profitable for a capitalist landowner, and it was probably the source of many arge fortunes in the later republic.

2. *Slave-labour.*—Agriculture needed larger quantities of labour than it was possible to get from the free population of Italy. In southern and central Italy, where the estates of the wealthy Romans were mostly to be found, the countryside had been most heavily devastated during the Hannibalic war, and

the wars of the early second century continually kept 100,000 Italians (mostly of the peasant class) on military service abroad. But these wars also produced slaves, who were prisoners of war. The capitalist landowners not only absorbed the greater number of the war captives, but stimulated the regular slave-trade of the Mediterranean regions into activity. Slaves offered several advantages : they were not liable to be called away on military duty ; they could be fed on the coarsest food and made to work hard. Wherever slaves could be put to work in gangs, they were distributed into regular squads under a foreman, and each labourer was carefully selected, in accordance with his physique and mentality, for his particular task. But the disadvantages in slave labour soon showed. The early Roman slave-masters frankly treated their staff as mere animals, and relied upon the fear of punishment by scourging or chaining to make them work. The food and clothing of the slaves, though adequate in quantity, were of the coarsest type ; their sleeping-quarters were often underground. Their work, besides being unending, was monotonous ; opportunities of family life were denied to all except the bailiff ; and their chances of eventually buying their freedom (by saving up their little *peculium*, or pocket-money) were small. Under such conditions the thought of rebellion was never far from the minds of the slaves, and although Italy escaped a slave-war on a large scale in the second century, there were frequent minor rebellions. But the principal weapon of the dissatisfied slave was passive resistance. He got even with his master by stealing his property or handling it negligently ; as soon as the foreman's eye was off him he slackened his work. It therefore required constant personal attention on the part of the owner — which few of the capitalist landlords could give — in order to maintain work on the estate at a profitable level of efficiency. At best, the labour of slaves was economical for only as long as their initial cost remained low.

While the wealthier Romans took their barbarian war-captives to their *latifundia*, they retained in their town houses the Greek slaves. The Greek captives not only did the humble jobs of the great households, but held semi-professional positions as secretaries, teachers and physicians; and the women slaves found additional occupations in spinning and weaving.

In comparison with the condition of the rural slaves, the lot of the town slaves was an enviable one. The task of each town slave was seldom heavy; the secretaries and other brain-workers might be virtually as free as tutors and confidential clerks at the present day. The household slaves, moreover, had the opportunity of catching the master's eye and of earning special rewards for good service. They might obtain permission to enter into a matrimonial union (*contubernium*), or they might earn a liberal allowance of pocket-money (*peculium*).

The domestic slaves, it is true, were at the mercy of the personal whims of cruel masters. The slave-owners for their part, with a staff of submissive slaves to gratify their every desire, stood in danger of losing their habits of self-help and self-control. On the other hand, household slavery was one of the principal channels by which Greek culture came to Rome. As a confidential secretary or tutor, the Greek war captive gave to his master's family a close and constant contact with the Greek civilisation.

3. *Industry and Trade.*—Italian industry changed little in the third and second centuries. In Rome the wealth gained by the war did not increase manufactures. Tarentum never recovered from its losses in the Hannibalic war, but Capua remained a thriving town : by the side of its ancient industries in pottery and bronze new manufactures of furniture and perfumery were established there. In the second century Campania definitely outstripped Etruria as the industrial centre of Italy. Puteoli took over part of the Tuscan iron industry, and Pompeii rose in wealth by the sale of its textiles.

A considerable volume of new trade was attracted to Italy, though little came from Italy. Apart from the bronzes of Capua and the olive-oil of the Campanian *latifundia*, the exports of Italy were insignificant. On the other hand, Rome now imported large quantities of grain from Sicily, and took most of the produce of the Spanish silver mines. The capital itself, together with the new *latifundia*, regularly bought slaves from Delos, which became the collecting-point of the slave-trade.

Roman policy was not directed to commercial objects. The Roman nobility took little personal interest in overseas trade; still less did it wish to establish a trade monopoly for those of lower rank. The settlements made by the Senate with the conquered and allied peoples showed the same disregard for trade. These treaties did not as a rule give any special privilege to Roman or Italian men of business. After the Second Punic War the Senate even stopped protecting Italian traders against pirates. Under these conditions the transport of the Mediterranean remained in the hands of Greeks and Phoenicians. Italian merchants established themselves in considerable numbers at Delos; but the majority — despite the name of 'Romans' which the Greeks gave them — came from Campania and the Greek cities of the south rather than from central Italy; and the principal port by which overseas products flowed into Italy was Puteoli, a town whose people were mostly Greek or Campanian. The port of Ostia at the Tiber mouth was still quite undeveloped.

But in their financial operations the Romans left the Greeks and Orientals far behind them. The concentration of this business in Roman hands was a natural result of the wars of conquest, which had the effect of accumulating the Mediterranean's stocks of gold and silver at Rome. The wealth of capital which Roman money-lenders and tax-collectors had gave them an advantage over their competitors which sometimes amounted to a monopoly. But the success of the Romans in money-dealing was largely due to their better organisation.

The business of money-lending was mostly in the hands of individual capitalists. In Italy their opportunities were restricted by the fourth-century laws against the taking of interest; in the provinces they might be limited by the governor's edict to a mere 12 per cent, but they found borrowers (such as hard-pressed tax-payers) willing to offer 24 per cent or even 48 per cent.

The profits gained by the Romans from their conquests, raised them to a level of material prosperity exceeding that of any other Mediterranean people. The soldiers were paid off with handsome war bonuses, and often received a land allotment into the bargain. The senatorial class derived wealth from the proceeds of their war booty, from the administration of provinces, and from the scientific development of their *latifundia*. The fortune of P. Licinius Crassus (consul in 131), who was estimated to possess a hundred million sesterces, was no doubt exceptional at this stage of Roman history. But it is noteworthy that Aemilius Paullus, the victor of Pydna, was not thought wealthy, although he possessed one and a half million sesterces, a sum which any nobleman of the fourth or third century would have regarded as immense.

But the outstanding feature of this period was the rise of a new middle class, the Equites or Equester Ordo, which took the lead in capitalistic enterprises of all kinds, whether of land improvement, or building or of traffic in goods and money. The term Equester Ordo, which originally had been applied to the men who served as cavalry in the army and voted in the *equitum centuriae*, was subsequently extended to all those citizens whose wealth qualified them for such service. Finally it came to include all persons possessing not less than 400,000 sesterces, who stood outside the ranks of the governing aristocracy. In the second century the number of these Equites was sufficient to constitute them as a distinct social class.

### CHAPTER IX

# 133–90 B.C.

## Part 1 : *Politics at Rome*

### (A) *133–132 B.C.: Tiberius Gracchus*

THE period of comparative calm through which Roman domestic politics had moved since the end of the Conflict of the Orders ended in 133 with the tribunate of Tiberius Gracchus, who made the first really formidable attack upon the privileges of the nobles.

As the son of the elder Sempronius Gracchus, a strong conservative, and of Cornelia, the daughter of Scipio Africanus, Tiberius seemed hardly the man to lead a revolution. As an officer in the Third Punic War, he had been first over the wall of Carthage. With such an ancestry and such a personal record, Tiberius had merely to observe the Roman nobleman's ordinary code of 'good form', and his career was assured.

The reasons that impelled Tiberius to turn against his own class may partly be found in the influence of his Greek teachers. But no doubt he learnt more from current events than from any man's theories. He had noted the shortage of peasants in Etruria, a land of large estates tilled by slaves. In Spain he had observed the deterioration of the Roman soldiery, and he had sought its cause in the decline of the Italian yeoman class. An even better proof of the dangers of slavery had been offered to him by a recent rebellion in Sicily, where the slaves had risen in 135 against their Greek and Roman landlords. Their forces were estimated at not less than 60,000, and it was not until 133–132 that the island was pacified. So Tiberius became a land-reformer and a revolutionary politician.

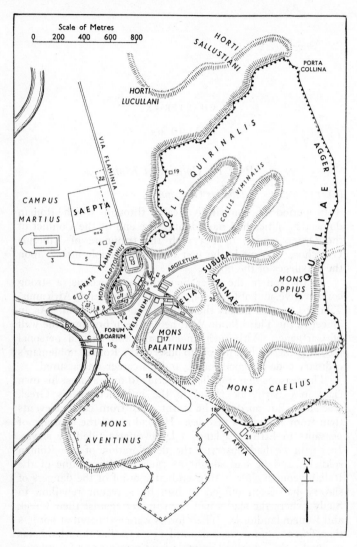

REPUBLICAN ROME

Elected tribune for 133, Tiberius brought forward a bill for making allotments out of the large area of public land which the republic had acquired after the Second Punic War. Of this territory he offered to leave in the hands of the existing occupiers a piece of 300 acres each (the maximum which in strict law might be held by a single tenant), and an additional 150 acres for each of two sons; the rest he proposed to distribute to new tenants. He made the new allotment-holders pay a small rent, and promise not to sell their land for a certain number of years. By way of compensation for the disturbed tenants, some of whom had considerably improved the land occupied by them, he gave them a permanent lease, free of rent, of the land left to their hands, which they could pass on to their children.

This was not in the least a revolutionary measure in itself, but merely resumed, after a brief interruption, the traditional Roman policy of land settlement. A couple of similar bills had recently been brought forward by Scipio Aemilianus' friend C. Laelius (c. 150), and by P. Licinius Crassus (145), though neither of these reformers persisted in the face of opposition from the occupying tenants. Tiberius had an assurance of support from some leading members of the nobility,

1. Theatre and Porticus of Pompey, and Temple of Venus Victoria.
2. Porta Triumphalis.
3. Porticus Octavii.
4. Temple of Bellona.
5. Circus Flaminius.
6. Porticus Metelli.
7. Temple of Apollo.
8. Forum Holitorium.
9. Porta Carmentalis.
10. Temple of Jupiter Optimus Maximus.
11. Temple of Fides.
12. Temple of Ops.
13. Temple of Juno.
14. Temples of Fortuna and Mater Matuta.
15. Ara Maxima Herculis.
16. Circus Maximus.
17. Temple of the Magna Mater
18. Porta Capena.
19. Temple of Salus.
20. Temple of Tellus.
21. Temple of Honos and Virtus

JULIAN BUILDINGS

22. Saepta Julia.
23. Theatre of Marcellus.

BRIDGES

a. Pons Fabricius.
b. Pons Cestius.
c. Pons Aemilius.
d. Pons Sublicius.

including Appius Claudius Pulcher, the Princeps Senatus (the senior member on the roll of the House), P. Licinius Crassus, the wealthiest Roman of his day, and P. Mucius Scaevola, who was consul in the year of Tiberius' tribunate and probably helped him with the bill.

If Tiberius had followed the usual practice of submitting bills to the Senate before presenting them to the Assembly, they might have been accepted by the nobles. But he chose to act like C. Flaminius, whose land law had been carried in 232 without the Senate being consulted. The Senate naturally resented such treatment and used its normal method of checking the powers of a difficult magistrate — a veto by another official. When Tiberius' law was about to be read to the Tribal Assembly, a fellow-tribune named M. Octavius stopped the proceedings with his veto. Tiberius now prepared for a fight with the Senate. He agreed to discuss the situation with the House ; but tempers had by now risen to such a point that talk was useless. Tiberius reassembled the Tribal Assembly and got Octavius removed from office. This course was wholly unprecedented, but Tiberius had the support of all the land-hungry citizens and could use their votes to overbear opposition. Without further protest from the Senate, Octavius was replaced by a more favourable tribune, and the agrarian bill was made law. To give full effect to the measure, a permanent commission was set up, of which Tiberius himself, his younger brother Caius, and Claudius Pulcher were the original members, and which had power to decide all disputes arising out of the redistribution of land.

The agrarian commission now got to work, and allotments were made in various districts of Italy, but especially on the outskirts of the central and southern Apennines. An attempt on the Senate's part to starve it of funds was defeated by a new law, in which Tiberius proposed to use the money from the kingdom of Attalus for the commission. The mere threat to legislate again over the heads of the senators made them throw open the treasury for Tiberius' benefit. But Tiberius henceforth lived in fear of the nobility. To protect himself against attack he offered himself for a second tribunate ; but in so doing he raised another constitutional question. Elec-

tion to the same magistracy in two successive years was forbidden by the Lex Villia of 180; although it was not quite
certain whether the tribunate came under the scope of this
measure. Moreover, Tiberius found his supporters melting
away from him. The other tribunes and the urban proletariate soon lost interest in a cause that was of no personal
concern to them, and the rustic voters, who had previously
flocked to Rome in his support, were busy with the harvest.
The nobles might have defeated Tiberius and recovered their
power by strictly lawful methods. But some over-zealous
senators lost their heads. Led by the ex-consul Scipio Nasica,
they made a rush at Tiberius, and before his friends could
rally round him they clubbed him to death.

(B) *132–123 B.C.*

The lynching of Tiberius was followed by attacks on the
part of the Senate against his supporters. In 132 the consul
P. Popilius was directed to hold a trial, at which men who
had talked of violence were sentenced to death. Scipio
Nasica was made safe by an honourable exile, in the form
of a diplomatic mission to the new province of Asia. In 131
another political murder was threatened by a tribune named
C. Atinius, who had a personal grievance against the censor
Metellus Macedonicus; but his colleagues stopped him, and
for the time being no further violence was committed.

But the Senate took no steps to thwart Tiberius' land commission. With Licinius Crassus to replace Tiberius, the
commission carried on, and the consul Popilius not only co-
operated with it, but boasted publicly of his collaboration.
Thus the nobility made it clear that its opposition had not
been directed against the land law as such, but against the
methods by which it had been forced through.

In 131 a tribune named C. Papirius Carbo introduced
secret voting at legislative assemblies of the people. At the
instance of Scipio Aemilianus, the nobles defeated an attempt
by Carbo to allow re-election to the tribunate; but after
Scipio's death they allowed Carbo's measure to be carried by
some other tribune.

Among the many political issues raised by Tiberius

Gracchus the most important related to the Italian allies. The occupiers of Roman public land who were brought under the scope of his agrarian bill were not only Roman citizens, but Latins and Italians. As the Gracchan commissioners approached the limits of the land which they could profitably take from Roman occupiers, they began to lay hands on the pieces held by non-citizens. But some corporate allied communities had leases of this land, guaranteed by treaty ; they complained that the commissioners were overriding these agreements. In 129, therefore, Scipio Aemilianus got the Senate to transfer the settlement of disputes about land held by non-citizens from the Gracchan commission to one of the consuls. This brought the work of the commissioners to a standstill. Shortly after this, Scipio was found mysteriously dead, though no evidence of foul play was produced.

The grievances of the Italian allies against the Gracchan land-commission also brought up the more general question of their enfranchisement. In 125 M. Fulvius Flaccus, who was consul in that year, tried to solve the Italian question at one blow by means of a bill which offered enfranchisement to all the allies ; or, in case any should prefer to retain their communal independence, the right of appeal against Roman magistrates on the same terms as Roman citizens. Flaccus was plainly acting in the interests of the land commission, of which he and Carbo had recently become members (in place of Claudius Pulcher and Crassus, now dead). But he also had the honest intention of dealing with Italian franchise on its own merits.

The bill of Flaccus was not even put to the vote. To the nobility it meant the creation of a mass of voters who stood outside their patronage and might prove less manageable. Living at a distance from Rome, the new citizens might indeed choose not to use their votes often, yet they would remain a danger. To the urban proletariate, who thought of their franchise as a ticket with coupons attached for cheap corn, Flaccus' measure seemed bad : for the more citizens there were, the less cheap corn would be available for each citizen. The Senate, fearing that the Italians would flock to Rome and force or frighten the voters into passing Flaccus'

bill, instructed the tribune Iunius Pennus to introduce a bill
to throw out all non-citizens from Rome. At the same time
it offered Flaccus a tempting military command. He yielded
and went to southern France to achieve distinction in war.

For the moment the Italians had been outwitted. Yet their
interests were not wholly disregarded. The censors of 125
(Cn. Servilius and L. Cassius) showed unusual generosity in
testing the claims of applicants for registration as citizens, so
that the roll of citizens leapt up at one bound from 318,000
to 394,000. One Latin town, the colony of Fregellae, broke
into open revolt, but the rest of the country remained quiet,
and the unsupported rebels were soon beaten. Once more
the nobles had shown discretion in the hour of victory, and
by their judicious tactics they had disarmed opposition for
the moment. But the campaigns of Tiberius and of Flaccus
were a prelude to a more sustained assault delivered by
Caius Gracchus in 123–122 : it was in these years that the
ascendancy of the Senate was for the first time put to a
serious test.

## (c) *123–122 B.C.: Caius Gracchus*

The younger of the Gracchi was but twenty-one years of
age at the time of his brother's tribunate. But he took his
seat on the land commission at its beginning, and he gave
support to the reforms of Carbo and Flaccus. Foreseeing
their danger, the nobles endeavoured to cut short his career
by prosecuting him on various charges ; but he cleared himself
without difficulty and was returned tribune for 123.

Caius Gracchus was a man of wider imagination and of
deeper passions than his brother, and a very good public
speaker. He was re-elected tribune for 122 without opposition, so that for a year and a half he remained in a position of
great power, which he used to carry out a very full programme
of legislation.

Caius reinforced the agrarian act of 133. He exempted
from distribution certain portions of public land — presumably the more highly cultivated pieces in Campania, which
brought in a big rent to the treasury — but he restored to the
commission the judicial power which it had lost in 129. Thus

F

strengthened, the members of the commission resumed their work on a more ambitious scale. Caius also arranged for the construction of new roads, whose quality was equal to that of the best military highways. He also planned the foundation of colonies at Tarentum and Capua, and probably also on other Italian sites. But Caius' most notable scheme in fulfilment of his brother's policy was for an overseas colony named Iunonia, on the territory of Carthage, which had become Roman public land in 146. In the name of a fellow-tribune named Rubrius, he introduced a bill for the carving-out of this estate into six thousand allotments, which he proposed to give not only to Romans, but to land-hungry men from all Italy.

For the relief of those who preferred to take their chance in Rome he brought forward a law for the regulation of the city's corn supply. The cost of grain at Rome fluctuated wildly, and times of surplus in Rome were followed by seasons of high prices. No adequate storage accommodation had been provided. Caius arranged for the purchase of the overseas crops in bulk by the state, and for delivery at public warehouses in Ostia ; and from this store a fixed monthly ration was to be sold on demand to any Roman citizen at a low and unvarying price.

Caius first attacked the illegal practice by which the Senate had authorised the consul Popilius in 132 to constitute a special court with powers of capital punishment. This was now declared a punishable crime ; Popilius was prosecuted before the Tribal Assembly and driven into exile.

A second law was directed against the abuses which had crept into the jury-court for the trial of provincial governors on the charge of extortion. The natural sympathy which jurymen drawn exclusively from the Senate felt for culprits of senatorial rank had resulted in the acquittal of men whose guilt was obvious. An act of Caius made the senatorial jurors liable to prosecution. But in his second tribunate he abolished the senatorial juries altogether and transferred the court *de rebus repetundis* into the hands of the Equites. The juries of the court *de rebus repetundis* came mostly from that section of the Order which got its wealth from tax-farming and other financial operations. This group had interests in the provinces which were likely to bring them into conflict with the senatorial governors, and might be inclined to condemn rather than to acquit.

Another law prevented the Senate from taking into account personal likes and dislikes in its annual selection of two consular provinces for the outgoing magistrates of the rank and ordained that in future the selection must be made before the actual election of the consular pair to whom the provinces thus chosen would fall due. Since the elections of magistrates in the later republic were normally held six months before their entry into office, the effect of this was that the Senate had to make its choice of consular provinces at least eighteen months beforehand.

By a new law the freedom from tribute which the Senate had given to the cities of the former kingdom of Pergamum, was withdrawn from all but a few towns. This was because Caius needed to compensate the treasury for losses due to his corn law and colonial schemes. Instead of leaving the collection of the tribute of Asia in the hands of the several towns, he laid down that the rights of tax-gathering in all the cities of the province should be put up for auction at Rome, so that in effect he created a monopoly for the Roman tax-farming companies.

In 122 Caius had as a fellow-tribune M. Fulvius and now revived Flaccus' bill for the enfranchisement of the Italians. But this, the most statesmanlike of all his measures, proved the first step towards his downfall. During his second term of office the support which he received from Flaccus was offset by the subtle attacks which another tribune, M. Livius Drusus, carried on against him in collusion with the Senate. Drusus sought to outbid Caius in popularity with a rival block of laws whose object was to prove that he, not Caius, was the people's friend. He amended Caius' agrarian law by relieving the allotment-holders of the rent imposed upon them. He improved upon Caius' colonial projects by proposing no less than twelve settlements in Italy, to which the very poorest citizens were to be admitted.

In the meantime Caius' popularity had lessened. The

contents of his franchise bill were as unpopular as ever to the Roman voters, and the consul C. Fannius appealed quite frankly to their instinct not to spoil a good thing by making it too common. Finally, the Senate instructed the consuls to prohibit any of the allies from appearing within five miles of Rome on the day of the voting. Under these conditions Drusus was able to oppose the franchise bill with a direct veto.

After the defeat of the franchise act, commons and nobles combined to get rid of Caius altogether. In the summer of 122 the electors refused him a third tribunate, and the Senate instructed a new tribune, M. Minucius Rufus, to propose the abolition of the Lex Rubria, by which the colony of Iunonia was to be constituted. Minucius' bill was passed, but in the meantime Caius and the Senate had fought with other weapons.

While Minucius' law was under discussion, an appeal to force was made by Flaccus and Caius' associates, who occupied the Aventine hill with armed bands. In reply, the Senate passed a resolution which declared that the state was in danger, and asked the consuls and other high magistrates 'to see to it that the republic take no harm'. By this decree, which subsequently received the name of *senatus consultum ultimum* ('final decree of the Senate') and by repeated use became a common form, the Senate in effect promised its moral support to magistrates who used force against those endangering the state. On the strength of this the consul L. Opimius succeeded in raising enough troops to overwhelm the partisans of Caius. Flaccus was cut to pieces, and Caius himself only escaped Opimius by suicide. Opimius made arrests among Caius' followers and executed over 3000.

(D) *122–103 B.C.*

After the death of Caius Gracchus the senatorial aristocracy returned to power unopposed. In 120 L. Opimius was prosecuted by a tribune for putting citizens to death without a trial, but the Concilium Plebis was persuaded to acquit him. His acquittal gave the Senate confidence to make regular use of the *senatus consultum ultimum*.

In the following ten years the policy of the Senate was mainly directed by M. Aemilius Scaurus, who combined an

appearance of old-fashioned dignity with an open mind.
Scaurus' policy was in favour of a good understanding with
the Equestrian Order. It was probably on his advice that the
Senate accepted the main results of Caius' legislation, just as
it had previously tolerated Tiberius' land commission. Caius'
scheme of corn distribution was cut down but not totally
abolished. The colony of Iunonia was not established :
nevertheless the land commission was allowed to make individual allotments on the territory of Carthage. Colonial
settlements were also made at Narbo, Tarentum and other
Italian sites in accordance with Caius' law. About 120 the
land acts of Tiberius and Caius were amended by a law
permitting allotment-holders to sell their land, which accordingly began to pass back into the hands of big landowners.
Soon after (probably in 118) the land commission, which had
attained the limit of its usefulness, was ended. In 111 a
general law was passed, by which all the public land in Italy,
except a few reserved territories, was converted into private
property.

After the Gracchi, opposition to the Senate continued, and
opponents of the nobility became commonly known as
*populares*, 'men of the people'; the nobles themselves
became known as the *optimates*, the party of the 'best
people'. One of these new leaders of the opposition was
C. Marius, native of a small town called Arpinum whose
citizens had received the full franchise. Praetor in 115, he
married into the family of the Iulii, an ancient patrician *gens*.
His service in the Jugurthan War made him hope for a consulship, which he obtained in 108 by adopting the tactics of mob-
oratory and attacking the nobility — amongst them his old
commander Q. Metellus. The Tribal Assembly, against the
wishes of the Senate, appointed him to take command in
Africa. This set a dangerous example, and led ultimately to
the overthrow of the Senate by military commanders whom
it could not control.

In 106 the consul Q. Servilius Caepio carried a bill by
which the control of the court *de rebus repetundis* was handed
back from equestrian to senatorial juries. But in the same
year there was new hostility to the Senate, because of the

failure of its representatives in the Cimbric wars. In 105 and
the next four years the Comitia Centuriata re-elected Marius
to five successive consulships without asking the Senate to
suspend the Lex Villia, which declared such a practice illegal,
and the Tribal Assembly, taking senatorial privilege into its
hands, appointed him commander on the northern front.

Servilius Caepio was rightly singled out as the person
chiefly responsible for the catastrophe of Arausio. The Tribal
Assembly deprived him of his proconsulship, and a tribune
named Cn. Servilius Glaucia made an attack upon him by
procuring the repeal of his recent judiciary law and handing
the court *de rebus repetundis* back to the Equestrian Order.
In 103 both Caepio and his colleague Manlius were exiled.

### (E) *103–99 B.C.: Saturninus and Marius*

The law under which Caepio and Manlius were condemned
was enacted in the same year by a tribune named L. Appuleius
Saturninus. Appointed quaestor at Ostia in the previous
year, Saturninus sought election to the tribunate of 103 and
became the greatest popular agitator since Caius Gracchus. In
order to strike more effectively at Caepio and Manlius, he
created a new crime, 'lessening the majesty of the Roman
people' (*maiestas populi Romani imminuta*). The charge of
*maiestas* was vague and under cover of it any unpopular person
might be brought to court. In subsequent trials it was often
used as a make-weight or a substitute for more definite charges.

In two further measures Saturninus revealed himself as a
social reformer of the Gracchan type. He reintroduced Caius'
system of monthly corn-distributions at the same moderate
price. To provide for those of Marius' soldiers who had a
claim to a pension after the Jugurthan War, he carried a law
that gave them allotments of sixty acres each in the province
of Africa. Saturninus' legislation was remarkable for the
systematic violence which he used to force it through. After
first successfully turning a mob upon a colleague who had
vetoed his allotment law, he made use of fists and sticks and
stones in political battles. In 102 he defeated an attempt by
the censor Metellus Numidicus to remove him from the
Senate by setting thugs upon him ; in the next year he used

thugs to break up the Tribal Assembly, before which he was being accused of having insulted the envoys of King Mithridates. In the same year he got his re-election to the tribunate by hiring thugs to murder one of his competitors.

In his second tribunate Saturninus again lent his services to Marius. After his victory over the Northmen Marius enjoyed vast personal prestige. But he was lacking in political ideas. His only thought on his return to Rome was to find land for his soldiers and a fresh military commission for himself ; and he left it to Saturninus to make the necessary laws. In 100 B.C. Saturninus brought forward three laws on Marius' behalf. One gave allotments for the veterans on land in southern France ; another arranged for the foundation of colonies in Sicily, Achaea and Macedonia. A third law planned a general attack upon the pirates of the eastern Mediterranean. It was understood that Marius was to be the commander of the expedition, and a war against King Mithridates was to follow. In fear of a senatorial counter-attack Saturninus added to each of his laws an oath of obedience to its terms which every senator had to swear or go into exile. In the colonial law provision had been made for allotments to Latins and Italians (who had contributed their full share to Marius' victories), and for giving full Roman franchise to a select number of them. This had the effect of bringing back the urban proletariat to the side of the nobles, so that Saturninus had to use Marius' veterans to defeat the town mob in a battle fought in the Forum with legs of chairs and tables.

After this Saturninus took to assassination. In order to rid his friend Servilius Glaucia, who was trying for the consulship of 99, of a competitor, he procured the death of the ex-tribune C. Memmius by means of a gang of thugs. He lost the support of Marius ; the Senate declared an emergency and summoned Marius to exercise his consular powers for the safety of the state. In obedience to this call Marius penned up Saturninus on the Capitoline hill and drove him to surrender. An angry crowd killed him, Glaucia and several other agitators.

Marius looked on helpless while the Senate abolished Saturninus' laws. Though allotments were probably provided for the veterans of Marius, the projected attack against the pirates was allowed to drop out of sight. Soon Marius left Italy, leaving the Senate once more in possession of the political field.

### (F) 99–90 B.C.: Livius Drusus

The stormy opening of the first century B.C. was followed by an interval of calm. But a crisis which had been gathering in the last thirty years came upon the Senate unawares. The demand of the Italian allies for the Roman franchise was raised again. In the Jugurthan and Cimbric wars the allies had contributed their full share to the Roman victories, and the career of Marius, who came from an obscure country town, showed that Italians were just as fit to hold high command as Romans. In 100 their expectations had been raised by Saturninus' colonial act and large numbers of Italians had flocked to Rome to clamour on behalf of it. But in 99 Saturninus' law was repealed, and his followers were expelled from Rome under a law brought forward in 95 by the consuls L. Licinius Crassus and Q. Mucius Scaevola.

In 91 a nobleman named M. Livius Drusus (son of the tribune of 122) held a tribunate. Drusus, though a supporter of senatorial government, was thoroughly in earnest about reforms which had become urgent. In hopes of getting the Popular Assembly to swallow a bitter pill, Drusus began by offering it a few spoonfuls of jam. In the first place he revived his father's colonial law and Saturninus' corn law. To meet the costs, he brought forward a third bill for the debasement of the silver coinage. After this Drusus brought forward his real programme of reform. The first bill was connected with a recent scandal in the court *de rebus repetundis*. In 92 an equestrian jury had pronounced an ex-consul named P. Rutilius Rufus guilty of extortion in the province of Asia. Rutilius had recently stopped the agents of the Roman tax-farming companies in his province from abusing the powers placed in their hands by Caius Gracchus. In defence of their profits the *publicani* got him prosecuted and condemned against all principles of justice. His case gave definite proof that Caius Gracchus' reform of the court *de rebus repetundis* had been a change for the worse ; instead of guilty men being acquitted, innocent men were being punished.

Drusus proposed to share control of the court between senators and Equites. He also wished to include 300 Equites into the Senate, an arrangement which would have doubled the Senate's numbers. But the Equites were more angered by losing control of the courts than pleased by the chance of seats in the Senate, and the nobility did not want to buy back its judicial privileges at the price of allowing Equites in the Senate. Drusus had to sweep away his opponents by force. He then produced his most important project, which aimed to confer full Roman franchise upon the Italian allies. Senators and Equites united in opposition, and the urban voters joined them. Meanwhile ' Committees of Action' were being set up in various allied towns, and a Marsian chieftain named Q. Pompaedius Silo actually started out for Rome with an armed band, though on second thoughts he turned back. The consul L. Marcius Philippus pretended to believe that Drusus had plotted with Pompaedius, and got from the Senate a declaration that the laws already carried by Drusus were unconstitutional. Soon after, one of his supporters killed Drusus. As a further protection against fresh franchise acts, a tribune named Q. Varius carried a bill for the trial of persons suspected of conspiracy with the Italians.

The Italian Committees of Action, abandoning the hope of agreement, were organising a war to get the franchise by force. In the Picenian city of Asculum a Roman agent, named C. Servilius, so provoked the townsmen that they replied with a massacre of all resident Romans. This outrage wrecked in advance a final attempt by the allies to reach agreement with the Senate. In the winter of 91–90 both sides made open preparations for war.

The war could have been avoided, if Rome had realised the motives behind the demands of the Italians. They had remained strikingly loyal to Rome in her earlier wars — particularly when Hannibal was raging up and down Italy — and by bearing the brunt of battle had helped to save the mother city. As a reward they not unjustifiably hoped, if not for political voting power at Rome, at least for those rights of citizenship which would check the abuses which Roman magistrates and others practised on them. By granting the protective rights of citizenship, rather than the vote, Rome could have avoided a long, hard struggle. This is perhaps a typical case where the Romans' imagination failed them.


## Part 2 : *Foreign Wars*

### (A) *The War against Jugurtha*

In North Africa the empire of Numidia, after the death of Massinissa's successor Micipsa in 118, was left to Micipsa's three sons — Adherbal, Hiempsal and Jugurtha. Jugurtha murdered Hiempsal, drove Adherbal out of Africa. Adherbal came to Rome to plead his cause, and thus opened a 'Numidian question' which troubled the republic for the next ten years. The Senate arranged a division by which Adherbal received the eastern and richer half of Numidia. But Jugurtha resumed war against his brother and besieged him in his residence at Cirta (112). When he captured the city he gave his troops permission to massacre the Italian residents. After this atrocity the Senate had to act.

In 111 the consul L. Calpurnius Bestia began the operations against Jugurtha with a vigorous attack into Numidia, only to find that with his heavy infantry he could make no impression upon the nimble Numidian horsemen. He accepted an offer of negotiations from Jugurtha and granted him an armistice. But this let loose a storm of protest at Rome. A tribune named Memmius claimed that the Senate had been bribed by Jugurtha, and eventually all classes agreed that he should be forced into unconditional surrender.

In 110 the consul Sp. Postumius Albinus, with a force of 40,000 men, rushed into another offensive against Jugurtha, but accomplished even less. He soon returned to Rome on some excuse leaving his brother Aulus in charge of his troops. The new commander's plan, which aimed at seizing Jugurtha's chief treasure-castle at Suthul, was sound, but after a vain attempt to capture Suthul he was tempted into pursuit of the king in person. By this time the winter campaign and heavy rains had so undermined the discipline of his army that Jugurtha was able to force it to surrender. The king spared the lives of the defeated legions, but he allowed himself the luxury of making them pass under a yoke of spears.

The news of Aulus Albinus' failure raised more indignation at Rome against the whole nobility. A special court was set up to investigate recent cases of aristocratic corruption : the jury were derived from the Equestrian Order. The court satisfied itself of the guilt of several leading senators : Aulus Albinus' brother Spurius, Calpurnius Bestia and even Opimius were sent into exile. It is open to doubt whether any of these men had actually been bribed by Jugurtha's money. But with each decade the reputation of the ruling class for financial honesty was wearing thinner, and the charges of bribery at Jugurtha's hands had been repeated so often that they came to be accepted. But the Senate's critics were content to leave to the Senate the more difficult task of carrying on the war.

In 109 the African army was taken over by the consul Q. Caecilius Metellus. The new commander belonged to a family which had been acquiring a commanding influence in the Senate. By his conduct of the Jugurthan war Q. Metellus temporarily won back the reputation of the aristocracy for military ability. He completely restored discipline among the Roman troops. But since the best infantry could not bring Jugurtha's light horse to battle, Metellus resumed the policy of attacking the king's strongholds. He took several fortified towns, including the capital city of Cirta, and towards the end of 108 he reduced Jugurtha to an offer of submission. But he could not obtain the personal surrender of the king, who eventually made good his losses by hiring troops from the Gaetulian tribes on his southern border, and by making an alliance with Bocchus, the king of Mauretania (Morocco).

By 108 public opinion at Rome again became impatient. The new leader of opposition, C. Marius, was appointed to take command on the African front. A change in established military custom was made by Marius in preparation for the following year's campaign. In view of the growing diffi-culty of obtaining willing recruits for overseas service among the Italian peasants, he quietly disregarded the rule which prescribed a small property qualification for admission to the army, and enrolled volunteers among the members of the urban lower classes.

Marius' first task in Africa, the training of this new type of recruit to the high standard of a Roman legionary, was accomplished by him with great success. Though he made great demands on the fortitude of the troops, he had a rough humour which seldom failed in its appeal to Italian soldiers. His strategy was merely that of Metellus on a bigger scale, but with larger forces at his disposal he was able to penetrate Numidia more thoroughly. In 107 he cut through to Jugurtha's southernmost stronghold at Capsa and destroyed it. In the following year he made a bold advance six hundred miles to the west of the Roman province, and there captured the king's chief treasure-house. This last success compelled the king and his Mauretanian ally to stake their last chance on pitched battles. During Marius' retreat they twice delivered a desperate attack upon his marching columns, yet they were eventually driven off with heavy loss.

The steadiness of the Roman troops virtually decided the war. Bocchus now made up his mind that the Romans were the winners and opened negotiations. Marius left the bargaining in the hands of his quaestor L. Cornelius Sulla, a member of a patrician family who had shown promise as a soldier in the recent battle. Sulla conducted the discussions with admirable tact and declared that Bocchus could only earn the friendship of the republic by handing over Jugurtha to Rome. Bocchus obediently kidnapped Jugurtha, who was brought to Rome to be executed (105). Bocchus received from the Senate a large slice of Jugurtha's dominions. The province of Africa remained as before ; the Roman treasury collected no fine, and the only gain from the war was to the Equites, who were able to resume their trade in Africa.

## (B) *The Invasion of the Northmen*

Towards the end of the second century central and western Europe were thrown into temporary confusion by the migrations of two tribes, the Cimbri and Teutones, who had been driven out of their homes in Jutland and Frisia. After long

years of wandering along the Elbe and Danube, the Cimbri
and Teutones fell in with a Roman force under the consul
Cn. Papirius Carbo, who had been sent to bar their further advance, in 113. The Northmen were attacked by Carbo : they
beat off his attack, but did not resume their march towards Italy.
After four years' march round the Alps they invaded eastern
France. Near the borders of Gallia Narbonensis they met a
second Roman army under the consul M. Iunius Silanus.
They made a request for land within the Roman borders and
an offer of mercenary service under the Roman standards
(109) : but the Senate refused. Proving their military worth,
the Cimbri and Teutones attacked Silanus and broke his
army at the first charge.

After two years in central France, the Northmen returned
with reinforcements and now did not hesitate to cross the
Roman boundary. The Senate took this invasion seriously.
It ordered a large fresh levy and sent the consul Cn. Manlius
Maximus with these new drafts to join Caepio, who was
already in Gaul. The Cimbri and Teutones made fresh
overtures for a grant of land, which was again refused. But
Manlius failed to maintain discipline among his men, and
Caepio refused to co-operate loyally with the consul, so that
the invaders, giving battle near Arausio, were able to hurl
back the Roman forces, section by section, against the river,
with huge losses. This was the most disastrous Roman defeat
since Cannae.

The way to Italy was now clear to the Northmen ; but the
prestige of Rome still overawed them. The Teutones resumed
their travels in Gaul, while the Cimbri moved off to Spain,
thus giving the republic a period of three years to prepare.
During this interval Marius, whom the people appointed to
the command on the northern front immediately after his
return from Africa, electing him consul five times (104–100),
trained another proletarian army.

In 102 the Northmen reunited for an attack upon the Romans.
They planned to advance upon Italy on three fronts. While
the Teutones proceeded by the direct route through southern
France, the Cimbri undertook to retrace their steps along the
northern edge of the Alps in order to enter Italy by the valley

of the Adige, and the Tigurini to invade Venetia by way of the Julian Alps. This threw the main weight of the Northmen's attack in 102 upon the main Roman army under Marius in the Rhône valley. For the greater part of the year Marius allowed the campaign to drag on, so as to harden his own troops and take full measure of the enemy; but once he saw his way clear, he struck. He overtook the Teutones and fought them on a site near Aquae Sextiae (Aix). Not only did he win, but hardly an enemy escaped, so that Marius' soldiers made a haul of prisoners exceeding all previous captures.

The defence of Italy was given to Q. Lutatius Catulus, a nobleman more skilled in literature than in warfare. Catulus took up a position in the narrow valley of the upper Adige, but soon hurriedly withdrew his troops to the south bank of the Po. Fortunately the invaders made no serious attempt to cross that river or to capture the neighbouring cities. Once more, therefore, Marius was given time to retrieve the Roman losses. In 101 he joined Catulus, bringing the combined Roman forces to a total of 55,000 men. As in the previous season, he waited a long while before he struck. Eventually he met the enemy near Vercellae. The Roman troops outlasted the enemy and ended the day in a slaughter and slave-haul rivalling that of Aquae Sextiae. In the same year Cornelius Sulla drove off the Tigurini in the eastern Alps. Thus the northern peril dissolved as if by magic.

## (c) *Marius' Army Reforms*

In throwing open the legions to proletarians on terms of voluntary enlistment, and training his recruits up to the standard of regular soldiers, Marius took the decisive step in converting the Roman army from a conscript force into a standing force of professional warriors. The Roman legion of the first century differed from its predecessors in its equipment and organisation. All ranks alike were armed with pilum and long-sword, the division into three lines of *hastati*, *principes* and *triarii* was abolished, and for tactical purposes the maniple was superseded by the cohort of 360 to 500 men. The new-style legionaries were highly-trained duellists, whose technique in cut-and-thrust was modelled on that of the gladiatorial schools, and they developed an *esprit de corps* which did not exist in the old-time army. By these reforms Marius not only won his own victories, but prepared for those of his more famous successors.

## (D) *The Slave War in Sicily*

The concentration of Roman troops on the northern frontiers gave another opportunity for a slave rebellion in Sicily. In this province the larger estates had been partly restocked with free men kidnapped and reduced to slavery by the pirates of the eastern Mediterranean. In 104 a decree of the Senate called upon all provincial governors to make a search for such persons and to restore them to freedom ; but in Sicily the influence of the slave-owners had prevented its enforcement. The kidnapped men thereupon took their cause into their own hands, and carried with them the rest of the slaves (103). The revolt was headed by two leaders, Athenion and Salvius. These chieftains organised the rising in a methodical manner, and for three years the Roman governors were left with insufficient troops to make definite headway against them. In 101, however, the arrival of Marius' lieutenant, M'. Aquilius, with a detachment of the army from Aquae Sextiae, ended the war.

ITALY 90–60 B.C.

# CHAPTER X

# 90–60 B.C.

## Part I : *Rome and Italy*

### (A) *The Italian War*

AT the outbreak of war in 90 the rebel coalition consisted of the Vestini, Picentes, Marrucini and Frentani along the Adriatic seaboard, the Marsi and Paeligni in the central Apennine massif, the Samnites, Hirpini and Lucanians in the southern highlands. The revolt never spread to northern Italy, and it scarcely touched Etruria and Umbria. Latium and the Greek cities of the coastland were loyal to the Romans throughout. Within the rebel area there also remained loyal groups, where the inhabitants were bound by economic ties to Rome, or the local aristocracies were clients of the ruling families of the capital.

But the rebellion was supported by some of Italy's best fighting troops, with veterans from Marius' armies and leaders who had been *praefecti* of the auxiliary forces. Also, the rebels achieved a greater measure of co-operation than might have been considered possible. They combined to form a confederation, whose government was established at Corfinium, the chief place of the Paeligni, which formed a natural centre of communications within the rebel area. To this meeting-place the constituent peoples sent 500 delegates to form a federal senate. The more northerly tribes, which had by now adopted Latin as their official tongue, fought consistently for the attainment of the Roman franchise. The Samnites, who still retained their Oscan dialect, eventually aimed at complete independence. Nevertheless the Italian senate managed to put 100,000 men into the field and to find money and supplies for them. Since none of the mountain peoples could have possessed any large stocks of wealth, the success of the confederacy in financing a war on such a scale was a very notable achievement.

At Rome the Senate was given a free hand to direct operations, and it showed no lack of energy. It raised at least fifteen legions and a total force of some 150,000 men. But it allowed political considerations to dictate its choice of generals. It withheld the high command from Marius, and also from two other winners of previous wars, P. Licinius Crassus and T. Didius. These three veterans were attached as *legati* to the two consuls, L. Iulius Caesar and P. Rutilius Lupus, to whom the supreme control of the Roman troops was entrusted, although neither of them had sufficient military experience for such a task.

In 90 the Confederates maintained the initiative, but they did not play for a quick decision. Instead of a rapid concentration of forces at Corfinium and a drive at Rome itself along the line of the Via Valeria, they attempted to dislocate the enemy defence by capturing its centres of communication, and to extend the revolt into the Italian lowlands.

In view of the wide area of operations, both sides divided their front into two sectors with a separate commander-in-chief. In the northern zone Rutilius Lupus was faced by the

Marsian chief Pompaedius Silo; in the southern sector L. Caesar stood against the Samnite C. Papius Mutilus. On the southern front the Confederates captured the colony of Aesernia. Meanwhile Papius in person broke into Campania, whose man-power and wealth made it a valuable prize. He won over Pompeii, Nola and other towns of southern and central Campania, but L. Caesar drove him back from Capua, the chief arsenal of the Romans in southern Italy. Other Confederate leaders made successful raids into Apulia and Lucania, where they took several of the larger towns, including the colony of Venusia.

In the northern area the rebels laid siege to the colony of Alba Fucens and defeated the Roman armies in two battles, in the earlier of which the commander-in-chief, Rutilius Lupus, lost his life. In the Picentine territory a Roman *legatus*, named Cn. Pompeius Strabo, raised a considerable force on his private estates in that region and besieged the city of Asculum. The Romans appeared to be holding their own more successfully in the central Apennine region than in the south. The war in Italy was also a cause of grave financial distress at Rome. The strain which it imposed upon state finances drove the Senate to authorise a heavy debasement of the silver coinage, a further reduction in the weight of the copper money, and the sale of public land.

At the end of 90 it had become clear that the Romans could not afford to let the rebellion spread any further. The Senate therefore instructed the consul L. Caesar to bring forward a bill giving franchise to all those Italians who had remained loyal to Rome. This law had the effect of giving full Roman status to the Etruscans and Umbrians, and to the allies of Latin status. In 89 Pompeius Strabo, now consul, rewarded the semi-Celtic population of Transpadane Gaul by promotion to the Latin status. In the same year — presumably when the Confederacy first began to show signs of cracking — two tribunes, named M. Plautius and C. Papirius, carried a new law whose effect probably was to grant full citizenship to every freeman in peninsular Italy and in Cispadane Gaul. But a real and serious limitation was imposed on this law (the Lex Plautia Papiria) by a clause which confined the new franchise-holders to some eight or ten tribes specially constituted for this purpose, so that their collective voting power should always be inferior to that of the older citizens.

In selecting commanders for the campaign of 89 the Senate again took political considerations into account. It transferred Marius' forces to one of the new consuls, L. Porcius Cato. This general was soon killed. But his colleague, Pompeius Strabo, made a successful drive from the Adriatic which gave him possession of Corfinium and defeated the Marsi. Asculum became the rallying-point for all available forces, both Roman and rebel, in the north. The inhabitants held out until the end of the year, but after its surrender the rebellion in the north was rapidly stamped out.

In the south the army of L. Caesar was taken over by L. Cornelius Sulla, who opened his campaign with a decisive victory in southern Campania over the Samnite forces. After this success he was free to recover all the ground lost in Campania and Samnium as far as Bovianum Vetus, where the Confederates had set up their parliament after the fall of Corfinium. Though Bovianum fell into his hands, he was eventually held in check by the Marsian general Pompaedius Silo, who had escaped from the northern war. But the death of Pompaedius Silo in 88 ended the war as such, though a few rebel towns held out.

## (B) *Sulla and His Enemies in Rome*

1. *Marius.*—In 88 all the questions of domestic politics were raised by a tribune named P. Sulpicius Rufus. His programme included a bill to distribute the newly enfranchised Italians among all the pre-existing thirty-five tribes, and a proposal to transfer the command in the future war against Mithridates from Sulla to Marius. Having distrusted Marius in the Italian War, the Senate passed him over as a candidate for the command against Mithridates. His successful rival, Sulla, had to wait long for the consulship which he assumed at last in 88, and his eventual promotion over the head of Marius was a due reward of merit. But Marius did not abandon his claim to an eastern command. In 88 Marius was half forgotten by the people to whom he had once been a hero ;

but he could still count on the support of the Equites, who knew by past experience that he would protect their interests better than a senatorial representative, and it was no doubt through them that Sulpicius now became his supporter.

The programme of Sulpicius was both defended and defeated by organised violence. The Senate authorised the consuls to proclaim a *iustitium* or general suspension of public business ; but Sulpicius met the Senate by open force. Amid the rout of the Optimates a son of Sulla's colleague Q. Pompeius Rufus was killed, and Sulla himself only escaped by a prompt surrender to Marius. In return for Marius' protection the consuls cancelled the *iustitium* and allowed Sulpicius' measures to be carried into law. In 88 Marius carried his point by the same weapons with which he had defeated the Senate in 100 ; but in the event his agent Sulpicius was disarmed as thoroughly as Saturninus before him.

For the moment Sulla had been reduced to a plain consulship. But though legally deprived of the six legions which had fought under him in the Italian War and had been detailed to serve with him against Mithridates, he still held them by the bond of his personal authority, for he had endeared himself to them by a devil-may-care manner, which appealed to the new professional soldier more than the old Roman *gravitas*. In Campania he invited them to follow him in a march upon Rome. They made him master of the city before Marius and Sulpicius could collect a force of defence.

Sulla used his victory in this, the first civil war of Roman history, to abolish Sulpicius' legislation and to insure himself against future attacks. He got the Comitia Centuriata to deprive the Tribal Assembly of its powers and give to itself all power of law-making ; but at the same time it made its own acts subject to the Senate's veto. Sulla also reduced the maximum rate of interest to one-tenth. Though he did not interfere with the consular elections, he compelled one of the successful candidates, L. Cornelius Cinna, to swear that he would maintain the new political settlement. Lastly, he attempted to disarm Pompeius Strabo by transferring the command which he held to Pompeius Rufus. Sulla then left Italy for the next four years. Sulpicius was presently hunted down and put to death, while Marius had several hairbreadth escapes from his pursuers and finally took refuge in Africa.

Sulla's example of insubordination proved more potent than his support of the State. When Sulla's colleague Pompeius Rufus called upon Pompeius Strabo to take over his command, Strabo got his troops to kill Rufus and the Senate did not dare to call him to account.

In 87 the consul Cornelius Cinna reintroduced Sulpicius' redistribution bill in favour of the Italians. In the battle in the Forum the Italians on whom he was relying suffered defeat at the hands of the urban proletariate. Cinna went round Latium and Campania calling the Italians to arms, and at Capua he persuaded a Roman army to join the Italians. On his way back to Rome he joined with Marius, who had meanwhile landed in Etruria with another unofficial force recruited among his old soldiers in Africa, and was swelling his numbers with slaves from the neighbouring *latifundia*.

The fortifications of the city were strengthened and a call for aid was sent to Pompeius Strabo. But Strabo lost precious time in haggling for a second consulship as the price of his assistance. In the meantime Cinna and Marius had encircled the city, and towards the end of the year Rome surrendered to them.

The re-entry of Cinna and Marius into Rome was marked by scenes hitherto unknown among the Romans. The leading members of the aristocracy were put to death, often by mere murder. Marius' resentment of past injuries now made him lust for blood. The terror was eventually ended by Cinna. For the next year Cinna and Marius declared themselves consuls without an election, but a few days after his entry upon his seventh consulship Marius fell ill and died.

2. *Cinna and Carbo.*—Cinna now became the virtual dictator of Italy. Sulla's legislation was swept away, the redistribution bill of Sulpicius was re-enacted, and censors were elected to carry out the registration of the new citizens in all the thirty-five tribes. The new register was not completed until 84, yet the principle of equality between the new citizens and the old was now established. The relief of debtors was accomplished, on a far more generous scale than

in Sulla's recent law, by a new measure in the name of
L. Valerius Flaccus, the successor of Marius in the consulship,
which remitted three-quarters of all outstanding obligations.
On the other hand, the financial interests were appeased by
the calling in of plated coinage and a better system of control
over the moneyers' operations.  Reforms were made of special
benefit to the money-dealers of the Equestrian Order and in
general to all those who had suffered from the recent uncertainty of Roman coin-values.

The ensuing three years (86–84) were a period of tranquillity, yet Rome and Italy lived under the shadow of civil
war.  The consular elections were either not held or were
a mere formality, for Cinna reappointed himself for 85 and
84, and selected his colleague Cn. Papirius Carbo.  Cinna
and Carbo thus retained the right of levying troops and
decision between peace and war.  On his return to Rome
Cinna virtually declared war upon Sulla by declaring him an
outlaw, and he prepared an army with open orders to engage
King Mithridates and a secret commission to attack Sulla.
The commander of this force defeated Cinna's purpose and
in 85 the Senate exchanged messages with Sulla with a view
to peace.  But Carbo continued to levy troops and Sulla was
compelled to keep his forces together.  In this atmosphere
the negotiations with the Senate were broken off, and in 83
the Roman civil wars began in earnest.

Carbo produced some 100,000 soldiers, but these troops
were not fit to fight at the beginning of 83, when Sulla landed
at Brundisium.  Members of the aristocracy who had been
outlawed flocked to join him.  Metellus Pius, who had fought
with distinction in the Italian War, rejoined him from Africa,
and M. Licinius Crassus, a son of the consul of 97, returned
to him from Spain.  But Sulla's most valuable recruit was a
son of Pompeius Strabo.  This youth raised three legions
among his father's old soldiers in Picenum and put this force
at Sulla's disposal.  With these reinforcements Sulla's army,
now more than 50,000 men, began its second march upon
Rome.  Carbo sent forward two armies under the consuls
L. Cornelius Scipio and C. Norbanus.  Both consuls in turn
offered battle, but Norbanus was heavily defeated, and Scipio

saw his legions charmed away from him with promises of higher pay.

In the winter of 83 Carbo gained the Samnite cantons as allies. His colleague in the consulship, an adoptive son of Marius, lured his father's veterans back to the standards by the magic of his name. The Marian forces of 82 were far more efficient than those of 83.

At the outset of 82 the war front extended from Campania to the northern Adriatic. But Sulla advanced towards Praeneste and, hardly pausing to take possession of Rome, hurried on to Etruria, where Carbo was stationed with his reserve forces. The remaining Marian forces, left unsupported, were defeated by Sulla's lieutenants, Crassus, Pompey and Metellus. With enemy armies closing in on all sides, and his own supporters deserting, Carbo lost his nerve and fled from Italy. Some of the Marian troops joined with the Samnites, and their combined force, estimated at 70,000 men, made a sudden pounce on Rome. But in the battle of the Colline Gate, outside Rome, the last Marian army was destroyed.

The last actions of the civil war were fought in the western provinces. In Spain an old officer of Marius, named Q. Sertorius, was overcome by Sulla's deputy, C. Annius. Sicily was rapidly cleared by Pompey, who caught and killed Carbo. In Africa Cn. Domitius Ahenobarbus had raised a considerable force, but was defeated in 80 by Pompey. By the end of 80 the entire Roman empire was at Sulla's disposal.

### (c) *Sulla's Rule in Rome*

The first use to which Sulla put his victory was to murder members of the defeated party, in which reprisals he and his officers took vengeance on their private enemies. Sulla posted up from time to time lists of names, with a declaration that the men thus 'proscribed' were outlaws and that a price would be paid for their heads. The reign of terror lasted far into the following year. This system of mass-murder was now directed particularly at the members of the Equestrian Order who had helped the Marian leaders. The executions at Rome were reproduced on a minor scale in such Italian towns as had shown sympathy with the Marians, and territory of the

Samnites was given over to Sulla's soldiery to devastate from end to end. The total number of persons killed amounted to several thousands. From the slaves of the murdered men Sulla recruited a corps of 10,000, whom he freed in his own name and kept as a private bodyguard.

In order to keep the promises of pay and pensions which he had made to his troops, Sulla confiscated the estates of the persons on his proscription lists. Plenty of men who had taken no part in politics suffered death because of their wealth alone. Sulla also took large tracts of land from Italian cities guilty of helping the Marians. The land was used to provide for 120,000 discharged soldiers. Further supplies of money, which he used to reward his personal associates, were raised from the cities of the empire and the allied kings.

Sulla fully realised the need of setting the Roman government once more on a legal basis. Shortly after his return to Rome he bade the Senate appoint its senior member, L. Valerius Flaccus, as a temporary ruler or 'interrex' and instructed Valerius to carry two acts through the Comitia. One of Flaccus' measures made legal the recent executions and confiscations. The other revived the obsolete office of the dictator and gave it to Sulla for the purpose of reforming the republican constitution.

By virtue of his dictatorial power Sulla carried a programme of legislation even more comprehensive than that of Caius Gracchus. But he brought back the Senate's right of veto upon legislation and added considerably to its members. He introduced 300 new members into it, and for the future he provided that seats should be assigned to all ex-quaestors. Since the number of the quaestors was now to be fixed at twenty, the ultimate effect of this rule would probably be to maintain the normal membership at about 500. Sulla's primary object in filling out the ranks of the Senate was no doubt to provide a larger number of persons qualified to sit in the jury-courts. But since his new members were all recruited from the Equestrian Order, Sulla in effect carried out a partial amalgamation between the Equites and the senatorial aristocracy. Furthermore, since it may be assumed that the Equites to whom he gave promotion were not drawn from the financiers at Rome (whom he hated), but from the 'country members' of the Order, who filled the chief positions in the Italian towns, Sulla's reform of the Senate had the result of drafting a large Italian element into it. But Sulla provided no means of ensuring that these *novi homines* ('new men') should pass on to the higher executive offices. Thus the senatorial nobility succeeded in retaining the chief magistracies in its own hands, and in resuming control of the Senate Sulla struck a direct blow at the tribunes, who lost their unrestricted power of carrying laws in the Tribal Assembly, and an indirect one at military adventurers like Marius, who could no longer use tribunes to get anything refused to them by the Senate. He also abolished the tribunes' right to prosecute before the Tribal Assembly; he placed restrictions on their veto, and prevented them from holding a praetorship or other high office.

Sulla made no other important change in the magistracy. To provide for additional chairmen of jury-courts, he raised the number of the praetorships from six to eight; to keep pace with recent increases in the number of the provinces, he brought the quaestorships up to the total of twenty. A more important measure regulated the *cursus honorum*. By this act Sulla removed the absolute veto on a second consulship, but revived the older rule prescribing a ten years' interval between two consulships. He increased the number of the pontifices and of the augurs to fifteen each, and restored to them the full right of co-opting new members.

Sulla did not withdraw the recent grants of Roman franchise from Italian towns and many voluntarily remodelled their constitutions, so as to adapt them more closely to the Roman pattern. He made a new province by detaching Cisalpine Gaul from peninsular Italy and providing it with a garrison and governor. The justification for this was the need of a permanent defence force in the sub-Alpine regions: ten years previously a band from Raetia had sacked Comum at the southern end of L. Como. The total number of Roman provinces was thus raised to eleven, of which seven (Sicily, Sardinia et Corsica, Hispania Citerior, Hispania Ulterior, Africa, Gallia Transalpina and Gallia Cisalpina) were situated in the western Mediterranean, and four (Macedonia, Asia, Cilicia and the half-formed province of Cyrene) in the east. Sulla prohibited provincial governors from making war beyond the borders of their province without authorisation from the Senate or the people. Apart from this regulation, he made no big alteration in provincial administration.

Since the institution of the *quaestio de rebus repetundis* in 149, several other law courts had been appointed on the same pattern; under Sulla the number of the *quaestiones* was raised to seven, and in all the *quaestiones*, old and new, the jurors were appointed from the Senate, and the Equites were completely excluded.

Sulla remained dictator for three years. But he gradually became less dictatorial in manner, as his power grew less. In 82 he put to death a distinguished officer, named Q. Lucretius Ofella, who had defied him by standing for the consulship against his orders. In 80 he tried to refuse Pompey a triumph on his return from Africa, but when Pompey stood by his demand and did not disband his troops, the dictator gave way. When Pompey further asserted his independence by supporting M. Aemilius Lepidus for the consulship of 78 against Sulla's wish, Sulla could do nothing. In 79 he resigned his dictatorship and withdrew to a country estate in Campania, and in 78 he died.

Sulla stands in a line with Scipio Africanus and Caesar as one of the outstanding figures of the Roman republic. He was capable of hard work, had an unshakeable faith in his own luck, which he openly proclaimed in 82 by the adoption of the cognomen 'Felix' (the fortunate), and in war showed the same boldness of initiative, the same uncanny influence over his troops as Africanus and Caesar. He anticipated the Roman emperors in maintaining a bodyguard and striking coins with his own name and effigy. Yet he did not take the decisive step of attaching his army to himself on a permanent footing, and in retiring into private life he appointed no successor to his position. Like many practical men and most Romans, he lacked imagination. He wished to buttress the Senate, but did not take adequate measures for a regular infusion of fresh blood into the senatorial aristocracy; nor did he devise efficient safeguards against generals who wished to seize military power.

After Sulla's rule the ordinary routine of administration fell by common consent into the hands of the aristocracy, who continued to monopolise the highest offices and to dominate the Senate. But the Senate took no efficient steps to prevent disorder and made no attempt to carry on Sulla's work of reconstruction, but drifted along from one crisis into the next.

## (D) *Lepidus*

Immediately after Sulla's death, one of his officers, a member of the high nobility named M. Aemilius Lepidus, tried to repeal his former chief's acts. Elected consul, Lepidus brought forward in 78 a programme which included the restoration of the tribunate to its former status. The Senate played into his hands : it gave him a commission to quell a local uprising near Florentia, where some of the landowners had forcibly expelled the colonists of Sulla. Once out of the Senate's reach, Lepidus joined the rebels and started another revolt in northern Italy by his agent, M. Iunius Brutus. He then moved in upon Rome with his troops. Fortunately for the Senate, the veterans of Sulla, who had an obvious interest in checking Lepidus' propaganda, made a prompt rally round the other consul, Q. Lutatius Catulus, and round Pompey, who shared the command of the defence. In northern Italy Pompey drove Brutus into Mutina and made him surrender. Meanwhile Lepidus made a dash for the capital, but was defeated in a battle near the Janiculan Hill. He died shortly after in Sardinia.

The rising of Lepidus was followed by six years of calm, during which the nobles made a few concessions. In 75 they acquiesced in a measure brought forward by a consul, C. Aurelius Cotta, by which the tribunes were now allowed to proceed to higher magistracies.

## (E) *The Slave War in Italy*

In 73 a band of gladiators, led by a man named Spartacus, broke loose from its barracks at Capua. His ranks were joined by many thousands of runaway slaves, and in 73 they defeated with ease some hastily-levied defence troops ; in 72 they beat off in succession the armies of both consuls and of the governor of Cisalpine Gaul ; and between their victories they marched the length of Italy, plundering the country estates. The way now lay open to their native lands beyond the Alps, and Spartacus urged them to take their chance ; but they refused and drifted aimlessly about the rich countryside. Sulla's former lieutenant, M. Crassus, collected a force of some 40,000 men, and after a campaign in southern Italy, Spartacus was finally rounded up in Apulia, where he died with most of his men in a hard-fought battle (71). Of the surviving slaves, six thousand, whose masters could not be found, were exhibited on crosses set up like telegraph posts along the whole length of the Via Appia.

### (F) *Pompey, Crassus and Caesar*

1. *73–66 B.C.*—While Crassus was running down the last of the fugitive slaves, Pompey brought back his victorious forces from Spain and took part in the man-hunt. He was thus able to keep his army in being and to gain political power from it. Pompey, a man of conservative outlook, wanted a distinguished military reputation and the honourable position of *princeps* or 'leading man' in the governing class. But he was the son of Pompeius Strabo, a military adventurer who had used his army as an instrument of personal advancement, and the pupil of Sulla ; and at the age of twenty-five he had not hesitated to threaten Sulla with his soldiers. After the rebellion of Lepidus he had delayed disbanding his forces and he was appointed to high command in Spain partly because he threatened the Senate. Pompey's failures in Spain, for which he sought to blame the Senate, drove him into political opposition. In 73 he opened negotiations with a tribune named C. Licinius Macer, with a view to changing Sulla's constitution. On his return to Italy in 71 he manœuvred his troops within striking distance from Rome, and from this commanding position he asked the Senate for leave to stand for a consulship in spite of the Lex Annalis of Sulla. Coming from a man who had not yet stepped on the lowest rung of

the *cursus honorum*, this claim was even more unreasonable than Lepidus' demand for a second term of office in 77.

Crassus' well-trained army was a fair match for Pompey's men and had Crassus now dared to fight he might at one blow have made Sulla's constitution safe, and have won for himself the position of *princeps*, which he wanted as much as Pompey. But Crassus was cautious in the use of force, though bold in the field of finance, in which he had acquired vast wealth. Distrusting his chances of success against Pompey, he allied with him; though he needed to wait but one year to be qualified for a consulship, he faced the Senate with a claim to share Pompey's privilege. The Senate gave way and the Popular Assembly elected both of them to the consulship of 70. The two rivals soon dismissed their forces and co-operated in carrying fresh laws.

Pompey left one of his new laws in charge of the praetor L. Aurelius Cotta, who carried it through the Popular Assembly. This provided that the jury-courts, which Sulla had transferred back to the Senate, should in future be shared in equal proportions between these and the Equites, together with the next wealthiest class, the so-called *tribuni aerarii* ('tribunes of the treasury', perhaps originally paymasters in the army, but now including those whose income lay between 300,000 and 600,000 sesterces). In the interval since Sulla's dictatorship the senatorial juries had again acquired a bad reputation for indulgence to those of their own order. The most famous of these cases was tried in the summer of 70. A former governor of Sicily named C. Verres, who had plundered his province in the most outrageous fashion, had been charged at Rome by the Sicilians, who gave their case to a young barrister named M. Tullius Cicero.

Cicero came from the local aristocracy of the small Volscian city of Arpinum. His ambition to rise was intense; he staked his chances on success at the Roman bar, which had by now become sufficiently important to provide a new avenue to political distinction. Clever and highly educated, he rapidly came into notice as a lawyer and a man of letters. Shortly before the death of Sulla he had caused a mild sensation in the courts by opposing one of the dictator's most influential favourites ; and in 70 he won the case of the Sicilians against Verres.

The admission of the *tribuni aerarii* to the jury-courts shows that one object of the Lex Aurelia was to arrange a more equable distribution of jury service, which was a burden as well as a privilege.  But the law did little to improve the quality of Roman justice ; the reformed *quaestiones* could no more be trusted to give an impartial verdict than their predecessors.  Pompey's chief reason for supporting Cotta's law was to get the political support of the Equites.

The consuls also arranged for a revision of the Senate lists. A pair of censors named L. Gellius and Cn. Cornelius Lentulus, the first to be appointed since 86, expelled no less than 64 members.  They were acting under orders, and both of them subsequently held commands under Pompey, no doubt in acknowledgment of service rendered.

But Pompey and Crassus brought forward in person the most important measure of the year, which restored to the tribunate all the powers held by it before the laws of Sulla. In this act we may discern Pompey's real object.  After his quarrel with the Senate in 73 he could no longer count on its support, so he was driven to follow the example of Marius in looking to tribunician legislation for his commissions.  He had no immediate campaign in view, but he declined the usual proconsular term in a province in order that he might be in Rome to seize any future chance of an important command. He had not long to wait, for in 67 the raids of the pirates upon the corn supply of Rome created a demand for military action against them.  A tribune named A. Gabinius, acting on a hint from Pompey or guessing his purpose, framed a bill to confer upon him an *imperium infinitum* ('command without limit') on the Mediterranean Sea.  The nobles, led by Catulus, opposed this and a tribune named L. Trebellius used his veto. But the Senate had already created a similar post for M. Antonius in 74 ; and in any case the people of Rome were not in the mood to listen to counter-argument.  Trebellius withdrew at the last moment, and Gabinius' bill was passed over the Senate's head.

Another law of Gabinius, by which the command against

Mithridates and Tigranes was withdrawn from Lucullus and given for the time being to Acilius Glabrio, was no doubt intended to prepare for passing it on to Pompey later. Early in 66 the tribune C. Manilius presented to the Tribal Assembly

BUST OF CICERO

the bill which gave Pompey his general commission to settle the affairs of the Near East. This project was even less pleasant to the nobles than the Lex Gabinia, but it received strong support from the Equites. Their case was put by Cicero, who had often defended the interests of the Ordo Equester in the courts, and now came forward as their spokesman in high politics. The Lex Maniiia was therefore carried.

2. *66–63 B.C.*—After Pompey's departure to the east it was realised that the Gabinian and Manilian laws had placed the republic in his control. The Senate had no policy; but Crassus, whose feud with Pompey had been postponed rather than ended, intended to act. His first thought was to obtain a foreign command, if necessary as a base of operations against Pompey. In 65 he took advantage of a sudden vacancy in the governorship of Higher Spain to press upon the Senate the appointment of his agent, Cn. Calpurnius Piso. Crassus, who had used his wealth to bribe poor members of the House, had enough influence to carry his point, and Piso went to Spain as *quaestor pro praetore*. His stay in the province, however, was cut short: he was killed by a Spaniard whom he had insulted and Crassus made no attempt to find a substitute for him.

Crassus' next move was to gain control of Egypt by means of a bill to be passed in the Tribal Assembly, by which the kingdom of the Ptolemies was to be converted into a Roman province and an agent of Crassus was to be sent to take it over. With Egypt in his grasp, Crassus might meet Pompey on equal terms and his agent, a young nobleman named C. Iulius Caesar, was a better man than Piso. This project of Crassus was legally defensible, for the reigning monarch, Ptolemy XI (Auletes), held his throne only by a doubtful title, and the Roman republic could claim Egypt for itself on the strength of a will (also doubtful) by a former king; it was economically attractive, for the Ptolemies possessed large treasure. But his bill was rejected: mainly due to Cicero, who was on Pompey's side and spoke against it.

After this second set-back Crassus found a new agent in L. Sergius Catilina who was resolved to stick at nothing in order to win a consulship. In 66 he offered himself as a candidate, but was not allowed to stand, so he laid a plot to murder the successful candidates as they entered on their consulate in 65; but his plan was easily frustrated. He escaped prosecution through the influence of Crassus, and in 64 he was admitted to the competition. But Catiline now found himself competing with a *novus homo* who was striving with equal determination to break into the aristocracy, M. Tullius Cicero. In any event Cicero could count on the votes of the Ordo Equester, and on those few votes which were awarded on personal merit. He also set himself to win the support of the nobles by playing upon their fears of Catiline, or of a political coup by Crassus. Cicero was elected with C. Antonius as his colleague. Crassus' intentions in helping Catiline to the consulship are not clear, but his object may have been to have a man who would not hesitate to use his consular power to mobilise Italy against Pompey, as Carbo had in 83 against Sulla.

In 63 Crassus got a tribune, P. Servilius Rullus, to introduce a harmless-looking bill for an extensive redistribution of land in Italy and the provinces. The hidden purpose of this was to concentrate in the hands of the men who allotted the land — whom Crassus controlled — all territory which Pompey might want for his soldiers, so that he would have to buy it on Crassus' terms. But this subtle intrigue was unmasked by Cicero and the bill was withdrawn. After this Crassus made no further attempt to insure himself against Pompey. Crassus did not desire a civil war and was aiming at a bargain with Pompey rather than a battle.

The year 63 also marked the advent to high office of C. Iulius Caesar. Like Sulla and Catiline, Caesar came from a patrician family which had dropped out of the inner circle of the nobility. For his political advancement he had relied on his powers as an orator, though he had no clear-cut political programme, and he was heavily in debt to Crassus. But in 63 he snatched for himself the office of Pontifex Maximus, with the help of a tribune named T. Labienus, and in the same year he was elected praetor. He was now emerging as a responsible statesman.

Catiline persisted in trying for the consulship. At the elections of 63 he staked his chances on a programme of *novae tabulae* ('new accounts'), a general cancelling of debts. With this policy he was making a general bid for the votes of a large and growing section of the nobility who were in debt. But the Ordo Equester, who were owed money rather than owing to others, stood almost solid against him. The balance was definitely turned against him by Cicero, who again contrived Catiline's defeat at the elections.

G

In the autumn of 63 Catiline planned a coup in Rome with the help of some Sullan colonists in northern Etruria, who were engaged to march in upon the capital on the day appointed (October 27th). Of this plot sufficient details leaked out to justify the Senate in proclaiming a state of emergency (October 21st). Cicero left Catiline free, on the chance of his obtaining more evidence about his plans. Catiline arranged a plan of wider scope — to distract the government's attention with rebellions in every part of Italy, while he marched in upon the city with an army from Etruria. Cicero still did not dare to proceed against Catiline in person. On the following day Catiline, who had listened to the consul's angry speeches in the Senate, left Rome to muster his forces in Etruria.

But some associates of Catiline passed on their information to Cicero, who seized the ring-leaders without delay and faced them with evidence which the whole Senate accepted as con-clusive (December 3rd). Two days later he reassembled the Senate, in order to obtain its consent for the summary execu-tion of his prisoners — a procedure which he considered necessary to the republic, but dangerous to himself, for it was a matter of doubt whether a consul, even in an emergency, could legally kill without trial Roman citizens who were not actually in arms or an immediate source of danger. In this debate one senator after another voted for immediate action, until Caesar made the strange counter-proposal that the prisoners should be detained for life. Whatever Caesar's motives, he completely turned the tide of the discussion, until a tribune-elect named M. Porcius Cato rallied the Senate to its earlier opinion. Cicero obtained the Senate's authorisation and executed the prisoners on the same day. Left to his own resources, Catiline's only salvation now lay in flight from Italy. But he was headed off by one army under Q. Metellus Celer in an attempt to cross the Apennines, and killed himself and his remaining supporters by a hopeless attack upon a second pursuing force under M. Petreius near Pistoria.

3. *62–60 B.C.*—In 63 Cicero had attained the goal of his personal ambitions and had become the man of the hour. In the following years he made his only practical attempt at con-structive statesmanship. Having rallied against Catiline all

the more solid elements in the Roman state that stood to lose by civil disorder, he conceived a more permanent 'Concord of the Orders' or 'of all Good Men', and more particularly strove for an enduring agreement between the senatorial nobility and the Ordo Equester. In this he reserved for himself the position of manager, but Pompey was to be the figurehead. Though Cicero's programme was in fact unrealistic, it at least seemed to offer a guarantee against further political chaos. Moreover, the idea of setting up Pompey as the defender of the constitution was not fantastic. On his return to Italy at the end of 62 Pompey surprised everyone by disbanding his troops as soon as he landed at Brundisium, and at his first meeting with the Senate he addressed it with courtesy.

But Pompey's gesture of friendship was ignored. With perverse obstinacy the Senate refused the reasonable demands which he laid before it. Led by Lucullus, Crassus and Cato, it delayed the ratification of his settlement of the Near East, and the urgent business of providing pensions for his soldiers. When Pompey tried to introduce a land law into the Tribal Assembly, the nobles continued their obstruction in the Forum. Here the urban voters gave Pompey such poor support that he withdrew his bill and waited on events.

After a year of provincial administration in Further Spain, Caesar returned to Rome in 60 to try for the consulship. Cicero, who was quick to recognise in him a man of outstanding power, hoped that Caesar too might be trained into a defender of the established order. But the Senate was less anxious to convert him into a 'Good Man' than to pay off old scores against him. It denied him the triumph which he claimed for some minor victories in north-west Spain. Worse still, in anticipation of his election to the consulship, it made an extraordinary arrangement by which the consuls of 59, instead of taking up the usual provincial appointments, were to stay in Italy as 'commissioners of forests and cattle', a routine office of third-rate importance. This last decision was nothing less than a declaration of war upon Caesar, who had discovered his military talents in Spain and was determined to test them more thoroughly on a wider field. He at once offered an alliance to Pompey, with a view to action

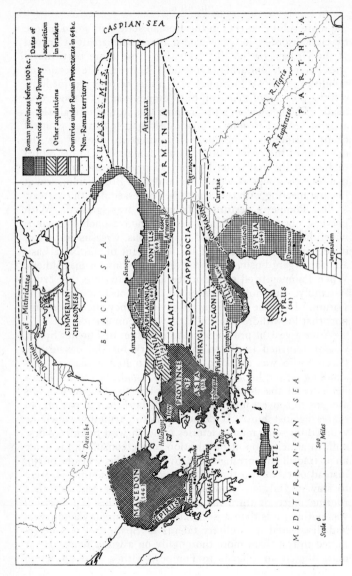

| Roman provinces before 100 B.C. | | Dates of |
| Provinces added by Pompey | | acquisition |
| Other acquisitions | | in brackets |
| Countries under Roman Protectorate in 64 B.C. | | |
| Non-Roman territory | | |

CASPIAN SEA

CAUCASUS MTS.

Artaxata

ARMENIA

Dominion of Mithridates

CIMMERIAN CHERSONESE

BLACK SEA

Sinope

Amastris

PAPHLAGONIA (64)

PONTUS (64)

Lesser Armenia

Tigranocerta

CAPPADOCIA

COMMAGENE (64)

Antioch

SYRIA (64)

Damascus

R. Tigris

R. Euphrates

PARTHIA

Carrhae

BITHYNIA (74)

GALATIA

PHRYGIA

LYCAONIA

CILICIA (102)

Jerusalem

CYPRUS (58)

PROVINCE OF ASIA (133)

Troy

Ephesus

Pisidia

Pamphylia

Lycia

Rhodes

Hellespont

MACEDON (146)

EPIRUS

ACHAEA

CRETE (67)

MEDITERRANEAN SEA

Scale 0     500 Miles

R. Danube

GREECE AND ASIA MINOR IN THE FIRST CENTURY B.C.

against the Senate. Pompey accepted, and married his daughter Julia into the bargain. Caesar also sought the support of his former patron Crassus, and of Cicero, whose oratorical ability he recognised as valuable. Crassus renewed his partnership, if only to safeguard himself against Pompey ; but Cicero refused to help Caesar in an enterprise which threatened to lead him into the path of revolution.

The 'First Triumvirate', as the alliance between Caesar, Pompey and Crassus is called, was plain to all at the beginning of 59, when Caesar entered upon his first consulship. He at once brought forward a land law, by which he provided for Pompey's veterans. After a vain attempt to get his law discussed in the Senate, he submitted it to the Popular Assembly. His colleague L. Calpurnius Bibulus, assisted by several tribunes and by Cato, used every possible form of obstruction against it, so he brought in some of Pompey's old soldiers, who swept away opposition by physical force and got the law passed. After this display of determination, Caesar began a wide programme of legislation, which was submitted partly in his own name and partly in that of the tribune P. Vatinius. He obtained ratification for Pompey's settlement of the Near East, and Ptolemy Auletes bought recognition from the Roman people in return for an enormous bribe to Caesar and Pompey. Caesar also strengthened the law against extortion in the provinces, and he provided for the official publication of all acts of the Popular Assemblies and resolutions of the Senate. Lastly, Caesar obtained for himself, by the agency of Vatinius, the governorship of Cisalpine Gaul and of Illyria for a term of five years, reckoned from the 1st of March 59. Later in the year he took advantage of a sudden vacancy in Narbonese Gaul to get this province too. Thus Caesar kept his promises to Pompey and got for himself a provincial command.

## Part 2 : *Foreign Wars*

### (A) *Mithridates and Tigranes*

1. *90–80 B.C.*—While the Romans were emerging from the Italian War, only to plunge into their first civil wars, they

also became involved in a conflict with their most formidable enemy in the eastern Mediterranean, King Mithridates VI of Pontus. Before 100 B.C. he had occupied Galatia and Cappadocia, and remained in undisturbed possession until 95, when Nicomedes II of Bithynia directed a complaint to the Senate. The Senate ordered Mithridates to evacuate Cappadocia. Two years later the king endeavoured to steal back into Cappadocia through the agency of his son-in-law, King Tigranes of Armenia; but this was promptly checked by Sulla, who was then acting as governor of Cilicia (92).

But the outbreak of the Italian War gave the king a new opportunity. In 91 or 90 he expelled Nicomedes' successor (also called Nicomedes) from Bithynia, and he reoccupied Cappadocia. The Senate sent M'. Aquilius to put Nicomedes back on the throne. Mithridates withdrew without a battle; but for his services in restoring Nicomedes Aquilius had demanded a fee which Nicomedes could not pay. Aquilius pressed him to raise funds by raiding Pontus. Again Mithridates offered no resistance, but his patience at last gave out; and once he made up his mind that the Romans were determined to fix a war upon him, he struck first and struck hard.

Mithridates swept Aquilius and Nicomedes out of Bithynia; then turning southward he ended the campaign with a drive through the province of Asia, where the towns readily came over to him on a promise of lighter taxation. Apart from a few places on the south coast and the city of Rhodes, he carried Asia Minor in a single whirlwind invasion. After this easy triumph Mithridates gave orders for the simultaneous massacre of all the Italians in Asia. Most of the Asiatic cities carried out the king's command, a strong proof of the unpopularity of Roman rule.

Mithridates now prepared for an invasion of Europe. He won over Athens, where his agent Aristion led a revolution, and his admiral Archelaus attacked Delos, where all the Italian residents were killed, and occupied the Piraeus (the port of Athens). From this base he captured all southern and most of central Greece. The Roman troops from Macedonia could do no more than defend Thessaly against Archelaus.

In 87 Sulla landed in Greece with an army of five legions, or 30,000 men. He besieged Athens and Piraeus and took them in 86. The main Pontic army was advancing through Thrace and Macedonia, and threatened to take the Romans in the rear. Eventually both sides concentrated their strength for a set battle at Chaeroneia. In this battle Archelaus assumed the chief command on Mithridates' behalf and had the advantage of numbers on his side. But Sulla held a flying corps in reserve, and he threw it into action with such good judgment that he converted the battle into a rout, in which Archelaus' army was virtually destroyed. But a reinforcing army engaged Sulla at Orchomenus. Here Sulla put the enemy to flight with a well-timed cavalry charge, stormed their camp and made an end of Mithridates' expeditionary force.

In 87 Sulla made a slow advance towards the Dardanelles. In the meantime a counter-offensive in Asia had been opened by a second Roman force under the consul L. Valerius Flaccus, which Cinna had sent out. Flaccus had secret orders to attack Sulla, but he was killed in a mutiny instigated by his legatus, C. Flavius Fimbria, who now took command. In 85 Fimbria invaded the province of Asia, and after an easy victory over a reserve Pontic army, which he caught by surprise on the banks of the Rhyndacus, he expelled Mithridates from his residence at Pergamum. In the summer of 85 Sulla made peace with Mithridates at Dardanus (near Troy). The king agreed to evacuate all conquered territory in Asia Minor, to surrender his Aegean fleet, and to pay a moderate fine.

As soon as the peace was signed Sulla caught up Fimbria and overawed his troops who deserted to Sulla. Fimbria took his own life ; his troops were left under Sulla's legatus, L. Licinius Murena, to hold down the province of Asia. The cities of Asia submitted readily to Sulla. But they were held strictly to account for the massacres of 88 B.C. and the enormous sum of 20,000 talents, representing five years' tribute and the costs of the war, was demanded from them (84 B.C.).

2. *80–63 B.C.*—Mithridates refrained from any overt hostility until 74, when he made a sudden invasion of the Roman territory in Asia. . This was partly intended to prevent a Roman occupation of Bithynia, which the childless King

Nicomedes III had recently left to Rome in his will. Two Roman legions were stationed in the province of Asia ; but these were caught off their guard, so that the king was able to overrun Bithynia without opposition. The whole burden of the war fell upon Cotta's colleague L. Licinius Lucullus, whom the Senate had appointed to the provinces of Asia and Bithynia (74).

Mithridates sent his fleet on into Greek waters ; with his land forces he invaded the province of Asia and laid siege to Cyzicus. Lucullus succeeded in cutting Mithridates' communications, and in 74–73 the king attempted to retreat, but nearly all his men were overtaken and destroyed. In the spring of 73 Lucullus followed up this success with a naval victory off Lemnos and now the way was open for an invasion of Pontus.

In the autumn of 73 Lucullus made a dash through Galatia into the valley of the Lycus, in the heart of Mithridates' realm. After a second winter he eventually gained a victory near Cabira. Mithridates again escaped, but he was left without an army or a kingdom. His son Machares, whom he had placed in charge of his European dominions, declared against him, and his relation Tigranes, the king of Armenia, to whom he fled, held him virtually as a prisoner.

The Romans could take the fortified towns of Pontus at their leisure, a task which they completed in 70. Lucullus returned to the province of Asia, where there was a financial crisis. Condemned by Sulla to a fine of 20,000 talents, the cities of Asia had paid the Roman treasury by borrowing from private money-lenders at a high rate of interest. Under this scheme their debt swelled up to the huge total of 120,000 talents. The cities became bankrupt. By reducing the sum to 40,000 talents and arranging for repayment by instalments, Lucullus set the province back on the path to prosperity.

By the end of 70 all Asia Minor was at Rome's disposal. Yet Lucullus, judging that nothing was settled so long as Mithridates was not dead or in Roman hands, determined to obtain his surrender from the king of Armenia, even at the cost of another war. Tigranes, on coming to the throne in 95, at once followed the example of his father-in-law Mithridates in delivering nicely timed attacks upon his neighbours. Since 92, when Sulla compelled him to withdraw for the time being from Cappadocia, his attacks upon Roman allies had not been challenged by the Senate. Though Tigranes had not helped Mithridates against Lucullus, he now stood firm against the demand for his surrender. But Lucullus decided to fight : in 69 he crossed the Euphrates and invaded Armenia.

Lucullus had no commission from the Senate to make war upon Armenia, and no more than 160,000 weary and half-willing soldiers to oppose to Tigranes' far superior forces. But he made a direct march upon the fortress of Tigranocerta and though heavily outnumbered obtained the victory in a few minutes' fighting. Tigranes' empire was brought down like a house of cards, and Tigranocerta fell into the hands of the Romans. In 68, by the advice of Mithridates, Tigranes drew the Romans on by a continual retreat towards his capital at Artaxata. Lucullus was within striking distance of Artaxata when his troops refused to advance any further. He retreated to Mesopotamia : Mithridates returned to Pontus and opened a guerrilla war on the Roman lines of communications. Had Lucullus now received reinforcements from Rome he might even yet have defeated both the kings. But in 67 Lucullus was robbed of what troops he had left. At Rome his attack upon Tigranes, and his settlement of the debt question in the province of Asia, were criticised. The Senate took from him the provinces of Asia and Cilicia, leaving him Bithynia and the command of the Roman field forces (69–68) ; and in 67 the concentration of all the spare military resources of the empire in the hands of Pompey cut off all sources of fresh supplies.

Lucullus' lieutenant, C. Triarius, fought Mithridates on unfavourable ground and was defeated near Zela. Lucullus fought on but his army began to melt away, and the new governors of Cilicia and Bithynia, to whom Lucullus turned for assistance, found excuses for staying in their provinces. He made a stand in the valley of the upper Halys, but he could not prevent the kings from regaining full possession of their dominions. A law brought forward at the beginning of 66 gave Pompey general powers against all the enemies of Rome in

Asia, and authorised him to make a general settlement of affairs in the eastern Mediterranean. At this time Pompey was in Cilicia. He now moved forward to the Halys and sent Lucullus home.

In 66 Mithridates lost the support of Tigranes, who was called away to fight Parthia. Outnumbered by Pompey's force of more than 50,000 men, he fell back and tried guerrilla strategy. But Pompey hemmed him in and at a site near the future town of Nicopolis the Romans caught up and slaughtered the last Pontic army. Mithridates, as usual, escaped and raised fresh troops among his European subjects (65–63): but he used so much severity in doing so that he caused a rebellion, led by his own son Pharnaces. At Panticapaeum he took his own life (63).

## (B) *Sertorius*

Before the death of Sulla, the Marian leader Sertorius recovered his foothold in Spain. He acquired an authority over the Spaniards such as no native chief possessed, so that they flocked to his standard to fight a Roman's battles. In 80 Sertorius raised a rebellion among the Lusitanians, by which a further nine years of Spanish wars were begun. In 79 and 78 Sulla's colleague Metellus Pius failed to defeat him and in 77 Sertorius became strong enough to hold Metellus in southern Spain, while his flying columns overran the central and northern plateau as far as the Pyrenees and occupied most of the eastern coast. On the east coast he came into touch with the pirates and he made an agreement with King Mithridates, who gave him financial and naval support.

After the death of Sulla the government could have made an honourable end of the Spanish War by offering to restore Sertorius. But with misplaced loyalty to Sulla's memory it carried on the conflict. At the end of 77 it sent heavy reinforcements to Spain under its best general, Pompey. In 76 and 75 the main scene of operations in Spain lay along the east coast, from which Pompey sought to expel Sertorius. In 76 Pompey was defeated near Lauro. In 75 Metellus definitely recovered southern Spain for the Senate by a victory near Segovia. After this success he again marched east to take Sertorius in the rear; but once more Pompey would not wait for his partner, and in consequence lost a second battle near the river Sucro. At the end of the year Sertorius still held the best part of the rich coast-lands near Valentia. But the Senate sent Pompey fresh supplies, and a fleet which effectively cut off Sertorius from his allies on the high seas.

With their forces now more than 50,000 men, Pompey and Metellus recovered one town after another in 74 and 73, so that the remaining enemy forces were gradually pushed into the Ebro valley. Finally in 72 M. Perperna, who had consistently failed Sertorius in battle and could not forgive his chief for winning victories, murdered him and took over his command. Pompey made short work of him, and brought the long war to an end.

## (c) *The Pirates*

Shortly after the death of Sulla the Senate was called upon to grapple more seriously with the problem of the pirates of the Mediterranean, whose activities had begun to threaten vital Roman interests. They had recently started to organise themselves into fleets that did not shrink from attacking or blackmailing entire towns. As their power grew, they took less care to avoid offence against Rome. They held to ransom Roman citizens of high rank; they roamed the western seas, which they had previously left alone, and they allied with Sertorius in Spain. In 78 the ex-consul P. Servilius opened a methodical attack by land and sea on the pirates in Lycia; in 76 he expelled them from Pamphylia and in 75 from western Cilicia. But before he could deliver his final assault he was recalled, and the Mithridatic war in 74 reorganised the Roman forces in Asia Minor.

Meanwhile the pirates scattered over the Mediterranean in quest of new bases. In 74 the Senate established a garrison at Cyrene, which was now definitely constituted as a Roman province. In the same year the Senate gave a special command to the ex-praetor M. Antonius, with unlimited powers of getting ships and ship-money, in every country of the Mediterranean. But Antonius was at a loss to organise his movements effectively against his enemies. In 74 and 73 he partly cleared the western seas. But before his task in the west was completed he transferred his fleet to the Aegean, where he suffered defeat in Cretan waters at the hands of a pirate battle squadron (72), and died shortly afterwards. His fleet was thereupon disbanded.

The following years mark the highest point of the pirates' power. In 69 they sacked the harbour of Delos. The chief scene of their activities was the coast of Italy, which they attacked from Brundisium to Ostia. They captured two praetors, attacked a Roman fleet in 68 at Ostia, and intercepted the corn supplies of Rome. Famine at Rome drove the people to take the direction of the pirate war out of the Senate's hands. In 67 the Tribal Assembly gave the imperium which Antonius had enjoyed to Pompey.

Pompey recruited a fleet of 270 warships and 100,000 legionary infantry. Closing the straits between Sicily and Africa with a strong cordon, he cleared up the western seas in forty days. By a similar movement he drove the Levantine pirates to their last refuge in western Cilicia, where strong infantry detachments demolished their castles. In three months Pompey was able to report all clear, and although piracy again raised its head here and there, it ceased to be a general menace. Pompey crowned his success by the leniency with which he treated his captives. The greater number were set up by him as honest peasants or traders in Cilicia or elsewhere.

## (D) *Pompey's Settlement of the East*

In the intervals between his campaigns and in the following year, Pompey was occupied with the political settlement of the Near East. Tigranes was left in possession of Armenia and had part of his conquests in western Mesopotamia confirmed. Pharnaces retained his father's dominions in Europe. On the other hand, he excluded the dynasty of Mithridates from Asia Minor. Finally, he took Syria out of the hands of the remaining Seleucid princes. He made the Seleucid territory into a new province named Syria. At the same time he enlarged the province of Cilicia by adding to it the previous no-man's-lands along the coast of Asia Minor as far as Lycia and the interior up to the central plateau.

In the provinces created or enlarged by him Pompey adopted the policy of the Hellenistic kings in helping the growth of towns. It is estimated that in Asia Minor and Syria he founded or restored some forty cities, whose inhabitants were supplied by the refugees of the recent wars, and by the populations forcibly removed by Tigranes to Tigranocerta. He also made the more privileged towns of Asia Minor pay taxes : Rhodes and Cyzicus were the only two which escaped.

Pompey's fame as a conqueror put Lucullus into the shade. His military reputation was earned cheaply, for none of his wars had put his military skill to a severe test. But his political settlement was of lasting importance. It consolidated Roman authority in the East ; it brought to the treasury huge war spoils, and it raised the annual revenue of the republic from fifty to eighty-five million denarii (£2,000,000 to £3,400,000). In return the peoples of the Near East received security. The pacification of Asia Minor was nearly complete ; Syria was saved from anarchy ; and the Levantine coasts, the greater part of which now stood under direct Roman rule, were made secure against piracy.

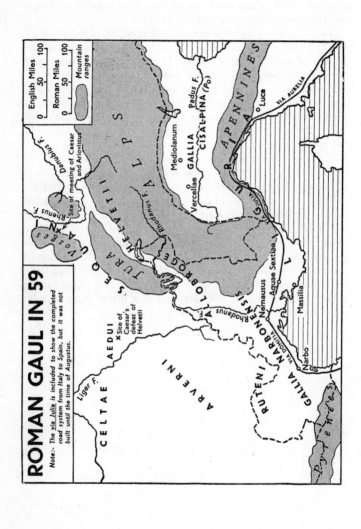

# ROMAN GAUL IN 59

Note:— The *via Julia* is included to show the completed road system from Italy to Spain, but it was not built until the time of Augustus.

English Miles
0   50   100

Roman Miles
0   50   100

Mountain ranges

Rhenus F.

Site of meeting of Caesar and Ariovistus

Danubius F.

V O S E G U S

J U R A

H E L V E T I I

S E Q U A N I

A L P S

Rhodanus F.

Mediolanum

Vercellae

GALLIA CISALPINA

Padus F. (Po)

Luca

VIA AURELIA

A P E N N I N E S

Julia

Aquae Sextiae

Massilia

ALLOBROGES

Nemausus

via Domitia

Rhodanus F.

GALLIA NARBONENSIS

Narbo

RUTENI

ARVERNI

P y r e n e e s

CELTAE

AEDUI

Liger F.

×Site of Caesar's defeat of Helvetii

### CHAPTER XI

# 60–44 B.C.

## Part 1 : *Caesar in Gaul*

### (A) *Background History*

IN making first choice of Cisalpine Gaul for a provincial command Caesar was partly guided by politics. Being so near, it allowed him to keep an eye on events in the capital. Whenever he could safely leave Transalpine Gaul, Caesar spent his winters in his Italian province, performing the routine duties of a governor and receiving visits from his agents and associates in Rome. But he was also alive to the military opportunities which Cisalpine Gaul offered. The inclusion of Illyria in his proconsular command, and the position of his troops at the beginning of 58, when three of his four legions were stationed at Aquileia, indicate that his original plan of operations may have been to extend the Roman frontiers north-eastward beyond the Carnic Alps. But the province of Transalpine Gaul in fact became the starting-point of his campaigns.

Transalpine Gaul's population consisted of 'Ligurians'; of the Celts, who entered Gaul from southern and western Germany in the first half of the first millennium, and of Iberians who passed from Spain into Gascony and Languedoc during the fifth or fourth century; and of Belgae, a mixture of Celts and Germans who crossed the Rhine and occupied the districts north of the Seine and Marne *c.* 200 B.C. Among these the Celtic element predominated. Except in Aquitania (south-western Gaul) the Celtic language was in general use and the governing class was of Celtic stock.

The civilisation of the Gauls was more advanced than that of any European people beyond the Mediterranean coast.

Intensive agriculture was practised in many districts of Gaul : several improvements in the ordinary process of ploughing which eventually reached the Roman world were of Gallic origin. Also the Celtic peoples had become highly skilled in metal-working and Gallic swords had no rivals but those of Spain. From the sixth century, when the Greek colony of Massilia was founded near the Rhône estuary, trade began to follow the river valleys of Gaul. From the third century Greek coins were widely current ; after 200 Roman denarii came into use. By the time of Caesar carriage-roads had been made, and the trading centres along them were growing into permanent towns. Writing was as yet unknown in Gaul.

The political organisation was essentially aristocratic. Kingship still prevailed among the Belgae, but in central Gaul it had disappeared after 100. The Druids formed an influential religious body ; they exercised a formidable right of religious excommunication ; they executed criminals and war captives. But they never assumed the direction of state policy. The nobility provided the flower of the Gallic armies, annual magistrates and governing councils. By the first century the Gauls had made far greater progress towards national unity than their Spanish neighbours. But rivalry between the various tribes was sometimes carried to such a length that one Gallic state would call in foreign aid to defeat another. The Gallic armies had good equipment, and their cavalry, which was supplied by the nobles, was superior to that of the Italians. But the infantry was badly trained, and discipline was poor. By 100 B.C. Germanic peoples had begun to invade the home of the Celts between the Main and the Danube, and in this region a confederacy of nomadic tribes known as the Suebi was preparing for a further advance into France and western Switzerland. Meanwhile the Arverni and the Sequani (between the Saône and the Rhine) called upon the Suebi to help them against their neighbours on the lower Saône, the Aedui. The Suebic chief Ariovistus, a very able man, assisted the Sequani to overcome the Aedui ; but he kept part of his allies' territory in Alsace as the fee for his services. Meanwhile on the left bank of the Rhine the Helvetii, a Celtic tribe which had recently been pressed back from southern Germany into

Switzerland, prepared to move across the territory of the Aedui to a new home near the Atlantic coast. Information of these movements had been given to the Senate by the Aedui, who asked for Roman aid. The Senate, however, did nothing definite.

## (B) *58–56 B.C.*

At the start of 58 Caesar was still lingering near Rome when news was brought that the Helvetii were about to cross the Rhône near Geneva and to cross the Roman province on the way to western France. With the legion that was stationed in the Transalpine province he hastened to the threatened point, but the Helvetii found an alternative route across the Jura and the land of the Aedui, who again asked for help. In answer Caesar at first told the Helvetii to halt. But when the Helvetii refused, he advanced across Aeduan territory to meet them with his four original legions (now concentrated along the Rhône) and two newly-recruited ones. Near Bibracte he was counter-attacked and nearly defeated; but his legionaries saved the battle. After this the remnant of the Helvetii agreed to return to their homes.

The vigour with which Caesar had thrown back the Helvetii opened the eyes of the Gallic chief. Gauls from all parts of the country now joined the Aeduan leader Divitiacus in asking his aid against Ariovistus, but Ariovistus openly stated his intention of extending his conquests to the Atlantic. The Roman army fell into a panic when it received orders to move forward to the Rhine. But Caesar made his men face up to the Suebi in a set battle at the foot of the Vosges (near Cernay), where the Suebi were defeated. Their confederacy fell to pieces, and a long period of security set in for the Gauls along the middle and upper Rhine.

At the end of 58 Caesar committed himself to the conquest of all Transalpine Gaul and placed his legions for the winter at Vesontio (Besançon) in the territory of the Aedui and Sequani. In 57 all the Belgic tribes except the Remi (near Rheims) took the field against Caesar, who advanced as far as the Aisne. Caesar had ascertained that the Gallic army was too big to get enough supplies, and simply waited for it to disperse for lack of provisions.  Once the Gallic retreat began, Caesar pressed the pursuit and in a lightning campaign captured the greater part of what is now northern France.  In the extreme north of Gaul an alliance headed by the Nervii offered a more stubborn resistance.  On the banks of the Sambre Caesar was surprised by their tribal army and lost his army in a confused and desperate hand-to-hand encounter.  Thanks to their better battle-discipline, and to Caesar's presence of mind in extricating them out of their disorder, the legions managed to win in the end.  After this the Belgae were conquered within the same year.  While Caesar was in the north of Gaul, P. Crassus made an easy progress along the western seaboard from Normandy to the Garonne and received the submission of the peoples of this coast with scarcely a blow struck.  Crassus' unprovoked attack upon the peaceful Atlantic populations proved beyond all doubt that Caesar was now aiming at nothing less than the complete conquest of Gaul.  It also revealed his plan of campaign : he was encircling the inland in order to subdue it at his leisure.

At the end of 57 Caesar may have thought that all Gaul had been pacified.  But in 56 the Atlantic peoples, led by the Veneti of Brittany, reasserted their independence.  But Caesar took the Veneti in the rear with a fleet which he had hurriedly built on the Loire.  The resourcefulness of the Roman admiral D. Brutus, who improvised scythes on long poles to cut the enemy rigging, and a fortunate calm which left the Gallic ships motionless, put the Veneti at the mercy of the Romans.  The rebellion of the Veneti was punished by Caesar with wholesale executions and enslavements.  In the same season P. Crassus continued his march from the Garonne to the Pyrenees and conquered the small and weak Aquitanian tribes without any serious struggle.  Towards the end of 56 Caesar occupied all the northern coast between Brittany and Flanders.

(c) *55–49 B.C.*

In 55 Caesar was attacked by two German tribes, the Usipetes and Tencteri, in northern Belgium.  Caesar met their leaders at a conference, took advantage of an accidental breach of the armistice, arrested the chiefs in his camp, attacked their unsuspecting followers, and hunted down the whole tribe, to the last woman and child. He followed up this massacre with an invasion of Germany. But after a brief period, in which he failed to force the Suebi or any lesser German tribe to fight, or to collect any profitable plunder, he returned to Gaul.

In 55, and again in 54, Caesar made similar exploratory expeditions across the English Channel. Roman interest in Britain was largely economic, for the island was thought to be rich in pearls and precious metals. In the campaign of 55 Caesar took a small force with him, and only achieved a landing-place on the east coast of Kent. But in 54 he returned with five legions and made a stay of two to three months, during which he was engaged in some hard fighting. His main opponent was a chief named Cassivellaunus, who had recently subdued the neighbouring tribe of the Trinovantes in Essex. Caesar easily defeated the Britons in battle and captured Cassivellaunus' stronghold, but his fleet suffered losses by tide and wind, and there was little plunder. Cassivellaunus surrendered : but he was never, in practice, under the power of Rome.

Gaul had remained quiet in 55 and 54, but discontented. In the winter of 54 Ambiorix, king of the Eburones (in the Ardennes), ambushed and destroyed one and a half legions. This disaster led to rebellions in northern Gaul, and another legion under the command of Q. Cicero was besieged in its camp by the Nervii. But Caesar relieved Cicero and in the summer of 53 he overcame the rebels.

After a winter spent in Cisalpine Gaul (53–52), Caesar returned to meet a more powerful enemy and a more formidable rebellion. This was directed by an Arvernian chief named Vercingetorix, who was acknowledged as commander-in-chief of nearly all the peoples between Loire and Garonne. Vercingetorix imposed a Roman strictness of discipline upon his troops. The Gauls had at last produced an army and a leader that could meet Caesar on equal terms.

In the spring of 52 Caesar made an attack on Arvernian

territory, and thus cleared his path to the Seine valley, where he concentrated his forces. He crossed the Loire and besieged Avaricum. Here Vercingetorix attempted to starve out Caesar's army, but the attackers broke into the city and replenished their supplies. From Avaricum Caesar pushed on to Gergovia, in the heart of the Arvernian country, but in an attempt to capture it his troops got out of hand and were hurled back with considerable loss. After this all the Gallic tribes except three joined the rebels. Caesar's position was now all the more critical, as he had sent back four legions under T. Labienus to northern Gaul. He escaped Vercingetorix and rejoined Labienus : and stayed long enough in northern Gaul to reorganise his cavalry. Then an attack by Vercingetorix upon Gallia Narbonensis made him return for the defence of the province. For the moment all the work of the past six years seemed wasted. But a battle near Dijon, where Vercingetorix was roughly handled by Caesar's substitute cavalry, gave back the initiative to Caesar.

After this reverse Vercingetorix committed the fatal mistake of retiring behind the walls of a hill-city named Alesia. Caesar besieged Alesia : other Gallic chiefs came to the rescue of Vercingetorix, but the Romans held firm until Alesia was starved into surrender. After the surrender of Vercingetorix the independence of Gaul was lost. Caesar spent the last year of his proconsulship in making friends of his former enemies. For the time being he left the tribal governments undisturbed, and the tribute which he imposed was small. On these terms the Gauls made a quick and lasting peace with him. In 49 he could safely withdraw the greater part of the Roman forces and enrol Gallic auxiliaries to fight his personal battles in a civil war.

For Caesar his term of command in Gaul was the turning-point in his career. The plunder which he got was enough to pay off his enormous private debts and enabled him to use bribery in Rome on a scale comparable to that of Crassus. He held an invincible army that was ready to follow him anywhere. Above all, it was as proconsul of Gaul that he 'found himself' and brought into full play his powers as a soldier and administrator. From this point Caesar's actions betoken a leader who is serenely conscious of his superior genius.

## Part 2 : *Politics at Rome to 49 B.C.*

(A) *58–57 B.C.*

During Caesar's absence in Gaul the senatorial nobility continued to secure most of the high magistracies for its own candidates, and it could still strike at its opponents in the courts of law. But the ultimate decision on all questions of importance henceforth rested with one or other of the three members of the Triumvirate. Yet the Triumvirate was continually hampered by mutual suspicions among its three partners and was never free from the danger of falling to pieces.

Suspecting that Pompey and Crassus could not be trusted to play their appointed part in safeguarding him against the nobility, Caesar had secured the services of a disreputable but talented adventurer named P. Clodius, who became for a year and a half the uncrowned king of Rome. Appointed tribune for 58, Clodius made himself popular with the mob by means of a law substituting free gifts of public corn for the previous sales at reduced prices. He also ran a trained and permanent army of expert gangsters and thus carried without opposition a supplementary programme to the legislation of Caesar and Vatinius. As a precaution against obstructive magistrates he limited the right of religious obstruction to augurs and tribunes. With the object of depriving the nobility of its ablest spokesman, he drove Cicero from Rome with a law which 'deprived of fire and water any person guilty of killing a citizen without a trial' — an obvious allusion to the ex-consul's proceedings against Catiline's accomplices. In a third bill he again killed two birds with one stone by deposing the king of Cyprus (a younger brother of Ptolemy Auletes, who had not followed the Egyptian king's good example of buying recognition from the triumvirs), and by sending Cato away from Rome with a commission to take over the late monarch's treasure.

So far Clodius had served Caesar well. But he lost his head and prepared for his own downfall by turning his gangs

upon Pompey. Pompey formed an opposition army of
ruffians under another politician named T. Annius Milo, and
called his veterans to his aid. In the summer of 57 Clodius
lost his power. A law sponsored by Pompey authorised
Cicero's return from exile and a triumphal reception was
given to the orator at his home-coming.

Pompey thus gained more power at Rome than he had
enjoyed since his consulship. In 57 he received a commission
to relieve Rome of a sudden shortage of grain. In the following
winter he declined the command of an expedition to reinstate
Ptolemy Auletes who had been expelled by his subjects. Yet
Crassus still thought he desired a high military command.
This renewal of the ancient feud between Pompey and
Crassus was the signal for an assault upon the Triumvirate.
Cicero, who still nursed the hope of detaching Pompey, sought
to drive a wedge between him and Caesar by proposing the
partial repeal of Caesar's land legislation on the chance that
Pompey might be willing to jettison Caesar's measures if only
his personal interests in them were safeguarded.

## (B) 56–52 B.C.

At this time (March 56) Caesar had not yet left his winter
quarters in Cisalpine Gaul, but was stationed at Ravenna, only
200 miles from Rome. After a meeting with Crassus, he
asked Pompey to a conference at Luca, the southernmost town
in his province. At first Pompey hesitated, but eventually he
went. Here the three partners patched up their quarrels and
settled the Roman empire for years to come. In anticipation
of their coming to terms a crowd of more than a hundred
senators flocked to Luca to show their support.

From Luca Pompey and Crassus returned together to
Rome to carry out the agreements made at the conference.
A polite warning stopped Cicero from proceeding with his
attack upon Caesar. Pompey and Crassus then got themselves
made consuls for 55, and fulfilled their part of the bargain by
carrying a law to prolong Caesar's proconsulship in both the
Gauls for another 'quinquennium' ('five-year period'), the
terminal date apparently being fixed at some point in 50 or
early 49. The passing of the Lex Licinia Pompeia was stoutly

resisted by the aristocracy, but Pompey on this occasion did
not hesitate to use violence to fulfil his promises to Caesar.
In return for their services a tribune named C. Trebonius got
proconsular commands for Pompey and Crassus.  Crassus
chose for himself the province of Syria.  Pompey took the two
provinces of Spain under his general control, but he himself
stayed at Rome.  The principal result of the conference of
Luca was that Caesar had enough time to complete the
conquest of Gaul, thus giving the chance of raising armies to
his partners, and to Pompey the sole control of affairs in
Rome.  Crassus' governorship of Syria gave him a free hand
to deal with Parthia.  Parthia was a monarchy whose kings,
the Arsacids, left the outlying provinces of their realm in
the hands of dependent princes.  The Parthian infantry was
weak, but the mounted forces were exceptionally strong.  The
Parthian nobility provided a corps of heavily armoured
knights ; their followers were skilled riders, and could shoot
arrows to deadly effect while pretending to flee.

Crassus had under his command not less than 35,000 men,
almost all legionary infantry.  He crossed the Euphrates in 53
and had reached the neighbourhood of Carrhae when he met
an experimental Parthian army of 10,000 mounted archers.
Selecting their own range, the archers steadily shot down the
helpless Roman infantry.  The survivors fell into such a state
of demoralisation that, although the Parthians did not press
them closely on their retreat, they compelled their commander
to surrender.  Crassus was killed by a Parthian officer, and
his army was carried off into captivity.  A bare 10,000 regained
the Roman frontier.

In 54 and 53 the republic drifted into chaos.  Pompey left
events to take their course, though the Senate dared not move
freely during his presence at Rome.  Bribery was practised
on a large scale, and the tribunes' veto was misused with
such persistency to obstruct the elections that the years 53
and 52 began with an interregnum.  The Senate passed a
resolution that in future ex-consuls should not proceed to their
provinces until five clear years had elapsed from their consulate;
but this was totally inadequate for the prevailing confusion.

The disorder culminated early in 52 in a fight between the

gangs of Milo and Clodius, in which the latter was killed, and in an outbreak of rioting, in the course of which Clodius' gang burnt down the Senate-house and other buildings in the Forum. The Senate passed an emergency decree, by which Pompey was charged with the restoration of order. It went on to recommend that Pompey should be elected 'sole consul', and under this title the people gave him a virtual dictatorship, such as Sulla had held. Pompey carried stricter laws against bribery and breaches of the peace, which he applied with severity against Milo and other agitators. This kept Rome quiet until the next civil war.

In the same year Pompey confirmed by legislation the resolution of the Senate prescribing a five-year interval between a consulship and a proconsulship. By agreement with Caesar, who was expecting a second consulship in 48 (with a further military command to follow), he arranged for the ten tribunes to carry a law to excuse Caesar from having to appear in person as a candidate, so that he might, if necessary, carry on his work in Gaul. Finally, the Senate agreed to prolong Pompey's command in Spain for a second term of five years (presumably reckoned from some point in 52).

In 54 the death of Caesar's daughter Julia removed the only bond of sentiment between Pompey and his partner; and in the following year the death of Crassus at Carrhae removed a possible counterbalance to Pompey within the Triumvirate. Pompey for the time being gave no sign of disloyalty to Caesar. In 53 he lent Caesar one of his Spanish legions; in 52 he showed due regard to his partner's interests in his legislation. But the accumulation of power in his hands during this year gave impetus to a political campaign against Caesar, into which Pompey was drawn. Since 59 a group of aristocrats, among them M. Cato and L. Domitius, had been plotting. Cato had demanded that Caesar should be handed over to the Usipetes in retribution for his treachery towards them. In 54 the nobility was successful in a prosecution of Pompey's friend Gabinius on a charge of extortion in Syria, and this minor triumph suggested a hopeful method of attack upon Caesar himself. Yet they had no armed force behind them. Pompey's dual command in Spain and Italy, however, inspired Caesar's enemies with a new plan of campaign. Pompey, it was assumed, must be jealous of Caesar's victories in Gaul, and fearful of his ambitions for the future. The extremists in the Senate now wanted to prolong their alliance with him until they should have got rid of Caesar.

## (c) *51–49 B.C.*

Early in 51 Caesar, scenting danger, sent a request to the Senate for a further prolongation of his command in Gaul to the end of 49, so as to close the gap between his proconsulship and his second consulship (due to begin on January 1st, 48) and to leave his enemies no time to prosecute him. This proposal was rejected by the consul M. Claudius Marcellus, a determined enemy of Caesar, and Pompey maintained a silence which the extremists took as a sign of encouragement. In May 51 Marcellus made a counter-proposal, that Caesar's term be curtailed so as to expire on March 1st, 50. But his motion was not carried.

On March 1st, 50, the consul C. Marcellus again pressed for Caesar's early recall, and Pompey now declared himself in favour of giving Caesar no less, but also no more, than his legal due. But the motion was vetoed by a tribune named C. Scribonius Curio, a bankrupt young nobleman whom Caesar had bought at an enormous price to defend his interests. The Senate then called upon Caesar and Pompey each to surrender one legion for service against the Parthians. Since Pompey, as expected, chose to surrender one of his legions from Spain, which he had lent to Caesar in 53, the result of this deal was that Caesar lost two legions. After their arrival in Italy, the troops handed over by Caesar were kept there at Pompey's disposal. But in a renewed debate on Caesar's term of office Curio insisted that Pompey's double command in Spain and Italy should not be allowed to run on beyond Caesar's term in Gaul. This was entirely reasonable, and it received a hearty welcome from all those who dreaded civil war. Put to the vote on December 1st, Curio's motion was carried by 370 votes against 22. To the extremists, however, this solution was not acceptable, for without Pompey's forces to bring him to court and see that strict justice was done they feared that Caesar might still evade punishment.

On the next day Marcellus appealed to Pompey to ignore constitutional scruples and to 'save the republic' by mobilising his troops in order to bring immediate pressure upon Caesar. Pompey allowed himself to be persuaded. From this moment the result was settled, for Caesar replied by summoning his legions from France to his winter quarters near Ravenna. At the eleventh hour Caesar made several earnest attempts to reach a compromise. Late in December he offered to surrender Transalpine Gaul at once and his other province on the day of his election to a second consulship (in summer 49). Pompey showed signs of entertaining this offer, but Marcellus refused. On New Year's Day 49 Caesar repeated Curio's proposal of joint disarmament, but Pompey himself now declared that he expected the Senate to stand firm. Interpreting this hint as a command, the House rejected Caesar's offer and proceeded to nominate L. Domitius to Transalpine Gaul and an ex-praetor to the Cisalpine province, with orders to take over at an early date (presumably before summer 49). In the next few days Cicero, who had just returned from a term of proconsular duty in Cilicia, reopened negotiations. But the extremist party, now headed by the consul L. Cornelius Lentulus, cut these discussions short. On January 7th the Senate, still under pressure from Pompey, passed the Decree of Emergency, and handed the republic to the care of consuls and proconsuls, which meant, in effect, to Pompey. Three days later Caesar was told of this. For one anxious hour he reflected in solitude ; finally he made his reply by crossing the Rubicon (the frontier stream) and invading Italy. He made six further offers in the course of the next eighteen months ; but some of these were rejected by Pompey himself, others by the escort of extremists that stood guard over him.

## Part 3 : *The Civil War*

(A) *49–48* B.C.

1. *Italy and Spain.*—At the crossing of the Rubicon, Caesar's total force fell short of 50,000 men, and not more

than one legion was stationed with him at Ravenna. On the other hand, Pompey had at his disposal the entire resources of the Roman empire outside Gaul. But while Caesar's soldiers were seasoned veterans and ready for a rapid concentration on the war front, his rival's army was hardly yet in being. In Italy Pompey had hardly any trained troops except the two legions recently handed over by Caesar; the rest were recruits who for the moment lay scattered over the whole of the peninsula.

The first week of the campaign of 49 decided the fate of Italy. Taking the fullest advantage of Pompey's slowness, Caesar seized two of the principal Apennine passes into Etruria without a blow struck. Pompey fell back from Rome to Capua. Caesar advanced down the east coast of the peninsula, and his remaining legions from Transalpine Gaul soon arrived. The Italian campaign resolved itself into a race for Brundisium, which was won by Pompey. Embarking with great skill, Pompey drew off the whole of his remaining forces, amounting to some five legions, and shook off the pursuit of Caesar, who had no ships to follow him across the Adriatic. Thus Caesar's attempt to end the war without a battle failed, and Pompey was left at leisure to reorganise his army for a second campaign. Yet within two months Caesar had carried all Italy with scarcely any loss to his side.

The remainder of 49 was spent by Caesar in securing Italy before making a fresh advance against Pompey. Returning to Rome from Brundisium he found that most of the higher magistrates and the leading senators had left the city with Pompey. He got a praetor named M. Aemilius Lepidus to assemble some members of the Senate, but it was by mere right of conquest that he broke into the treasury, which the Pompeians had not wholly emptied when they left the city. But Caesar was at any rate able to show that he was not a revolutionary, out for booty and blackmail. His soldiers had observed

Money struck by Caesar in 49, out of the gold reserves raided by him on his return to Rome

good discipline, and the campaign of early 49 had none of those horrors that had marked the struggle between Marians and Sullans.

In Africa the governor P. Attius Varus had declared against Caesar and the Numidian king, Juba I, was his personal enemy. Caesar gave the command against them to the ex-tribune Scribonius Curio. Curio made a hasty dash into the valley of the Bagradas in pursuit of a Numidian force, which drew him into an ambush. Curio himself was killed, and two of the Caesarian legions were destroyed. His failure to secure Africa in the campaign of 49 had an important bearing on the later stages of the civil war, and for the time being it deprived Rome of one of its sources of corn-supply. But a food crisis in the capital was averted by the speedy capture of Sicily and Sardinia, which the Pompeians abandoned without a struggle.

The principal operations in the second campaign of 49 were conducted in Spain, where Pompey's men, L. Afranius and M. Petreius, commanded five legions. Caesar led a force of six legions against them. He found the Pompeian army firmly entrenched in a prepared position at Ilerda in the valley of the Sicoris (a tributary of the Ebro), which he could not hope to storm without heavy losses. But in forty days he dislodged them by means of his Gallic cavalry, headed off their retreat to the Ebro, and finally made them give in. This scared the remaining Pompeian forces in Spain to a speedy surrender.

2. *Dyrrachium and Pharsalus.*—Pompey had his head-quarters at Thessalonica. He withdrew the Roman garrisons from the eastern frontiers, so as to make up a total force of eleven legions. From the east he collected cavalry and a fleet far outnumbering the few ships of Caesar. At Dyrrachium on the Adriatic seaboard he formed a base for the recapture of Italy in the following campaign.

But early in 48 Caesar crossed the Adriatic, escaping the Pompeian blockade squadron. Pompey would not risk a pitched battle. With seven legions Caesar now tried to make a quick end to the war by besieging Pompey at Petra (close to Dyrrachium). But he was compelled by shortage of food, by

Pompey's skill as a general, and by the destruction of his transport ships to slip away to the cornlands of Thessaly where he found provisions for his half-starved men. Pompey followed him to Thessaly. He still distrusted his chances in open battle, but the nobles in his camp put pressure upon him and persuaded him to stake everything on a quick finish. On an open site near Pharsalus he drew up a battle-line of 35,000 to 40,000 men, against which Caesar could put no more than 22,000 into the field. His plan was to use his infantry to hold Caesar's in the front and his powerful cavalry to take him in flank and rear. But the cavalry was held up by specially picked infantrymen, whom Caesar had placed. The Pompeian horsemen fled. As soon as he had brought the enemy attack to a standstill Caesar threw in his remaining reserves. The Pompeian infantry fled, and at a loss of not more than 1200 men, Caesar killed not less than 6000 Pompeians and captured 24,000.

(B) *47–45 B.C.*

1. *Egypt and the East.*—After the battle of Pharsalus many Pompeian officers and admirals surrendered to Caesar. But in Greece and the Balkans a group of nobles collected the remnants of Pompey's army and embarked for Africa. Pompey had fled to seek protection with the young king, Ptolemy XII (son of Auletes). But the ministers of Ptolemy got rid of their embarrassing visitor by murdering him. Caesar stayed in Alexandria to collect the fee which Ptolemy Auletes had promised to pay for his recognition, and to settle a dispute between Ptolemy XII and his sister Cleopatra. Caesar gave such offence to Ptolemy's ministers that they set the royal army upon him and kept him blockaded in the palace quarter of Alexandria through the winter of 48–47. With a force scarcely exceeding 3000 men, Caesar became involved in street-fighting against the Ptolemaic troops, reinforced by the mob of Alexandria.

Caesar escaped with the help of troops collected in Cilicia and Syria by Mithridates of Pergamum, a son of a wealthy Pergamene. In the spring of 47 Mithridates got past the frontier-gate of Pelusium to the apex of the Delta, where

Caesar, eluding the patrols of Ptolemy, joined him. A few days afterwards the war was ended in a pitched battle near one of the western Nile arms, in which the royal camp was stormed by Caesar's troops and Ptolemy XII killed. The crown went to his younger brother, Ptolemy XIII; but the effective ruler of Egypt was Cleopatra, who had gained Caesar's favour during the siege of Alexandria.

In the summer of 47 Caesar began his return journey. From Syria he proceeded to Asia Minor, where he conducted a campaign against Pharnaces, son of Mithridates, who had re-occupied Pontus during the campaign of Dyrrachium. It was a hard-fought contest, and the placard which Caesar exhibited at his subsequent triumph, containing the telegraphic message *veni vidi vici*, hardly did justice to Pharnaces' soldiers. Yet this ended Caesar's five-day war in Asia Minor.

2. *Thapsus and Munda.*—At the end of 47 Caesar embarked for Africa. In this province the remnants of the Pompeian forces had been put together into ten new legions, to which King Juba brought a reinforcement of four Numidian legions trained by Italian officers, and the cavalry of the Pompeians had been raised to a strength of 15,000. For Caesar the African war was a race against time. Once he was surprised and nearly beaten by a strong cavalry division under Labienus; but he struggled through to shelter without any serious loss. After the arrival of his later convoys, which brought his numbers up to a total of eight legions, he tried to get his enemies to fight a pitched battle. His opportunity came during the siege of a city called Thapsus. By the rapidity of his attack he broke into the enemy line and rolled it up before it had completed its formation. During the pursuit Caesar's troops got out of hand and refused to take prisoners, so that Thapsus ended in a blood-bath. The last notable casualty was M. Cato, who had been left in charge of the Pompeian garrison at Utica, and who committed suicide. The younger Cn. Pompeius in Spain had been engaged after Pharsalus in raising new forces. After Thapsus he was re-inforced by refugees from Africa under Labienus and his brother Sextus and his army grew to fifteen legions, mostly made up of native recruits.

Caesar took the field with eight legions. He accepted a battle on ground which compelled his legions to deliver their attack uphill. The action of Munda was one of the hardest fought of Caesar's battles; but in the end he overthrew an enemy flank, and the fight was won. Though Sextus Pompeius lived on to wage new wars with Caesar's successors, no other important Pompeian officer survived the disaster of Munda, and the Pompeian troops were slaughtered indiscriminately. In March 45 Caesar had become the master of the Roman empire.

## Part 4 : *Caesar in Power*

### (A) *Reforms and Reconstruction*

1. *Rome and Italy.*—From the time when he re-entered Italy with his invading legions Caesar was at pains to show that he had no intention of repeating Sulla's methods. The first few weeks of his campaign in 49 proved to the Italians that they need fear no confiscations or plunderings. In this year and the next the captured enemy troops were either dismissed without harm or enrolled in new Caesarian legions. After Pharsalus all the adherents of Pompey who sought Caesar's mercy were pardoned and many of them were advanced by him in their political careers. M. Brutus, who had fought at Pharsalus, and C. Cassius, one of Pompey's best admirals, were promoted to praetorships in 44. Cicero, who had joined Pompey in 48, was granted a free pardon. Caesar's policy was justified by its results. The building of a temple to the 'Clemency of Caesar' was the most sincere of all the compliments which Senate and people paid to him in return.

In the days of Caesar the city of Rome had a population not far short of a million. There was serious overcrowding in its central quarters; and the difficulties of keeping the mob in order had been too great for the senatorial government. The scheme for reconstructing the centre of the city, which successive emperors carried out in the next two centuries, originated with Caesar. He also banned all private clubs, except associations of artisans and traders, and religious groups, such as the Jewish synagogues. He was the first, and perhaps the only, Roman statesman to deal effectively with the question of the idle mob. He reduced the number of those who got free corn from 320,000 to 150,000; he sent 80,000 of the disqualified recipients to his new colonies overseas. To ensure a more regular supply of corn he made plans for a better harbour at Ostia.

On his return to Rome in December 49 Caesar carried a bill to give full franchise to the people of Transpadane Gaul, partly in recognition of the valuable service which his Transpadane soldiers had given. Caesar's interest in the removal of constitutional absurdity is also shown in two statutes for the regulation of municipal government in Italy. In one of these acts he laid down uniform rules for the municipal *cursus honorum* and admission to the local senates; in the other he made arrangements for a more accurate and punctual municipal census.

As a financier Caesar was generous and efficient. His entertainments of the Roman mob, the handsome bounties and pensions for his soldiers, and his schemes of new public works, were expensive; and a permanent new burden was laid by him upon the treasury when he raised the yearly pay of the troops from 120 to 225 denarii. For this money he confiscated the estates of Pompeians who delayed their surrender after Pharsalus and imposed heavy fines upon the African and Spanish towns that had shown sympathy with them. After his return to Rome from the east he raised large sums by sales of privileges to dependent kings and cities. Thus he not only cleared himself of his debts, but accumulated a fund of 175,000,000 denarii in the treasury and of 25,000,000 for himself. From the plentiful stocks of precious metals in his possession he made the first regular gold coins at Rome, the *aurei* or equivalents of 25 denarii. Caesar also set right the Roman calendar based on the calculations of Sosigenes, an Alexandrian man of science. With a slight modification introduced in 1582 by Pope Gregory XIII, this calendar is still in use.

2. *The Provinces.*—In 77 and 76 Caesar prosecuted two of Sulla's governors; as consul in 59 he had tightened the law

relating to extortion. After Pharsalus he reduced the taxation of Asia and perhaps of other eastern provinces, which had suffered heavily from Pompey's officers, and transferred the rights of collection from Roman tax-farmers to the municipal governments. He limited the term of ex-praetors in the provinces to one year and that of ex-consuls to two, for fear of ambitious governors doing what he himself had done.

With these incidental innovations Caesar hardly touched the fringe of administrative reform in the provinces. Nevertheless his dictatorship was a period of fundamental importance in the history of the provinces, because at this time the first clear gaps were made in the barriers which had hitherto separated the provincials from the Italians. The Senate had not been able to prevent a considerable emigration of Italian peasants and traders but it disliked their settlement abroad, and only in rare cases had it sanctioned colonies on foreign soil. Caesar, on the other hand, kept the tide of emigration flowing fast. He drained off to the provinces the superfluous proletariat of Rome, and he pensioned off the greater number of his old soldiers with grants of provincial land — only a few had allotments on Italian soil. To all these overseas settlements he gave the status of Roman or of Latin colonies, and he gave similar privileges to some of the older groups of Italian residents abroad. Twenty colonies were constituted by him in the provinces, and more than 100,000 Roman citizens received new homes from him in foreign parts. In Spain his principal foundations were Hispalis (Seville) and Tarraco (Tarragona); in Gaul, Arelate (Arles) and Nemausus (Nîmes); in Africa, Cirta and Carthage. Since the time of Marius, Roman generals had made occasional grants of Roman citizenship to troops, but such enfranchisements had remained few and far between. Caesar, on the other hand, enfranchised *en masse* an entire legion which he had recruited in Narbonese Gaul. He also allowed for the future enfranchisement of all doctors and teachers living in Rome and he gave Roman or Latin status to citizens of several provincial towns. The first towns to receive full Roman franchise were Gades (Cadiz) and Olisipo (Lisbon) in Spain. Besides enrolling in the Senate many *novi homines* from the municipalities of

H

Italy, Caesar admitted to it some men of Narbonese Gaul, and got a tribuneship for a Spaniard, L. Decidius Saxa. This policy of gradually breaking down the distinction between Italians and provincials, and of converting the Roman empire from a military dominion into a commonwealth, was his most important contribution to Roman statesmanship.

Caesar had foreseen the need of extending the Roman frontiers in the Danube region as early as 58. An expedition which A. Gabinius led in 48–47 ended in disaster ; his successor, P. Vatinius, held the Delmatae in check, but did not gain ground.

Though the Parthian king Orodes had never followed up his victory at Carrhae, he had offended Caesar by agreement with Pompey during the civil war, and in 45 he gave support to a mutinous governor of Syria. Caesar conscripted 10,000 horsemen and an auxiliary force of archers to reinforce his legionary troops on the Parthian expedition ; instead of invading Babylonia, he intended to strike through Armenia and he was allowing himself no less than three years (44–42) to carry the war to a conclusion. In southern Russia he allowed Pharnaces to keep his throne. After the death of this ruler, who was supplanted *c.* 45 B.C. by his son-in-law Asander, he told Mithridates of Pergamum to add Pharnaces' possessions to his kingdom in Pontus, but he gave Mithridates no military support. Had Caesar been able to carry out his schemes of further conquest, he would no doubt have advanced the Roman boundaries in the east.

## (B) *Political Powers and Death*

The praetor Lepidus got Caesar made dictator in 49 B.C., and he had the office confirmed in 48. It was generally believed that he would not destroy the general framework of the republican constitution. Yet after his return from Africa in summer 46 it began to be thought that he might not follow the example of Sulla in abdicating his emergency powers. Although his dictatorial powers gave him ample authority, he took many additional offices and insignia. He held a consulship in 48, 46, 45 and 44, and a *praefectus morum* ('prefect of morals') with censorial powers in 46–44. In 44 he became a tribune. In the new calendar he allowed the month 'Quintilis' to be renamed 'Iulius'. His head appeared on coins and he allowed his statue to be set up in temples. His raising the number of aediles from four to six, of praetors from eight to sixteen, and of quaestors from twenty to forty might suggest on first impression that he intended to give more scope and a wider range of functions to the republican executive. Yet in 47, 46 and 45 he made no arrangements for the election of officials (other than tribunes) for the current year until summer or autumn, and he virtually appointed all the higher magistrates in advance by his personal recommendation. The routine business of administration, so far as it was done at all, was in the hands of Caesar himself or of his Magister Equitum ('Master of the Horse'). Caesar showed respect for the Senate, but deliberations on important matters of state were held in private, and to these he did not summon men like Cicero who were steeped in the senatorial tradition. His chief confidants were two equites, L. Oppius and C. Cornelius Balbus.

On February 14th, 44, Caesar assumed a new dictatorship, which was to be not merely of indefinite but of perpetual duration. On the same day he put on the purple robe of Rome's early kings instead of the purple-edged toga of the magistrate, and he replaced the magistrate's chair of ivory with a gilt throne. About this time he also accepted an official cult of himself at Rome, and allowed Antony to be appointed as his priest. These innovations placed Caesar's intentions beyond the range of doubt: he had come after all to destroy, not to reconstruct, the Roman republic.

On the precise form of his new monarchy Caesar had evidently not made up his mind at the time of his death. He toyed with the title of *rex*. On February 15th he refused a diadem offered to him by Antony; yet when a Sibylline oracle was interpreted to declare that none but a king might defeat the Parthians, he arranged for a formal motion in the Senate that he should adopt the royal name outside of Italy — an impossible compromise. In September 45 he had selected a possible successor to his kingship by adopting his grand-nephew, C. Octavius, in his testament; but the will was kept secret. In Rome a voice here and there might hiss at the name of *rex*; but the mob in general had no regard for republican tradition; it judged political actions by their material results, and by this standard Caesar's monarchy had every prospect of gaining its approval. The Senate, once the chief guardian of republican tradition, was being gradually transformed into the instrument of Caesar's will. Its membership, now raised to 900, consisted largely of Caesar's nominees. Indeed the Senate had virtually egged Caesar on to assume a crown by the number and the extravagance of its compliments. Yet individual senators resented Caesar. To Cicero, the dictator was henceforth 'the tyrant', and this opinion was widely echoed. The need of striking the blow for freedom quickly became clear when Caesar declared his intention of leaving Rome on March 18th. A group of sixty to eighty champions of the republic laid a plan to assassinate him at the Senate on March 15th. The originator of this plot, C. Cassius, and its figure-head, M. Brutus, were Pompeians, but the majority of their accomplices were former officers of Caesar. The conspiracy included men with personal grievances against the dictator, and some who hoped for a better career under a republic. Yet several of the ringleaders, such as D. Brutus and C. Trebonius, who had sided with Caesar in the civil war still stood high in his favour. Though vague rumours leaked out about the conspiracy, these were not sufficient to turn Caesar back from the place of meeting on the Ides of March — a room which was part of a stone theatre built by Pompey. There, unarmed and unattended, Caesar was quickly killed under a rain of dagger-thrusts.

Coin struck by M. Brutus to pay
his troops, 43–2 B.C.

### CHAPTER XII

## 44–31 B.C.

# Part I : *The Death of the Republic*

### (A) *The Rule of Antony*

THE senators who had killed Caesar went out to spread the glad news in the Forum ; but they found it almost deserted and from the few bystanders they drew but the faintest of cheers. Fearful for their own safety, they withdrew to the Capitol. Thus the conspirators let the initiative pass into the hands of Caesar's chief assistants, M. Aemilius Lepidus and M. Antonius. At the time of Caesar's death Lepidus, who was about to take up the governorship of Gallia Narbonensis and Hispania Citerior, had at the gate of Rome a legion of recruits waiting to proceed to France. He brought a detachment of these troops into Rome and prepared for an attack upon the Capitol. But he allowed affairs to be taken out of his hands by Antony, and a few days later he withdrew to his province. M. Antonius was, like Sulla and Caesar, a member of an ancient family ; he found his true vocation as a lieutenant of Caesar in Gaul. His strength and good humour endeared him to the troops, and his resourcefulness in the field commended him to Caesar, who promoted him to be his chief deputy in the civil war. In 44 he was Caesar's partner in the consulship. In fear for his own life he spent the Ides of March in hiding. But in the following night he got hold of Caesar's papers, which the dictator's widow, Calpurnia, willingly entrusted to him ; on the next day he took over the control of affairs from Lepidus. He held back Lepidus' soldiers and convened the Senate for the next day. On March 17th the senators carried the proposal of Cicero that the conspirators should receive pardon, but voted a public funeral for the dead dictator. The sight of Caesar's body and blood-stained toga, the recital of his will and a speech by Antony combined to stir the assembled crowds to frenzy, and the conspirators now fled from Rome to escape lynching.

Until the end of April 44 Antony persevered in his policy of compromise : the agreement between Antony and the Senate saved Rome from chaos after the Ides of March and suggested that the republican constitution could and would be restored. But at the end of April the situation was given a new turn by the arrival in Italy of Caesar's adopted son and heir, C. Octavius. Octavius was descended from a family of the Volscian town of Velitrae, recently passed from equestrian to senatorial rank. He was connected with the Julian gens by the marriage of his grandfather with a sister of Caesar. In 46 the dictator had met him; in 45 he had sent him to Apollonia in Epirus to begin his military training, and altered his will in the young man's favour. At the time of Caesar's death, Octavius was only eighteen. He suspected that he might have been remembered in his will and returned to Italy. Discovering that he was Caesar's heir and had been adopted as his son, he went to Rome where he took the name of C. Iulius Caesar Octavianus, and visited Antony to claim his share of the dictator's estate. Antony tried to bluff him out of his rights by a rude refusal, but found Octavius to be equally tough-minded. In May 44 a duel began between Antony and Octavian, in which the latter attempted to steal the sympathies of Caesar's old soldiers from Antony by the magic of his new name. Antony sought to protect himself against future attacks by means of a law which gave him a five years' command in Cisalpine and Narbonese Gaul and authorised him to transfer Caesar's legions from Macedonia to his new provinces.

In July 44 Antony quarrelled with M. Brutus and Cassius. The two chief conspirators objected to the provinces assigned to them for the next year — the Senate had given Crete to Brutus and Cyrene to Cassius — and asked for more important commands for themselves. Antony replied with threats which led Brutus and Cassius to believe that their lives were in danger. They resolved to arm in self-defence, and abandoned Italy in order to raise forces in the east.

Cicero had fallen into a state of despondency about the future of the republic, and had again retired from public life. On September 1st Antony took offence at his absence from the Senate. On the following day Cicero appeared in the House, and in the absence of Antony delivered his so-called *First Philippic*. Its effect was to irritate Antony into a violent reply which in turn startled Cicero into his last great political effort. He prepared at leisure the pamphlet known as the *Second Philippic*, in which he branded Antony as an immoral and ambitious traitor. In October Antony prosecuted Octavian on a false charge. Octavian called Caesar's veterans to arms, and the magic name of Caesar which he bore helped him. Several thousands of old soldiers joined him ; of the four legions which Antony had got from Macedonia two eventually went over to his side ; but neither would take the risk of striking the first blow. Antony diverted his troops to Cisalpine Gaul, which he had decided to take over from D. Brutus.

D. Brutus received instructions from Rome to hold firm. After Antony's departure for northern Italy Cicero returned to the city and launched his crusade in defence of the republic. He opened his campaign on December 20th with the *Third Philippic*, and in quick succession he delivered to Senate or people eleven further calls to action. By the force of his oratory he carried his point and attained a power such as he had never wielded before.

On December 20th Cicero got the Senate to agree that D. Brutus should stay on in his province until further notice. On January 1st, 43, in the *Fifth Philippic*, he urged that all the recent legislation of Antony, and in particular his claim to Cisalpine Gaul, should be repealed, and proposed that Octavian should be accepted as an ally against Antony, with the rank of propraetor. The Senate sent Antony a command to keep his hands off Cisalpine Gaul, made an ally of Octavian, and ordered the new consuls, A. Hirtius and C. Vibius Pansa, to raise additional troops.

Meanwhile Antony closed in upon D. Brutus and besieged

him in the town of Mutina. In reply to the Senate's demands he offered to evacuate Cisalpine Gaul at once, and Narbonese Gaul at the end of five years. But the Senate, instead of testing Antony's sincerity by further negotiations, repealed his legislation and proclaimed a state of emergency (February 43). Antony tried to starve out Brutus before the relief armies came. But Brutus was still holding out in April, when Hirtius and Pansa joined Octavian near the city. Antony sustained a serious defeat and retreated into southern France.

The Senate now took the extreme step of declaring him a public enemy. But Antony succeeded in joining with the reinforcements which his lieutenant, P. Ventidius, had been recruiting in Picenum ; by continuing his march into France he was able to win over to his side the governors of Gaul and Spain. In 43 Lepidus was stationed in Gallia Narbonensis with an army of seven legions, which included some of Caesar's best troops. Two other armies of considerable strength lay in Hispania Ulterior and in Gallia Comata (the newly-conquered part of Gaul) under two former officers of Caesar, C. Asinius Pollio and L. Munatius Plancus. To all these commanders Cicero sent dispatch after dispatch, exhorting them to support the republic. But each in turn, when confronted by Antony, deserted to him. Antony in effect became the sole commander of twenty-two legions. In the late summer of 43, Antony occupied Cisalpine Gaul without opposition. Decius Brutus, left unsupported, tried to escape to Macedonia. His army deserted him and he was killed by a brigand chief.

## (B) *The Second Triumvirate*

Hirtius was killed in action at Mutina and Pansa died of his wounds, so that Octavian was able to control the whole of the relief army. Octavian would not and could not combine with D. Brutus, the assassin of Caesar. At his first appearance in public life he had come forward to avenge Caesar. He therefore disregarded an instruction from the Senate to join with Brutus and to let Brutus have the chief command. The Senate treated him with disdain and refused to pay his army.

In July 43 Octavian decided to break with the Senate. He asked for one of the vacant consulships but the Senate rejected his ultimatum. Octavian marched on Rome, which he entered without opposition. At the consular elections Octavian was elected. His first act was to carry through the Popular Assembly a law to repeal the amnesty for Caesar's assassins, all of whom were declared outlaws. Since the two chief conspirators had powerful armies, another civil war was inevitable. He had already made offers to Antony via Lepidus, and after his return to Rome he repealed the sentence of outlawry on Antony, and met him and Lepidus at Bononia. The three chiefs there agreed upon a common future policy.

Antony, Lepidus and Octavian had a law passed which made them *triumviri rei publicae constituendae consulari potestate* ('board of three men to settle the constitution, with consular power') for five years. From this titulature it might be inferred that the object of their special commission was to wind up a state of war, after the manner of Sulla and Caesar. In point of fact, it was intended to give them an absolutely free hand in prosecuting further wars of their own making, and it threw the rule of the Senate and ordinary magistrates permanently out of gear. The fiction of popular election was still maintained, but the higher magistrates were nominated by the Three and functioned under their orders. The Senate was packed with their supporters.

The first practical demonstration of the new dictatorship was a wholesale political massacre. Three hundred senators and two thousand Equites were killed. A few of the victims eventually obtained a pardon, a great many more found refuge outside of Italy; but the slaughter was on a scale recalling that of Sulla's proscriptions, and it had even less excuse. The reason for this massacre was chiefly the need to raise without delay the enormous sums of money which both Octavian and Antony required to keep their promises to their troops.

The Triumvirate of Antony, Lepidus and Octavian was unstable. But its associates defined their spheres of power on geographical lines. They kept Italy as a common possession, so that each of them was free to raise troops and keep his own legions there : they shared out the man-power and the money of the western provinces between them. Antony took Gallia Comata, Lepidus Gallia Narbonensis and the two Spanish provinces, and Octavian was promised Sicily, Sardinia and Africa. Octavian also married Antony's stepdaughter Clodia. But for the time being the chief bond of union between the triumvirs was the need to reconquer the eastern provinces from M. Brutus and Cassius.

Brutus went first to Greece, where he gathered round himself a corps of officers. With this force he took over the province of Macedonia and won over the troops of P. Vatinius in Illyria. In February 43 he received from the Senate the legal status of a proconsul of Macedonia and Illyria. He then moved to Asia Minor to meet Cassius. In the meantime Cassius had returned to Syria, and persuaded all the soldiers there to serve under him. In taking command in Syria he was taking the place of Antony's colleague Dolabella, who had been legally appointed to govern this province in 44, and left Rome towards the end of 44 to take possession. On the way to Syria Dolabella made a surprise attack on another conspirator, C. Trebonius, who had held the province of Asia since 44, and killed him. He was declared an outlaw by the Senate, and Cassius received a commission to make war upon him with the Syrian armies. Cassius was able to besiege his enemy in the Syrian port of Laodicea, which he captured after a short siege. Dolabella committed suicide (summer 43). After the fall of Laodicea, Cassius co-operated with Brutus in taking possession of all Asia Minor. By the end of 43 the two arch-conspirators had acquired control of all the eastern provinces, and the support of all the dependent monarchs except Queen Cleopatra. They also had a powerful fleet.

Antony, unable to cross the Adriatic in the face of the enemy fleet, summoned Octavian to his aid. The combined forces of the two chiefs broke through the blockade and advanced without opposition as far as Macedonia. But here they were held by the armies of Brutus and Cassius, which had entrenched themselves in an impregnable position at Philippi. Antony forced Brutus and Cassius out of their entrenchments and first defeated the divisions of Cassius, who killed himself. Antony tempted Brutus to a second engagement which Antony won outright. Brutus in turn took his own life; the greater number of his high officers were executed after surrendering. Of the republican forces the fleet alone survived the disaster of Philippi.

## Part 2 : *The Victory of Octavian*

(A) *42–40 B.C.*

Antony and Octavian now got rid of their partner Lepidus. Octavian took Spain from him; Antony helped himself to Transalpine Gaul, but surrendered Cisalpine Gaul, which was treated from now on as part of Italy. The power of Antony within the Triumvirate was now at its height. As the victor of Philippi he could dictate his terms to Octavian, who had been little more than an onlooker. He reserved for himself an attractive occupation in the east; he relieved Lepidus of all active duties, and he gave Octavian a difficult job in Italy. This was to pension off some 100,000 soldiers, whose services were no longer required after Philippi. The confiscations of land which Octavian carried out in 41 for this purpose made him hated in Italy. Also, he was hard driven by Antony's wife Fulvia and by his brother L. Antonius. They pretended to share the indignation against Octavian; and they promised the soldiers far more handsome bounties from Antony out of the spoils of the gorgeous East. But they acted too quickly. In autumn 41 L. Antonius concentrated the troops which he commanded in his brother's name at Praeneste and made a dash upon Rome, where he promised to the people that Antony would restore the republic on his return, and obtained authority (probably in the form of a *Senatus Consultum Ultimatum*) to fight Octavian. But Octavian's troops stood firm by him in the hour of crisis, and while L. Antonius was in Rome, he made sure of his communications through northern Italy with Spain, to where he had recently sent the major part of his legions under an officer named Q. Salvidienus. Salvidienus returned to Italy, and with a friend of Octavian, named M. Vipsanius Agrippa, besieged L. Antonius in the Etruscan hill-city of Perusia. L. Antonius was starved into surrender (winter 41–40). Octavian sent part of his victorious troops to occupy Gaul and thus gained control over all the western half of the Roman empire in Europe.

Antony returned in 40, and when Octavian's commander at Brundisium refused him admission, he landed troops close by and blockaded the town. But eventually the triumvirs came to an understanding. Antony kept all the eastern provinces, but left Gaul and Spain in Octavian's hands, together with Illyria. Lepidus was confirmed in possession of Africa. In place of Fulvia, who had died at an opportune moment, Antony married Octavian's sister Octavia.

## (B) *40–36 B.C.*

1. *The War with Sextus Pompeius.*—Sextus Pompeius, son of Pompey, had been commissioned by the Senate in 43 to take command of the remains of Caesar's navy. After the fall of the republic he took possession of Sicily with Caesar's ships. After Philippi he took over the greater part of the surviving fleet of the republicans, and in 40 he disturbed Octavian by intercepting the corn supplies of the capital. Sextus gave support to Antony in the War of Brundisium, in which he added Sardinia to his possessions. Despite the efforts of Antony he was not admitted to the peace-treaty ; but in the following year he reduced Rome to such a state of famine that Octavian had to negotiate with him. At a conference near Misenum, in which Antony acted as peacemaker, Octavian agreed to recognise Sextus as a proconsul of Sicily and Sardinia on condition of his stopping the blockade of Rome. But these conditions were not strictly observed by either side and Octavian grabbed the island of Sardinia from a traitorous vice-admiral of Sextus. At this time also he married a lady named Livia, who already had one son (the future emperor Tiberius) from her former husband, Tib. Claudius Nero, and was expecting another (Nero Claudius Drusus).

In 38 Octavian made for Sicily with two squadrons from the Etruscan ports and from Tarentum, but mistimed his movements, so that Sextus was able to defeat the attacking fleets. He lost more ships in a storm, and disorder spread over Italy. Antony returned from the east to help and met his partner at Tarentum. In return for 120 warships, Octavian promised to give Antony 20,000 Italian troops. At the same time the Triumvirate, which had legally expired at the end of 38, was renewed to the end of 33. While the conference of Tarentum was dragging along, Agrippa was constructing a new fleet and patiently training its crews. Octavian's preparations went on for the whole of 37. In an attempt to attack Sicily with three separate fleets in 36, the squadron under Octavian's personal command was defeated near Tauromenium. But Agrippa landed troops on the northern shore and joined with Lepidus, who had meanwhile landed at Lilybaeum. With the enemy armies closing in upon his main base at Messana, Sextus had to fight a set battle at Naulochus, near the Straits. Each side had three hundred ships. Agrippa had chief command of Octavian's fleet for boarding operations. In the end all except seventeen of Sextus' vessels were captured or driven ashore. Sextus in person escaped to Asia Minor, where he was eventually killed. With 500 to 600 warships and 45 legions at his disposal, Octavian had so far outdistanced Antony that his partner could no longer catch him up. Thus secure, Octavian could afford to be kinder now. The Italians began to look to him as the restorer, not of the old republican liberties which seemed too much to ask for, but of orderly government. When Lepidus tried to assert himself by claiming Sicily, but was promptly deserted by his troops and disarmed, Octavian not only spared Lepidus' life, but allowed him to remain Pontifex Maximus. On his return to Rome the Senate gave Octavian the rights of a tribune, a sincere compliment; and Octavian undertook to restore the republic in due course.

2. *Antony in the East.*—After the battle of Philippi Antony made a tour of the eastern provinces, where he raised money from the unfortunate inhabitants for their unwilling submission to the exactions of Brutus and Cassius. This he intended to use for a war with the Parthians. He sent for Queen Cleopatra. At the time of Caesar's death Cleopatra was in Rome, presumably for the purpose of strengthening her hold on the throne of Egypt. After Caesar's murder she returned to Alexandria, where she killed her brother Ptolemy

XIII. In return for money Antony hunted down and executed her younger sister and rival Arsinoe.

Then King Orodes of Parthia made an attack upon Roman territory. He entrusted his forces to his son Pacorus and to a Roman refugee, Q. Labienus. Entering Syria at the head of a foreign army, Labienus won over the Roman garrison and captured the entire province (40 B.C.). Later in the same year he overran Asia Minor, while the forces under Pacorus broke into Palestine and carried off its ruler Hyrcanus. At the end of 40 the Roman empire had lost most of its Asiatic possessions. In the following two years, however, reinforcements sent by Antony under Ventidius swept the invaders back as fast as they had come. Labienus evacuated Asia Minor and the Parthians were driven from Syria. In 37 another general of Antony, C. Sosius, recaptured Jerusalem from Parthia. Herod, who had seen Antony and Octavian during a visit to Rome in 40, became its king.

In 36 Antony decided to make for the Persian plateau by way of Armenia. He arrived in Media Atropatene and laid siege to its chief town Phraaspa. But he was not able to capture it. In autumn 36, having neither provisions nor shelter for the bleak winter of northern Persia, he abandoned the siege and retreated through Atropatene and Armenia. He saved the greater part of his force. In 33 he advanced once more to the borders of Atropatene, but problems in Italy obliged him to turn back. Antony had missed his opportunity of eclipsing Octavian.

(c) *36–30 B.C.*

The year 36, which was a turning-point in Octavian's upward career, also marked the first stage in Antony's downfall. He fell under the influence of Cleopatra. The Parthian invasion had made him more dependent on her financial assistance, and he was already bewitched by her charms. The growing influence of Cleopatra over Antony was revealed by his attendance at the unending court festivities in Alexandria. He also declared that one of the queen's children, a youth named Ptolemy Caesarion, whom she had destined to be her successor in Egypt, was the son of the dictator Caesar. Antony also laid himself open to a more damaging attack by the so-called 'Donations of Alexandria'. On setting out for the Parthian expedition Antony made promises to enlarge Cleopatra's kingdom ; in 34 he confirmed and extended his grants. He gave away Media, Armenia and Parthia to any future sons of Cleopatra and himself and portions of Palestine and Nabataean Arabia to the queen in person. In addition, Antony made free with entire Roman provinces. Cyprus, Cyrene and southern Syria he gave to Cleopatra, northern Syria and Cilicia he kept for Caesarion. Had all these transfers of territory been carried into effect, the result would have been disastrous for the Roman empire.

Hitherto Antony and Octavian had co-operated fairly well. Cleopatra helped to sever their alliance. After 35 B.C. Antony refused to see Octavia and in 33 he consented to become Cleopatra's prince consort by Greek law. This may be regarded as the turning-point in the relations between the triumvirs. In 33 Octavian attacked and abused Antony. In this war of words, however, Antony at first held his own, but in summer 32 the news of Octavia's divorce and the publication of Antony's will, whose contents two deserters from Alexandria revealed to Octavian, at last turned the tide. The will disclosed Antony's wish to be buried at Cleopatra's side and completed the process of converting public opinion in Italy into Octavian's favour. Octavian was elected consul for 31 and obtained a formal declaration of war against Cleopatra. No direct measures were taken against Antony ; but since the Triumvirate had now expired, he became in the eyes of the law a mere soldier employed by the enemy queen. Octavian's diplomatic triumph was complete.

Octavian had material as well as moral advantages. In infantry Antony was fairly matched with Octavian, for he still had thirty legions, but he was definitely inferior at sea. Though he had raised the total number of his fleet to 500, Octavian probably had close on 600 ships of approximately equal tonnage, and his admiral, Agrippa, was the greatest naval tactician in Roman history. Moreover, the presence of Cleopatra in Antony's camp — for the queen had insisted on taking the field in person — was resented by many of Antony's officers, and weakened their loyalty. At the end of 32 Antony had moved forward as far as Greece. The site of his advanced base was on the bay of Actium. Octavian's troops meanwhile lay near the harbours of Brundisium and Tarentum. In 31 Agrippa succeeded in intercepting the enemy reinforcements and supply columns. At the same time Octavian's army harassed Antony's communications by land. Towards the end of summer Antony tried to retreat to Asia Minor. On September 2nd, 31, he came out of the bay with a fleet of two hundred galleys. His plan of escape was to sail away before the brisk sea breeze. Whether his fleet got out of hand, or disloyalty had spread among his officers, his order to hoist sail was badly obeyed. Cleopatra's squadron of sixty vessels broke through, and Antony slipped away to follow her with a few more ships. The remainder of his fleet became involved in a confused fight, and part of it was destroyed by fire.

In the actual engagement Agrippa inflicted no crushing losses. Yet the battle of Actium was decisive. The break-away of Antony after Cleopatra suggested to his suspicious followers that he had deliberately deserted them, and gave them a valid excuse for deserting him. His fleet at Actium surrendered to Octavian at once, and the army also. Antony and Cleopatra escaped to Egypt, but his troops everywhere made a prompt surrender, and Octavian entered Egypt without opposition. Antony and Cleopatra took their own lives. A few of Antony's officers were put to death but many were spared. Cleopatra's children by Antony were allowed to survive, but Caesarion, as a possible claimant of the Ptolemaic throne, was removed. Having abolished the Ptolemaic dynasty, Octavian turned Egypt into a Roman province and carried off the royal treasure. His victory was the most complete in the long series of Roman civil wars, and it was the most profitable.

## Part 3 : *Economic Conditions by the End of the Republic*

### (A) *Agriculture*

A change in the ownership of land in Italy and in some of the provinces had taken place. In Italy 120,000 allotments were provided by Sulla, 80,000 by Caesar, 170,000 by Octavian. But the disturbance created by these was less violent than might be thought. Many of the military settlers left the former owners in actual possession. Others sold their plots to rich traders, who were as eager as ever to convert their money into land. There is little evidence at this period of a rapid growth of latifundia, or of a squeezing out of the smaller peasants. In one respect the small proprietors of the first century were better off than those of the preceding age, in that they were no longer called upon to perform long spells of compulsory military service.

In the provinces large areas of land passed into the hands of men of Italian birth. Roman capitalists occupied land in Sicily and especially in northern Africa; and it was on the latifundia of the new Italian landlords that the vine and the olive were grown in Spain. The old soldiers of Marius were settled in Africa, and probably also in Narbonese Gaul. Caesar paid off most of his troops with Gallic or Spanish land. In 43 L. Plancus founded a veteran colony under the Senate's direction at Lugdunum; and Octavian used Narbonese Gaul to provide for the soldiers disbanded after Actium. Civilian settlements were made by Caesar at Carthage, Corinth and in Spain. The emigration from Italy is proved by the big recruitment of Italian soldiers in the provinces. Metellus Scipio raised several legions in Africa, and the younger Cn. Pompeius in Spain; the elder Pompey and Antony recruited Italian residents in the east.

Labour for the Italian latifundia was supplied by slaves. But the slave revolts in Sicily, and still more the war of Spartacus in Italy, had shown up the danger of large numbers of slaves, and some Italian landowners partly replaced their slaves by free farmers (*coloni*), who paid a rent (usually in money) in return for the use of the land. But the use of *coloni* was only small. The foreign wars and the slave trade still supplied plenty of labour, most of which continued to be used on the land. In most provinces, however, the Roman landowners used mostly *coloni* or free wage-workers.

In Italy methods of cultivation changed little. The capitalist landowners extended and improved the orchard farming which had been introduced in the second century. Before the end of the first century the best Campanian wines, such as those of the Ager Falernus and Mons Massicus, were as good as the choicest wines of Greece. North Italian wines were produced for export to Gaul and the Danube lands. After the opening up of the Near East by the Roman armies, oriental fruits and plants were farmed in Italy. Near Rome and Campania market-gardening, poultry-farming, bee-keeping and the cultivation of flowers made handsome profits.

## (b) *Industry and Trade*

Outside Italy industrial activity in the first century was small. In the eastern Mediterranean the continuous drain of wealth caused by the civil wars and the plunderings by Roman officials disorganised trade and industry. But there was great building activity, and skilled Greek craftsmen brought new prosperity to two ancient Italian industries, pottery and bronze. About 100 B.C. Capua exported bronze cooking utensils, wine-jugs and lamps to supply northern Europe as well as Italy. The Etruscan town of Arretium produced good imitations of Greek pottery. But the distribution of wealth in Italy was too unequal to provide a large market for sale, and no great fortunes were made from manufactures.

The commerce of the Mediterranean suffered from the political chaos of the later republic and from piracy. In its western countries the growth of trade was mainly due to the Italian middle class. The new business of providing Rome with corn was taken up by Italian merchants, who organised exportation from Sicily and Africa. In 113 the Numidian town of Cirta contained many Italian residents. In 46 the Italian trading community virtually controlled the city of Utica. The exportation of Italian wine and bronze-ware to Gaul and the Danube lands was carried on by Italian merchants. In the eastern Mediterranean the commercial activity of the Italians was greatest in Asia Minor, though the Levantine centres of production still had a monopoly at Alexandria and Rhodes.

The Roman business world continued to be chiefly concerned with money-dealing. The farming of provincial taxes

became much larger and each new conquest in Asia increased
it.    In Rome itself the opportunities of profitable money-
lending were restricted, but provincial cities and dependent
kings now began to use Roman money-lenders to pay off their
debts to the republic.    The high rates of interest demanded
(usually from 24 to 48 per cent) gave sufficient cover.    With
the first century the age of the millionaire at Rome began.
The triumvir M. Crassus, whose real estate alone was worth
50,000,000 denarii, had more than twice the wealth of his
ancestor P. Crassus, the richest Roman of the Gracchan
period.    But these huge fortunes were in a small number of
hands.    Rich men formed an insignificant minority in comparison with the 320,000 proletarians who were in regular
receipt of free corn *c.* 50 B.C.

Territory annexed (or bequeathed) to Rome by 44 b.c.
(numbers signify date of annexation)

Territory under Roman Protectorate in 44 b.c.

167

Lissus 146 Philippi

Dyrrachium Thessalonica

Brundisium Apsus

Apollonia Pharsalus

Corcyra

Actium

Sinope

Heraclea 64 Zela

74

133

64

Antioch 64

58 Laodicea

67

Alexandria

CYRENAICA

74

Coin of Augustus

### CHAPTER XIII

# AUGUSTUS

### (A) *Augustus and Caesar*

PERHAPS the strongest card in Octavian's hand had been that he bore the name, and consequently the prestige, of Caesar. Yet in his political arrangements and behaviour he used Caesar's career as an example of what not to do, more than as a model to be followed. Undoubtedly the thought foremost in the minds of contemporary Romans could be expressed in the obvious question: 'Will Octavian be another Caesar?' This question Octavian answered by a definite 'No'.

Caesar had not been a bloodthirsty tyrant: but he had been a tyrant, and had underestimated the importance which contemporary Romans attached to constitutional form. His signs of megalomania, his ambition, his perpetual dictatorship, and his general carelessness for outward appearances all seemed intolerable to the outraged aristocrats who assassinated him. Augustus, though we may consider him inferior to Caesar in many respects, took immense pains to avoid Caesar's error: and it was his superiority in this vital respect which enabled him to succeed where Caesar had failed.

Augustus, of course, always held a virtual monopoly of the real power — chiefly by retaining control of the legions. He governed by persuasion, but it was the sort of persuasion no wise man would resist. But he succeeded in inducing a general acquiescence in his system. For this he used three main methods :

1. He took a good deal of trouble to disguise his power beneath constitutional forms. On paper at least, he never held any office which could not be paralleled in republican history — and often refused offices, such as the dictatorship, which could be so paralleled. He used the powers of wholly respectable republican officials — of the consulship, the tribunate, the censorship, and so on. In theory his title of *princeps* ('first citizen') was only a courtesy title, and carried no legal power with it : he was *princeps inter pares*, 'first citizen among his equals'. To Caesar's quality of clemency he added the quality of tact.

2. He relied upon the greater efficiency of his regime to make itself felt, and hence to make the regime popular. The more centralised control of affairs under the personal supervision of himself and his staff was, of course, a much more efficient system than the haphazard government of an oppressed and anxious Senate : and anyone who had lived through the previous decades of civil war and senatorial incompetence would easily see the superiority of the Augustan system.

3. He relied on the natural supporters of the regime to defend it against actual or possible criticism on the part of the nobles. These supporters derived mainly from the middle class, a group which had long felt itself under-privileged when compared either with the senatorial aristocrats or with ambitious war-lords like Sulla, Marius, Pompey and Caesar. Much of his propaganda was directed towards emphasising the virtues of his regime which would appeal to this group : peace, sound morality, economic prosperity, and above all the real possibility of middle-class Romans bettering themselves in one of the many careers which Augustus threw open to them.

All these methods, as we shall see, paid off handsomely. Plots against the Augustan regime were infrequent, and effectively crushed : the criticism of the nobles was at least muffled : and the loss of completely free speech and open government was compensated by the obvious merits of the system. It is arguable that Caesar could hardly have succeeded in doing this, and that Rome was not yet ripe in 44 B.C. for an autocracy, however skilfully disguised. Certainly the bloodshed between 44 B.C. and 29 B.C. gave Augustus two advantages : first, a great many nobles who might have caused trouble had been killed in battle or by proscription : and second, Rome in general was far more ready to have civil peace at any price. But this hardly diminishes the greatness of Augustus' achievement and of his statesmanship.

(B) *Constitutional Settlement*

In the summer of 29 Octavian had the entire military strength of the empire at his disposal ; and he brought with him the treasure of the Ptolemies, which enabled him to pay off the troops and left him with a surplus for distribution to the people. It was now thirty years since the republican government had been in anything like normal working order ; the memory of liberty was becoming faint, and the nobles who had been the most active guardians of the republican tradition had been reduced in numbers and strength by the civil wars. Above all, Octavian was now welcomed as the Prince of Peace who had ended a period of civil war.

Octavian might have tried to set up an absolute monarchy in 29 with far greater chances of success than Caesar in 44. But he attempted a compromise, in which his guiding principle was to reserve for himself the military and foreign policy of the empire and a general supervision over the civilian administration, but to hand over the details of civilian government to two privileged classes of public servants, the *senatorius ordo* and the *equester ordo*. In 32 he had carried on with his triumviral powers. From 31 to 28 inclusive he assumed the quasi-dictatorial powers which attached to the consulship when reinforced by a *senatus consultum ultimum*.

In 29 and 28 he obtained for himself and Agrippa a special grant of censorial power, which he used to reduce the Senate from 1000 to 800. In 18 he cut the membership down to 600. He brought back the Sullan system of automatic recruitment from ex-quaestors ; but he restricted the right of seeking the quaestorship to the members of a limited *senatorius ordo*, and he made admission to this order dependent on personal integrity, a term of military service, and the possession of a minimum of 800,000, subsequently raised to 1,000,000 sesterces. For entrance into the *equester ordo* the property qualification remained, as before, at 400,000 sesterces. In practice, the two orders came to be mostly recruited from the governing classes of the Italian towns. The *senatorius ordo* tended to become a hereditary body, as indeed Octavian meant it to be. It naturally included all the survivors of the old governing families ; yet its membership was drawn from a far wider area than that of the republican nobility.

In 27 Octavian made a formal offer to resign all his offices. The Senate rejected his proposal and by that fact recognised him as indispensable. Having thus acquired moral authority to continue in office, he came to terms with the Senate in regard to the future division of political functions. On January 16th, 27, the Senate, acting on a suggestion from him, gave him the new cognomen of 'Augustus'. The new name sharply distinguished him from Octavian, the triumvir and military despot.

In the new sharing-out of power the Senate received back into its hands the supervision of Rome and Italy, and of one-half of the provinces. It resumed control of Sicily, Sardinia and Corsica, southern Spain (henceforth known as 'Baetica'), Illyria, Macedonia, Achaea (or Greece, which was now constituted as a separate province), Asia, Bithynia, Crete and Cyrene (which were combined into a single province), and Africa. Later it surrendered Sardinia and Corsica, and Illyria ; but it obtained Cyprus and Gallia Narbonensis. Its members lost the right of sitting as jurors in the criminal courts — a privilege now shared by the *equester ordo* with people possessing the lower property qualification of 200,000 sesterces. The number of the magistrates was again fixed on a similar scale to that of the later republic ; but the age-limit for the quaestors was lowered to twenty-five, and for the consuls to thirty-five. In 27 and the following four years, Augustus continued to hold successive consulships, and either by *imperium proconsulare*, or *imperium consulare*, he retained all the provinces which he had not handed back to the Senate. The acting governors in the imperial provinces received his directions from Rome.

In 23 Augustus resigned the consulate which he had held continuously since 31, and henceforth resumed it only on rare occasions. But he brought into active use the *tribunicia potestas* ; by virtue of this power he convened the Senate and presented legislation to the Tribal Assembly of the people and over the senatorial provinces. He had a direct proconsular authority over the provinces outside senatorial control ; in 18, 13 and 8 B.C., and again in A.D. 3 and 13, he obtained a formal renewal of his *proconsulare imperium*. By the redistribution of provinces in 23 Augustus took for his share northern and western Spain (henceforth known as Hispania Tarraconensis and Lusitania), Gallia Comata (subsequently divided into the three separate provinces of Aquitania, Lugdunensis and Belgica), Sardinia and Corsica, Illyria, Galatia, Syria and Cilicia (which were combined into one command), and Egypt. All provinces created after 23 were also included in his sphere of power.

Augustus had the right of presenting candidates for magistracies by direct nomination and to nominate the jurors for the *quaestiones*. All incoming magistrates swore an oath to observe all his decrees ; and he obtained special authority to conclude treaties with foreign powers, without submitting them to Senate or people.

Augustus claimed that in 27 he had 'handed back the republic to the authority of Senate and people', and that he had reduced himself to the status of a magistrate. On inscriptions and coins, and in the literature of the day, his settlement was hailed as a 'restoration of the republic'. This assertion contained some truth. From 27 B.C. Augustus was an official who, in theory, held his power by gift of the Senate and people, and subject to the sovereignty of the laws. His powers were for the most part covered by precedents from the history of the later republic. Successive consulships had been held by Marius ; proconsulships in several provinces and over long terms of years had been accorded to Lucullus. Caesar and

Pompey ; and Pompey had set an example of governing provinces while still in Rome.

In 23 and again in 19 B.C. riots in Rome, probably due to food shortages, made the Senate give to Augustus *imperium consulare*. He refused offers of a dictatorship. He kept the Senate informed of his own decisions and consulted it on questions of policy. In contrast to Caesar, Augustus was at pains to maintain the outward appearance of a republican magistracy. He carried no insignia except those of a consul (which he was authorised to retain after 23). His house on the south-eastern edge of the Palatine resembled the mansion of a great nobleman rather than the palace of a king. Though Augustus maintained a bodyguard, he made it as inconspicuous as possible ; to all comers he was 'citizen-like' in his bearing. Lastly, the title of *princeps* or 'first citizen' under which he summed up his position was wholly in keeping with republican usage. But Augustus controlled the entire armed forces of the state and most of its money. Every Roman soldier continued to take the oath of allegiance to him and to look to him for his material rewards, as in the days of the Triumvirate, and all acting commanders of Roman armies were his subordinates. Augustus never surrendered this power ; in the last resort he held the power of life and death over all the inhabitants of the Roman empire. In effect, the *princeps* was swallowed by the *imperator*, and the name of 'emperor', by which the modern world usually calls Augustus and his successors, indicates the real position. Moreover, the new *senatorius ordo*, whether from lack of experience or by a sheer failure of nerve, failed to provide a better administration than that of the republican nobility, and the Senate gradually withdrew the various administrative services of Rome from the magistrates under its direct control and transferred them to new officials nominated by the emperor. Once Augustus was recognised as the supreme power in the state, he found himself saddled with an increasing number of cases which proceeded not merely from the provinces under his direct control, but from the senatorial provinces, and from Rome and Italy ; so that the imperial court of appeal gradually established itself as a regular part of the constitution.

Lastly in 12 B.C. the office of Pontifex Maximus was offered to Augustus and accepted.

### (c) *The Civil Service*

Augustus started a special civil service of his own, which expanded under his successors into the most extensive bureaucracy of ancient times. For the administration of the provinces of which he was proconsul, he appointed acting governors called *legati Augusti pro praetore* or (as in Egypt) *praefecti*; and to these he attached a staff of *procuratores* as his financial agents. In Rome there was a civil service under *curatores* or *praefecti*. These imperial officials were recruited from the senatorial and the equestrian orders, on the general principle that governorships of provinces and high military posts should be reserved for senators, while the civilian functions were mostly given to men of equestrian rank. The new officials carried on their work from year to year and received a generous salary. Many of the imperial officials made a life's career of their administrative work, and most of them served long enough to acquire special skill in their duties. The gradual substitution of a professional public service for the amateur magistracy of the republican period was one of the most far-reaching of all the constitutional changes made by Augustus : it put into the hands of the emperors a far more powerful machine than the Senate ever possessed.

Augustus held at his disposal a large staff of ex-slaves of his household who served as his accountants and secretaries. Though these assistants were technically his private servants, they formed the nucleus of a large and important branch of the civil service. Two *praefecti praetorio* ('prefects of the pretorian guard') held command of a corps of nine battalions, each of five hundred picked soldiers, who acted as the emperor's guards and as his servants. In addition to their strictly military duties, the *praefecti praetorio* carried out the functions of imperial chiefs-of-staff. A masterful personality in this position might become in effect a prime minister. Augustus entrusted it only to men of equestrian rank.

Though Augustus did not form a Privy Council, he laid the

foundations of such a body.   In 27 B.C. he set up a committee
of the Senate, consisting of the two consuls, of one representative from each of the other magistracies, and of fifteen private
members selected by lot, for a period of six months.   In A.D. 13

STATUE OF AUGUSTUS IN THE VATICAN

he added to this committee members of the imperial family
and other members of the equestrian order, and he carried
out its recommendations without submitting them to the
Senate for confirmation.   Augustus also convened from time
to time informal *consilia* for law suits, according to the ordinary

custom of the republican magistrates. From these two sources the *Consilium Principis* was eventually derived.

The difference between political theory and practice in Augustus' constitution became the cause of many misunderstandings between the emperors and the Senate, and the uncertainty placed a severe strain upon both. But the vagueness of Augustus' constitution had this great merit, that it conformed to the sound Roman tradition of making political changes by slow and gradual steps. He achieved lasting results, for his scheme of government survived for more than two centuries.

### (D) *Rome and Italy*

With Agrippa's help Augustus did much for the city of Rome. He built another aqueduct, organised a fire-brigade and appointed a *praefectus* to take care of the corn supply. He cut down the number of those receiving free corn to 200,000 (between 5 and 2 B.C.). In public entertainments Augustus accepted the republican nobles' policy of keeping the town mob amused. He left the old-established *ludi* (circus races and dramatic performances) in the hands of the aediles and praetors, but he provided other amusements out of his own purse. The gladiatorial contests became almost an imperial monopoly.

To repress riots he reaffirmed Caesar's ban on *collegia*, but organised a police force. For public peace he made permanent the office of the *praefectus urbi* and equipped him with three *cohortes urbanae*, each one thousand strong, and organised in military fashion. The urban cohorts could be reinforced by the nine *cohortes praetoriae*. Henceforth the mob of Rome was kept well under control.

Italy now included Cisalpine Gaul and had some ten million free inhabitants. The government of the 474 separate towns had by now become sufficiently standardised and brought into line with the central administration at Rome. In addition to the settlements of veterans made during the Triumvirate, Augustus established several military colonies after the battle of Actium, including Ateste, Augusta Praetoria and Augusta Taurinorum. He arranged for large numbers of young men

from the leading municipal families to join the senatorial and
equestrian orders at Rome. By this gradual but far-reaching
process the Italians became in the fullest sense the partners of
the Romans in the government of the empire. The emperor
gave money for building to many individual towns, and he
undertook to carry out a thorough repair of the road system,
which had received little attention since the days of Caius
Gracchus. Augustus paid out of his own purse the costs of
reconstructing the via Flaminia. He created in 20 B.C. a
permanent board of *curatores viarum* ('supervisors of the
roads').

But Augustus' principal gift to Italy was greater public
security. A special force of police was formed by the emperor
to patrol the country districts. A greater and more permanent
cause of insecurity was removed when Augustus extended the
Roman frontier beyond the Alps and thereby gave Italy two
centuries of freedom from foreign invaders. During the
reign of Augustus Italy as a whole made a rapid recovery from
the disorders of the triumviral period ; but its northern
regions in particular profited by the establishment of the
imperial peace.

## (E) *Moral, Social and Religious Laws*

Owing to the civil wars of the first century the population
of the country had suffered heavy losses, and the general un-
settlement of the period had weakened the old traditions of
Italian family life. Partly to ensure an adequate number of
citizens, and partly to reinforce his political regime by a soundly
established morality, Augustus used his tribunician power in
19 B.C. and after to make a number of marriage laws. By
these all unmarried men above a certain age were required to
marry, and all widowers below a certain age were required
to re-marry within three years, while to those who had three
or more children rapid advancement in their public careers
was offered. A new law on adultery reaffirmed the right of a
father to kill both the guilty parties, and of a husband to take
the life of the adulterer, and made unfaithfulness a public
crime as well as a private offence. Persons convicted of
adultery became liable to banishment to some small island.

THE *ARA PACIS*—*TERRA MATER* AND THE SYMBOLS OF PEACE AND PLENTY

Augustus' marriage-code was not successful, and was never enforced in any consistent manner.

Augustus maintained the restrictions which barred freed-men from the *cursus honorum* in Rome or the Italian munici-palities. But he gave them compensation by inventing some minor offices which were wholly or mainly confined to their class. In Rome he created the *vicomagistri*, local officials who assisted in the fire-service and had charge of the *ludi com-pitalicii* (local games). In many Italian and some provincial towns he encouraged the *Seviri Augustales* (or *Augustales* for short), six minor officials, mostly freedmen, who took control of some of the public entertainments. The *Augustales* were expected to subscribe freely to the festival funds out of their own pockets ; but wealthy freedmen (of whom there were many) willingly paid to get on a higher rung of the social ladder.

Augustus systematically repaired disused temples in 28 B.C. As Pontifex Maximus he carefully supervised the worship of Vesta and arranged a performance of the Ludi Saeculares ('hundred-year games') in 17 B.C. The festival, to which all Italy had been invited, lasted three days. Its main episode was a rite in front of Apollo's new shrine on the Palatine, at which a chorus of youths and maidens sang an ode composed for the occasion by Horace, and the sacrifice was offered by Agrippa and Augustus in person.

These and other measures, among which should be noticed his use of inscriptions on coinage and his patronage of out-standing authors whom he persuaded to write in support of his regime, formed a vital part of Augustus' propaganda. He worked hard at winning support by propagandist methods for the regime, and its stability was to a large extent due to their success.

## (F) *Frontiers of the Empire*

Augustus knew that Rome had reached the turning-point in its history, at which foreign warfare would in general be too expensive. Beyond the existing boundaries of the empire there were hardly any states left with gold and silver, or wide areas of good soil to repay the costs of conquest. Towards

I

## THE ROMAN EMPIRE
### under Augustus, Trajan and Hadrian

Roman Miles
0  50 100   200    300    400

English Miles
0  50 100   200    300    400

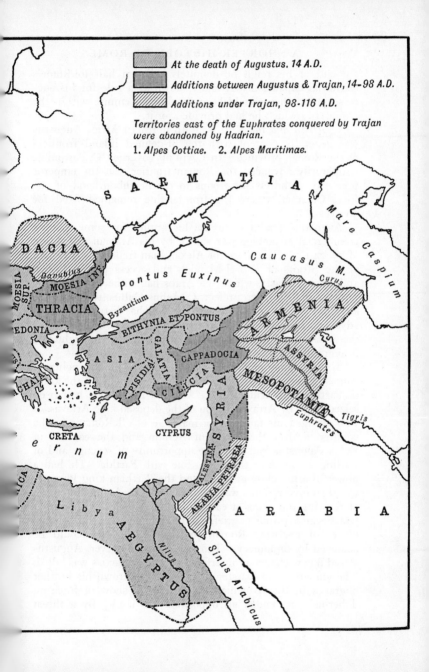

At the death of Augustus, 14 A.D.

Additions between Augustus & Trajan, 14-98 A.D.

Additions under Trajan, 98-116 A.D.

Territories east of the Euphrates conquered by Trajan
were abandoned by Hadrian.
1. Alpes Cottiae. 2. Alpes Maritimae.

SARMATIA

Mare Caspium

DACIA

Danubius

Caucasus M.

MOESIA INF.

Pontus Euxinus

Cyrus

MOESIA SUP.

THRACIA

Byzantium

ARMENIA

EDONIA

BITHYNIA ET PONTUS

ASIA

GALATIA

CAPPADOCIA

ASSYRIA

PISIDIA

MESOPOTAMIA

ACHAIA

CILICIA

SYRIA

Euphrates

Tigris

CRETA

CYPRUS

PALESTINA

ernum

ARABIA PETRAEA

ARABIA

ICA

Libya

AEGYPTUS

Nilus

Sinus Arabicus

the end of his reign he definitely called a halt to Rome's territorial expansion and laid it down as a rule for his successors that they should keep the Roman empire within the boundaries which he had provided for it.

1. *Africa and the Red Sea.*—In northern Africa Augustus was generally content with the ill-defined inland frontiers of the Roman province. In Egypt his governor, C. Petronius, temporarily advanced the Roman frontier, but the emperor presently withdrew his troops to the neighbourhood of the First Cataract, where the frontier-line remained fixed for 300 years.

Augustus' readiness to use his armies for some definite commercial advantage was shown by his Arabian expedition of 25–24 B.C. To secure for Alexandrian traders the freedom of the Straits of Bab-el-Mandeb and access to the Indian and Somali coasts, which the Arabs had hitherto barred, he directed the Egyptian prefect, C. Aelius Gallus, to invade the kingdom of the Sabaeans (in the Mocha district). Gallus advanced from the Nabataean port of Leuce Come as far as the Sabaean capital, Mariaba. The Sabaeans were frightened into granting a free passage to the Straits.

2. *Asia Minor and the Euphrates.*—In the eastern policy of Augustus the chief problem lay in his relations with the kings of Parthia and Armenia. In Armenia the throne had been seized in 33 by Artaxias, a son of the deposed king Artavasdes who avenged his father by a massacre of all Romans in the country. After the battle of Actium and the capture of Egypt Augustus had a unique opportunity of revenge and of settling accounts at the same time with Parthia. He had a powerful army close at hand, and the Parthian king Phraates was then involved in a war. But the emperor had no intention of reviving the plans of eastern conquest which had brought Crassus and Antony to grief, and he reckoned that the essential object of restoring Roman prestige in the east could be achieved by diplomacy. Ten years later, however, Augustus seized a new chance of interference, when Artaxias was killed. The emperor sent his stepson Tiberius to crown his brother Tigranes in the Armenian capital, and a show of force on Tiberius' part ended all opposition (20 B.C.). By a threat

of invasion Tiberius obtained from the Parthian king the surrender of all his Roman prisoners and all the captured ensigns.

After the death of Tigranes (*c.* 6 B.C.) Armenia again came under Parthian rule ; yet the emperor did nothing till his grandson Caius Caesar, in 1 B.C., put another pro-Roman prince (Ariobarzanes) upon the Armenian throne.

The dealings of Augustus with Armenia and Parthia might be described as a half-hearted compromise between a resumption of Caesar's and Antony's plans of conquest, and a frank abandonment of Armenia to Parthian overlordship. But the latter course, which was ideally the best solution of Rome's eastern problem, might have given serious offence at Rome ; the former was a gamble for a stake of very doubtful value. In the event, Augustus secured the Roman frontier against invasion, and made adequate amends for past Roman defeats, without any heavy expenditure in men and money.

In Asia Minor there was a group of rebels in the Taurus mountains. In 25 B.C. Augustus annexed Galatia and took over responsibility for the peace of the mountain region. At some date between 12 and 4 B.C. he told the governor of Galatia, P. Sulpicius Quirinius, to seek out the principal bandits, the Homonadeis, in their lairs on the high border-lands towards Cilicia. After several campaigns Quirinius finally pacified this district.

3. *Western Europe.*—In Spain Augustus finally conquered the peoples of the northern and north-western mountain border in a hard and merciless warfare lasting from 26 to 19 B.C. The task was completed by Agrippa, who transferred the mountain peoples to the Castilian plateau.

In Gaul Caesar had done his work so thoroughly that after his death no big rebellion took place. In Aquitania minor campaigns were fought by Agrippa in 39 and by M. Valerius Messala in 30. But Augustus' task in Gaul was administrative rather than military. During his reign some twelve new towns were founded in various parts of the country.

A journey to Gaul and Spain which the emperor under-took in 27–26 B.C. gave rise to rumours that he was about to invade Britain. But Augustus never departed from Caesar's final decision to leave Britain to its own devices, for the characteristic reason that a conquest and occupation of that country would be too expensive. On the other hand, Augustus seriously contemplated the conquest of Germany. For some thirty years after Caesar's death the Rhine frontier had proved itself an adequate barrier against German invasions of Gaul. In 16, however, an attack by the Sugambri and other peoples of the middle Rhine resulted in the loss of a Roman legionary standard. This served as an excuse for a systematic invasion of German territory by the Romans. Augustus' policy was primarily intended to put Gaul beyond the reach of German attacks. Its other intention was probably to establish a new frontier (presumably along the Elbe), so as to cut off the sharp angle between the Rhine and the upper Danube (to which the Roman boundary had by now been advanced). About this time Augustus' reorganisation of the Roman army had been completed and his stepsons Tiberius and Drusus had reached a sufficient age for the conduct of a major campaign.

In 12 B.C. and the next three years Drusus overran Western Germany as far as the Elbe. His fleet sailed out of the Rhine and the Zuyder Lake through a specially constructed canal into the North Sea, and opened up relations with the seaboard tribes of the Batavi and Frisii, who were enrolled as allies on condition of supplying auxiliary troops to the Roman army. The death of Drusus on his return from the Elbe in 9 B.C. ended the first stage of the Roman invasions. His place was taken by his elder brother Tiberius, who consolidated the previous gains (8–7 B.C.). In 5 B.C. a general named L. Domitius Ahenobarbus discovered a new line of advance into Germany from the upper Danube by the valley of the Saale and made a reconnaissance beyond the Elbe.

In A.D. 4 and 5 Tiberius resumed his summer marches across western Germany. In A.D. 6 Tiberius planned another movement, whose object was to conquer the Marcomanni, the only German people this side of the Elbe that lay outside the reach of the Romans. After the campaigns of Drusus this tribe had been withdrawn by its ruler Maroboduus from the lower Main to Bohemia, where it conquered or displaced the Boii enemies. Maroboduus introduced Roman equipment and Roman discipline into his army of 75,000. Tiberius attacked him with two large forces. One army under his personal leadership advanced northward from Carnuntum on the middle Danube, while the other followed the Main in an easterly direction. The two arms of the Roman pincers had nearly closed upon Maroboduus when a serious revolt in Tiberius' rear compelled him to retreat.

Since 12 B.C. Germany, to the north of the Main and to the west of the Elbe, was being gradually reduced to a province. Lacking towns and wealth, it could not yet be brought within the framework of ordinary provincial administration, and no permanent Roman camps were established in it. But the country was regularly patrolled by Roman troops. German chieftains looked after the altars set up for the worship of the emperor, their sons served in the Roman auxiliary forces, and the folk appeared to be submitting to Roman rule. But at the end of his reign the ageing Augustus undid the work by sending out an unsuitable governor, P. Quintilius Varus. Varus' folly started a revolt among the Germans. In A.D. 9 a young chieftain of the Cherusci named Arminius, who had served in the Roman forces and had been admitted to the Ordo Equester, organised a rebellion in which he turned his knowledge of Roman warfare against his teachers. Enticing Varus into unfamiliar country between the Weser and the Ems, he virtually annihilated a Roman force of 20,000 men. Reinforcements were hurried to the Rhine, and the Romans could have recovered all the lost ground. But the disorder had so shaken Augustus that he made no serious effort to retrieve it ; at his death the line of the future Roman frontier remained unsettled.

4. *The Danube.*—At the end of Augustus' reign the boundaries of the empire in central and eastern Europe had been completely redrawn. In 35–34 the approaches to the St. Bernard passes were partly cleared by Valerius Messala ; in 25 his work was completed by Terentius Varro Murena. A high-road was now built across the Little St. Bernard, which was guarded by a military colony at Augusta Praetoria. In 14 B.C. the coastal frontier strip was finally cleared of Ligurian bandits. The Mt. Cenis route was left in the hands of a

trustworthy native chieftain named Cottius, but a detachment of Roman troops was kept at the border town of Segusio.

The security of the north Italian plain against the Raeti (who inhabited the central and eastern Alps) was achieved in the single campaign of 15 B.C. While Tiberius ascended the Rhine valley from the neighbourhood of Basle to Lake Constance, Drusus passed from the valley of the Adige into that of the Inn and the Danube. The two brothers occupied the country of the Vindelici, a Celtic tribe between the Rhine and the upper Danube, so as to extend the Roman boundary to the Danube. The territory became a separate province with the name of Raetia.

An advance of the Roman frontier from the line of the Save into Noricum and Pannonia was undertaken by Augustus about 16 B.C. Noricum was easily overrun and became a province. Pannonia required four years of hard fighting (12–9 B.C.) under the leadership of Tiberius. In A.D. 6 a rebellion led by a Pannonian chieftain, Bato, rose in Tiberius' rear while he was engaged in Bohemia. But Tiberius, with prompt support from the Roman troops in the Balkans, soon stopped the invasion. At Siscia on the Save he held up the main Pannonian attack. In A.D. 7 reinforcements from Italy and Asia Minor, which brought up the Roman forces to a total of nearly 100,000 men, enabled him to resume the offensive. Two campaigns brought about the surrender of the Pannonians. Pannonia became a separate province, and Illyria was shortly afterwards renamed Dalmatia.

The conquest of Raetia, Noricum and Pannonia completed a process of advancing the Roman frontiers to the Danube which had been begun on the lower reaches of that river immediately after the battle of Actium. In 29 Augustus gave some of the legions left over from the campaign of Actium to M. Licinius Crassus. With these Crassus conquered the Moesian and Thracian peoples bordering the Danube (29–28 B.C.). The Thracian tribes were for the present left under their own kings, but the Moesians of Serbia were incorporated into Macedonia. After a rising in 11–9 B.C., which was repressed by troops from Galatia, northern Thrace was absorbed into the kingdom of the Odrysae, whose rulers had been in

alliance with Rome for two centuries. For the defence of the
Danube a separate province of Moesia was constituted c. A.D. 6.

In making the Roman boundary along the Danube,
Augustus made a greater addition to Roman territory than any
Roman conqueror before or after him, and he established a
new frontier line whose vital importance was proved in later
Roman history. The new Danubian lands brought less economic profit to the Romans than Gaul, but they proved an
even more valuable recruiting area.

The conquests of Augustus gave the Roman empire a
nearly unbroken ring of easily defensible frontiers — oceans,
deserts and rivers. His policy of extending the empire to
certain well-considered limits, and no further, was fully
justified by its results.

### (G) *Military Reforms*

The number of the Roman legions, which in 31 stood as
high as seventy or seventy-five, was cut down to twenty-seven
or twenty-eight. On the other hand, the auxiliary forces of
light infantry and horsemen became a regular establishment.
At the end of Augustus' reign the Roman army numbered
from 250,000 to 300,000 men, of whom half served in the
legions and half in the auxiliaries. This force was only just
enough to hold a frontier line exceeding 4000 miles.

Augustus extended the Roman state's right to recruit
troops by compulsion to the provinces. It became common
to fill up the auxiliary troops from newly conquered territories
such as the Danube lands. But generally the voluntary system
of recruitment, which had plainly justified itself since the
time of Marius, was maintained. Italy was now showing the
bad effects of the decline in the number of its free farmers,
but its northern districts at least continued to be one of the
principal recruiting grounds of the legions. In the east the
legions had a large mixture of non-Roman elements, and
volunteers for the auxiliary units (usually cohorts of 500 or
1000 men) were enlisted from the less Romanised regions of
the empire (e.g. from Gallia Comata and the wilder parts
of Spain) and from some of the allied peoples.

After 14 B.C. military service was for a fixed period varying from twenty years in the legions to twenty-five in the auxiliary forces. In practice, however, men were often kept waiting for their discharge, because of the expense of giving them pensions. Though the custom of giving old soldiers allotments of land was sometimes kept up, it became more usual to pay them with money. The cash bonus for a private soldier was 3000 denarii, equivalent to thirteen years' pay. The auxiliaries were less well paid, and were entitled to pensions ; but it became the rule to reward them with Roman citizenship at the end of their service.

The more regular terms of service made it possible to keep the individual units in continuous existence. The legions became fixed units, received permanent numbers and distinctive titles ; they formed their own traditions and developed a strong *esprit de corps* and a healthy rivalry. The total number of the Roman military forces was kept steady, which permitted more scientific distribution. Most of the legions were concentrated near the Rhine and the Danube ; the only other districts which received strong garrisons were north-western Spain and Egypt. Everywhere else the Roman forces were reduced to a minimum. Only 5000 were stationed in Asia Minor, and 3000 in Judaea ; for the security of southern and central Gaul 1200 men at Lugdunum were considered sufficient. At the frontier stations the camps began to be laid out and furnished as permanent quarters for their garrisons.

The power and prestige which Augustus had enabled him to restore severity of discipline in the army. The troops were also trained to take a pride in their regiment and to feel an almost religious reverence for its standard.

Augustus did not create a complete professional body of officers, but kept most of the higher posts for the members of his own family, or for men of consular or praetorian rank, whose experience might be administrative rather than military. But the centurions, who continued to come from the ranks, and were transferred from one post to another by a carefully graded system of promotion, were highly trained professionals. In addition the *praefecti fabrum* (chief engineers) and their *praefecti castrorum* (quartermasters), whose position in the Roman army became increasingly important, were regular officers.

Augustus was the creator of the first regular fleet. In the Mediterranean Sea he maintained squadrons of cruisers to check piracy and patrol the routes of the corn-fleets, and he established naval bases at Misenum, Ravenna, Forum Iulii and Alexandria. In general, the crews were recruited from freeborn provincials, and the officers were mostly drawn from the same source. The terms of service were similar to those of the auxiliary troops.

## (H) *Provincial Administration*

In the days of Augustus the Roman empire contained at least 70,000,000 inhabitants, perhaps 100,000,000. Some three-quarters of this population were in the provinces, whose number had risen by the end of Augustus' reign to twenty-four or twenty-five. Apart from the new provinces formed by conquest, several others were made by the division of existing provinces of dependent kingdoms. Augustus made it a general rule to leave the native rulers of these in possession; but where the security of the frontiers or the kingdom's internal peace seemed to demand a change, he converted them into provinces. He gave Mauretania to a son of the Numidian king Juba, but took away Numidia, which he incorporated into the province of Africa. In Judaea he gave full power to King Herod. After Herod's death in 4 B.C. he allowed his three sons to divide his kingdom. The territory of Hispania Ulterior was divided into the senatorial province of Baetica and the imperial province of Lusitania. Gallia Comata was split into three provinces, Aquitania, Lugdunensis and Belgica. Achaea and Epirus were detached from Macedonia and had a separate governor.

The interest which Augustus took in the provinces was made clear by the long tours of inspection which he undertook. In 27–24 he visited Gaul and Spain; in 22–19 he went the round of the eastern provinces; in 15–13 he revisited Gaul. Similarly in 23–21 and again in 17–13 Agrippa was appointed by him to inspect the eastern provinces.

Augustus carried on the excellent tradition of respecting local customs and giving a large measure of self-government in the provinces. In the eastern provinces local bronze and small silver coins were allowed to circulate alongside the imperial money; in Gaul and Spain native bronze pieces continued to be made. In Gallia Narbonensis and several other provinces some cities had large territories attached to them. Town life in the provinces was also encouraged by the settlements of veterans made since the Triumvirate. Not less than forty colonies were established in the provinces between 43 and 30 B.C., and more than forty during the reign of Augustus. The emperor's most famous foundations included Vienna and Nemausus in Gaul; Barcino, Caesaraugusta and Emerita Augusta in Spain; Antioch and Lystra in Asia Minor; Carthage and Corinth in Africa and Achaea. In general, his settlements were in regions already colonised by Caesar, so as to reinforce the earlier settlements.

The most urgent problem for Augustus in the provinces was to check the alarming drain on their wealth. The eastern provinces in particular had been plundered by Brutus, Cassius and Antony, and the whole Roman empire was being threatened with bankruptcy. In the rates of provincial taxation the emperor made little change. With a view to the better apportionment of the fixed taxes he instituted a census in some, perhaps in all, of the provinces, and he made provision for a re-count at the end of every fourteen years. In his own provinces he gave direct control of the taxes to the magistrates of the cities; when private contractors were used he supervised their operations by a staff of *procuratores* or inspectors.

In the provinces of which he was proconsul, Augustus chose his legati or praefecti with careful regard to their individual capacities. The usual period of service was from three to five years, which gave the officials time to learn their duties thoroughly. The emperor paid his governors and other agents fixed salaries on a generous scale, so they had no excuse for private money-making. Lastly, by improving the road-systems in the provinces, he was able to keep in touch with his subordinates and check their mistakes before serious mischief was done.

In the senatorial provinces the governors continued to be selected from the ex-consuls or ex-praetors; each proconsul's office seldom exceeded one year. Augustus tried to create a new bond of loyalty among the provincials by religion. After Actium the worship of Augustus became widespread in the Near East. In 29 B.C. the cities of Asia went a step further in combining to offer him a temple at Pergamum in the name of the whole province. Augustus accepted the gift, on condition of the goddess Roma being joined with him in the worship. He allowed it to spread in other eastern provinces ; and eventually he took the initiative in introducing them into the western Mediterranean. In 12 B.C. his stepson Drusus dedicated an altar of *Roma et Augustus* at Lugdunum ; in 2 B.C. L. Domitius did the same on the banks of the Elbe ; other altars were set up at Tarraco, in the territory of the Ubii, and probably also at Nemausus. By the end of his reign, or not long after his death, an altar or a temple of *Roma et Augustus* had been set up in most of the Roman provinces. Augustus started provincial *concilia*, or parliaments elected by the several cities, which met once a year at the chief town of the province to choose a high priest of *Roma et Augustus* and to conduct the festival in their honour.

## (1) *Finance*

Augustus made no big change in the position of the *aerarium* (the treasury of the republic). The general costs of administration were covered, as under the republic, by payments from the *aerarium* at the Senate's order, and Augustus presented his accounts to the treasury officials like any other Roman magistrate. Though he insisted that the management of the *aerarium* should be taken out of the inexperienced hands of the quaestors and given to persons of praetorian rank, he did not claim any direct control over it for himself.

But most of the public income passed through the hands of the emperor into the imperial treasury (*fiscus*); for the payment and pensioning of the soldiers alone he took nearly three-quarters of the regular income. Except in Gallia Comata, Augustus did not increase direct taxation in the provinces. On the other hand, he created several new indirect taxes at uniform rates in every part of the empire : 1 per cent on market sales, 4 per cent on sales of slaves and 5 per cent on indirect legacies above 100,000 sesterces. These additional

taxes were hardly sufficient. The *aerarium* was often empty
and required a grant from the *fiscus*. The emperor also had
difficulties and it was not until A.D. 6, when the tax on legacies
began to pay for the pensions fund of the soldiers, that the
*aerarium militare* (as this fund was called) began to be built
up to the necessary level.

But Augustus had other sources to draw upon — a large
stock of gold and silver and several large estates and legacies left
to him by private citizens (which amounted to 1,400,000,000
sesterces). All the money that flowed into Augustus' public
or private account was administered by trained accountants
of his own domestic staff. His finances were so well ordered
that he was able to publish a yearly balance-sheet, and at the
end of his life he prepared a comprehensive survey of the
financial resources of the whole empire.

## (J) *The Succession*

Though in strict law Augustus was not entitled to assume
that the magistracy which he held would not lapse after his
death, in actual fact nothing was more certain than that his
place would need to be filled. He was determined that the
imperial power should, if possible, remain in his own household. But so long as his daughter Julia was unmarried, and
his stepsons Tiberius and Drusus were mere boys, Augustus
had to look beyond his family circle, and the claims of his
friend Agrippa were irresistible. Accordingly, when the
emperor stood at the point of death in 23, he handed his
signet ring to Agrippa. On his recovery he obtained for
Agrippa an *imperium proconsulare* over all the imperial provinces, which appeared to mark him out as the next emperor.
Yet in the same year a marriage which Augustus arranged
between Julia and his nephew, C. Claudius Marcellus (a son
of his sister Octavia by her first husband), was accepted by
Agrippa as a hint that he was to be passed over. However,
Marcellus died suddenly and Agrippa was married to the
widowed Julia. In 18 he was given *imperium* over all the
senatorial provinces of the east, and in 13 over the western
provinces. He also got the *tribunicia potestas*, so that he
became virtually the co-regent of Augustus ; finally, his two

eldest sons by Julia were adopted in 17 by the emperor under the names of Caius and Lucius Caesar. But Agrippa died in 12 B.C., before his sons had reached manhood. The emperor's stepsons, Tiberius and Drusus, had recently distinguished themselves in command of the Roman armies. In 11 B.C. Augustus required Tiberius to divorce his wife, a daughter of Agrippa by an earlier marriage, in order to become the third husband of Julia; and he married Drusus to his niece Antonia, a daughter of Antony and Octavia. The choice between these two candidates was made in 9 B.C. by the death of Drusus. In 6 B.C. the claims of Tiberius to the succession seemed to have been finally recognised when the emperor obtained for him a grant of *tribunicia potestas*. But in the same year Tiberius left home and for the next seven years he lived at Rhodes.

In 5 B.C. the emperor introduced C. Caesar to public life, and he appointed him to be consul in A.D. 1 at the early age of twenty. After three years' interval L. Caesar was promoted to the same honours. Tiberius received permission to return to Rome in A.D. 2, but was barred from further political activities. But the death of L. Caesar in A.D. 2, and of C. Caesar two years later, reduced Agrippa's family to his widow Julia, to a daughter of the same name and a younger son named Agrippa Postumus. In contrast to his father the younger Agrippa had a nasty character, and the two Julias were immoral. In 2 B.C. Augustus banished the elder Julia to the island of Pandateria; in A.D. 7 he sent her daughter to a similar place of exile and banished Agrippa Postumus to the island of Planasia. Tiberius was left as the only possible heir to Augustus, for in A.D. 7 Drusus' son, Nero Claudius Drusus (afterwards known as Germanicus), had not yet come of age. After the death of C. Caesar accordingly Augustus adopted Tiberius and restored his tribunician power. In A.D. 13, when the aged emperor's strength showed signs of failing, he gave Tiberius an unlimited *imperium proconsulare*. Augustus had given each of his potential heirs in turn a thorough training in the art of government. In this respect Tiberius was perfectly qualified to carry on Augustus' work, and the first and most important succession between emperors took place without a hitch.

### CHAPTER XIV

# THE EMPIRE, A.D. 14–68: CONSOLIDATION

## (A) *The Emperors*

THE first fifty years after the death of Augustus were a period of transition. The four emperors whose reigns fill this half-

century formed a dynasty (the so-called 'Julio-Claudian' dynasty), for all of them were related by blood to Augustus or to his third wife Livia. This hereditary transmission of power was due to the great prestige of Augustus. No later dynasty of emperors lasted for more than two generations.

Head of Livia personifying Pietas

1. *Tiberius* (*A.D. 14–37*).—Tiberius Claudius Nero was a son of Livia by her first marriage, and the adopted son of Augustus. He had a strong sense of duty and all-round ability as a soldier and administrator. But he had a cold and reserved manner and had accepted the imperial power unwillingly. The successor to Augustus was bound to have an unpleasant job. The benefits of the new order were beginning to be taken for granted, and enthusiasm was giving way to boredom. Tiberius' position was difficult. Senators plotted against him, and his own family and friends were constantly at war with him. Augustus had said that the future emperor should in turn adopt his nephew Germanicus and arrange the next succession in his favour. Although Tiberius had a son of his own by his first wife, Drusus II, he agreed, and after the death of Augustus he gave no sign of going back upon it. Drusus II was a popular figure at Rome, but he lacked the

prestige and experience of Germanicus. Germanicus for his part was content to wait for the imperial power (Tiberius was fifty-five in A.D. 14). But his death in A.D. 19 made a crisis in the imperial family. His widow Agrippina convinced herself that Tiberius had poisoned him, and henceforth she fought against the emperor.

After the death of his own son Drusus II in A.D. 23, Tiberius recognised Agrippina's children, Nero and Drusus III, as heirs to the empire. But trouble was made by the emperor's *praefectus praetorio*, L. Aelius Seianus. The son of a professional administrator, who had held the praetorian prefecture at the beginning of the reign, Seianus was quickly promoted

Head of Drusus
(brother of Tiberius)

Head of the Elder
Agrippina

to his father's office, and Tiberius gave him great confidence. Seianus roused the emperor's suspicions against Agrippina's family and against several prominent senators. Agrippina's hostile attitude to the emperor certainly laid her open to accusations of conspiracy. After the death of his mother Livia, Tiberius struck. In 29 he got from the Senate a sentence of banishment against Agrippina and Nero; in the following year he sent Drusus after them.

The object of Seianus in removing Agrippina's family was to make himself the successor of Tiberius. In 23 he had made himself virtually master of the city of Rome by concentrating the whole of the praetorian cohorts (who had been in scattered billets) in a large camp on its eastern outskirts. In 26 he got

Tiberius to prolong a holiday on the island of Capri, so as to keep him out of touch with events at Rome. He was given the proconsular *imperium*, a distinction which seemed to point to further promotion. But Tiberius would give Seianus no definite promise of the succession, and in 31 Antonia, the widow of the emperor's brother Drusus, revealed to him the intrigues of Seianus against Agrippina and her family. Tiberius secretly instructed an officer named Sertorius Macro to command the praetorian cohorts and to steal them from Seianus with the offer of a special bonus. At a meeting of the Senate the presiding consul read a long letter from Capri, which denounced Seianus as a traitor. The Senate passed sentence, and he was executed. Unable to overcome his distrust of Agrippina and her sons, Tiberius put them to death or drove them to suicide.

Prosecutions for treason or disloyalty became common in the later years of his reign. Taking advantage of the emperor's suspiciousness, politicians in pursuit of personal aims, or fortune-hunters who wanted the customary fee for a successful prosecution (one-quarter of the condemned man's estate), laid accusations of treason (*perduellio*) or more often of *maiestas*. This was a dangerously vague charge, but the accused persons were given an opportunity of speaking in their own defence ; Tiberius allowed the Senate to acquit, and even to proceed against an obviously mischievous prosecutor, and he sometimes spoke in favour of the accused or stopped the trial with his tribune's veto.

In the last ten years of his reign Tiberius was absent from the capital; he retired to Capri. Though he still guided the administration with occasional letters, he postponed the appointment of new officials and let the troops go unpaid. At the emperor's death in 37 no definite choice had been made of a successor. By the deaths of Drusus II and of the two eldest sons of Germanicus the field had been narrowed to Germanicus' youngest son Caius and to the emperor's grandson Tiberius Gemellus. Tiberius named them as equal heirs.

2. *Caligula* (*A.D.* *37–41*).—The praetorian prefect Macro, whose support had been won by Caius, at once submitted his name to the Senate, and the Senate accepted. Caius Caesar,

or Caligula ('Little Boot', as his father's soldiers had nick-named him after the boots which he wore as a small boy in Germanicus' camp), was received at Rome as a welcome relief from the stern and suspicious regime of Tiberius. The young emperor at first gave promise of fulfilling the wildest hopes of the Romans. He adopted his cousin Tiberius Gemellus, recalled exiles and repressed informers; he gave renewed personal attention to the government, and displayed a shrewd judgment and a ready wit. But he lacked training in adminis-tration and spent far too much money. A bad temper made him unco-operative with the Senate, and he murdered all possible rivals. Within a few months he put to death Tiberius Gemellus and Macro without a trial. By this he provoked several real conspiracies, in which senators of old republican families co-operated with military officers. In 39 the com-mander of the legions on the Upper Rhine, Lentulus Gaetulicus, laid a plot, the detection of which provoked further executions, and two sisters of the emperor, Agrippina II and Julia, were sent into exile. But the disloyalty spread to the praetorian cohorts. In 41 a tribune of the Guards named Cassius Chaerea stabbed him in a quiet corner of the palace grounds.

3. *Claudius* (*A.D. 41–54*).—After the murder of Caligula some of the guardsmen found the uncle of the dead emperor, Tiberius Claudius Drusus in hiding. They saluted him as a brother of their former favourite Germanicus and car-ried him off to their camp, where he was pressed to accept the imperial power from them. Claudius gave his consent, but kept the soldiers loyal by the promise of a special bonus. This was the first of many deals by which the throne was bought and sold in the camp market. In the meantime the

Head of Claudius

Senate had begun to debate on the choice of a new emperor. Its discussions were cut short by the Guards. After a brief show of resistance the Senate gave the imperial power to Claudius.

On his accession Claudius had taken no part in public life. He was handicapped by illness which, in the judgment of Augustus and Tiberius, disqualified him from political service. But he had many new ideas, and a shrewd practical sense and a genuine concern for efficiency in administration. Augustus and Tiberius had chosen their political associates from the Senatorial and Equestrian Orders : Claudius found them in his own household. The earlier emperors recruited their secretaries and accountants from their domestic staff, but they only did routine work. Claudius sought their guidance on questions of high policy and of appointments to the chief executive posts. In the later years of his reign no Roman of high rank possessed influence equal to that of Callistus, the *praepositus a libellis* (examiner of petitions), of Narcissus, the *praepositus ab epistulis* (chief secretary), or of Pallas, the *praepositus a rationibus* (chief accountant), all of whom were freed slaves. The influence of these freedmen was greatly resented. Pallas and Callistus died richer than the triumvir Crassus.

The last two of Claudius' four wives were Valeria Messalina and the younger Agrippina (whom he had recalled from exile soon after Caligula's death). Messalina was immoral. Agrippina had a lust for power. Both used their influence with the emperor to remove those who stood in their way. In the second year of Claudius' reign the governor of Dalmatia, Camillus Scribonianus, had combined with a nobleman named Annius Vinicianus in a plot. In 48 another nobleman, C. Silius, was tempted by Messalina to take Claudius' place, but the freedman Narcissus summoned the Guards and executed both.

By his marriage with Messalina Claudius had a daughter, Octavia, and a son, Tiberius Claudius, surnamed Britannicus after the emperor's victories in Britain, who became heir. But Britannicus was opposed by Agrippina, who was determined to make her own son by a previous marriage, L. Domitius Ahenobarbus, the next emperor. She got Claudius to adopt her child (who was renamed Nero Claudius Caesar). Claudius died suddenly (A.D. 54), but Agrippina, however, had already come to an arrangement with the praetorian prefect Afranius Burrus, who now presented Nero to his troops. The Senate for the third time confirmed the choice of the praetorian cohorts.

4. *Nero (A.D. 54–68).*—Nero was only sixteen. Agrippina became involved in a struggle for power with Burrus and the prince's tutor, L. Annaeus Seneca. Burrus and Seneca asserted themselves against her attempt to control political affairs. They carried with them the young emperor, who soon tired of his mother's rule. Agrippina then tried to back Britannicus; but Burrus commanded the praetorian cohorts and the sudden death cf Britannicus in 55 removed the only possible rival to the emperor. Three years later she brought on a new conflict by

Head of Nero, and on the reverse the Temple of Janus

backing Nero's wife Octavia against his mistress, Poppaea Sabina. Poppaea had set herself to marry the emperor and under her influence he was persuaded to kill his mother. The murder was carried out by a freedman named Anicetus who broke into her house and had her battered to death. The emperor felt no remorse.

The emperor's first impulse after the death of his mother was to fulfil his artistic ambitions. In 59 and 60 he started two new festivals, the Iuvenalia (to celebrate the first clipping of the imperial beard) and the Neronia — contests of charioteering, music and dancing. At these functions he gave a public exhibition of his singing.

During the ministry of Seneca and Burrus the government of Nero followed a cautious but efficient administrative routine. The emperor's behaviour did not give rise to serious scandal. But the death of Burrus in 62, followed by the retirement of Seneca, whose position at court now became insecure, marked a turning-point in Nero's reign. In the same year Nero got rid of his wife Octavia ; he banished her and shortly afterwards put her to death, then married Poppaea. One of the two praetorian prefects whom he appointed in place of Burrus was Ofonius Tigellinus, and under his influence the government became an irresponsible despotism.

Nero now became wildly immoral, and almost mad. Also his career as a circus and opera performer caused him to neglect urgent public business and made him spend far too much money. Lastly, in the later years of Nero the terror of treason trials was renewed. In order to raise new money, Tigellinus played upon the emperor's fears and got him to unleash the professional informers. Under Tigellinus' regime the charge of *maiestas* was now expanded to cover every manifestation of freedom. Usually the accused received a curt order to commit suicide without the chance of offering a defence. Among those who were compelled to take their lives was Seneca. Nero was especially fond of convicting men of wealth, and in 65 some twenty men of senatorial or equestrian rank made preparations for his assassination. The ring-leader, C. Calpurnius Piso, was a wealthy noble. But the real driving force of the movement proceeded from Faenius Rufus, the colleague of Tigellinus in the command of the Guards, and from several subordinate officers. But the plot failed.

Nero then had news that the governor of Gallia Lugdunensis, C. Iulius Vindex, was persuading his colleague in Hispania Tarraconensis, Servius Sulpicius Galba, to champion the 'human race' against the emperor (March 68). Galba followed the lead of Vindex. Vindex collected a large following in his own province, but his Gallic birth made the German legions suspicious: they attacked his Gallic recruits and made short work of them. After this Vindex took his own life.

Yet the army that had destroyed Vindex was infected by his disloyalty to Nero. It made an offer to its commander to continue its march to Rome and to make him emperor. For the moment indeed the commander, Verginius, refused.

But the rebellion revived disloyalty among the praetorian cohorts at Rome. Their new commander, Nymphidius Sabinus, backed Galba, and won over his men by money. Tigellinus did not protect Nero, and the Senate deposed the emperor and sentenced him to execution. Deserted by all, the emperor after long hesitations took his own life (summer 68).

## (B) *The Constitution*

At the death of Augustus his system of government had won general approval, and a restoration of the republic was out of the question. The Senate gave Tiberius' powers to him for life, and these were voted *in toto* to each new emperor. Under these four emperors a process of constitutional development went on, by which effective political power was still further concentrated in their hands.

In the first year of Tiberius' reign the election of magistrates by the Popular Assemblies was discontinued, so that the Comitia henceforth were merely called upon to accept candidates approved by the emperor and the Senate. In the reign of Tiberius the legislative functions of the Comitia also lapsed and no serious attempt was ever made to revive them. The common citizens could still give expression to their political opinions by organised clamour at the public festivals.

No important change was made in the functions of the surviving magistrates. Of all republican institutions, the Senate showed the greatest vitality. Under the Julio-Claudian emperors it not only kept the rights given to it by Augustus, but had its range of functions enlarged. It continued to supervise the magistrates in Rome and in the Italian towns, and the proconsuls in the more peaceful provinces. It was consulted by the emperors on general questions of policy and of fresh legislation. Only under Caligula and in the later days of Nero was its liberty of speech endangered. Tiberius transferred to the Senate the choice of the annual magistrates, which he withdrew from the Comitia, thus giving it powers which it had never claimed under the republic. These powers, it is true, were exercised subject to the emperor's will: and the consulships, at any rate, always remained in his control.

Tiberius definitely constituted the Senate into a high criminal court of law. Its power extended to all cases in which the accused was a person of high rank — a member of the ruling family, of the equestrian class or of its own order. On the other hand, the Senate in debate often refused to commit itself. If the emperor attended in person, senators would hang on his every word and gesture in order to ascertain his views and echo them ; if he was absent they found excuses for coming to no decision at all.

For advice on more important questions, the emperors were driven to rely on their personal friends or on their Privy Council. Under Tiberius the *consilium principis* ceased to be a mere committee of the Senate, as under Augustus. It came to include Equites, and as its members were no longer changed from year to year, but served for long periods, they had great power. Under Claudius the Council began to replace the Senate as a court for the trial of high political criminals.

A great development in the civil service took place under Claudius. The number of the *procuratores* who collected taxes and rents on the emperor's account was considerably increased, and their powers were enlarged by the transfer of law-suits between the *fiscus* and the taxpayers from the governors' court to theirs. Several new administrative bureaux were created in the same reign. Claudius no doubt acted on the advice of his freedmen, who brought to their own work a professional training. From this point of view his reign is an important link in the transition from a republic to a centralised monarchy.

Under the Julio-Claudian dynasty the imperial household began to look like a royal court. Though their domestic staff did not yet include personages of high social rank in the office of a Lord Chamberlain or Chief Steward, the menial functionaries attached to the palace grew into a veritable army. The freedmen and slaves now included a considerable number of skilled industrial workers, who carried out constructional repairs.

Lastly, Claudius took the cognomen of Caesar, which had hitherto belonged to the Iulii. His example was followed by later emperors, so that these came to be known as the ' Caesars '.

## (c) *Frontiers of the Empire*

With one exception, the successors of Augustus took his advice not to extend the Roman empire beyond its existing boundaries. Tiberius would not trust himself to wage war on his own responsibility, and the next three emperors were unfit to command armies. But emperors who did not take command had reason to fear that conquests achieved by other generals might lead to military revolutions, like those which had destroyed the rule of the republican Senate. So the warfare of the first half century after the death of Augustus was mainly defensive ; in this period the Roman army began to stop being a field force and to become a frontier garrison.

1. *Africa.*—At the end of his reign Caligula caused a rebellion in Mauretania. Under Claudius the revolt was suppressed, mainly by the services of C. Suetonius Paulinus (41–42). Claudius made the kingdom into two provinces, known as Mauretania Caesariensis and Tingitana. *Praefecti* were appointed to supervise the tribal governments and to recruit for the Roman auxiliary forces.

War was waged under Tiberius against a Numidian chieftain named Tacfarinas. After four years' campaigning (17–20) the Senate asked Tiberius to take charge. Tacfarinas was finally run down and put to death by an imperial officer, P. Cornelius Dolabella (24). Caligula transferred the command of the African forces to an imperial officer, leaving the civil administration in the hands of the senatorial proconsul.

2. *Judaea.*—In the eastern Mediterranean the chief area of disturbance under the early emperors lay in Palestine, where the Jewish population hated Roman rule. Under Augustus the Roman governors of Judaea had instructions to allow for the people's religion. At Jerusalem the High Priest, assisted by his council, the Sanhedrin, exercised the usual powers of local self-government. In recognition of this the clergy and landowners accepted Roman sovereignty. But the Jewish people in general hoped that the day of freedom from foreign rule might be near. They thought that the promised Messiah would be a liberator like Samuel and David. In A.D. 6 they opposed the Roman census officials, and robbers, who disappeared into the desert when pressed hard by the Romans, continually infested the country. In 40 Caligula, who ordered the Jews to set up his statue in the Temple at Jerusalem, nearly caused a general rebellion in Palestine. Thanks to the governor of Syria, P. Petronius, the emperor relented.

Judaea was entrusted to a governor of procuratorial rank, under the general supervision of the *legatus* of Syria. The procurators were often bad. In 66 there was a rising at Jerusalem. The Jews besieged the Roman garrison and massacred it. The procurator Florus looked on quite helpless, and the *legatus* of Syria, Cestius Gallus, who brought up an army of some 30,000 men and began to besiege the citadel at Jerusalem, abandoned the siege and made a retreat out of Palestine. After this, the rebellion swept over the whole of Judaea and spread to Galilee and parts of Transjordania, and the various towns of Palestine became battlefields.

But Nero gave a special *imperium* over Syria and the nearby provinces to an officer named T. Flavius Vespasianus, who had a good military record, and was considered a reliable man. With more than 50,000 men Vespasian systematically conquered Galilee in 67 and the Transjordanian lands in 68, so as to encircle the rebels in Judaea. At the end of Nero's reign Palestine as a whole had been recovered by the Romans.

3. *Armenia and Parthia.*—In Asia Minor the coastland of Lycia and Pamphylia was made into a separate province in 43. In 17 Tiberius reduced the kingdom of Cappadocia to a province, so as to strengthen the Roman frontier along the Euphrates.

In Armenia and Parthia the successors of Augustus carried on his policy of maintaining Roman authority with the smallest possible military effort. The Parthian kings also did little. At the death of Augustus the Parthian ruler, Artabanus III, was not yet established firmly, and Armenia was in a state of chaos. Yet Tiberius made no move until 18, when the Armenian nobility invited a prince from one of the lesser dynasties of Asia Minor to become king. The emperor appointed Germanicus to give the crown to him at Artaxata. The new king, Artaxias, reigned until 35. At his death the Parthian king, Artabanus, got one of his sons to seize Armenia for himself. Tiberius got a man named Mithridates to beat the Parthian troops out of Armenia and secure the throne for himself.

Caligula kept Mithridates in Rome and Artabanus occupied Armenia. Claudius at first succeeded in reinstating Mithridates with the help of a small Roman force. But in 52 or 53

THE EASTERN FRONTIER

Mithridates' nephew, Radamistus, invaded Armenia and treacherously killed his uncle, who received no support from the neighbouring Roman governors. Thus the Romans played into the hands of a new and able Parthian king, Vologeses I, who helped the Armenians to get rid of Radamistus and replaced him by his own brother, Tiridates (53–54).

In 54 the Roman governor of Cappadocia, Iulius Paelignus, was replaced by an officer named Cn. Domitius Corbulo. After a year of hard training, the Roman general made a bold march into the valley of the Araxes. In two rapid campaigns he captured and burnt Artaxata, and marched to Tigranocerta (58–59). From this base he overran Armenia during the next summer, so that Tiridates evacuated his kingdom. In 60 Corbulo settled the Armenian question for the time being by enthroning a prince named Tigranes.

In the following year a direct clash between Romans and Parthians occurred. Corbulo remained inactive in Syria, while the new governor of Cappadocia, L. Caesennius Paetus, allowed himself to be surprised by Vologeses and was compelled to surrender (62). The Romans evacuated Armenia, of which Tiridates now resumed possession (62–63). Corbulo was now created general of all the forces on the Euphrates. With an army of 50,000, Corbulo resumed his invasions of Armenia in 64, but he did not fight seriously. The demonstration brought a new peace offer from Vologeses, and Tiridates agreed that he should receive his crown from the emperor in person. In 65 and 66 the Armenian king journeyed to Rome, where he was crowned by Nero. The friendly relations thus established lasted for half a century.

In 64 Nero made the kingdom of eastern Pontus part of the province of Galatia. The Roman government took over the royal fleet and the duty of patrolling the farther end of the Black Sea. Fifty years of warfare on the Armenian and Parthian front left the Roman boundaries more or less as they were. But from the time of Nero the Roman garrison along the Euphrates frontier was permanently increased at the expense of the Rhine and Danube frontiers.

4. *The Danube.*—In the Balkan regions a revolt in the kingdom of Thrace in 25 was suppressed by the governor of

Macedonia, Poppaeus Sabinus. In 46 Claudius made Thrace a province under a procurator. The northern part of the Thracian kingdom was attached to the province of Moesia. At this period a forward thrust by a nomadic folk from the central Asiatic grass-lands, the Alans, was giving rise to a movement of peoples across the Russian plains, and was exerting pressure upon the populations near the Danube estuary, which threatened to overflow into Moesia. About 62 a governor of Moesia, named Tib. Plautius Silvanus, relieved the strain on the Roman frontier by settling 100,000 Dacians on the southern bank of the Danube. Apart from these movements on the Moesian border, the Danube lands enjoyed half a century of freedom from war.

5. *Germany.*—The reign of Tiberius opened with three years of heavy fighting in northern Germany, where Germanicus conducted expeditions. In 14 he went into the basin

THE GERMAN FRONTIER

of the Lippe, where he devastated the land and butchered its inhabitants. In 15 and 16 he used the Rhine fleet to transport a division of his army through Drusus' canal to the Ems, so as to join the main division marching up the valley of the Lippe. In 15 the combined forces reached the scene of Varus' disaster and interred the remains of the fallen Romans ; in 16 they advanced beyond the Weser and defeated the Cherusci in two battles. Germanicus now had hopes of completing the reconquest of western Germany in one further campaign. But Arminius succeeded in holding the north German tribes together, and the Romans had serious losses by battle and shipwreck. At the end of 16 Tiberius recalled Germanicus and definitely gave up the conquest of Germany.

The Rhine borderland was made into two military zones, known as Germania Superior and Inferior, whose headquarters were at Moguntiacum and Vetera. The forts on the Lippe were abandoned. In 28 Tiberius made no move when the Frisii of the North Sea coast expelled their Roman *praefecti*. The Roman armies on the Rhine front remained quiet for half a century.

6. *The Conquest of Britain.*—Invitations to interfere in British affairs were presented to the emperors by several lesser chiefs who felt the growing power of Cunobelinus' dynasty. Cunobelinus' son, Caratacus, increased his power. But the motive of Claudius probably was to obtain a military reputation for himself.

In 43 an army of 50,000 men under A. Plautius landed in Kent and crossed the Thames. After the arrival of the emperor, who took part in the campaign, the Roman troops defeated Caratacus in a battle and captured his capital, Camulodunum. While Claudius returned to Rome to celebrate, his lieutenants rapidly overran East Anglia and the south coast. Though the future emperor Vespasian had to fight many battles in a westward march along the Channel, in other regions several chieftains made immediate submission. By 49 the Romans had reached the Severn estuary and the Wash. Plautius' successor, P. Ostorius Scapula (47–52), completed without much difficulty the conquest of the English lowlands between Severn and Trent. He defeated Welsh border tribes called together by Caratacus, and sent him as a prisoner to Rome — where Claudius treated his captive with all due honour. But he made slow progress in south Wales.

Suetonius Paulinus resumed warfare in north Wales. In 61 Suetonius was preparing to capture Anglesey, when a rebellion broke out in his rear. In East Anglia Roman tax-collectors and money-lenders had been too ruthless to the tribe of the Iceni. At the same time the Trinovantes of Essex were complaining of Roman colonists established at Camulo-dunum. Under the leadership of Boudicca, the widow of the East Anglian king, the rebels took Camulodunum ; they drove back a legion under Q. Petilius Cerealis and, though they could not prevent Suetonius from cutting his way back to Londinium, they eventually took this town and its neighbour Verulamium. All the three towns were burnt to the ground, and their Roman inhabitants were massacred. But the rebels played into Suetonius' hands by engaging him in battle on a site of his own choice. Though the Roman force only numbered 10,000 to 15,000 men, by perfect battle discipline it put the enemy host to complete rout, and the death of Boudicca left the Britons without a leader. After a while Nero recalled Suetonius, and under the next governors the English lowlands as far as the Humber and the Dee settled down under Roman rule. The kingdoms of the Iceni and others became part of the Roman province.

### (D) *Provincial Administration*

Under the Julio-Claudian dynasty the number of the Roman provinces increased. Of the new provinces Britain alone was acquired by conquest. The two Mauretanias, Cappadocia, Thrace and the Alpes Cottiae were formed out of kingdoms whose dynasties died out or were deposed. Raetia was detached from Gallia Belgica under Tiberius or Claudius, and Pamphylia was separated from Galatia under Claudius.

The new system of administration which Augustus had devised remained more or less unchanged. A fresh ground for complaint was given to the provincials when Roman officials forced them to undertake tax-collection and other public duties. Augustus' successors did not do periodical tours of inspection in the provinces, and thus kept no check upon the Roman officials. The worst mischief was usually done by the lesser officials, which suggests that too little care was taken in filling the lesser posts.

Roads helped trade and frontier defence. In the Danube lands Tiberius created a system of highways ; and two new metalled roads across the Alps were built by Claudius. Tiberius checked an over-zealous prefect of Egypt, who had sent more than the due amount of tribute to Rome. In 17 the same emperor came to the assistance of twelve cities of Asia Minor which had suffered severely from earthquakes by stopping all their taxes for five years. In 15 the provincial councils of Macedonia and Achaea asked him to transfer their territories from senatorial to imperial control. Tiberius agreed, but Claudius handed back the two provinces to the Senate in 44. Above all, Tiberius and Nero encouraged the provincial parliaments to watch over the Roman officials. Members of the *concilia* collected evidence and presented it at Rome to the emperor or the Senate. In most of the recorded cases, which were especially frequent under Nero, the *concilia* obtained a sentence of exile or of expulsion from the Senate against the person accused by them.

Tiberius merely maintained Augustus' practice of giving Roman citizenship to demobilised soldiers. His successors, however, struck out a new line. Caligula had spent his childhood with his father on the Rhine frontier ; his sister Agrippina was a native of the Rhineland. Claudius was born in Gaul at Lugdunum, and he realised clearly that the partnership of Rome and Italy, which had produced the Roman empire, must be succeeded by a partnership of Italy and the provinces, if that empire was to last. Seneca came from Corduba in Spain and Burrus was probably a native of Vasio in southern Gaul. Under Claudius several colonies were established in Noricum and Pannonia, and two cities were founded, Colonia Claudia Camulodunum and Colonia Claudia Agrippinensis. To Claudius a number of the native towns in Noricum and in Mauretania owed their Roman franchise. The same emperor also used his authority as censor in 48 to place on the list of the Senate several chiefs from the tribe of the Aedui in

Central Gaul. Under Nero the Alpes Maritimae and the Alpes Cottiae on the Italian borderland received the Latin franchise.

## (E) *Finance*

Under his successors, Augustus' financial system became more centralised in the hands of the emperors. Tiberius increased the imperial finances by various methods. But his concern for the newly established *aerarium militare* tempted him to delay the discharge of soldiers, which led to a brief mutiny of the Rhine and Danube armies in the first year of his reign. Yet to actual distress Tiberius gave prompt and generous relief. At the end of his reign the total assets in the emperor's balance-sheet is stated to have amounted to £27,000,000, five or six times his annual income.

Tiberius' savings were spent in three years by Caligula. Taxation, which had been slightly lowered under Tiberius, was increased. But Caligula's new taxes were removed by Claudius, under whom the treasury was again made financially sound. Under Claudius all the income of the Caesars went into a single *fiscus*. At the same time a special fund was set apart to provide for the costs of the imperial household and to prevent confusion between the public and the private accounts of Claudius. This tightening of the control over the tax-gatherers was Claudius' chief contribution to financial reform. Its effect was reinforced by the gradual increase in the income of the newer imperial provinces as their economic development progressed. The emperor's money therefore soon recovered from Caligula ; but the *aerarium* began to go bankrupt. In the early part of Nero's reign the *fiscus* made an annual grant of some £60,000 to the *aerarium*. In return, the collection of the indirect taxes that flowed into the *aerarium* was placed under the control of imperial officials. In the first half of Nero's reign the *fiscus* had a surplus, which served not only to subsidise the *aerarium*, but to provide special money for the victims of natural calamities. But under the regime of Tigellinus the imperial finances were plunged into bankruptcy. Nero did not reimpose Caligula's taxes ; but he devalued the coinage. The aureus and the denarius were lightened in

K

weight. This had no immediate effect, but it was the beginning of a process which eventually produced financial chaos. But neither this nor the confiscations of rich men's estates could check the drain on the *fiscus*. At the end of Nero's reign the pay of the troops had been delayed, and the loyalty of the Roman army was fatally undermined.

## (F) *Economic Conditions*

1. *Agriculture.*—In Italy the Second Triumvirate had brought about an extensive change in the ownership of land. The general effect of this redistribution was to break up the larger estates into smallholdings, and the tendency for these to be reabsorbed into *latifundia* was checked by Augustus' policy of giving free loans to rural landowners. The imperial estates and the estates of the wealthiest Romans were in the provinces rather than in Italy. The typical Italian estate of the first century A.D. was a holding of medium size, in which the middle class invested the profits of commerce or manufactures : though the large ranches of the later republic did not disappear.

When Augustus called a halt to Roman conquest and suppressed piracy in the empire, he cut off the main sources for the supply of slaves to Italy, and thereby created a new labour problem. Nor did slaves work well, unless carefully watched. The main source of supply from the time of Augustus consisted of home-bred slaves, and the Italian landlords under the early emperors used more female labour on their estates ; for each child reared the women workers received money, and they could look forward to personal freedom as the reward of having three children. The treatment of the slaves was more humane and intelligent. With these improvements the slave estates in Italy could still be efficient ; under an expert landlord they might make a good profit.

So long as Rome made the provinces give it wheat, the Italian countryside merely grew for its own consumption. Experiments were made here and there, but in general it was the least fertile portion of the land that was left over for the growth of corn, and the methods of tillage were not improved.

But the typical Italian ranching system had reached its maximum under the republic, so that no further change was made here.

The growing demands for wine and oil were met by the provinces. But the finer brands for the tables of the rich were supplied by Italy, whose products now competed on equal terms with the Greek. A vineyard was regarded as the safest investment. Campania still flowed with wine and oil ; the region of the Alban mount became a second centre for the production of vintage wines ; and the trade led to an increase of vineyards in the Po valley and of olive-growing in Istria. The place of Sicily as Rome's principal granary was taken by Africa and by Egypt. The cultivation of Egyptian wheat for export was restored by Augustus to a high level.

On the European continent the cultivation of the land was hardly enough for local needs. But the borderlands of the western Mediterranean now began to rival Italy in food production. Emigration to these regions had been greatly increased by the colonial settlements of Caesar and Augustus ; and a medium-sized farm, cultivated by free native tenants under the active supervision of the Roman proprietors, was the normal type of holding. In North Africa wheat-growing was increased, so that the district became one of the chief sources of supply for Rome. The principal products of the western Mediterranean lands, as of Italy, were wine and oil. In Gaul the olive was grown with more success than the vine.

2. *Industry and Trade.*—The benefits of the new system of government gave impetus to the commerce and manufactures of the Roman empire. Never before had the Mediterranean lands enjoyed such security and freedom. Restrictions on travel within the empire were almost unknown : a merchant might travel its length from the Euphrates to the Thames without being called upon to produce a passport. The Roman network of roads, and the establishment of Roman camps and colonies on the outskirts of the empire, opened up many new markets. Rivers were systematically exploited for commercial purposes. The Baetis was navigated as far as Hispalis, the Rhine up to Cologne. Lutetia, which had been nothing

THE ROMAN THEATRE AT ARAUSIO (ORANGE)

more than a tribal capital, began to attain importance as a river-port.

The early Caesars took economic advantages more into consideration than the Senate of republican days. Augustus' Arabian expedition was frankly directed to commercial gain ; his treaties with Parthia almost certainly made provision for trading in the interior of Asia ; and he discussed trade questions with the envoys from India. The emperors also increased their income by exploiting industry. They acquired large mining fields in the provinces ; in Italy they manufactured pottery. The example set by the emperors was followed by men and women of high standing at Rome. One of the largest brick-factories of Rome was in the possession of a leading senator named Domitius Afer.

Though the period of the Roman emperors saw no new technical inventions, new industries sprang up in the north and the south of Italy. Earthenware was made at Mutina and Aquileia. Pompeii in the south, Parma, Mediolanum and Patavium in the north, produced woollen goods. The Campanian cities introduced glass-blowing into Italy, and Rome began to supply its own enormous market in the more specialised industries, such as paper-making and work in the precious metals.

The manufactures of the Levant became prosperous under the early emperors. They maintained their hold on local markets, supplied Rome with luxury wares and found new markets in the east. The new glass industry prospered in Phoenicia and at Alexandria ; a fashion for half-silk goods benefited Cos and other cities of Asia Minor. In the European countries the mining industry maintained its former importance. In Spain the lead ore of Andalusia increased in value as the towns of the west followed the example of Rome in laying down water-pipes, and the discovery of tin mines along the western coast made the Spanish peninsula the chief source of supply. The iron mines of Noricum remained highly productive, and the varied mineral resources of Illyria were energetically exploited after the Roman conquest. Gaul developed pottery and textile manufactures.

The foreign trade of the Roman empire expanded rapidly

in the first century A.D. In Britain the Italian or Gallic merchant began a peaceful penetration half a century before the military occupation by the Roman legions. Along the Rhine and upper Danube the emperors discouraged commerce, but in the days of Nero a new trade route was opened by a Roman in search of amber, who found his way from Carnuntum to the eastern Baltic. The exploration of the North Sea by the Roman fleets opened up a new waterway from the lower Rhine to Germany and Scandinavia, by which the bronze of Capua and other metal ware was carried to these countries.

During the reign of Augustus the main routes from the Euphrates to Seleucia (near Bagdad), and thence to Merv and Kandahar, and to the Persian Gulf, were surveyed for the benefit of Mediterranean traders. The sea route to India was now thrown open to sailors from the Mediterranean. Pioneers discovered short cuts to central and southern India; under Claudius or Nero occasional adventurers touched Ceylon or

THE PERISTYLE OF THE HOUSE OF THE VETTII AT POMPEII

THE PONT DU GARD, NEAR NÎMES

crept up the Bay of Bengal. These explorations led to the growth of a regular traffic between the Mediterranean lands and India. Before long the Indian trade became huge.

A new sea route was opened along the east African coast. No attempt was made under the early emperors to explore the interior of Africa. But trade in the Roman empire also grew fast. The wine and oil of the Mediterranean lands went with the legions across Europe. The vases of Arretium travelled to the Rhine and to Britain, to Spain and Morocco, and eastward as far as the Caucasus. The bronze pots and pans of Capua have been found in the Black Sea regions, in Wales and in Scotland.

The new inter-provincial trade was not confined to luxuries. It included cooking vessels, tiles and common lamps, and wine and oil.

The massacres of Roman traders during the revolts of the Pannonians in A.D. 6, of the Gauls in 21, and of the Britons in 61, suggest that the ruthless and greedy money-lending of republican days was still being practised in the provinces; but the general improvement in the condition of the provinces reduced the opportunities of the tax-gatherers. But the growth of trade and industry brought with it a greater demand for business capital, and thus gave scope for a new kind of money-lending at moderate rates for productive purposes.

Workers in the provinces and the Italian country towns were mostly free, but in Rome slaves were more numerous. Many of the town slaves rose to the position of foremen or managers in business. Many of those engaged in manufactures and trade were freedmen.

### CHAPTER XV

# THE EMPIRE, A.D. 68–180: STABILITY

## Part 1 : *A.D. 68–96*

(A) *Civil War*, *A.D. 68–96*

TIBERIUS made no attempt to meet the legions in his later years by going the rounds of the camps. Except for Claudius' flying visit to the war-front in Britain, none of the next three emperors saw any active service, and Nero's only absence from Italy was on a theatrical tour. On the other hand, the money which Augustus' successors gave to the praetorian cohorts showed the dependence of the emperors on their household troops and made the frontier armies jealous. Finally, in delaying the pay and pensions of the soldiers Nero made them disloyal.

1. *Summer 68–January 69.*—With the death of Nero the Julio-Claudian dynasty became extinct, and the hereditary principle of succession could not be continued. The imperial power was given to Galba by the Senate, and the news was brought to him. He at once set out for Rome, but before he could make good his position he had to dispose of two possible rivals. In Africa there was the military commander Clodius Macer; Galba had him killed. In Lower Germany the commander-in-chief, Fonteius Capito, was killed by his own subordinate, Fabius Valens, without waiting for Galba's orders. But now Nymphidius Sabinus suddenly repented of his choice of emperor. Nymphidius had made Tigellinus resign and was expecting to have the whole command of the praetorian troops. On hearing that Galba, before leaving Spain, had appointed Cornelius Laco to the post, Nymphidius tried to make himself emperor. But the soldiers killed him.

For the moment Galba controlled all the Roman military forces.

On taking up his duties as emperor Galba tried to improve the finances and discipline in the army. But he lacked judgment, and at the age of 71 he could not cope with his new duties. He was also unfortunate in his advisers, some of whom became very unpopular. He recalled Verginius from his command in Upper Germany : another error of judgment,

Head of Galba                                 Head of Vitellius

for Verginius alone had sufficient authority to hold the Rhine armies in check, and the generals whom Galba sent to replace him and Fonteius Capito — Hordeonius Flaccus in Upper Germany and A. Vitellius on the lower Rhine — were totally unable to restrain the soldiers. The effective command on the German front now fell into the hands of two divisional officers, Fabius Valens and A. Caecina, who were quite prepared to march on Rome.

2. *January–July 69.*—On January 1st of 69 the legions of Upper Germany refused to renew their oath of loyalty to Galba ; those of the lower Rhine followed suit. At the news Galba rightly judged that his only chance would be to nominate a co-regent and successor. But the emperor chose a young man named M. Piso Licinianus, who was acceptable to the Senate but meant nothing to the troops. Galba incidentally gave offence to M. Salvius Otho, the former governor of Lusitania, who had been the first army commander to proclaim

his loyalty to the new emperor. Otho made offers to the praetorians, who accepted him. On January 15th, 69, they acclaimed Otho emperor in their camp and marched in upon the Forum, where they killed Galba.

Otho's bid for power was accepted by the Senate and by most provincial governors. On January 3rd, 69, Fabius Valens, who had killed Fonteius Capito, got the army of the lower Rhine to accept its own commander, A. Vitellius, as emperor, and the forces of Upper Germany agreed. While Vitellius stayed behind to form a reserve army, Caecina and Valens at once moved off with the flower of the Rhine armies, and the death of Galba did not stop them.

The strength of the Vitellians, amounting to some 100,000 men, was barely equal to that which the emperor had, but they were the best of all the Roman armies ; they had the highest morale and the best leaders. Moreover, Otho's troops were scattered over a wide area and could not be concentrated before summer.

The plan of campaign of the Vitellians was bold. Valens and Caecina were each to lead thirty to forty thousand men across the Alps before the winter snows had melted, and to join in Transpadane Italy. They accomplished their march without serious loss or delay, and their intact armies joined at Cremona.

The division of Caecina, which was the first to emerge on the plain of northern Italy, made an attempt to force the line of the Po without waiting for the troops of Valens ; but it was held up between Placentia and Cremona, where Otho's force made a stand. With the arrival of Valens' division the Vitellians were considerably stronger than their enemy. Otho foolishly refused to wait for more troops, and fought the Vitellians near Cremona. He was defeated and committed suicide. At the news of Otho's death the Senate accepted Vitellius without waiting for orders.

After the battle of Cremona the Vitellian leaders attempted to make their victory secure by drastic measures against the defeated Othonians. The praetorian guard was disbanded, the Illyrian legions, which had arrived in Italy, were sent back, and their best centurions were put to death. Vitellius was a weak and foolish man. He plunged the Roman treasury further into bankruptcy, and allowed his troops to get rid of all discipline.

Moreover, the Vitellians did not control the remaining military forces of the empire. Their arrogance angered the armies on other fronts, and the execution of Otho's centurions scared the officers into rebellion. The first challenge to Vitellius' authority was made in the eastern provinces. The prefect of Egypt, Tiberius Alexander, and the governor of Syria, C. Licinius Mucianus, put forward as rival to Vitellius the commander of the forces in Palestine, T. Flavius Vespasianus.

3. *July 69–Summer 70.*—On July 1st, 69, Tiberius Alexander got his troops to take an oath to Vespasian. A few days later Vespasian's own forces and all the governors and dependent kings in the East followed suit. Vespasian based his strategy on starving Rome into submission by cutting off its supplies of grain from Egypt. While he proceeded to Alexandria to organise this, Mucianus made a leisurely march through Asia Minor towards Europe, taking with him an army of some 20,000 men. But the legions of the Danube anticipated Mucianus. At the first news of Vespasian's proclamation as emperor the legions of Pannonia and Moesia accepted him and marched on Italy. The leader was a subordinate officer in the Pannonian army named Antonius Primus.

In the late autumn of 69 Primus set out on a fast march to Rome. Disregarding Mucianus' instructions to wait, Primus pushed forward into the plain of northern Italy. With a force which never exceeded 50,000 men, he found the Vitellians unprepared. While the emperor entertained himself, Valens was ill and Caecina in despair. Under new officers of their own choice the Vitellian soldiers prepared to make a stand on the line of the middle Po. The rival armies came upon each other between Cremona and Bedriacum. The Vitellians probably had superior numbers, and they fought with determination ; but the Danubian troops broke through and completed their victory by storming the enemy camp. A massacre of the defeated troops followed.

The governors of the western provinces now accepted

Vespasian. Primus made a dash for Rome, and annihilated the Vitellians. The emperor himself attempted escape, but was killed. The entry of the Danubian troops into the capital started a new reign of terror. Fortunately Mucianus soon came to Rome and controlled the troops, who returned to their stations on the frontier. On the arrival of Vespasian in Rome (in the summer of 70) Mucianus in turn retired into the background.

Meanwhile a second rebellion broke out in 69 on the Rhine border, organised by a Batavian chief named Iulius Civilis. In autumn 69 the civil war in Italy gave Civilis his opportunity. He declared for Vespasian, and in his name attacked the Vitellian garrisons on the lower Rhine ; but he soon showed himself opposed to any Roman authority.

Early in 70 two chiefs of the Gauls, Iulius Classicus and Iulius Tutor, came to terms with Civilis. The entire line of the Rhine to Strasbourg or Basle had now been lost to the Romans, and the tribes on the Gallic side of the river supported Classicus or Civilis.

But the rebel Gallic leaders could not control Civilis and his German allies, whose object was complete independence. The German and the Gallic armies parted company, and neither party made preparations for Vespasian's counter-attack.

In summer 70 an army which Mucianus had formed from the remaining Roman garrisons in Europe took the field against the rebels under the command of Q. Petilius Cerialis. At the approach of Cerialis the legionaries deserted back to the Roman side. Cerialis, in a hard-fought battle, destroyed the Gallic empire. After another fight near Vetera, where he met a German army under Civilis, Cerialis drove the Batavians back upon their own territory. He obtained the surrender of the Batavi by an offer of easy terms.

As insurance against new civil wars, Vespasian broke up the large camps on the Rhine and Danube frontiers. The legions were spaced out in separate camps, where they had less opportunity of realising their strength or of making trouble. He also moved the auxiliary troops from their native districts to distant frontiers, and transferred their command from native chieftains to Roman officers.

(B) *The Emperors*

1. *Vespasian* (*A.D.* 70–79).—The founder of the 'Flavian dynasty', T. Flavius Vespasianus, was a fair representative of the new middle class of Italy. At the age of sixty (which he

Head of Domitian          Head of Vespasian

Head of Titus and on the reverse two captive Jews
under a palm-tree

reached in 69) he had gained much experience but little distinction.

The new emperor was an administrator rather than a statesman, and had little imagination. But he was well fitted for his task, which was not to devise a new government but to give the existing machinery a fresh start. He worked hard, and spared neither himself nor his subordinates; he was firm, sane, and had a sense of humour. By these virtues he established his authority firmly and assured the succession to his two sons.

2. *Titus* (*A.D. 79–81*).—Vespasian's elder son, Titus, had brains and good looks. He caught the world's fancy, but he died young. His reign of two years was too brief to show its future possibilities.

3. *Domitian* (*A.D. 81–96*).—The younger son, T. Flavius Domitianus, was as silent as Titus was gay. Vespasian and Titus gave him consulships and other empty marks of honour, but neither would entrust him with military commands or other responsible offices. This made Domitian sour and distrustful. When his brother's sudden death left the imperial power in his hands he exercised it in a despotic fashion. He insisted on being called not *Caesar* or *princeps* but *dominus et deus*. His manner made him one of the most hated of Roman emperors ; yet it was justified by his abilities. If to him the state was a mere machine, at any rate he was an efficient driver. While he lacked his father's sense of humour, he inherited his industriousness and calm good judgment. Domitian completed the work of restoration which Vespasian had successfully begun.

4. *The Opposition.*—By putting the Roman world in order Vespasian earned great popularity. Titus was popular also, but there was opposition and in the later years of Domitian the atmosphere became thick with plots.

In 79 A. Caecina attempted to snatch the succession from Titus by bribing the household troops. But Titus, who was chief of the Guards, put him to death. In 88 the commander of the army on the upper Rhine, L. Antonius Saturninus, tried to march on Rome, but having no more than two legions he was defeated by another division of the Rhine forces under L. Appius Norbanus.

Opposition was offered by some obstructive philosophers of the Stoic and the Cynic sects. The Stoics and Cynics made a virtue of personal independence. Several of their leading members now criticised Vespasian and Domitian. Their opposition seems to have been directed against Vespasian's determination to treat the office of emperor as a hereditary possession ; but their general attitude was one of obstruction. By their sheer insistence they broke the patience of Vespasian, who expelled them from Italy, and put to death a senator named Helvidius Priscus. The less long-suffering Domitian twice renewed his father's expulsion order (which had been ineffective) and caused the Senate to condemn on a charge of *maiestas* two members of their order.

A more dangerous kind of opposition to the Flavian emperors took the form of conspiracies by discontented senators, who resented the attitude of Domitian to their order. These tried to kill Domitian. During the early part of his reign Domitian took no special precautions against assassination ; but after a rebellion by Saturninus in 88 he gave free rein to the professional informers, and the Senate was once more called upon to condemn its own members on charges of treason or *maiestas*. Domitian's executions created an additional sense of personal insecurity among the senators, out of which arose fresh plots. Domitian fell a victim to a plot by his wife Domitia. Under her instructions a palace servant named Stephanus stabbed the emperor while he was reading.

## (c) *The Constitution*

The constitutional powers which the Senate gave Vespasian were afterwards enlarged in accordance with the policy of the Flavian emperors. A far-reaching change was the revival of the censorship by Vespasian in 73, and its permanent occupation by Domitian from 84 to his death. The most important use of their censorial power was to create new senators by the process of direct nomination. The purpose of the Flavian emperors was to include men of tried ability (such as equestrian members of the administrative service) who were past the usual age for holding a quaestorship and qualifying for a seat in the normal manner. By this the Flavian emperors gave wider effect to Claudius' policy of filling the Senate with men of provincial origin. Like Claudius, they used their censorial powers with discretion, restricting their selection to the more highly Romanised districts of the Latin-speaking West, in particular to Gallia Narbonensis and to Hispania Baetica. But they gave a sufficiently strong lead to future emperors to ensure that their policy should be carried on.

However, Vespasian and Domitian used the Senate to choose individual members for their administrative service, rather than as a corporation with important collective functions. The attitude of the Flavians to the Senate was shown with brutal candour by Domitian. While Vespasian consulted the House, Domitian seldom summoned it except to give information, and took away the illusion that it was the emperor's partner rather than his servant. He therefore earned the hatred of the Senate as no previous emperor had done.

In the civil wars of 69 the value of the civil service was clear. While the emperors came and went, the professionals, for the most part, kept their posts and preserved a great measure of continuity in the administration. Under the Flavian emperors they had the same strict supervision as in the best days of Augustus and Tiberius ; no emperor showed better judgment in selecting his administrators or more firmness in controlling them than Domitian. The supply of suitable candidates for an administrative career had now increased, so that the emperors had less need to give public duties to their domestic staff. The Flavians transferred most of the secretarial and financial work to men of equestrian rank.

Vespasian frankly treated the imperial office as a hereditary property. In order to remove all doubts, he ruled in partnership with his eldest son. He gave Titus the consulate, the censorship and the *tribunicia potestas*, appointed him sole commander of the praetorian cohorts and gave him a general right of control over the administration. Despite their distrust of Domitian, his father and brother recognised him as heir. Domitian executed two of his cousins, Flavius Clemens and Flavius Sabinus, on a charge of conspiracy ; but he arranged one or other of Clemens' young sons to be his successor.

## (D) *Rome and Italy*

In the city of Rome the Flavian rulers introduced a new age of great activity. Domitian began a new festival of Jupiter Capitolinus and in 88 he conducted another celebration of the *ludi saeculares*. On the other hand the immorality of Nero's reign was firmly suppressed. The supply of corn, which Vespasian went to Alexandria to organise, suffered no further interruption. A special merchant fleet was arranged by him for the regular transportation of grain to Rome.

The traces of the civil war in Italy were soon obliterated, but in 79 Mt. Vesuvius, which had remained quiet since the prehistoric age, broke into sudden activity and buried three cities, Herculaneum, Pompeii and Stabiae, under a rain of volcanic dust.

### (E) *Finance*

The financial chaos resulting from Nero's extravagance and the civil wars was a big problem for Vespasian. It required some £40,000,000 to make the state finances sound. Vespasian raised the rates of existing taxes and invented new ones. He took back most of the large estates in Egypt which earlier emperors had given to their friends. He set up commissions to recover public land which private landowners had secretly stolen.

Vespasian had not made extravagant promises of money to his troops and was thrifty in his personal life. By good management he restored the imperial finances, and raised sufficient funds to carry out an extensive programme of new buildings and to give money for higher education.

Titus was not so economical, and Domitian, to ensure himself against fresh military mutinies, raised the annual pay of the legions from 300 to 400 denarii. But he slightly reduced the numbers of the army. The general administration of Domitian was successful.

### (F) *The Provinces*

For the Roman provinces the Flavian era was on the whole an age of prosperity. In 69 the provinces suffered from Vitellius' and Vespasian's armies, and during the reign of Vespasian they were severely taxed in order to clear off the debts of the Roman treasury. But they escaped the havoc of actual battle ; and they had uniformly good administration.

The Flavian emperors did not pursue a vigorous policy of colonisation in the provinces ; but they carried their enfranchisement a considerable stage further. In 73–74 Vespasian gave Latin rights to the entire Spanish peninsula, whose towns now had a constitution of Italian type. The main purpose of this was to give recognition to the progress which Romanisation had made in Spain, and to get the leading men of the Spanish towns into the administrative service of the empire.

1. *The Jewish War.*—Vespasian's war against Vitellius in 69 gave the Jews a year to recover. But in 70 Titus, taking over his father's command, captured Jerusalem after a siege of six months. The surviving population of Jerusalem was mostly reduced to slavery, and a Roman legion was permanently stationed on the site. The Sanhedrin was abolished and the Temple, which had been burnt down in the siege, was not allowed to be rebuilt.

2. *Britain.*—In 70 or 71 Vespasian appointed Petilius Cerialis to be governor of Britain. Advancing from his old quarters at Lindum, Cerialis defeated the Brigantes (between the Humber and the Tyne), and probably founded Eburacum (York), which subsequently became the military headquarters of Britain. Thus the Romans completed the conquest of the English plain. Cerialis' successor, Sex. Iulius Frontinus (*c.* 74–77), resumed the advance into Wales. Frontinus' work was carried on by Cn. Iulius Agricola (77–78), who conquered the coast of North Wales to Caernarvon.

After two campaigns in Wales Agricola made the first Roman advance into the northern hill-country. He made a base at Newstead and a chain of signalling towers between the Clyde and the Forth, but could not invade, for Domitian refused the necessary reinforcements. But in the next two seasons (82–83) Agricola resumed his advance into Scotland. In 83 he won a battle over the combined chiefs of the Caledonian tribes of the Highlands, and the fleet sailed to the extreme north of Scotland. In 84 Domitian recalled Agricola. The three legions stationed in Britain remained on the English plain ; the auxiliary cohorts were distributed over Wales and garrisoned northern Britain as far as Stirling and Perth.

As an administrator, Agricola set an example of fair dealing which won him the confidence of the natives, and by his personal encouragement he got the chiefs to adopt a Roman way of life. Under his governorship Britain entered upon a period of economic development, and was for the first time brought fully within continental European culture.

3. *Germany.*—On the German frontier the Flavian emperors

THE 'SAALBURG', A RESTORED FORT OF DOMITIAN ON MT. TAUNUS

carried out the same policy of advance as they adopted in Britain.
In order to cut off the sharp angle of the Rhine at Basle, and
to hold the line of high ground beyond the middle Rhine, they
took the Taunus Mountains and the Black Forest into their
system of defences. This was begun by Vespasian, who conquered the Black Forest land as far as the river Kinzig ;
Domitian extended the frontier to the Neckar. Raids by the
Chatti on the middle Rhine were punished by two expeditions
under the emperor himself (83 and 89). Domitian prolonged
the forward zone to the north side of the Main. At the end
of his reign the Roman frontier road ran from Bonn round
Mt. Taunus and down the Neckar valley to a point north of
the Danube (near Lorch), where it met a road extending along
that river in front of Raetia. These roads were guarded at
close intervals with watch-towers which were connected by
roads with the advanced camps of the auxiliary cohorts.
Within the area a mixed population of Celts and Germans
made permanent settlements, and in the Black Forest area a
new centre for the worship of the emperors was established
at Arae Flaviae.

4. *The Danube.*—The civil wars of 69 did not bring the
Roman frontiers on the Danube into any serious danger.
Raids by the Suebi into Raetia were stopped in 74 by the
troops from Upper Germany under Pinarius Clemens. In
the winter of 68–69 heavily armoured Roxolanian horsemen
from the Russian plain crossed the frozen Danube for a raid
into Moesia ; but they were checked by a thaw, in which the
mud made them easy victims to the Roman infantry.

During the reign of Domitian a new danger arose from
the reunion of the Dacian tribes under a chief named Decebalus. He formed a national Dacian army and trained it in
Roman fashion. In 86 Decebalus broke into Moesia and
overwhelmed the Roman garrisons. Domitian's praetorian
prefect, Cornelius Fuscus, brought reinforcements from the
middle Danube and invaded Dacia, but was defeated. Two
or three years later another general, named Tettius Iulianus,
renewed the invasion of Dacia and defeated Decebalus.
Domitian fought in person against a coalition of German
tribes, the Suebi, Quadi and Marcomanni on the middle

Danube, but was defeated. Though he could have recovered, he thought the whole war too expensive, and he arranged a peace with Decebalus by which Decebalus kept his territory and acknowledged himself a dependant of Rome (89).

Domitian fortified the Danube front against further attacks. He concentrated a force of nine or ten legions in a chain of camps along the river, extending from Vindobona, Carnuntum and Aquincum to Troesmis. He also divided Moesia into two separate provinces, Superior and Inferior.

5. *The East.*—The Parthian king, Vologeses, threatened to invade Syria in 76, but was deterred by its governor, M. Ulpius Traianus. This was followed by thirty-five years of peace between Romans and Parthians.

In 72 Vespasian deposed the kings of two small border states, Commagene and Armenia Minor, so as to bring the entire middle reach of the Euphrates under direct Roman control. New legionary camps were established at Melitene and Satala, and roads were built to connect them with Syria and the Black Sea.

## Part 2 : *A.D. 96–180*

### (A) *The Emperors*

1. *Nerva (A.D. 96–98).*—After the death of Domitian, one of the Praetorian commanders, Petronius Secundus, kept the Guards in check, while the Senate made its first free choice of a successor. The imperial power was transferred to a senior senator named M. Cocceius Nerva.

The new emperor (96–98) was a very able lawyer. He was skilled in administrative routine, but he was too old to guide the state firmly through a political crisis, and he had no prestige among the soldiers. The chief problem of his reign was whether he could keep the army under control. In 97 the praetorian troops demanded the execution of Petronius Secundus. Nerva had to give way. Realising the need for force, he won the support of the commander in Upper Germany, M. Ulpius Traianus (Trajan), by adopting him and making him co-regent. Nerva ruled under the shelter of

Trajan's legions, and after his death in 98 Trajan succeeded him without opposition. Though Nerva's call to Trajan was an emergency measure, it set a new precedent for the regulation of the succession. The next three rulers followed Nerva's example of adopting a man of ability to succeed them. This method saved the Roman world for a century from further succession-crises and gave it five good emperors.

Head of Trajan and on the reverse Trajan's bridge over the Danube

Head of Hadrian

2. *Trajan* (*A.D. 98–117*).—Trajan was first and foremost a military man, who commanded the respect of the soldiers, and had no need to bribe them. His tolerance and courtesy were welcome to all, in particular to the Senate. Trajan selected a distant relative named P. Aelius Hadrianus to succeed him.

3. *Hadrian* (*A.D. 117–138*).—Hadrian was one of the ablest of Roman emperors. He lacked personal magnetism, and he

possessed a gift of making enemies which was absent in Trajan; yet soldiers and civilians alike felt that his was a master hand. Two years before his death Hadrian adopted a young man named L. Ceionius Commodus Verus. The death

BUST OF HADRIAN

of Verus in 138 compelled Hadrian to make a second choice. On this occasion he played for safety by selecting a senator of high rank named T. Aurelius Antoninus.

4. *Antoninus (A.D. 138–161).*—In character and abilities Antoninus (138–161) was like Nerva. Though old he was capable of competent government.

5. *Aurelius (A.D. 161–180).*—Hadrian required Antoninus

to adopt a son of L. Verus, and one of Antoninus' own nephews
named M. Annius Verus (and renamed M. Aelius Aurelius).
Of the two candidates for the succession to which Antoninus'
choice had been limited, the latter was rightly preferred.
M. Aurelius, it is true, insisted on his adopted brother being
given equal rights, so that until the death of the younger Verus
in 169 the imperial power was held by two men.   But the co-
regent left all power and responsibility in the hands of M.
Aurelius, who in effect ruled as sole emperor from 161 to 180.

M. Aurelius was braced by his Stoic teaching to shoulder
manfully the burden of his position, and he spared himself
neither at home nor in the field of war.

## (B) *The Constitution*

In this period misunderstandings between emperors and
Senate, which had caused mutual irritation under Domitian,
gave way to an agreement which was not seriously disturbed
before the death of M. Aurelius.   The emperors always kept
the Senate informed of their decisions.   They submitted
legislation to it for approval.   Nerva, Trajan and Hadrian
swore not to put a senator to death except by the Senate's own
sentence after a free trial.

The emperors of the second century dispelled the atmosphere of conspiracy.   At the beginning and the end of
Hadrian's reign, it is true, persons of high rank were executed
on a charge of treason.   In 118 four of Trajan's right-hand
men, including his two chief military assistants, Cornelius
Palma and Lusius Quietus, were arrested by the praetorian
prefect Caelius Attianus, and sentenced to death by the Senate,
in the absence of the emperor.   In 136 a brother-in-law of
Hadrian named Servianus was put to death on a charge of
conspiring to make his grandson Fuscus emperor.   In this
case there can be little doubt that a real plot was formed.   In
175 the governor of M. Aurelius in the east, Avidius Cassius,
had himself proclaimed emperor, but he obtained little support from his troops and was easily suppressed.   In these rare
conspiracies the ruling motive was personal ambition rather
than political discontent.

But the emperors were equally careful to retain in their

hands all the powers exercised by the Flavian dynasty. Though they did not formally assume the office of censor, they used censorial power. Trajan and his successors introduced into the House members from Asia Minor and other eastern countries, where the Greek-speaking populations were beginning to take a more active interest in the Roman administration. By the end of the second century the Senate had become fairly representative of the empire as a whole, but it was now of small practical importance, except as a panel for the recruitment of high imperial officials. But the main feature of the Roman government in the second century was the further growth and more complete organisation of the civil services. This was mainly the work of Hadrian. To cope with the imperial correspondence, Hadrian divided the secretariat into two separate departments, for the Latin and the Greek letters respectively. To speed up civil law in Italy, he divided the country into four judicial districts and appointed to each of these a permanent official who took over cases from the praetors at Rome and heard appeals from the municipal courts.

Under Trajan and Hadrian the freedmen of the imperial household played little part in public administration. The higher administrative posts that were not reserved by tradition for senators were given to members of the equestrian order. Regular 'promotion ladders' were set up. A mark of this more rigid organisation now appeared in the honorary titles which the imperial officials of equestrian rank began to add to their names — a practice which grew up in the later years of the second century. Officials of the third grade (e.g. the financial *procuratores*) henceforth styled themselves *viri egregii* ; on rising to the next higher posts, such as the *praefectus annonae* ('prefect in charge of the corn supply'), they became *viri perfectissimi* ; those who rose to the summit of the equestrian career by appointment to the command of the household troops were *viri eminentissimi*. At the same time a distinction between civilian and military careers, which the early emperors had not drawn sharply, was established within the equestrian ranks of the imperial service. In the military branch of the service the imperial officials rose from the tribunate of a legion or the 'prefecture' of an auxiliary cohort to the governorship of a frontier province. In the civil section they took up a minor financial or judicial post and ascended to a high administrative function at Rome.

Under Hadrian the annual edicts of the praetors at Rome, and the edicts of the provincial governors, were cast into final shape by a distinguished lawyer named Salvius Iulianus. Interpreting and expanding Roman law was done by the *Consilium Principis*, to which the chief lawyers of the day were regularly invited.

The Comitia now ceased to be a law-making body. Its place was taken by imperial commands, whether in the form of general edicts (with or without the Senate's confirmation), or of decisions in answer to questions from the imperial officials.

## (c) *Finance*

The emperors all followed the good example of Vespasian and Domitian in giving nothing away to favourites. But in their outlay for public purposes they were liberal and at times even lavish. Trajan reduced the money usually paid to the praetorian cohorts by a new emperor, but the next two emperors paid them an unnecessarily high price. Nerva made permanent loans from the *fiscus* to Italian landowners, on condition that they should pay interest at the moderate rate of 5 per cent into the treasury of their town, and that the towns should use the money for maintenance allowances for the children of needy families in their territory. These were loans extended by Trajan, Antoninus and M. Aurelius, and the service of this fund was placed on a permanent basis by Hadrian. Trajan made special provision for the distribution of free corn at Rome to 5,000 needy children. Yet none of these emperors cut down the feeding of the multitudes in Rome ; indeed Trajan spent considerable sums on additional distributions of wine and oil to the people of Rome, and the next three emperors were even more extravagant.

Though Antoninus and M. Aurelius spent little on public works, the three previous emperors carried out extensive building programmes in Rome. Nerva spent money on the repair of the Italian main roads. Trajan improved communications between Rome and Brundisium by constructing a new high-road across the Apennines ; also he spent large sums on harbour works at Ancona, Centumcellae, and especially at Ostia. Hadrian also spent a lot on public works in the provinces.

But slight reductions in taxation were made. Trajan and Hadrian allowed many taxes to go unpaid and Nerva abolished the Jewish tax to Jupiter Capitolinus. Freedom from tribute was also given to towns that had been harmed by fires or other natural calamities. A lot of money came to the *fiscus* when Trajan brought back the treasures of the Dacian monarchy to Rome, and the Dacian mines provided a big additional income. But the sound state of the imperial finances was mainly due, as in the reigns of Augustus and Vespasian, to a regime of internal peace and sound administration.

The emperors of the second century made no great changes in Augustus' system of taxation. The direct taxes were taken by the local authorities, but from the time of Trajan or Hadrian the responsibility for their collection was fixed on a special body selected from the senators of each community. The indirect taxes remained in the hands of private contractors, but the companies of *publicani* were replaced by individual collectors, who were residents in the district under their charge, and were no longer required to pay the total amount of the tax before collecting it. Imperial *procuratores* supervised their operations. This method for the gathering of indirect taxes was borrowed from the method of rent-collection which had gradually come into use on the imperial estates under Hadrian. On these estates a *conductor* ('contractor') let most of the land to cultivating tenants (*coloni*) and collected their rents for the emperor. In return the *conductor* was entitled to get from the *coloni* a certain amount of labour on part of the land which he himself used.

For disputes between tax-payers and the *fiscus* a special court of appeal was set up at Rome by Nerva. The president of this court was a magistrate of republican type, and had no interest in upholding the previous decision of the procurator's court ; but from the time of Hadrian imperial officials were appointed to argue the case of the *fiscus* both at Rome and in the provinces.

In the second century the *fiscus* could not sustain any heavy additional burden. The wars of Trajan meant getting more money from the provincials. To meet the Marcomannic Wars, M. Aurelius sold the crown jewels and devalued the coinage by 25 per cent. But usually the *fiscus* more than paid its way. Under Antoninus its surplus again rose to the sum of 2700 million sesterces (*c.* £27,000,000), which it had not reached since the time of Tiberius.

## (D) *The Provinces*

In the second century the town life of the empire reached its furthest limits. The growth of city life at this period was a natural process, for though Trajan started many colonies (especially in Thrace), the founding of new cities by government action ceased soon after. But the emperors gave the status of a colony or a municipium to many native towns, wherever these had sufficient Roman or Hellenic culture.

The general political development of these towns was the same as that of Rome in the second century B.C. Political power came into the hands of ruling aristocracies, mostly the local landowners, though rich traders and industrialists would have less difficulty than at Rome in entering the governing circles. In many cities of the first and second centuries A.D. the *plebs* still had a real choice in the appointment of magistrates. But the senates eventually acquired the right of appointing the magistrates and selecting their new members.

So long as these aristocracies were efficient, the Roman government gave them a free hand. But in the second century in some districts (notably in the eastern provinces) Roman force was required to keep public order. The commonest failure of the cities was financial inefficiency. In 109 Trajan appointed a special commissioner, Quintilius Maximus, to cure the financial disorders of the cities of Achaea, and Caecilius Secundus to Bithynia, with powers to overhaul the municipal accounts. The same emperor appointed *curatores* to take charge of the finances of individual Italian towns. Imperial control over local finances, once introduced, tended to become a regular practice.

Trials before the Senate in the days of Trajan show that

the proconsuls of senatorial provinces, if left to their own devices, were still able to govern oppressively. But Trajan supervised the provincial governors, which he himself appointed with great care.

Hadrian made systematic tours of inspection, in which he visited almost all the empire. He made a grand tour of the empire in 121–126, travelling to the Rhine and Danube fronts, Britain, Spain, Mauretania, Africa, Asia Minor and Greece. In 129–134 he made a similar journey through the eastern provinces as far as Egypt. Of the twenty-one years of his reign Hadrian spent more than half outside Italy. Though his travels, incidentally, served to gratify his curiosity as a sightseer and to provide an outlet for his restless activity, their main purpose undoubtedly was to give him a first-hand acquaintance with provincial government in all the three continents. To supplement his own investigations, he required his officials to furnish him with detailed reports on territories not visited by him. By these means he had a firm grasp of the actual conditions of the various provinces, and was able to exercise more effective control than any previous emperor.

The example of Hadrian was not followed by Antoninus, who never left Italy, except for one visit to the eastern provinces. But M. Aurelius frequently inspected the Danube lands and spent two years (175–176) on a general tour round the eastern Mediterranean. The provinces received more personal attention than ever before from the emperors of the second century.

In the second century the enfranchisement of the provinces was carried on. Trajan and his successors all had provincial blood in their veins. Trajan was born in a town of southern Spain named Italica. Hadrian's family came from the birthplace of Trajan, and M. Aurelius from the neighbourhood of Corduba. Antoninus was born at Lanuvium, but his place of origin was Nemausus in Narbonese Gaul. They followed the example of the Flavian rulers in granting 'Latin rights' as a half-way house to full Roman status. These grants were chiefly made in the Danube lands and in the eastern provinces. The final step of giving full Roman citizenship to all free men of the empire, which was taken early in the third century,

THE 'PRAETORIUM' OR HEADQUARTERS OF THE
CAMP AT LAMBAESIS

may be regarded as the sequel of the franchise policy of Trajan
and his successors.

1. *Africa.*—The Mauretanian provinces were the scene of
wars. In this district the process of settlement had not been
carried beyond the coastal border, and the nomadic tribesmen
of the hills made occasional raids on the plains. During his
visit to Mauretania in 123 Hadrian endeavoured to extend the
area of effective occupation to the ledge of the Atlas plateau.
But the inland tribes, reinforced by Gaetulian raiders from the
oases of the western Sahara, returned to the attack every now
and then. Between 144 and 152 the small Roman garrison
was kept occupied by continuous raids, and another series of
raids took place between 170 and 176, in the course of which
even Spain was attacked.

About 100 the frontier of the province of Africa, which had
long been the line of Lake Tritonis and Mt. Aures, was carried
westward and southward to the salt lakes. Under Hadrian the
headquarters of the Roman legion in Africa were removed
from Theveste to Lambaesis.

2. *Armenia and Parthia.*—On the eastern border of the
empire advances were carried out by Trajan; but these were

for the most part lost by Hadrian. In 105 Trajan took over the kingdom of the Nabataean Arabs, whose position had a high commercial value. The Nabataean territory was made into a separate province of 'Arabia', but the territory of Damascus at its northern end was attached to Syria.

Towards the end of his reign Trajan abolished the Euphrates frontier which Augustus had fixed. This change of policy was provoked by a Parthian king named Chosroes. Trajan declared Armenia a Roman province (114).

In taking over Armenia Trajan committed himself to a further extension of the Roman frontier into Mesopotamia, so as to cut off the angle between Armenia and Syria. Continuing his advance into Parthian territory, he occupied the western end of Mesopotamia, whose kings, left unsupported by Chosroes, made feeble resistance or came to terms at once. After a winter spent in the construction of a transport fleet on the middle Euphrates, the Roman forces made a parallel march in two divisions along each of the Mesopotamian rivers, but united to attack Chosroes' winter capital at Ctesiphon. The Parthian king fled, and Trajan sailed down the Tigris to the Persian Gulf (115–116). He now gave Ctesiphon and Babylonia to a son of Chosroes named Parthamaspates, and made the territory between the middle Euphrates and Tigris into an additional province of Mesopotamia. But now rebellion broke out. Seleucia and other occupied cities rose in revolt, and in Judaea a rebellion had been pre-arranged with the Parthian king (117). Thanks to a Mauretanian chieftain named Lusius Quietus, who held the main line of retreat through central Mesopotamia, Trajan safely regained the Euphrates. Had he lived he would no doubt have resumed the attack ; but his eastern policy died with him.

In order to concentrate an overwhelming force against Armenia and Parthia the emperor had reduced garrisons on other fronts beyond the margin of safety. His new frontier in the east followed no natural line of defence and required a larger permanent garrison than the valley of the Euphrates. The first act of Hadrian, therefore, was to abandon Trajan's conquests, so that Chosroes got back his lost provinces and Parthamaspates was transferred to the vacant throne of

Armenia. In 130 Hadrian paid a personal visit to Chosroes and confirmed the arrangement. In 155 it was threatened, when a new Parthian king, Vologeses III, invaded Armenia, but on being warned by Rome he withdrew. In 161, however, Vologeses returned and put on the throne an Arsacid prince (another Pacorus) in Armenia after two victories over the governors of Cappadocia and Syria, who had met him with inadequate forces. In 163–164 a large Roman army under the direction of Avidius Cassius and of Statius Priscus, overran Armenia and Mesopotamia in much the same way as Trajan. In 163 Priscus captured and burnt the Armenian capital Artaxata. In 164 Cassius followed up a successful battle at Dura-Europus on the Euphrates by capturing the twin towns of Seleucia and Ctesiphon, both of which he destroyed. In 165 Vologeses agreed to leave Armenia in the hands of another Arsacid named Sohaemus. The kingdom of Osrhoene in western Mesopotamia became a Roman dependency. By this arrangement M. Aurelius, while keeping to the line of the Euphrates, straightened his frontier by cutting off the bend in its middle.

3. *Judaea*.—In 116 the Jews rebelled over a wide area ; they gained the upper hand in Cyprus and Cyrene, and held down the Roman troops in Palestine and Egypt. But the end of the Parthian War in 116 left Trajan free to recover Palestine and crush the rebellion in Egypt and Cyrene. Enough Jews survived to rebel again under Hadrian. In the early part of his reign this emperor had upheld the rights of the Jews at Alexandria, but during his second tour through the eastern provinces he got the idea of solving the Jewish problem by forcing them to mix with their neighbours. He founded a Roman colony, 'Aelia Capitolina', at Jerusalem, an act involving the building of a shrine of Jupiter Capitolinus on the site of the Temple. The Jewish revolt which followed was confined to Palestine. Under a leader named Bar-Coceba the rebels attempted to wear out the Romans in a war of sieges and small skirmishes (131–134). But the Roman troops, strongly reinforced by detachments from other frontiers, recovered Palestine in the same methodical manner as under Vespasian. In 134 their commander, C. Iulius Severus, cut off and starved

L

TRAJAN'S COLUMN — SOLDIERS BUILDING A BRIDGE

TRAJAN'S COLUMN — THE FINAL ROMAN VICTORY

out one district after another, and in 135 he pacified the whole country. The Second Jewish War was in effect a man-hunt in which the Romans killed a large part of the population of Palestine. The surviving Jews were forbidden to visit Jerusalem except once in a year. But under Antoninus the attack which Hadrian had made upon the Jewish law was stopped. Those born in the Jewish faith were allowed their worship, and synagogues and schools were allowed to keep alive the national traditions. The Jews, though now a homeless people, were unimpeded in their religion, which enabled them to maintain themselves as a separate nation.

4. *Dacia.*—Trajan did not wait to give the treaty between Domitian and King Decebalus a full trial, but made immediate preparations for a new attack upon Dacia. Before his attack Trajan improved the connexions between Pannonia and Moesia by cutting a road along the Danube through the pass of the Iron Gates. In 101 the emperor invaded Transylvania by the Iron Gate pass in the Carpathians, while Lusius Quietus attacked from Moesia Inferior. Advancing by the valley of the Matisus, he expelled the Dacian defenders from a position at Tapae. In 102 he took a more southerly route, and captured a chain of fortified positions by siege warfare. After a final victory near the Dacian capital, Sarmizegethusa, Trajan obtained the surrender of Decebalus. He left the king in possession, destroyed some of his fortresses and placed Roman garrisons in the remainder.

After two years' secret preparations the Dacian king destroyed or besieged the Roman garrisons, and in 105 he broke into Moesia. The Second Dacian War was one of the greatest in Roman history, for Trajan commanded a force of twelve legions, a total strength of 120,000 men. After a campaign in defence of Moesia he re-crossed the Danube in 105 at a point below the rapids of the Iron Gates and re-entered Dacia. At the end of two hard-fought campaigns, and a second battle near Sarmizegethusa, Decebalus killed himself and his followers surrendered. In 107 Trajan made Dacia a Roman province.

Trajan's advance of the Roman empire across the Danube replaced a clear-cut frontier by a more vague one, and it increased the burden of defence. Hadrian prepared to evacuate Dacia, but on second thoughts kept it. To abandon Dacia would have been to desert the colonists whom Trajan had compelled to cross the Danube and settle there. In Dacia, native villages and Roman garrison centres presently developed into *municipia* and *coloniae*.

After Trajan's wars the Danube lands enjoyed some sixty years of almost unbroken peace. But under M. Aurelius the districts of the middle Danube were overrun by a coalition of German tribes.

5. *The Marcomannic Wars.*—After 150, disturbances on the eastern borders of Germany forced the tribes along the Danube border to seek a more secure place to live on its southern bank. In 167 two of the chief peoples of southern Germany, the Marcomanni and the Quadi, with some other tribes (including the Vandals), broke across the Roman frontier on the middle Danube. The invaders swamped the Roman garrisons and crossed the entire line of the river from Raetia to Moesia. At the same time the Iazyges, a nomadic tribe in the valley of the Theiss, overran Dacia. The Marcomanni and Quadi then attacked Italy, where they penetrated as far as Aquileia.

M. Aurelius raised money, and recruited troops from all classes (including slaves and gladiators). In 168 he set out in person for the Danube front, and he revisited it continuously until his death in 180. The Romans took advantage of disagreement among the invaders. By 175 the emperor had recovered the lost ground, and by 180 he had finally cleared them out of Roman territory and was preparing to advance the frontier to the Carpathians and the mountains of Bohemia by the formation of two new provinces, Sarmatia and Marcomannia. But after the emperor's death his plans were abandoned. By the terms of peace which his successor made, the Germans and Iazyges agreed to provide recruits for the Roman army, and not to approach within ten miles of the Danube.

6. *Britain.*—At the beginning of Hadrian's reign the forts beyond the Scottish border were definitely evacuated, and new lines of defence were organised on English soil. The

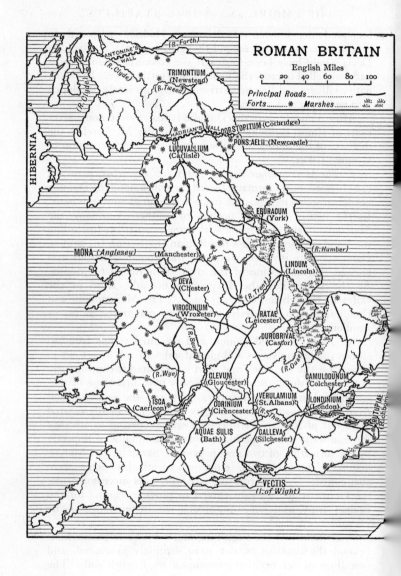

## ROMAN BRITAIN

English Miles

| 0 | 20 | 40 | 60 | 80 | 100 |

Principal Roads ......................
Forts .......... *      Marshes .......... ⸬⸬⸬

HIBERNIA

ANTONINE'S WALL
(R. Forth)
(R. Clyde)
(R. Tweed)
TRIMONTIUM
(Newstead)

HADRIAN'S WALL
CORSTOPITUM (Corbridge)
PONS AELII (Newcastle)
LUGUVALLIUM
(Carlisle)

EBURACUM
(York)

MONA (Anglesey)
(Manchester)
(R. Humber)
LINDUM
(Lincoln)

DEVA
(Chester)
(R. Trent)

VIROCONIUM
(Wroxeter)
RATAE
(Leicester)

R. Severn
DUROBRIVAE
(Castor)
(R. Ouse)

(R. Wye)
GLEVUM
(Gloucester)
CAMULODUNUM
(Colchester)

ISCA
(Caerleon)
CORINIUM
(Cirencester)
VERULAMIUM
(St. Albans)
LONDINIUM
(London)

RUTUPIAE
(Richboro')

AQUAE SULIS
(Bath)
GALLEVA
(Silchester)
(R. Thames)

VECTIS
(I. of Wight)

decision to abandon Agricola's gains followed a rebellion in northern Britain, in which one of the Roman legions, the *Nona Hispana*, was completely destroyed. A new position was taken up between the Tyne and the Solway. Hadrian visited Britain and planned a system, constructed in 122–127 under the governor A. Platorius Nepos. The chief element of this was a wall of solid stone extending from the estuary of the Solway to that of the Tyne, and generally following a ridge of higher ground. In this wall, or close by it, were constructed seventeen small forts and some fifty castles. At wider intervals bigger forts were built; and other forts along Solway Firth towards St. Bees Head protected the flank of the wall. The troops required to man these fortifications were mostly drawn from Wales and the Welsh border.

The solidity of Hadrian's wall plainly indicates that it was intended to mark the Roman frontier for all time. Yet a revolt by the Brigantes in northern England caused Antoninus to extend the military zone into Scotland. Under the governor Q. Lollius Urbicus (*c.* 142–143) a fortified line was established between the firths of Clyde and Forth. It occupied a commanding situation on a ridge of high ground, and it had the advantage over Hadrian's line of measuring only 36 miles instead of 73. But between 155 and 162 the Roman defences often had to be restored.

## (E) *The Army*

The rebellions and wars of this period showed up the numerical weakness of the Roman army. But the total number of the Roman forces was only slightly increased. The lack of a general reserve was partly met by sending detachments of legions from quiet to threatened fronts, and by better communications between the various sectors.

In the second century the transformation in the personnel of the army, which had begun in the days of Caesar and Augustus, was nearly completed. The scarcity of recruits from Italy was now such that only the praetorian cohorts were supplied from this source. The legions as well as the auxiliary units were made up almost wholly of provincials, many of whom were natives of the areas in which they served. But the

A ROMAN CAMP (HOUSESTEADS)

distinction between legions and auxiliaries was kept. Though the legions were rearmed with a lighter javelin (*lancea*) and a longer sword (*spatha*), so as to cope more effectively with cavalry, their equipment and drill remained the same, and the centurions who instructed and commanded them were ex-praetorians of Italian birth. Among the auxiliaries the numbers of the cavalry were increased, and new corps of archers were formed.

With the stabilisation of the frontiers, service in the Roman army tended more and more to be a routine of police patrolling. Legionary base camps and the forts of auxiliaries in advanced positions were built of stone and arranged with a view to the comfort of the garrisons. The Roman soldier of the second century was losing the mobility which he had in the days of Caesar and Augustus, but was still well trained. At the death of M. Aurelius the Roman army was as unconquerable and the peace of the Roman empire was as secure as ever.

## Part 3 : *Economic Conditions from A.D. 68 to 180*

### (A) *Agriculture*

In the central portions of the empire agriculture was not much changed, and no technical improvements were made. In Italy the typical form continued to be, as in the earlier part of the first century, the medium-sized plot acquired out of the profits of industry or commerce. For the cultivation of these estates slave labour was still in use, but it was giving way steadily to that of *coloni* or free tenants.

In Italy the planting of vineyards was carried to a point at which wine threatened to become cheaper than water, and ceased to pay. Though Italian agriculture had not yet reached the stage of decay, it did not share in the rising prosperity of the period. On the other hand, the provincial land was brought under more intensive cultivation, especially in the undeveloped countries on the outskirts of the empire. British regions became the chief centre of corn production in northern Europe. The wool industry which was England's main source of wealth in the Middle Ages was a legacy from Roman times.

GALLIC 'TERRA SIGILLATA'

'CASTOR' POTTERY

In the province of Belgica, the Roman camps along the Rhine stimulated corn growing. In the south of Gaul the production of wine was increased; while the Narbonese province supplied the Rhineland, Aquitania opened up a new market in Britain. The cultivation of the olive in south-eastern Spain and southern Tunisia was so great that these districts became the principal centres of oil production in the empire.

## (B) *Industry and Trade*

Better roads increased trade considerably. Even in remote country districts home production of ordinary articles ceased, and goods were bought from shops or factories. The technical processes of manufacture were not changed, nor the organisation of industry. But fresh sources for the supply of raw materials were found. An important new gold-field was developed in Dacia. In Britain the iron deposits of the Sussex Weald and of the Forest of Dean were worked intensively, and lead from the mines in the Mendips and Shropshire, in Flintshire and Yorkshire was exported.

The tendency of Italy to fall back in the economic race was even more marked in manufacture than in agriculture. About the middle of the first century the potters of Arretium began to lose their markets to their competitors in Gaul; in the second century the glass and bronze wares of Capua were replaced by Gallic products. In the east the old-established centres of industry maintained their power.

The most remarkable growth of industry took place in Gaul and the Rhineland. The glass industry, which was established at Lugdunum in the first century, moved northward to Normandy and across the Channel as far as the Mersey. But later in the second century the centre of the glass-making industry was Cologne. Above all, the potteries of Gaul had a huge output. At the end of the first century the centre for the manufacture shifted from Graufesenque to Lezoux in Auvergne; after 150 the headquarters of the industry moved on to Tres Tabernae. Each of these districts in turn supplied western Europe with the greater part of its fine table ware. A black

THE AQUEDUCT AT SEGOVIA

THE CORBRIDGE LION

pottery was manufactured near Tongres in Belgium, and a similar ware was produced in Britain, more particularly at Castor near Peterborough. In this period western Europe for the first time caught up with the lands of the eastern Mediterranean in industrial production.

Commercial relations with countries outside the Roman frontier were carried furthest in the second century. Ireland, Germany, Scandinavia, Denmark and the Swedish islands were all commercially linked with the empire ; and the main trans-continental road across the Parthian territory acquired a new importance at the end of the first century. During the last thirty years of the first century the Chinese emperors

THE ROMAN VILLA AT CHEDWORTH

THE ROMAN BRIDGE AT ALCANTARA

organised two trade routes to Bactra and Antiochia Margiana, where caravans from the Far East met the Greek or Syrian traders of Seleucia or the Mediterranean. Direct commercial relations between the Roman empire and China were hampered by the kings of Parthia. But in 97 a Chinese envoy named Kan-Ying got through to Antioch and obtained an interview with the governor of Syria. During the reign of Hadrian or of Antoninus individual Greek merchants got as far as the rim of the Tarim plateau (at Tashkurgan or Kashgar) and occasionally to China by this route.

But the Indian Ocean remained the chief road of commerce with the east. By the end of the first century individual Greeks had penetrated from the west coast of India to the capitals of the principal rajahs in the Punjab, the Dekkan, and the south of the peninsula. In the early or middle years of the second century Greek navigators explored several open-sea routes across the Bay of Bengal. In 166 Greek merchants visited the court of the emperor Huan-ti at Loyang and opened negotiations for a regular overseas trade between the Mediterranean lands and China.

Rome still kept the largest share of trade within the empire, and in the second century the population of Ostia rose to not less than 100,000. It handled a vast volume of goods.

### CHAPTER XVI

# THE EMPIRE, A.D. 180 ONWARDS: DECLINE

## Part 1 : *A.D. 180–234*

### (A) *Commodus (A.D. 180–192)*

IN promoting Commodus over the heads of several competent generals and ministers M. Aurelius no doubt relied on his son's willingness to keep these right-hand men in his service.

M. Aurelius' experiment was successful so far as frontier defence was concerned. In 180 the new emperor made a satisfactory peace with the Quadi and Marcomanni. In Britain Ulpius Marcellus defeated a Caledonian attack upon the Wall of Antoninus (*c.* 183), and a general named P. Helvius Pertinax suppressed a mutiny in the same province, which was probably due to a delay in providing the veterans with their pensions (*c.* 186). Commodus restored the rights of the cultivating tenants on the imperial estates in Africa, where the *conductores* had introduced a system of compulsory labour (182). In 186 he arranged a regular service of ships to convey the produce of Africa to Rome.

But in going back to the hereditary principle of succession, M. Aurelius erred. Commodus became wildly immoral. In 185 he gave the command over the Guards, together with the general control of policy, to a freedman named Cleander. After Cleander's fall the emperor set up and removed his praetorian prefects in quick succession, according to the will of his mistress Marcia. The imperial finances, which had already been burdened by the increase of the legionaries' pay from 300 to 375 denarii, rapidly went to rack and ruin. Judicial murders were arranged as in the worst days of Nero, in order to raise fresh funds by confiscations. Commodus' own contribution was to dress up like Hercules and to shoot animals, or kill them with a club at the public beast-hunts. For these achievements he rewarded himself with divine honours.

Commodus' reign was filled by plots and rumours of plots. In 183 an attempt by his sister Lucilla and her stepson Pompeianus to assassinate him caused many executions. On the last day of 192 the praetorian prefect Aemilius Laetus, with the help of Marcia, had Commodus strangled.

## (B) *Civil War* (*A.D. 193–197*)

The assassins had made plans for the succession, and their choice was one of M. Aurelius' right-hand men, Helvius Pertinax, who was accepted by Senate and soldiers. The new emperor at once took the reins into his hands, and in three months' time he had almost solved the most urgent problem of the state finances. With equal vigour he set himself to restore discipline among the household troops. At the same time he tried to get on well with the Senate and to strengthen its authority. But this threatened to undermine the position of Laetus who, after three months, had him murdered by the Guards.

When two candidates for the vacant throne offered themselves, the *praefectus urbi* Sulpicianus and a rich senator named Didius Iulianus, the household troops put the empire to auction and sold it to Iulianus for the promise of 25,000 sesterces (*c.* £250) per man.

But the troops on the frontiers confronted Iulianus with three rival candidates — Decimus Clodius Albinus in Britain, L. Septimius Severus in Pannonia Superior, and C. Pescennius Niger in Syria. Making a dash for Italy, Severus captured Rome in a bloodless campaign. The prefect Laetus came to terms with him. Iulianus was deposed and condemned to death by the Senate; his guardsmen carried out the sentence upon him (July 1st, 193).

## (C) *Severus* (*A.D. 193–211*)

Severus stayed only long enough to consolidate his position. But he found time to carry out an enduring reform by removing the praetorian cohorts and replacing them with soldiers drawn from the legions.

Severus gave Albinus a free hand in Britain, Gaul and Spain, and the title of 'Caesar', which had come by now to carry with it a claim to the succession. Then he advanced with the full strength of the Danube armies upon Niger, who had captured Asia and had thrown an advance force across the Bosporus. In the winter of 193–194 Severus dislodged Niger's troops from the Black Sea entrance by defeating them near Cyzicus and Nicaea, stormed his second line of defence in the Cilician Gates near Issus, and killed his rival on his final flight from Antioch to the Euphrates.

Head of Septimius Severus

In 196 Severus swung his troops back across Europe for the final round with Albinus. A victory near Lugdunum early in 197 left him master in the Roman empire.

1. *Military Policy.*—Severus took personal charge of the chief foreign wars of his reign. After the defeat of Niger, Severus had marched across the Euphrates and set up a Roman garrison at Nisibis, the chief town of Adiabene (195). In the autumn of 197 he expelled the Parthians from Osroene and Adiabene, and in 198 took Ctesiphon, which he reduced to ruins. Severus went so far as to reconstruct Trajan's province of Mesopotamia and to occupy it permanently with two legions; but he withdrew his troops from Babylonia.

In Britain, at the end of the second century, the Caledonians and a tribe named the Maeatae overran the north of England as far as York and Chester. The invaders were eventually persuaded by a bribe from the governor Virius Lupus to evacuate the land to the south of Hadrian's wall, but the Roman garrison did not reoccupy the frontier of Antoninus. In 205 an attack upon the Northumbrian wall was beaten off by the governor Alfenius Senecio; and in 208 Severus, despite his sixty-three years of age, arrived in person. For three years the emperor stayed in the province with his two sons.

Caracalla and Geta ; in 209 he made a determined attempt to crush the Caledonians and Maeatae. But he failed and, after his death at York in 211, his sons definitely evacuated Scotland and fixed the Roman frontier on the line of the Tyne and Solway.

In the reign of Severus the Roman army was increased by the creation of three new legions, of which two were stationed in Mesopotamia, and a third at Albanum (on the west bank of the Alban lake), where it served as a general reserve. In opening the praetorian cohorts to provincials, Severus thus enabled them to qualify for centurions' commissions (for a term of service in the Guards continued to be the usual method of rising to the grade of centurion). By this he removed the last privilege which Italians had held over provincials in the Roman military forces. He also removed the ban on marriage by soldiers serving with the colours. This prohibition, which had been reasonable enough so long as the Roman army was essentially a field force and the troops changed their quarters frequently, became both unfair and impracticable, as military service more and more took the form of frontier defence in permanent camps. Indeed marriage between soldiers on garrison service and the women of the neighbourhood had the advantage of providing the army with a good supply of recruits, for the camp-children usually followed the careers of their fathers. The conversion of the Roman army into a frontier-force was carried further by Severus when he offered hereditary leases of Roman crown lands to certain auxiliary units. Finally, Severus raised the legionaries' rates of pay from 375 denarii, at which figure Commodus had recently fixed them, to 500. This was probably intended to compensate them for a fall in the value of money, which seems to have occurred at this time.

Under Severus Numidia was detached from Africa ; Syria and Britain were divided into two. The partition of Syria and Britain, where his rivals Niger and Albinus had formerly held command, suggests that Severus was taking precautions against future pretenders by preventing the concentration of military power in the hands of any one provincial governor. This measure of insurance against civil war proved effective only so long as emperors took personal command of armies engaged in major wars and maintained their control over these. In making new towns in the provinces Severus carried on vigorously the policy of Trajan and his successors. It is probable that the British towns of Eburacum (York) and Lindum (Lincoln) owed their status as colonies to him. In Egypt Severus introduced a larger measure of self-government by providing Alexandria and the district capitals with senates.

In view of his African origin and his marriage with a Syrian wife, it was natural that Severus should favour the promotion of the provincials to a status of equality with the Italians. He admitted them in large numbers to his administrative service. A feature of his reign is the number of imperial officials from Syria and other eastern provinces. From their presence in the Roman administration it is clear that the Roman franchise had by then been extended to many towns of the eastern Mediterranean, and this was largely the work of Severus himself.

In the civil wars of 193–197 the districts through which the armies passed paid the usual heavy toll, but taken as a whole the provinces enjoyed the same good standard of administration as under Trajan and his successors. Severus kept his officials up to a high level of efficiency. The popularity of his dynasty in the provinces is proved by many monuments found in all parts of the empire.

2. *Internal Administration.*—Severus made an attempt to come to a good understanding with the Senate, and after the campaign against Niger he killed no more than one of his partisans. But after the war against Albinus, Severus reversed his attitude to the Senate, for many of its members had helped Albinus. Though he allowed thirty-five out of sixty-four suspects whom he put on trial for treason to be acquitted, he withdrew from the senators the right of trial in their own assembly. He abandoned all pretence of partnership with the senators, and he did not disguise the fact that the authority of the emperor was based on the support of the soldiery.

Severus gave preference in filling his administrative posts to persons of the equestrian order, whose previous training had been purely military. Though he did not directly replace the governors of the senatorial provinces with his own men, he prepared for their removal from the provincial government by setting deputy-governors of equestrian rank by their side. He abolished another surviving institution of republican times by closing down the standing jury-courts for higher crimes. Their entire range of duties was now transferred to the *praefectus urbi*, to whom all cases originating within a hundred miles of Rome were given, and to the *praefectus praetorio*, who took cases from the rest of Italy and from the provinces.

In the early part of his reign the emperor fell under the influence of his praetorian prefect C. Fulvius Plautianus, to whom he gave many powers. Plautianus controlled the *praefectus annonae*, and was made vice-president of the *Consilium Principis*. After the fall of Plautianus in 205 Severus divided the duties of the prefecture between two commanders of equal rank. For the judicial duties which now attached to the prefecture, the emperor appointed a distinguished lawyer, Aemilius Papinianus, to one of the vacant posts.

A result of the transfer of *quaestiones* to the imperial prefects was that the imperial examining magistrate had the same freedom of procedure as a consul of the early republic. This change was accompanied by the setting up of different scales of punishments according to the person of the criminal. The citizen body was divided into a class of *honestiores* ('the more honourable'), including members of the senatorial and equestrian orders, municipal magistrates and senators, and soldiers of all ranks, and another of *humiliores* ('lower class'). For the same crime a privileged offender might be exiled, an un-privileged one would be sentenced to penal servitude in the mines ; in capital cases the *honestior* would be put to death quickly and cleanly, the *humilior* might be thrown to the beasts. A person of higher status still enjoyed the right of appeal to the emperor, and he could not be tortured except in trials of treason or *maiestas* ; but these privileges were withdrawn from those of the lower order.

Severus saved the *fiscus* from the confusion into which Commodus had thrown it and finally left it in a sound condition. By raising the legionaries' rates of pay to 500 denarii, he placed a heavy additional burden on the tax-payers. At

Rome he built a new front to the palace of Domitian; he began the construction of a vast and luxurious new suite of baths; in addition to the customary distributions of grain, he gave the people free oil. In the provinces he spent large amounts on road repairs, and the costs of the postal service. But he had a large reserve of money in the *fiscus*, and large stocks of grain. The money came in part from the heavy fines which he had imposed upon the supporters of Niger and Albinus. These were put by him into a new fund, the *res privata*, which he treated as family property. He devalued the denarius, whose silver he reduced to 60 per cent.

### (D) *Caracalla* (A.D. 211–217)

Severus marked out his elder son for the succession by having the full imperial powers given to him, together with the title of Augustus. His son was hereupon officially re-named M. Aurelius Antoninus, but he went down in history by his popular nickname Caracallus or  Caracalla. Caracalla and Plautianus remained enemies until Severus removed Plautianus. Caracalla's position was assured; but at the end of his reign Severus associated his younger son, P. Antoninus Geta, with Caracalla as co-heir to the imperial power. On his death in 211 the feud threatened to lead to a fresh civil war; but in 212 Cara-

Head of Caracalla

calla murdered Geta. Caracalla ruled tyranically. He massacred Geta's supporters and a great number of the citizens of Alexandria. He raised the pay of the legionaries from 500 to 750 denarii, which soon converted his father's financial surplus into debt. He was driven to increase taxation, and to tamper with the coinage by issuing a new silver piece, the *Antoninus*, to which he gave a currency value of two denarii, although it weighed only five-thirds of a denarius.

In 212 he practically completed the extension of the Roman citizenship to all free men within the borders of the empire. The long-standing distinction between Italians and provincials, between conquerors and conquered, was virtually obliterated, and the Roman empire was definitely converted into a commonwealth of equal partners.

In Britain he surrendered all his father's gains. On the Danube front he fought two German tribes, the Alamanni and the Goths. The Alamanni were a coalition of displaced tribes in southern Germany. The Goths were an east German people who had moved from the lower Vistula to the Black Sea, and now met the Romans in Lower Moesia. Caracalla beat off the attacks of these tribes (213–214). In Armenia he deposed the king Vologeses and set up a Roman province (216). He made a raid across Adiabene into Media (216). In the next year he resumed operations, no doubt with the intention of carrying Roman arms beyond the farthest limits of Trajan and Severus. But a group of officers murdered him.

### (E) *Macrinus* (*A.D. 217–218*)

The ringleader of the conspirators, the praetorian prefect M. Opellius Macrinus, was a Mauretanian who had joined the Roman army as a common soldier. The army and the Senate recognised him as emperor, but he soon fell a victim to his own success. Resuming Caracalla's campaign against Artabanus, he lost two battles and was driven out of Mesopotamia. Fortunately for Macrinus, Artabanus, the king of Parthia, consented to a compromise. In 218 the troops at Emesa in Syria set up as a rival emperor a grand-nephew of Iulia Domna, the wife of Severus, who was now passed off as a son of Caracalla and assumed the name of M. Aurelius Antoninus. Though only fourteen years of age, and quite unknown outside Syria, the new Antoninus supplanted Macrinus after a short struggle.

### (F) *Elagabalus* (*A.D. 218–222*)

The new emperor took the name Elagabalus from the sun-god of Emesa, whose worship he introduced to Rome. He was immoral and a poor administrator. His masterful grandmother, Iulia Maesa, tried to restrain him, and herself took part in the debates of the Senate. Elagabalus tried to appease the rising anger of the people by nominating his cousin M. Aurelius Severus Alexander as his successor ; but when he tried to go back upon this arrangement the household troops murdered him.

## (G) *Alexander Severus* (*A.D.* 222–235)

Alexander Severus was only thirteen, but his mother, Iulia Mamaea, ruled him, and her son was an obedient pupil. Indeed Alexander never attempted to throw off her guidance, so that from 222 to 235 the Roman empire had the unique experience of being ruled by an empress.

Mamaea tried to get the Senate to reinforce the imperial authority, and rely on the civilian rather than the military element in the service of the government. She therefore confirmed the Senate's claim to hear all capital accusations against persons of high rank. But she used as her principal instrument of government a *Consilium Principis* on which lawyers and civilian administrators predominated, and a small subcommittee of that body, consisting entirely of senators. She appointed as praetorian prefect and head of the entire administration a distinguished lawyer named Domitius Ulpianus.

Under the rule of Mamaea the Roman empire enjoyed a dozen years of comparative stability. The administration of Alexander succeeded in avoiding any serious frontier disturbance for the first ten years of the reign. Its chief object was to win the general support of the civilian population. For the benefit of the Roman populace it provided, besides the regular gifts and public baths, a new scheme for the regulation of the city's supply services. It enrolled in special clubs all those in the industries and trades that provided for the needs of the capital, so that their work was carried on under continual official supervision. The Roman government had hitherto avoided interference in commerce and manufacture, but found itself committed henceforth to control. Alexander's government extended the assistance to towns in Italy ; it subsidised teachers and scholars ; and it cut down some taxes. The money was partly raised by further tampering with the coinage, in consequence of which the aureus was reduced in weight. But by rigid economy at court the imperial finances stood the strain.

The early years of his reign passed without serious disorder; but in 228 the prefect Ulpianus was murdered by his own men, and foreign war broke down discipline altogether.

About 230 the Parthian monarchy fell to pieces.  Its Arsacid dynasty was deposed by a rebellious leader in southern Persia named Ardashir (Artaxerxes), who overcame Artabanus V and Vologeses V, and gathered all the Parthian dominions into his hands.  The new 'Sassanid' dynasty was powerful.  In 231 the Persian king besieged Nisibis.  In 232 Alexander in person took charge of a Roman counter-attack. With the Armenian king Chosroes, he attempted a triple invasion of Persia through Armenia, Mesopotamia and Babylonia, in which he achieved success.

In 234 Alexander made preparations for a campaign against the Alamanni.  But the growing insubordination of his troops compelled him to buy them off with a bribe.  C. Iulius Maximinus started a riot in which Alexander and his mother were killed.

## Part 2 : A.D. 234 Onwards

### (A)  Civil War (A.D. 234–285)

1.  A.D. 234–253.—The fifty years that followed the death of Alexander Severus were a period of disaster and of crisis for the Roman empire.  C. Iulius Maximinus was an obscure provincial (from Thrace).  He was a competent soldier, and in 236–237 he restored order on the Rhine and Danube frontiers.  But the Senate soon withdrew its support.  After three years it faced Maximinus with an opposition emperor named M. Antonius Gordianus, the proconsul of Africa.  But Gordian was killed in a local war against the governor of Numidia, who took sides with Maximinus and won easily. The Senate set up M. Clodius Pupienus and D. Caelius Balbinus, as emperors.  Maximinus marched upon Italy from Pannonia, but he met with an unforeseen resistance.  The Italians rallied to the defence of the Senate and the praetorian cohorts gave support to the Senate against the legions.  At Aquileia Maximinus' army murdered him (June 238).

Then the Guards killed Pupienus and Balbinus and forced upon the Senate a new emperor, a grandson of Gordian, who was a boy of some fifteen years (July 238). This sudden fancy of the household troops proved wise, for this Gordian chose as his regent a capable man named C. Furius Timesitheus. In 243 the regent repelled an invasion by Ardashir's son Shapur, who had taken Antioch ; but his sudden death (by disease) in the same year put Gordian into the hands of M. Iulius Philippus, who stirred up a mutiny and took over from the young emperor. He made a peace with Shapur and came to an understanding with the Senate. But the habit of treason had now fastened upon the Roman army. An officer named C. Traianus Decius left his command in Dacia to invade Italy and made good his claim by killing Philip in a set battle near Verona (249).

In deserting his post on the Danube, Decius handed over the Balkan peninsula to a swarm of Goths and other tribes, which were now being driven on by the pressure of the Alans, a nomadic people from the Asiatic plain, to secure a permanent home on Roman territory. The new emperor hurried back but was twice defeated by a Gothic king named Cniva and died in the second encounter (251). The governor of the two Moesias, C. Trebonianus Gallus, got himself proclaimed emperor by his own troops and received recognition from the Senate on a visit to Rome. But his successor in the Moesian command, a Moor named M. Aemilius Aemilianus, who had driven Cniva out of Moesia (253), attacked Gallus. Another civil war in Italy ended in the defeat and death of Gallus at Interamna. Aemilianus now offered a partnership to the Senate imperial power ; but his own soldiers killed him. His place was taken by the last representative of the old republican nobility among the emperors, P. Licinius Valerianus.

2. *Valerian and Gallienus* (*A.D. 253-267*).—Valerian was a man of integrity who won the confidence of the Senate and restored some measure of discipline in the military forces. But the barbarians now took advantage of the complete disorganisation of the Roman frontier defences. The trickle of invaders now swelled into a flood. The line of the Danube was crossed at either end by Goths and Alamanni. On the

lower Rhine the Franks, a new tribe that had coalesced out of fragments of Cherusci, Chatti and other old opponents of Rome, broke in with devastating force (256). On the Euphrates front Shapur took his opportunity.

In 256 Shapur, having recently murdered the Armenian king Chosroes, again overran Syria and regained possession

Head of Gallienus

of Antioch. Against this invader Valerian took the field in person, while he left his son, P. Licinius Gallienus, whom he had nominated co-regent, to hold the European fronts. After some delay the emperor recovered Antioch (258) but later had to make peace. During the negotiations Valerian was kidnapped by Shapur and ended his life in captivity (259). In 260 the Persian king occupied Antioch for the third time and made a dash across Asia Minor as far as the Sea of Marmora. Shapur could now have proceeded to the systematic conquest of Asia Minor, had he not been attacked by an unexpected enemy.

This was the army of the city of Palmyra, which in the next twenty years played a big part in politics. Situated in the desert of northern Arabia, Palmyra was the principal station on the caravan route from Damascus to Seleucia, which offered the shortest way from Antioch into the Asiatic continent. With the growth of the trans-continental trade in the second century the city reached the summit of its prosperity. It was raised to the status of a Roman colony (probably by Hadrian or Septimius Severus), and its leading citizens, who were of Arabian race, but had Roman culture, received the Roman franchise. In a war between the Caesars and the Sassanids the economic interests of Palmyra naturally placed it on the side of Rome against the Persians.

The Palmyrene forces came to the rescue of the Romans in 260. Under the command of a nobleman named P. Septimius Odaenathus they drew Shapur away from Asia Minor by a counter-raid into Mesopotamia, and inflicted a defeat upon h.m which threw the Persians back upon the defensive. In 264 Odaenathus recovered Mesopotamia for the Romans. Gallienus allowed Odaenathus to assume the title of king in Palmyra and gave him command over the Roman forces along the Euphrates front and in Egypt. But after the death of Odaenathus in 266 or 267 the rising strength of Palmyra became a menace to Rome. Government was taken over by his widow Zenobia, whose personal ambition threatened Roman rule in the east.

While Valerianus was preparing to meet Shapur, Gallienus successfully beat back the Alamanni (256–257). But before he could bring relief to other fronts the Franks obtained a firm hold in eastern and central Gaul and in north-eastern Spain. About this time another newly formed German tribe, the Saxons of the Jutish and Frisian coasts, first crossed the English Channel with their pirate ships. In 258 the Goths repeated their attacks across the Balkans and took the city of Byzantium by a surprise attack. With a fleet of boats they crossed into Asia Minor, where most of the towns of Bithynia fell into their hands.

In 259 the capture of Valerianus left Gallienus at the mercy of many rivals. The majority were easily disposed of : often their own troops killed them. But in Gaul an officer named Latinius Postumus established his position firmly (260), and the provinces of Spain and Britain supported him. Postumus may have claimed the whole empire, but exercised control only over an *imperium Galliarum*, i.e. of western Europe.

Meanwhile the Alamanni crossed the Rhine in two columns, of which one overran the Rhône valley and Auvergne, while the other crossed the Brenner pass and ravaged Italy as far as Ravenna. These invaders were eventually defeated by Gallienus and his lieutenants. In the meantime Postumus turned aside to clear the Franks out of Gaul and Spain.

In 267 the Goths besieged Thessalonica, while an allied band of Heruli temporarily occupied Athens, but were soon driven out by the skilful strategy of an Attic commander named Dexippus. Gallienus in person defeated the raiders in the Balkans. But again Gallienus was distracted by disloyalty on the part of his subordinates. The officer whom he had left in charge of the war against Postumus, M'. Acilius Aureolus, abandoned his post in order to march upon Rome. Gallienus hurried back, but was killed by his own officers.

3. *Claudius and Aurelian A.D. 267–275*).—His immediate successor, an Illyrian named M. Aurelius Claudius, defeated Aureolus, and he had no difficulty in checking another Alamannic raid, which got no farther than Lake Garda. But in 269 he was troubled by a new Gothic invasion. Having explored the Balkan peninsula, the Goths had resolved to

Head of Claudius Gothicus                    Head of Aurelian

occupy it permanently. They crossed the Danube and sailed through the Bosporus into the Mediterranean as far as Cyprus. Thrusting in between their first and second wave of invaders, Claudius cut to pieces the second detachment at Naissus in the Morava valley while his naval squadrons made a combined drive against the sea-raiders. The invaders who did not die in the snows of the Balkan highlands made their surrender and were settled as *coloni* in the vacant spaces of the Danube provinces (269–270). This removed all danger from the Goths for a hundred years.

Shortly after this Claudius died of the plague. The troops in Italy put forward his brother to succeed him ; but they killed him on hearing that the army in the Balkans had proclaimed Claudius' right-hand man, L. Domitius Aurelianus. The first act of Aurelian was to complete the reconquest of the Danube line, the second was to recall the remaining Roman garrisons from the province of Dacia. Then the Alamanni attacked Italy (271). After a defeat, Aurelian destroyed the invaders.

Meanwhile Zenobia attacked Asia Minor. But she received no support from the Sassanids, and Aurelian's lieutenant Probus expelled her invading columns from Egypt (271). In the following year Aurelian swept the Palmyrenes out of Asia Minor and outmanœuvred them in a pitched battle at Emesa which gave him possession of Syria. He then put Palmyra under siege. The capture of Zenobia ended this campaign (272). Aurelian deposed Zenobia and put Roman troops in Palmyra. But his garrison was massacred in a revolt by the queen's relatives. The emperor returned and pounced on the rebel city before it was ready for him. Palmyra was completely destroyed by him (273).

Aurelian hurried his troops back to Europe in order to make an end of the *imperium Galliarum*. There in 269 Postumus died and three other rulers after him were removed in quick succession. Then the troops accepted a civilian emperor named C. Pius Tetricus. At Aurelian's approach he was forced by his army to make a stand, but he surrendered to Aurelian quickly (273). By his energy Aurelian had welded the Roman empire together once more. In 275 he was preparing to fight the Sassanid monarchy, when he was killed by his officers.

4. *A.D. 275–285.*—The Senate appointed Cornelius Tacitus. Tacitus took the field against some Goths and Alans in Asia Minor and defeated them. But the soldiers again killed the senator-emperor (276). The mutineers allowed the dead man's half-brother, M. Annius Florianus, to proclaim himself the next emperor, but killed him as soon as they learnt that the other armies of the east had set up a lieu-tenant of Aurelian, M. Aurelius Probus.

Head of Probus

Alamanni and Franks now attacked Gaul on a wide front and stayed long enough to capture seventy towns ; of all the Germanic invasions this struck the heaviest blow at the prosperity of Gaul. But Probus attacked the raiders and re-gained the line of the Rhine and upper Danube. After some minor campaigns on the lower Danube and in Asia Minor (278–279) he returned to Gaul, where an officer named Bonosus had proclaimed himself emperor (280). This man was suppressed; but in 282 Probus was killed by the Pan-nonian army.

The soldiers replaced Probus by M. Aurelius Carus, who had also proceeded from the school of Claudius and Aurelian. In the following year Carus attacked the Persian king Bahram, who had reoccupied Armenia and Mesopotamia, but after the capture of Ctesiphon he was murdered. The victorious army retreated under Carus' son Numerianus, who had been nominated co-emperor by his father. On the march Numerianus was killed, and in his place the praetorian prefect C. Aurelius Diocletianus was proclaimed (284). Diocletian had to fight Carus' elder son Carinus, who had been left in command in Italy. This war between the armies of east and west ended with a victory for Diocletian on the banks of the Margus in 285. With Diocletian the Roman empire returned for a while to settled government. In the previous fifty years eighteen emperors at least had been set up and knocked down.

## (B) *Diocletian* (*A.D. 285–305*)

Diocletian had no great gifts as a general; but he was a good organiser. He associated with himself an Illyrian named M. Aurelius Valerius Maximianus (286). In 293 he also gave C. Flavius Valerus Constantius and Galerius Valerius Maximianus a share of the imperial power. The division between Diocletian and his colleagues was made on a territorial basis. While Diocletian kept the eastern provinces, he assigned Italy and Africa to Maximian, the Danube provinces to Galerius and the western districts to Constantius. But while the primary ob-ject of this was military, it was also intended to provide for an orderly succession. While Diocletian and Maximian were

Head of Diocletian

joint emperors and shared the title of Augustus, Galerius and Constantius, who were styled Caesars, became heirs to the two senior rulers. Under Diocletian's supervision it worked well. By virtue of his personal authority he remained in effect sole emperor, while he secured the loyal assistance of the three ablest military commanders. Though he was not free from attempted rivals, these did not lead to any general civil war. In 286 M. Aurelius Carausius, who had been appointed to command the Channel fleet, used his naval power to proclaim himself 'Augustus' and set up a local empire in

Constantius, laureate. On the reverse side the walls of London. The city of London, personified in a kneeling figure, welcomes a Roman relief force

Britain. With the help of his fleet Carausius was able to defy Maximian, who made peace with him in 290. But after the death of Carausius, who was murdered in 293 by a subordinate named Allectus, the *imperium Britanniarum* collapsed before an attack by Constantius.

In the absence of civil war, Diocletian's colleagues were able to cope with frontier defence. Maximian and Constantius crushed invasions by the Alamanni in Gaul. On the Euphrates front Diocletian made a lucky peace in 284 with the Persian king Bahram, who yielded Armenia and Mesopotamia to the Romans; but in 296 he had to defend his gains against a new king named Narses. He entrusted the conduct of the Persian war to Galerius, who destroyed Narses' army. Diocletian enlarged the province of Mesopotamia so as to include the whole of the upper Tigris basin. The Roman gains in Mesopotamia were consolidated by a chain of forts.

M

The success that the system of Diocletian achieved was entirely due to the personal prestige of the emperor ; it was this, and not the system itself, that checked the ambitions of his colleagues. In 305 he resigned his office and forced Maximian to accompany him into retirement ; at the same time he promoted Constantius and Galerius to the rank of Augusti and appointed two new Caesars.

## (c) *A.D. 305 Onwards*

Galerius, who became the senior Augustus after the death of Constantius at York in 306, could not control the western half of the empire. In Gaul and Britain the troops of Constantius proclaimed his son Constantine emperor. Maximian's soldiers and the praetorian cohorts at Rome supported his son Maxentius, who seized Italy and Africa for himself and held these territories both against Galerius and against his own

BATHS OF DIOCLETIAN

father.   Diocletian did nothing ;  his death in 316 passed almost unnoticed.

In the west Constantine employed his troops for the time being in quelling disorders on the Rhine and in Britain.  But in 308 he had to fight Maximian, who had left Italy for Gaul. He put him to death in 310 on a charge of conspiracy. Maxentius then attacked Constantine (311).   In his duel with Maxentius Constantine had to fight superior forces, but his own troops were far better trained, and he conducted operations with a rapidity worthy of Caesar himself.   He crossed the Alps and won a battle at the Milvian bridge, at the gates of Rome (312).   This gave Constantine possession of all the western portion of the empire.

Meanwhile the death of Galerius in 311 had left the eastern provinces as a prize to be fought for by two of his former subordinates, Valerius Maximinus Daia, who held command in Asia and Egypt, and Valerius Licinianus Licinius, the ruler of the Danube provinces.   Licinius ended by driving his opponent across the whole length of Asia Minor to Tarsus. The sudden death of Maximinus put Licinius in possession of all the eastern provinces.   In 314 the first round in the final duel between east and west was fought in Pannonia, where Constantine defeated Licinius.   After nine years of uneasy peace Licinius lost a battle at Adrianople and abandoned Europe.   When Constantine pursued him across the Bosporus, Licinius surrendered and was put to death in the ensuing year.

In 323 the Roman empire was temporarily reunited under a ruler who made the last notable effort to buttress it against further dilapidations.   Constantine carried the reforms of Diocletian several stages further and he provided the Roman empire with a new capital.   From the time of the great invasions in mid-third century the emperors had spent most of their reigns on campaign, so that their visits to Rome were short.   In 330 Constantine definitely transferred the seat of government from Rome to Byzantium, which he rebuilt and renamed after himself.   Constantine also made the empire officially Christian.

A new round of civil wars after the death of Constantine kept the empire disunited, and its temporary reunion under

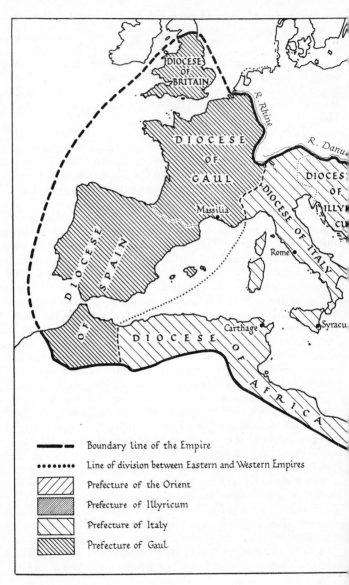

Boundary line of the Empire

•••••••• Line of division between Eastern and Western Empires

Prefecture of the Orient

Prefecture of Illyricum

Prefecture of Italy

Prefecture of Gaul

THE LA

Scale 0 250 500 Miles

DIOCESE
OF
THRACE
ippi

Byzantium

DIOCESE
OF PONTUS

CESE

DIOCESE
OF ASIA

OF

Antioch

R. Tigris

ACEDONIA

Babylon

R. Euphrates

DIOCESE OF THE ORIENT

Alexandria

R. Nile

Constantius (353–361) and Julian (361–363), and again under Theodosius I (395), merely emphasised the difficulty of holding it together. In 364 the brothers Valentinian and Valens made a division of the Roman dominions, by which the former took Italy and the western districts, while Valens received the eastern provinces ; Theodosius' two sons, Arcadius and Honorius, became the founders of two sub-empires in the east and west. In actual practice they became independent of each other, so that the history of the eastern and western divisions now ran on separate lines.

The east-Roman empire remained fairly free from civil wars and foreign invasions. It passed through a critical period after 378 when Valens was killed in a battle against an invading army of Goths at Adrianople ; but under his successor Theodosius the Goths were persuaded to settle down in the Balkan lands, and the Danube frontier was made firm again. A long period of comparative tranquillity followed. The code of Theodosius II on administrative law (A.D. 438) and the general code of Justinian (528–534) had their origin at Constantinople. But the separation of the eastern empire from Italy inevitably caused it to lose its Roman character. The Byzantine monarchy, which grew out of the east-Roman empire, was a Hellenistic kingdom, with a Christian church and a Roman law-book.

The separation of Italy and the western provinces from the eastern Mediterranean resulted in their bleeding to death. In the fifth century the western empire had German invasions at the same time as civil war. In 406 a rebellion by Constantine, who deserted his post in Britain in order to cut his way through to Rome, threw open all the frontiers of western Europe. In Britain the garrison maintained itself for some further years. But for lack of reinforcements it had to fall back from one position to another, so that by 450 Britain was left to itself. A few detachments also held out along the Rhine, but these could not prevent a continuous stream of German invaders from crossing the frontier. Between 409 and 419 northern Gaul was definitely conquered by the Franks, eastern Gaul by a lesser German tribe, the Burgundians, and Spain by the Suebi and Vandals. In 429 the

Vandals passed over to North Africa and turned its peaceful provinces into pirate bases, from which they cut off the sea-connexions between east and west in the Mediterranean lands. Meanwhile the Goths left their new homes in the Balkans in search of better land. In the first ten years of the fifth century they repeatedly invaded Italy, while the western emperor, Honorius, fled behind the marshes of Ravenna. In 408 the Gothic chieftain Alaric broke into central Italy ; in 410 he sacked Rome. After his death the Goths retired to Aquitania and founded a kingdom whose rulers came to a friendly understanding with the last Roman emperors of the west.

In 451 a Roman general named Aetius won the last triumph of Roman armies in the west when, with the help of the Goths from Aquitania, he beat off an invasion by the Hun chief Attila into central France. But between 470 and 490 the Franks and Goths shared out the remaining Roman provinces in central France and Provence. In 455 the Vandal Gaiseric made a sea-raid upon Rome and plundered the city so thoroughly that it remained henceforth half ruined. In 476 a German named Odoacer put to death the emperor Orestes and deposed his son, Romulus Augustulus. With this act the rule of Rome in the west was ended.

In the eastern Mediterranean the Byzantine monarchy was a direct continuation of the Roman empire on a small scale. After the break-up of the western empire it preserved Roman institutions for two further centuries, and kept the use of Latin in its courts. In the seventh and eighth centuries the Roman administration was replaced by a looser system and Greek replaced Latin as the official tongue. But the line of Roman emperors went on until the capture of Constantinople by Mohammed II in 1453. The Byzantine emperor Constantine XIII, who was killed at the fall of his capital, might consider himself a descendant of Augustus.

## (D) *Frontier Defence*

In the reign of Diocletian the Roman empire had almost recovered the ground lost in the mid-third century. With the exception of Dacia, no big piece of Roman territory had been

THE WALL OF AURELIAN

surrendered. The empire still exceeded the limits which Augustus had marked out for it.

The empire was also well fortified by A.D. 330. New chains of detached forts were drawn by Diocletian and Constantine along the Rhine and Danube. About A.D. 300 the English coast from the Isle of Wight to the Wash was safeguarded by forts against the Saxon pirates. In the early fourth century similar defences were established along the coasts of Wales and Cumberland. Behind the frontiers the towns in all the threatened areas were again making themselves secure with walls. Under Aurelian and Probus the city of Rome was provided with a line of ramparts, and Constantinople was supplied with defences that defied all attacks for nearly a thousand years. The Roman roads were still further extended by the emperors of the third century, and communications by river and sea were maintained by the Roman navy.

The weakness in the Roman army which the great invasion had shown was partly remedied in the later third century and under Constantine. After the defeats inflicted by the mounted troops of the Sassanids and of the Goths, Gallienus raised a strong corps of cavalry. To provide an adequate reserve, Diocletian began, and Constantine completed, a reorganisation of the entire Roman army, which was henceforth divided into two distinct branches: one to carry on the duties of garrison service at a particular frontier, the other as a general reserve, from which detachments might be sent at short notice to any front. Under this system the total numbers of the Roman army, which had crept up during the third century from 300,000 to 400,000, were raised by Diocletian to 500,000. From the time of Gallienus the high military commands were usually entrusted to men with a thorough military training.

For the recruitment of their armies Diocletian and Constantine relied first on the hereditary frontier men, who held their land under obligation of military service. Their next source was voluntary service ; as a last resort conscription was applied. The personnel of the Roman forces was worse than that of the armies of the first and second centuries. Since the two Severi, the frontier men included not only

Roman citizens, but a considerable number of German captives ; the volunteers came from the more backward portions of the Roman empire. The conscripts were not picked by the commanding officers but were supplied by the owners of the large estates, who naturally sent the least efficient. The Roman soldiers of the third and fourth centuries lacked the strict discipline of the recruits from Italy and the more Romanised provinces in earlier centuries. They refused to wear the same weight of armour, or to drill properly : and they were disloyal.

## (E) *The Constitution*

Even in this period of crisis Roman emperors moved slowly from precedent to precedent. But the rate of change was accelerated. The emperors of the third and fourth centuries assumed a consulship, and they had the *tribunicia potestas* ; for a full half-century after they had become Christians they continued to call themselves *Pontifex Maximus*. The Senate preserved and even added to its prestige. Its membership was now drawn from the great landowners of all parts of the empire, and from the higher ranks of the emperors' civil service. Under this system of recruitment the House had become fairly representative of the wealthier classes of the whole empire, and it stood for Roman civilisation in contrast with the growing barbarism of the military elements. In the fourth century a Senate was still thought necessary, so that Constantine had to create a duplicate of the Roman assembly at Constantinople.

On the other hand, the various republican magistracies had either died out before A.D. 300, or become merely honorary functions. The tribunate and the aediles, whose duties had gradually been absorbed by imperial prefects, ceased to be appointed in the reign of Alexander Severus. The consulate survived, even at Constantinople, where one of the pair lived after 330, while the other stayed on at Rome. But their last effective function, the presidence over the Senate, had been transferred to the *praefectus urbi*. The consulship, in effect, had become a title without an office. With the closing down of the jury-courts under Septimius Severus the praetors lost their occupation ; so too with the quaestors when the senatorial income from the provinces was cut off.

Until the later part of the third century the consuls and praetors passed on to the government of a province, as in the days of the republic. But in the days of the great invasions, the proconsuls were replaced by imperial officers. The withdrawal of the provinces from the Senate's sphere of control meant the loss of its chief source of income. Under Aurelian the *aerarium* was closed. Last, the Senate's authorisation was no longer required for the emperors. In 282 one of the soldiers' nominees, M. Aurelius Carus, neglected to apply to the Senate for his title. From that date the Roman emperors became autocrats ruling in their own right.

The emperors became autocrats in law as well as in fact. From the time of Aurelian the name of *dominus* crept in, and the name of *princeps* went out of use. But Aurelian deliberately assumed the trappings of Oriental despotism. Diocletian and Constantine created an elaborate code of court ceremonial on the assumption that their soldiers might be dazzled into obedience. Henceforth Roman emperors maintained a mysterious aloofness from their subjects ; they wore a diadem and robe of gold and purple.

But the principal difference between the constitution of Augustus and that of Diocletian or Constantine was that in the latter all pretence of a partnership in government had gone. In the fourth century the entire administration had been gathered into the hands of the emperor, and every official was his nominee.

Under Constantine the *consilium principis* was renamed *consistorium* and became a body with a fixed membership ; its functions were unchanged. The imperial civil service got bigger and it received a thoroughgoing reorganisation by Diocletian and Constantine. The increase was mainly due to the systematic splitting up of the provinces into smaller units. Under Diocletian the number of the provinces was raised to 60 or 70 ; eventually it grew to 116. The empire was mapped out into four 'prefectures' and twelve 'dioceses'. The *praesides* or *rectores*, as the governors of the individual provinces were now called, were subordinate to the *vicarii* of the dioceses, and the *vicarii* were under the direction of four *praefecti praetorio*.

Diocletian carried right through the principle of separating the military from the civilian offices. While the *rector* of a province had charge of law and taxation, a *dux* or *comes* took command of the garrison. Each province, diocese and prefecture had its own officials and a separate civil service.

In theory, the Roman executive was well organised in the fourth century. But its very size and completeness of organisation was a menace. The more powerful it became, the more easily was it able to elude control by the emperors. The higher officials sold appointments and promotions for bribes, and combined to plunder the populations in much the same way as proconsuls and *publicani* in republican days, but with more efficiency and greater impunity.

But the bureaucracy had to give way to unofficial superiors, the owners of the extensive *latifundia* which grew up after the invasions of the mid-third century. The proprietors of these large estates turned their tenants into serfs and gained great local powers. The *latifundia* of the later Roman empire thus came to form miniature states within the state.

## (F) *Finance*

From the time of the great invasions the economic prosperity of the empire fell sharply. But public expenditure still rose. More money was needed for Oriental luxury at court, a bigger bureaucracy and a larger army.

In the mid-third century the emperors seriously devalued the coinage. While the aureus was still further lightened, the denarius was progressively devalued until the time of Gallienus, when it became in fact a copper coin with a five per cent wash of previous metal. It caused endless confusion in the readjustment of prices and wages. The gradual renewal of gold and silver stocks from the time of Aurelian, and a slight improvement of the coinage by Diocletian and Constantine, led to a slow revival of confidence and a stable economy in the fourth century.

Diocletian reorganised the tax system imposts under three main heads. The principal source remained, as always, a tax on the produce of the soil. This tax was now extended to the landowners in Italy. Special taxes in money were imposed at irregular intervals upon traders and businesses. This scheme caused much injustice.

For the collection of these and all other services, Diocletian developed the system of corporate responsibility which had grown up in the second and third centuries. The whole *ordo senatorius* of each town was now responsible. In view of the general poverty of the cities, this was necessary ; yet it was the cause of much hardship, for the property qualification for admission to the local senates was now only twenty-five *iugera* (fifteen acres) of land, and many of the senators were poor. Consequently, though they were merciless in getting money from the ultimate tax-payers, they lived perpetually under the shadow of financial ruin. The officials and owners of *latifundia* had no responsibility and probably paid less than their fair share.

### (G) *Economics*

In the later days of M. Aurelius the prosperity which had set in under Augustus and endured through two centuries ceased. The Marcomannic Wars, followed by the civil wars at the end of the second century, acted as a brake on further progress. With the death of Alexander Severus, rapid decline and disintegration commenced, due to the continuous civil wars and foreign invasions of the third century. The effect of these was disastrous, because they became a normal condition of Roman politics. A sense of insecurity came over the population of the Roman empire about A.D. 250 and was never again dispelled.

The eastern provinces, which were less often invaded and had a longer tradition of industry and commerce than those of the west, recaptured some of their former prosperity. On the trans-continental route to China trade lingered on into the second half of the third century. The overseas commerce with the farther east fell away more rapidly. In the early third century the traffic with China by way of Malaya died out, and the Indian Ocean was abandoned.

North Africa remained productive to the end of the fourth

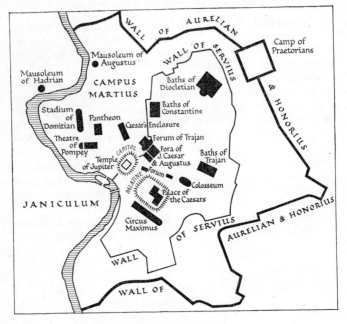

IMPERIAL ROME

century. Its decline dates from the sack of Rome by Alaric and the Vandal invasions of the fifth century.

In Britain a period of slow decline set in after 250; yet as late as 350 the wheat of eastern England was still being shipped to the Roman garrisons on the Rhine.

Under the shelter of the Roman camps and forts, areas of highly cultivated land remained here and there. But the total area of cultivation in the Roman empire got less and less. Large zones of frontier territory became waste. After 250 Spain had no surplus of foodstuffs to export to Rome. In Italy and even in Egypt good land went out of use. Aurelian and other rulers had to order the cities of the empire to find cultivators for their neglected fields.

But the effects of the chaos of the third century showed most clearly in industry and commerce. Craftsmen and the trades were more difficult to replace than farmers. Gaul and the Rhineland lost most of their manufactures and commerce. The glass industry of Cologne and the pottery industry of the western provinces fell to pieces after 250.

The economic disasters of the third century greatly reduced the numbers of the middle class which had done well in industry and commerce in the first and second centuries, and of the free cultivators on the land. In the third and fourth centuries the concentration of landed property into fewer hands increased. Need for protection against foreign invaders or against oppressive administrators drove many of the remaining small farmers to surrender their farms to their wealthier neighbours. The *latifundium* became the usual type of estate in the Roman empire.

The *coloni* were forced, in return for their protection, to remain permanently attached to the *latifundium*. Since the supply of slaves was now no longer adequate to the needs of the *latifundia*, the Roman government had to allow this new form of slavery, and by the time of Constantine it was being recognised in imperial legislation.

Industrial and commercial serfdom were also introduced into the Roman empire at the government's own initiative. In the fourth century a miller or a shipper was obliged by law to remain at his business for his lifetime and to train his sons to the same occupation.

### CHAPTER XVII

# ROME IN RETROSPECT

ROME began as a nation of peasants and farmers. Given an initial impetus by the Etruscans, and quickened by contact with the Greeks, its people still retained the virtues and defects which one might expect to find in a small agricultural community. But we stand amazed at the achievements of this community, whether we contemplate the length of Rome's rule, the width of her conquests, the stability of her imperial administration, the results of her artistic or literary efforts, or the richness and importance of the cultural movements and the efforts of the human spirit which she inspired or facilitated. Starting from a few huts on a couple of hills, a few arable fields ploughed by ignorant and superstitious peasants, she grew to be the richest city of the world — in a sense, the only city : and she instituted a way of life which still bears fruit in our time. From the appearance of Rome in the full light of history *c.* 500 B.C. to its ultimate disappearance *c.* A.D. 500 there is a thousand years of continuous history. This is un- paralleled in the affairs of men : it is a record.

As we contemplate the early history of Rome, it almost seems as if the Romans had in them some magical element, some divine spark, which the effects of heredity and environ- ment cannot account for. No doubt the Romans were born of good stock : no doubt their geographical position favoured them : no doubt the accidents of Etruscan proximity and the comparative weakness of her nearest neighbours helped her early development. But it is still hard to account for the fantastic determination, the incredible self-discipline, the amazing refusal to be defeated, which pulled the city time and time again out of a situation which would have permanently crippled any other state. This determination, together with the equally pronounced acquisitiveness and aggressiveness which the Romans displayed throughout their career, is part of the peasant-psychology which we have already mentioned : but it is as if these qualities had all been raised, by some historical accident, to the *n*th power.

Part of her early success is undoubtedly due to a virtue which she never lost, though was often slow to use : a virtue which, like so many other things, she may well have learnt from the Etruscans. Where other nations would have conquered and tyrannised, Rome allied. Though she always kept the pre-eminence in her treaties, yet the alliances were usually sufficiently genuine to allow her to draw on the man-power and resources of her neighbours, and thus to withstand the fiercest foes. Thus Hannibal might defeat one Roman army after another, but Rome could always produce a new one. Here Rome stands in sharp contrast with the Spartans of classical Greece, who, like Rome, had expanded their state by conquest, but who, unlike Rome, kept the conquered people in a state of near-slavery : so that their whole policy was dictated by the precarious position of tyranny, and the loss of even so few as 300 warriors caused them to sue for peace with Athens.

Moreover, the Roman army was a citizen army : it was not an army of mercenaries or slaves. In an important sense, the Roman army *was* the Roman state, just as the early *comitia* was an assembly of citizens in arms rather than a political body. Where the legions were, there was Rome. This remains true even after the Senate failed to control the usurping war-lords of the later republic : indeed, it is true in an even more real and brutal sense. The legions of Sulla, of Caesar, of Octavian, regarded themselves as Rome : they were its strength, and they gave their loyalty to their generals. And when Augustus flung the legions out to the imperial frontiers, it is no coincidence that much of the true history of Rome followed them, and that it is the growth of the provinces rather than of Rome herself which attracts our interest and our admiration.

But very quickly the tightly-integrated community of peasants began to change — and not always for the better.

Down to about 300 B.C., before Rome entered upon her wars outside Italy, one might well be satisfied with her progress. The sturdy plebeian peasantry had come to terms with the patrician ruling class, and gained from them sufficient concessions to play a real part in the government. But the disintegration soon began. The influence of foreign cultures, the influx of immense wealth from foreign conquests, the acquisition of vast numbers of slaves, and the total incompetence of the Senate to deal with the rapidly changing situation — all these played their part in removing the economic and moral framework which had held the community together. During this period the political diseases of Rome begin to fester: and after 133 B.C. they burst out into open sores.

This period of Roman history, though in many respects great and glorious, cannot be regarded as a successful lesson in internal politics. The senatorial government of the Roman republic proved itself a fairly efficient instrument of conquest, but an ineffective instrument of administration either in Rome itself or in the provinces. Rome was chiefly hampered by being, in origin and in essence, a class-conscious community. The government was an aristocratic one, and though last-minute concessions were made to the middle and lower classes, these classes never played any effective part in power politics. Certainly they were never absorbed into the government on a large scale. In many cities of classical Greece, by contrast, the existence of a strong middle class and its military importance to the state as heavy-armed hoplites ensured that the government remained to some extent associated with the interests of the governed: and at Athens, the similar importance of the lower classes, who manned the ships on which Athens depended for food and military security, resulted in an extreme democracy. But in Rome there was always an immense gulf between the rulers and the ruled. The *plebs* could not be brought into the area of power, and hence had to be placated by '*panem et circenses*'.

But the most dangerous (and ultimately fatal) symptom of this failure to integrate the social classes at Rome was the inability of the Senate to control war-lords like Sulla, Marius, Pompey and Caesar. Anyone not entirely loyal to the tightly-closed circle of patricians who ruled in the Senate would naturally probe the weaknesses of the system in order to gain power for himself.  Such a person might be of middle-class origin, a man who wished to compensate for his lack of nobility by making his mark in other fields, like Marius or Pompey : or he might be a patrician who was not content with the tentative and anxiety-ridden methods of the Senate, like Sulla or Caesar.  Since the Senate was in essence a conservative, unadventurous body, any adventurous and talented individual would be likely to come into conflict with it : and he would have the advantage that the people of Rome as a whole might well not be loyal to the Senate.  Thus the legions preferred to follow a general who led them to plunder rather than the weak dictates of the Senate, even if the city to be plundered was Rome itself.  For since the Senate refused them any share in the government, it could hardly expect to keep their loyalty.

Moreover, the Senate could hardly expect the people of Rome to admire its general administrative efficiency.  Designed by origin and nature to govern a small community of farmers, the patrician regime failed lamentably to govern the large city which Rome soon became, or the large section of the world which it soon conquered.  Elementary duties were neglected : there was no efficient police force or fire-brigade, the pirates were allowed to roam the seas unchecked, and the constant fluctuations in the price of corn were only one symptom of an unplanned economy.  For all this the conquests achieved by the Senate were poor compensation : for most of the booty fell into the hands of the patricians.  No efficient centralised administration dealt with the problems of provincial government, and the lack of effective communication between the Senate and the other classes allowed the situation to develop to a point where the Augustan autocracy became inevitable.

All this reminds us in certain ways of the political irresponsibility of the Greeks : it is, perhaps, as if the Greeks held the whole wealth and power of the world in their hands, and used it with the childishness which they generally displayed in their inter-state feuds.  Perhaps the Greeks were, indeed, indirectly to blame : for their effect on Roman civilisation was

considerable. In taking over the Greek-speaking easter
Mediterranean, the Romans had taken over an alread
existing commercial empire at once older and more sophisti
cated than their own. It is not till Greek culture reache
Rome that the selfless totalitarianism of the early republi
begins to degenerate into an individualism that reminds u
more of the Renaissance : Scipio Aemilianus was perhaps on
of the first figures who strikes us in this way, but there wer
plenty of other outstanding Romans who modelled themselve
on Achilles or Alexander rather than on the virtues of th
elder Cato. Greece provided Rome with a literature t
imitate, a philosophy to criticise, and in general with a cultur
which the Romans absorbed and rivalled : but the virtue
of government, administration and political success wer
purely Roman.

These virtues, though often hymned, are often disregarde
today. The chief Roman genius was for empiricism : that i
for the refusal to do anything else than to treat each case o
its own merits, the refusal to be doctrinaire or to follow blu
prints in political life. The Romans created and maintaine
the Pax Romana, not by insisting that the Roman religio
and way of life should be universally followed, but by requirin
only the minimum of conformity in their subject-peoples. Th
world has still not reached, or rather regained, the hig
standard of tolerance and the very real freedom which existe
under the Roman empire : freedom in religious and mor
practice, in decentralisation of control which permitted pr
vincials to run their own affairs, in speech and writing, i
trade and communication. In economic and military affai
Rome ruled with a strong hand : she insisted on money an
power, and often used brutal means to acquire and maintai
them. But she was not doctrinaire in her insistence on oth
matters. One could not be punished for being a Communis
or for not being a Communist, or for being a prostitute, 
for belonging to one religious sect rather than another. On
extreme cases, such as the Jews, were not covered by th
liberalism : and in such cases it could well be argued th
right was on the side of Rome.

The Romans, of course, were not idealists in any sens

They were highly acquisitive and aggressive, fond of money and power, not particularly religious, and not given to high-sounding morality : they felt little compunction about owning slaves, and kept women and children firmly in their place : and they were not greatly interested in anything which seemed to have no practical value. We are often inclined to undervalue them because their virtues are not flamboyant. If they could not build the Parthenon, they built the Pont du Gard ; and the functional efficiency of the latter should not blind us to its aesthetic merits. If they had no such colourful poets as Homer, Sappho and Aeschylus, they had poets with the power of Vergil, Horace and Catullus ; and it is the merest romantic prejudice to insist on the superiority of the former. If their philosophy was not as inspired as Plato's and Aristotle's, they created conditions in which equally inspired philosophers could think in peace ; and who shall say that this achievement is the lesser ?

Yet it remains true that with the Principate Rome seems to lose something of her drive, her forward-striving and pur-posive intensity. There were plenty of fruits to be reaped : for several hundred years the city and the empire continued in prosperity and safety. The world was secure for the Stoic and the Christian, for the peasant and the merchant, for the farmer on the frontier and for the rich man in Rome. Not till after A.D. 180 do we begin to be aware that the world which Rome built is beginning to come apart — that there is some-thing in the structure which will make the motto of '*Roma Aeterna*' into a lie. Yet even then we read of at least a century more of comparative stability ; and even when Rome falls, it does not fall because any alternative to the Roman way of life has seemed preferable : it falls at the feet of the barbarian.

Rome's initial impetus came from the acquisitive desires of a peasant people : it was the impetus of conquest. Having conquered, the Romans ruled wisely for the most part. They won their wealth, but maintained good government. But there it ended. The fatal aristocratic tradition which ruined the republic ruined the empire also in this sense : that the economy of the empire, and hence its sociology in general, was not forward-looking, because the tradition was one of aristocratic enjoyment and not of industrial expansion. The Roman empire never had an industrial revolution, and thus failed to follow one of the most important avenues which might have saved them from decadence. Their economy remained based on ownership of land : trade flourished, but the economic background as a whole remained stable.

It is at first sight surprising that the Roman world should not have become industrialised : one might have expected a practical people like the Romans to have succeeded where the more impractical Greeks failed. They had the resources, the time, the capital, the labour, and the political power. Their failure was partly due to the aristocratic tradition already mentioned, but other factors also played a part. The class of merchant-capitalists, though it prospered, was not so firmly established or so well integrated with the governing classes under the Roman empire as it was just before the industrial revolution in England. Moreover, there was little incentive for the ruling classes to support such a movement : the Romans already had as much wealth as they needed, and in particular an abundance of slaves made the solution of the labour problem too easy. In any case, for whatever reasons, the Roman economy never moved into the stage of full capitalism : instead, it slowly declined.

As a result, the impetus of conquest was never replaced by any other sociological drive. At first sight, the decision of Augustus to keep the empire within the Rhine–Danube frontier seems a good one from every point of view : it was financially wise, and it enabled him to dispense with a large part of his vast army and hence to remove much of the temptation to disloyalty on the part of ambitious generals. Within these natural boundaries the empire was manageable. But on a long-term view, the decision is more doubtful, for it also removed the driving force which, in leading Rome on to conquer more and more territory, had also imposed on her citizens a military and political discipline : the city had a *raison d'être*. After Augustus, imperceptibly at first but later only too obviously, the legions began to lose their verve, until eventually they became totally unlike the citizen force whose keenness, courage and incredible self-control had won Rome the world. They began to be replaced by local troops : they refused to carry the heavy equipment of the old-time legionary : and they lost the mobility and striking force which they once had. Moreover, the central administration, fearful of the national economy, more and more adopted a defensive attitude : and when the barbarians finally burst through the frontier, the intelligent observer could hardly have been surprised — any more than when the German panzer forces broke through the Franco–Belgian frontier in 1940.

But it is easy to be wise after the event : and difficult to imagine a world which knew only one mistress, and in which the name of Rome carried greater weight, and greater emotional overtones than the name of any other city has carried before or since. We forget the significance of Rome to the history of Europe only because we take it for granted : as we take for granted the system of Roman roads which laid the foundations of European communication, or the inventions of Roman architecture without which subsequent architecture could not have been created. We forget the corpus of Roman law, the notions of justice and equity on which most European codes are based : we forget the extent to which Christianity, and all other learning and culture, relied on Roman communications and Roman civilisation : we forget the Latin language, which long after the downfall of Rome remained the medium of all learning, and on which so many modern European tongues are founded. Much that the Romans have given the world may seem, like these inventions, very simple. But it is the simplicity which only comes from genius.

# RELIGION

In the early Roman community religious usage clearly reflected the agricultural basis of the people's life. Each household worshipped the protectors of its home and its livelihood : the Lares, who kept general guard over house and land ; the Penates, who watched over the grain-store ; Vesta, who fanned the glow in the hearth-fire ; Jupiter, the God of sun and rain ; Mars, who stirred the plants to life in spring ; and a host of other powers that aided or hindered the work of farmers, or guided the members of the family through the critical stages of birth and childhood, marriage and death. In his worship the peasant hardly looked beyond the practical needs of day-to-day life. His idea of the divine powers (*numina*) whom he addressed was hazy, and his conception of the next world was so dim that he could think of the dead (*manes*) only in a collective sense. His acts of worship consisted of a simple prayer and a ritual 'libation' (pouring-out) of milk or (more seldom) of wine, an offer of a cake or a sacrifical animal, on an altar of turf.

The religion of the state was similar to the private cults. The city of Rome gave public worship to Vesta, to the Lares and Penates, and to other guardians of fields and flocks, with ceremonies that did not differ much from those of the individual household. But certain of the rustic deities became protectors of the community as a whole in all its activities. Mars turned the tide of battle in Rome's favour ; Janus mounted guard over the city gates ; above all, Jupiter became the general watcher over Rome's welfare. At the end of the period of the kings, moreover, the official religion was elaborated under Etruscan influence. Their earliest temples were of Etruscan type.

At the close of this period the official Roman religion had acquired those permanent characteristics which no later influence was ever able to obliterate. It combined the practical give-and-take attitude of the Italian peasant with the ceremonial formalism of the Etruscans. Of all ancient religions it was the least emotional. The official Roman mind admitted a feeling of vague awe (religion in its original sense) in the presence of the deity, but it thought any unchecked display of emotion out of place in an act of worship. It was equally the most meticulous and conservative in its ritual. Even in the emancipated and irreverent days of the later republic ceremonial taboos inherited from the Stone Age were scrupulously observed. In this strait-jacket, Roman religion never became, like that of the Greeks, the mother of art, music and literature ; though it possessed a fundamental resemblance with the religion of the early Israelites, it never could produce a comprehensive and satisfying code of conduct. Yet for all its hardness and selfishness it was not lacking in social value. It fostered the idea of mutual obligation between man and man, and strengthened the feeling of partnership in a common cause.

In the fifth and fourth centuries Roman state religion came under Greek or Etruscan influence. Temples with proper images replaced the crude altars of an earlier age. The ritual of the Etruscans was used to reinforce the learning of the *augures*, and sons of Roman noblemen were sent to Tuscany to study. In 264 a member of a rising plebeian house, D. Iunius Brutus, introduced into Rome the Etruscan and Campanian custom of gladiatorial contests at the funeral of an important person. Greek influence is evident in the institution of state cults of Ceres, of Castor and Pollux, and of Hercules. The 'Sibylline books', a collection of oracles which had been brought to Rome under the last Tarquin, or perhaps in the early days of the republic, had been placed under the special care of a new body of priests who consulted the prophecies at the Senate's direction. With the Greek gods Hellenic forms of ritual, such as processions accompanied by music and dancing, were introduced.

But the ancient Italic religion of the home and of the fields and flocks remained the same, and the introduction of foreign usages into the Roman state cults was carefully supervised by the priests. While the ruling families at Rome were willing to admit foreign deities, they admitted them only on condition of their reducing rather than exciting popular emotion ; cults and beliefs which smelt of superstition were kept out.

As foreign influences upon the Roman world became more powerful, the Roman state-religion deliberately guarded itself against them. During the Punic Wars, it is true, the Senate allowed alien rites in order to put new heart into the people. In 249 and 207 it appointed special festivals of appeasement (*Ludi Tarentini*) to the Greek underworld deities, Pluto and Persephone ; in 216 it fulfilled the order of a Sibylline oracle which bade it bury alive two Greeks and two Gauls. In 217 the Italian thanksgiving festival of the Saturnalia became a Greek merry-making festival during which all doors stood open and masters changed parts with slaves. The decorous and dull ritual of various Roman state cults was made lively with processions, circus games and dramatic performances. The cheerfulness of the Greek ritual served the purpose of keeping the town mob amused and grateful to its noble patrons. In 205 an Oriental deity, the Phrygian nature-goddess Cybele or Magna Mater, was officially received into the Roman religion. By the help of King Attalus of Pergamum, Romans were able to bring home from her sanctuary at Pessinus a black stone in which the goddess was thought to live ; and an orgiastic type of ritual was established in her honour.

But the general policy of the governing class was to prevent alien influences from harming Roman religion. Though elements of Greek ceremonial were incorporated into official Roman cults, the practice of adopting new Greek gods into the circle of Rome's deities was almost discontinued. The only notable newcomer from Greek lands was Venus of Mt. Eryx in Sicily (217). The ritual of Cybele was admitted but no Roman citizen was allowed to officiate at her worship. Though the official Sibylline oracles might be consulted at moments of crisis by order of the Senate, private prophecies were suppressed. In 242 the Roman government went so far as to urge the allied city of Praeneste to close down the oracle of its patron goddess, Fortuna Primigenia. Attempts to introduce exotic worships of an exciting and unnerving character were punished.

The religious policy of the Roman nobles shows their readiness to exploit religion for their class. The subordination of the *res divina* to political convenience was frankly stated by the Aelian and the Fufian laws, which virtually allowed dishonest divination to suit politics.

An expulsion order by which the *praetor peregrinus* of 139 banished from Rome all astrologers and members of the Jewish sect shows that by then the city was becoming a missionary field for the religions and the philosophies of the Near East. But at this stage Oriental thoughts and faiths had hardly begun to work among the western peoples.

In the second century B.C. the republic was faced with the choice between the traditional Italic ways of life and the cosmopolitan (mostly Greek) civilisation of the eastern Mediterranean. Characteristically they made a compromise ; they adopted Greek culture, but not all of it. Of the many pupils of Greece, the Romans were the best ; they were not too proud to learn, and they learnt with their eyes open. In the second century the republic raised itself from the level of a police-state to that of a culture-state.

The religion of the Roman world under the later republic passed through a stage of stagnation, or decay. While the cults of the home kept their old vitality (of which the family altars in the houses at Pompeii and Delos offer visible proof), the worship of the state-gods was dying. No further deities of any importance were admitted and the *ius divinum* was becoming stereotyped. In the second century the *pax deorum* had become a conspiracy between the state-gods and the governing aristocracy for the maintenance of the latter's power ; in the first century it was turned to the selfish uses of individual politicians. Under such conditions the official worships lost much of their remaining hold on the Roman people. From the point of view of the ordinary citizen their chief function was to provide him with amusements at the public festivals.

The government of the later republic maintained the policy of discouraging new worships by private initiative. In 139 it expelled the first Jewish immigrants into Italy. In the first century it tolerated the synagogues set up by Pompey's prisoners of war from Palestine, and it did not formally outlaw the cult of the Egyptian deities Isis and Sarapis, which entered Italy *c.* 100 B.C. ; but it banned these foreign gods from the city to its outer precincts. So long as the Oriental element of the population in Italy remained small, these police measures proved effective. But the ban which Antony placed on the worship of the dead Caesar in 44 was lifted in 46 when the triumvirs started an official cult of *divus Iulius*. The great personality of Caesar made the Greek practice of offering divine homage to human beings, dead or alive, appear less strange to the Roman mind.

The age of Augustus saw the revival of one religion and the institution of another in the Roman world. The emperor made an attempt to breathe fresh life into the old state cults, and he became a god himself. Both these religious movements were honestly inspired, but the wave of sentiment which created them was soon spent. As the crisis through which Augustus had guided the Roman world passed away, the protecting deities of the state once again came to be simply taken for granted. Of Augustus' successors Claudius alone gave any personal attention to the state religion.

The feeling of gratitude to Augustus remained alive for a while after his death. Not only was the cult of *divus Augustus* officially established at Rome and in the provincial capitals (where it replaced that of *Roma et Augustus*), but permanent temples were constructed in many towns of Italy and the provinces at the wish of the inhabitants. During the reigns of Tiberius and Claudius altars were set up here and there to these rulers, or to popular members of the imperial family, like Livia or Germanicus. But the enthusiasm inevitably died down. Caligula forced his worship upon his subjects, and Nero requested the Senate to start an official cult of *divus Claudius* at Rome. But Tiberius and Claudius objected to the setting up of altars in their honour ; and the deification of Claudius after his death was generally looked upon as a bad joke. Emperor-worship maintained itself with the usual tenacity of an established religion ; but it soon became, like the cult of the older state-gods, a mere formality.

Meanwhile philosophy was ceasing to be widely studied, and in any case was coming to terms with religion. The atheistic creed of the Epicureans was dying out ; the Stoic school was accepting a supreme personal deity. From the time of Augustus the doctrine of astrology, which had been strong in the eastern Mediterranean since the second century B.C., spread to Italy, where it made converts in high society and among the emperors themselves. But astrology could not be a general substitute for religion.

Under the early emperors three religions could be singled out as holding the greatest promise for the future. In Hellenistic Greece the ancient Egyptian nature-goddess Isis had been transformed into a universal mother and well-wisher of mankind, who repaid her worship and the observation of a few simple rules of life (such as an occasional fast) with happiness in this world and the next. Her elaborate and emotional ritual was conducted by a professional clergy, but her worshippers, instead of merely looking on at the cere-monial, took an active part in it. The cult of Isis, and that of her male counterpart Sarapis, had a special attraction for mariners and merchants, who spread it in every Mediterranean port. From Campania, where temples of Isis were built at Puteoli and Pompeii in the later years of the republic, her cult spread to Rome. Though more than once banned from the capital by Roman governments, which disapproved of its noise and excitement, it always re-established itself. In 43 B.C. the triumvirs decreed a state temple in honour of Isis and Sarapis ; under Augustus and Tiberius this was simply disregarded, but it was carried into effect by Caligula.

The worship of Jehovah had become widely diffused over the eastern Mediterranean through the dispersion of the Jewish people in the Hellenistic period, and it had been introduced into Rome by the Jewish colony formed there in the last century of the republic. The political revolt of the Maccabees against the Seleucids had started a revival of religious enthusiasm, and of missionary activity among the

Gentiles. In the first century A.D. the cult of Jehovah had attracted to itself a large body of converts who regularly attended the synagogues, though they might not conform in all respects to the Jewish Law.

In the reign of Tiberius a Jewish prophet named Jesus proclaimed a new message. The crowds which Jesus attracted greeted him as a miracle-worker, and when he went on his prophetic mission to Jerusalem, the multitudes assembled there gave him a triumphal welcome as the son of King David (A.D. 33). The Jewish High Priest Caiaphas, who thought it his duty to defend Jewish orthodoxy, and feared that the disturbance over Jesus might be thought by the Roman governor of Judaea to be a rebellion, got Pontius Pilatus the procurator to sentence Jesus to the punishment of crucifixion (which the Roman courts usually pronounced upon slaves and other non-Romans of humble rank found guilty of rebellion or rioting). The death of Jesus attracted little attention at the time, but his disciples were heartened by a belief in his resurrection to keep his message alive, and eventually to set up a sect distinct from the parent Jewish church. Outdoing the Jews in zeal, these Christians carried Jesus' message through Asia Minor and Greece to Rome, and a recent convert named Paul laid the foundations of a universal Christian church by his missionary visits and letters. By 64 the Christians were numerous in Rome, and well known.

After about A.D. 70 the only philosophies that kept any vitality were those of the Stoics and Cynics. In the second century the Stoic school produced two of its greatest men, a Phrygian freedman named Epictetus and the emperor M. Aurelius. In humbler society wandering Cynic preachers could still attract attention with their doctrine of 'living according to Nature', by which they meant disregarding conventions and limiting one's own wants. But the teachers of the Stoic and Cynic schools, who insisted that virtue was its own reward, could not in the long run prevail against religious missionaries who were now proclaiming confidently a state of future immortality. Though Stoicism lived on in the Christian doctrine, which it influenced, it began to fade out after the death of M. Aurelius.

In the first and second centuries many of the provincial religions became merged in Roman cults. The gods of the peoples on the European continent disappeared before those of the Romans; the Carthaginian Moloch was swallowed by Saturn, and the Baals of Syrian towns were changed into Jupiters. Yet this involved little more than a change of name and perhaps of ritual. The established religions kept a firm hold. Domitian and Antoninus did their duties as chief pontiffs with scrupulous care and all the emperors from Vespasian to M. Aurelius, with the single exception of Domitian, were enrolled after death on the list of *divi*. Traditional conceptions of the underworld were still widespread, and even educated persons were reverting to beliefs and practices which they had abandoned or mocked in previous centuries. Oracles and omens were recovering much of their former authority. Books on the interpretation of dreams had a good sale; the temple of Apollo at Delphi once more attracted many clients, and another Apolline oracle at Claros, near Ephesus, attained celebrity in the second century. Stories of miraculous healings by pagan deities working through human agency were widely and unquestioningly accepted.

Yet the traditional religions were being eaten into by those newer worships which set greater tasks and offered higher rewards. The cult of Isis spread in the later first and the second century, together with that of Sarapis, to the northern outposts of the Roman dominions, to Cologne, London and York. But from the age of Antoninus it lost the lead among the pagan missionary religions to that of another Oriental deity, the Persian Mithras. Originally a mere sun-god, Mithras was transformed at the end of the pre-Christian era into a male counterpart of Isis. The cult of Mithras resembled the worship of Isis in its impressive ceremonial, conducted by highly trained priests, in its promise of future immortality, and in its possession of an ethical code. From the worship of the Phrygian goddess Cybele it borrowed a ritual of initiation by baptism with the blood of a bull. With the agreement or active support of the emperors of the second century, it was carried by the Oriental soldiers from camp to camp until it reached the Rhineland and Hadrian's Wall. But it also spread among the civilian population : it followed the Isis cult to Dacia and to Ostia.

The Jewish faith was kept alive in synagogues and schools, but after the political disasters which the Jewish people had suffered at the hands of the Roman emperors it ceased to be a missionary religion.

The eventual victory of Christianity was due to a variety of advantages which it held. The Christians provided themselves with an organisation better than that of all the other private religions. When the early Christian congregation broke away from the parent Jewish church, it lost all the advantages of membership in a well-regulated society. The first Christian communities were isolated cells under a rough-and-ready administration of elder members. But in the first century of their existence they set up a well-organised body of clergy possessing wide powers of discipline over the laity ; by the time of M. Aurelius the clerical hierarchy was complete in all essentials. Still more important was the creation of good communications between the several Christian communities. In the first century A.D. the only means of keeping touch between the individual churches was by irregular visits or occasional letters from authoritative leaders like Peter and Paul. In the second century the churches had a system of regular correspondence by representatives of neighbouring congregations. In the early years of the third century a critical step forward was taken, when in one Roman province after another the bishop of the 'metropolis' or principal town convened regular meetings of bishops from all the lesser cities. At these conferences provision was made for mutual financial support — a form of insurance whose value was often proved in times of persecution — and a uniform creed was formulated. Under the reign of Constantine there were also congresses attended by priests from more than one province. In 314 a gathering of bishops from the western churches assembled at Arelate ; in 325 a gathering of higher clergy from every part of the empire was held at Nicaea in Bithynia, whose work survives in the 'Nicene' creed. By 330 the administrative framework of the Church was complete.

The spread of Christianity was helped by a special literature.

N

The teaching of Jesus was soon set down in written records, of which the four Gospels, dated from *c.* 65 to 100, eventually came to be accepted as authoritative. By the time of Constantine these four books, together with other early records and epistles, had been collected to form the 'New Testament'; and the whole of this collection was made available to the western peoples in several Latin versions. The task of revising the Christian creed in the light of other systems of thought (the Stoic and Platonic philosophies) was begun in the epistles of Paul and carried on in the writings of various Church Fathers, mostly Greeks, among whom the Alexandrian bishops Clement and Origen (*c.* 200) were the pioneers. From the time of M. Aurelius the Church also kept its own historical records. In the days of Constantine a Palestinian bishop named Eusebius (264–340) collected the various traditions into a standard history of the Church.

Another branch of Christian literature was addressed to those outside the Church, in order to explain to them the Christian religion and to defend it against attack. The need of this was all the greater, as no other ancient religion had to encounter a more sustained opposition. The *De Civitate Dei* of St. Augustine (354–430) was accepted as the classic justification of the Christian faith. Though the Christian writers occasionally lost their patience, they maintained on the whole a tone of moderation and met their antagonists point by point. No other ancient religion was as fortunate as Christianity in the manner of its presentation.

The Christian like the Jewish religion was not content to share the world with other worships, but aimed at abolishing them altogether. This attack upon other gods was resented by those who wished to live and let live in matters of religion. Neither could the Jews and Christians escape by keeping aloof from society, for in an essentially sociable community such as a Greek or Roman city, self-isolation was disliked and suspected. But gradually Jews and Christians overcame much of their original unpopularity; by the time of Constantine individual Christians and pagans had no difficulty in making friends. But in the first two centuries the Christian communities were constantly liable to attacks by infuriated mobs, like those which have been directed against the Jews in medieval and modern times.

The attitude of the emperors to the Christians was not clear until the reign of Trajan. The execution of the Christians at Rome under Nero did not result in any general persecution. Under Vespasian the Christian community at Rome was fairly secure ; so too under Domitian. During the first half century after the crucifixion of Jesus the Roman governors in the eastern provinces took no active measures against the Christians, but at the end of the first century they executed quite a few. A justification for such punishments could be found in the laws of Caesar and Augustus against unauthorised associations, or in the refusal of Christians to worship the emperor.

About A.D. 110 Pliny, the proconsul of Bithynia, applied to Trajan for instructions in regard to the Christians. The emperor laid down the rule that Christians accused before a Roman court should be required to prove their loyalty by sacrificing to the emperor, and should, on refusal, suffer the penalties of treason, but that accusations against Christians must be left to private prosecutors.

The practical effect of Trajan's reply was that in the second century occasional executions of Christians continued. Occasional cases of mass-persecutions are on record. At Lugdunum an angry mob persuaded the governor to deal out death sentences to the victims. The third century opened with persecutions in Africa and Egypt ; but under Alexander Severus the Christians enjoyed safety.

But in 250 the emperor Decius, in a wild attempt to crush the general chaos of his time, commanded all Christians to give up their faith and to take part in pagan acts of worship. In 257 Valerianus repeated Decius' order. These decrees led to a considerable number of martyrdoms among the Christian priests. Yet the persecutions were too short to have any permanent effect. Public opinion was by now making peace with the Christians. During the next forty years the Christians were left safe, and were tacitly freed from the obligation to worship the emperor, so that they became free to join the army and the civil service ; under Diocletian they even rose to the position of provincial governors.

Yet between 303 and 311 they were subjected to a more persistent persecution than ever before. This renewed attack upon the Christians was all the more strange, as Diocletian had taken a Christian wife and was a tolerant man. The number of victims of the persecution under Diocletian and Galerius undoubtedly exceeded all previous totals. Yet the Christians once again found many loopholes of escape. Even in the eastern provinces, where Galerius supervised the execution of the decrees, the governors were slack in carrying out orders. In the west Constantius contented himself with closing the Christian places of worship, and Constantine gave complete toleration. Diocletian himself was doubtful, and in 311 Galerius frankly confessed his failure by cancelling the decrees against the Christians.

In 312 the conversion of Constantine to Christianity opened a new era for the Church. By the Edict of Milan, which was published in 313, in the joint name of Constantine and Licinius, the Christians were accorded complete freedom of worship and exemption from all pagan ceremonies in all the Roman empire. This decree was reaffirmed in 323 when Constantine became sole emperor. Two years later Constantine gave special facilities for Church priests to assemble at the Congress of Nicaea, and he took a personal part in the council. But Constantine's religious policy remained one of general toleration ; the persecuting activities of the Christian Church belong to later reigns.

In the days of Constantine Christianity was still a long way from being the universal religion of the Roman empire. Except perhaps in Syria, in Asia Minor and in the city of Alexandria, its adherents nowhere included more than half of the population ; in Rome and the west they were as yet a small minority. Yet they had planted their propaganda-cells in every province ; their clergy had constituted itself into a powerful aristocracy ; above all, they had captured a high proportion of the more thoughtful inhabitants of the empire. In the middle of the fourth century the emperor Julian, the last champion of the old order of things, had to admit that the ultimate victory of Christianity in the Roman world was assured.

# THE CITY OF ROME

IN general appearance the city of Rome was little changed between the expulsion of the kings and the third century B.C. After its demolition by the Gauls in 390 it was rebuilt haphazardly. The poor continued to live in huts. Stone was hardly used except for the foundations of houses, and roof-tiles only came in after 300. In the earliest days of the republic the construction of temples begun under the monarchy, and notably the great temple of Jupiter on the Capitol, was completed. Further building was stopped during the period of general poverty that followed ; but after 350 several new temples were erected from the sale of war-booty, in fulfilment of vows made before battle by the victorious Roman commanders. The gains of conquest were also applied to useful public works, such as road-making and the improvement of the water-supply. The censor Appius Claudius gave his name both to the Via Appia and to the Aqua Appia, the first Roman aqueduct. This channel was less than a mile in length ; but in 272 it was followed by the Anio Vetus, an aqueduct of forty miles, which brought an excellent supply of water from the Sabine hills.

In the third and second centuries the city of Rome outstripped all the towns of the west in size, and came near the Hellenistic capitals of Antioch and Alexandria. Its growing population now sought accommodation in large blocks of buildings (*insulae*), which were let off in flats or by single apartments. For the private mansions of the rich, dressed stone now came into general use.

The face of the city was greatly changed by the numerous public works constructed with private funds by the various war-winners, and with public money by the censors. Votive temples were still the commonest form of memorial. Greek influence was obvious in the numerous new *basilicae* or public halls which replaced the old rows of shops along the Forum and acted as markets and as courts of justice. The first of these purely Greek buildings, the Basilica Porcia, was erected by Cato (184) ; a second basilica was constructed jointly by the censors Aemilius Lepidus and Fulvius Nobilior in 179, and a third by Sempronius Gracchus in 170. The first of a typically Roman form of monument, the 'triumphal' arch, was set up in 120 by Fabius Maximus to celebrate his victory in Gaul. To sate the mob's appetite for amusements the censor Flaminius began the construction of a new circus in the Campus Martius (220).

The streets of Rome were repaved with blocks of hard lava from the Alban mount, and in 179 Aemilius Lepidus laid the foundations of a stone bridge (completed in 142), to help out the old trestle bridge which had hitherto carried all the traffic within the city. But nothing was done to widen or straighten the streets, and the Forum, with its narrow and irregular area of a hundred yards by fifty, was not enlarged to meet the growing needs of public life. On the other hand, the sanitation of the city was well cared for. Cato carried out a thorough repair of Rome's drainage system. In 144 the praetor Q. Marcius Rex provided for the construction of Rome's first high-level aqueduct, the Aqua Marcia, which conveyed the city's purest supply of water from the head of the Anio valley over a distance of thirty-six miles. In general, the public works of the second century reflected the traditional preference of the Romans for solid and useful rather than showy architecture.

Under the later republic the city of Rome outstripped all other Mediterranean towns in the size of its population, which now approached the million mark. Of the war-winners of this period, Sulla reconstructed the temple of Jupiter Capitolinus which had been burnt down in 83 and erected a *tabularium* (Records Office) on the Capitoline Hill. In the Forum Sulla rebuilt the Senate-house to accommodate its enlarged membership. To Pompey Rome owed its first stone theatre. Before the end of his term in Gaul Caesar began the construction of his chief architectural monuments, the Basilica Iulia and the Forum Iulium. The Basilica was a covered hall at the south-west end of the old Forum; the Forum Iulium was an enclosure, to the north-west of the old Forum, with surrounding galleries and a temple of Venus Genetrix in its centre. Both these buildings served as places of business and as courts of law. During his dictatorship Caesar arranged for the reconstruction of the Senate-house, another victim of the disorders of 52, and for the erection of a large covered enclosure for voters at the Popular Assemblies.

The censors of the later republic no longer made improvements or repairs out of the treasury; and the senatorial government remained blind to the need of controlling the vast building operations which the rapid growth of the urban population entailed. The poorer inhabitants of the city were being huddled together in crazy matchwood buildings of many storeys, whose rents soared as high as the buildings themselves. On the other hand, the outskirts of Rome now began to be laid out with pleasure grounds. The gardens of Lucullus and Sallust in the north, of Maecenas in the east and of Caesar across the Tiber provided a chain of parks around the city.

Augustus carried out a programme of repairs to the more dilapidated temples. In subsequent years he gave large sums from his private money to further reconstruction, to the completion of Caesar's unfinished buildings and to new ones. He made a regulation imposing a limit of sixty feet to the height of buildings. In continuation of Caesar's work, he laid out a second new Forum (the Forum Augusti, the ground-space for which he bought at a rate of £500 per square yard) to the north of the old Forum, and used the vacant land on the Campus Martius for other new constructions.

After the battle of Actium Agrippa took personal charge of the water-supply of Rome. In 19 B.C. he constructed a short new aqueduct, the Aqua Virgo, and erected the 'Thermae', an elaborate bathing establishment in the later Greek style, combining the modern swimming-pool and Turkish bath. After his death, in 12 B.C., his technical staff of 240 trained slaves was placed on the public pay-list, and the control of water-mains was permanently made over to an imperial officer. Before the end of Augustus' reign, water was laid on in most of the houses in Rome.

The Roman architects of the Augustan age not only employed white marble (from Carrara) for their columns, but made free use of coloured materials — yellow stones from Numidia, others with green streaks from Euboea or with purple veins from Phrygia. For this use of costly materials the emperor himself set an example in the temple which he dedicated to Apollo on the Palatine, as a thank-offering for his naval victories. The portico of this splendid building was in Numidian stone ; the shrine itself was of pure white marble.

The remains of the palaces built by the early emperors on the Palatine hardly convey an accurate idea of their architectural merits. Augustus' house (on the south-eastern edge of the Palatine) consisted of four blocks of apartments round a peristyle ; Tiberius' mansion, on the opposite corner of the same hill, conformed to the same plan, but Caligula added a new wing to it. The general plan of Nero's 'Golden House' has not yet been recovered.

In the later first and the earlier second centuries the emperors set an example of lavish expenditure on building. At Rome the Domus Aurea of Nero, which had become a public scandal, was demolished by Vespasian. Domitian reconstructed and enlarged the residence of Augustus. This now became the Domus Flaviana, which is the best preserved of the imperial palaces at Rome, the main building consisted of porticoed chambers in two storeys facing an inner quadrangle. The chief apartments of state were at either end : a dining-hall and a basilica, which the emperor used for his council. In Rome Hadrian made himself a mausoleum of such massive construction that in the Middle Ages it was used as a fortress.

The most useful gift of the Flavian emperors and their successors to the general public of Rome consisted of three new Fora. At the end of the Jewish war Vespasian built one with a Temple of Peace in the centre. Domitian and Nerva connected this new square with the Forum Augusti by the Forum Nervae or Transitorium. On the north side of Augustus' Forum Trajan cut away a bit of the Quirinal Hill to gain space for the roomiest of all the public squares at Rome, the Forum Traiani. This capacious place, which measured some 350 by 200 yards, contained in its centre a large covered hall, the Basilica Ulpia.

The Pantheon of Hadrian replaced an earlier temple by Agrippa, whose portico was left standing. The new temple was designed in the form of a rotunda spanned by a concrete dome 140 feet in diameter, with a 30-foot opening in the centre to let in the light. This dome, which was made to carry its own weight without any supporting columns, was the greatest achievement in ancient concrete construction.

Vespasian erected two other memorials of the Jewish War, the Arch of Titus and the Amphitheatrum Flavium. The amphitheatre was well worthy of its modern name, the 'Colosseum': it could accommodate at least 50,000 spectators.

Under Nerva and Trajan the last of the Roman aqueducts, the Aqua Traiana, was constructed; the daily supply of water to Rome now amounted approximately to one hundred gallons a head. With the completion of two new baths by Titus and Trajan the bathing facilities of the capital were enlarged to the same ultra-modern standard. In spite of extensive rebuilding the city still contained many narrow streets and slum areas. Vespasian and his successors did not build for the greatest welfare of the greatest number. But as a show-place Rome could now challenge the handsomest cities of the Hellenistic East.

The builders of the later empire possessed a technical ability as good as that of Agrippa's or Hadrian's architects: the vaults of the Basilica of Maxentius and Constantine will bear comparison, in point of height and span, with the dome of the Pantheon. Yet their work achieved its effect by mere bigness rather than by its good proportions and elegance of detail.

# LISTS

## A: CHRONOLOGICAL TABLE

### (A) 753 B.C.–A.D. 14

#### 1. INTERNAL HISTORY
##### (*Traditional or uncertain dates*)

B.C.

753 Romulus founds Rome
715 Numa Pompilius king
673 Tullus Hostilius king
642 Ancus Martius king
616 Tarquinius Priscus king (first Etruscan king)
578 Servius Tullius king
534 Tarquinius Superbus king
509 Expulsion of the kings

##### (*Probable or certain dates*)

451 Twelve Tables
449 Secession of the plebs
421 Number of quaestors raised to four : quaestorship opened to plebs
390 Gauls capture Rome, but bribed to depart
367 Proposals of Licinius Stolo and L. Sextius passed : magistracy reorganised
356 First plebeian dictator
351 First plebeian censor
339 Leges Publiliae
336 First plebeian praetor
312 Appius Claudius censor
300 Lex Ogulnia
287 Lex Hortensia
241 Number of tribes raised to 35 : *Comitia centuriata* reorganised soon after
c. 240 Two praetors appointed : *urbanus* and *peregrinus*

B.C.

232  Lex Flaminia *agraria* carried by the plebs

227  Addition of two praetors : beginning of organised provincial government

216  Q. Fabius Maximus last active dictator (in traditional sense)

197  Addition of two praetors : now six of these

180  Lex Villia annalis

167  Land-tax abolished

149  Lex Calpurnia *de rebus repetundis*

139  Lex Gabinia — introduction of voting by ballot

137  Lex Cassia

133  Tribunate of T. Gracchus : first civil bloodshed at Rome

132  Judicial commission of Popilius Laenas

131  C. Papirius Carbo fails to pass bill for re-election to tribunate

129  Judicial powers of T. Gracchus' land commission transferred to consuls : death of Scipio Aemilianus

125  Consulship of M. Fulvius Flaccus

123  Tribunate of C. Gracchus

122  C. Gracchus re-elected as tribune : probably first use of '*senatus consultum ultimum*'

107  C. Marius opened army to all citizens

106  Q. Servilius Caepio transferred courts *de rebus repetundis* to senate

*c.* 104  Servilius Glaucia re-transfers courts to equites

104–100  Marius successively consul : army reforms

103  Law '*de maiestate*' of Saturninus

100  Tribunate of Saturninus

91  Tribunate of Livius Drusus

91–88  Social War

88  Tribunate of Sulpicius Rufus : Sulla first Roman to march on Rome

87  Marius' reign of terror

86–83  Revolutionary government of Cornelius Cinna

83  Sulla lands at Brundisium

82  Battle of Colline Gate

81–79  Sulla dictator : constitutional reforms

77  Pompey defeats rebellion of M. Aemilius Lepidus

77–72  Campaigns of Pompey against Q. Sertorius in Spain

75  Tribunes allowed to hold higher offices

73–71  Slave War

70  Consulship of Pompey and Crassus : breakdown of Sulla's constitution

B.C.

- 67  Lex Gabinia
- 66  Lex Manilia
- 65  Proposal of Crassus for annexation of Egypt rejected
- 63  Cicero consul : Catiline's conspiracy overthrown : Julius Caesar elected *pontifex maximus*
- 60  First Triumvirate
- 59  Consulship of Caesar : Lex Vatinia
- 58  Tribunate of P. Clodius : Cicero and Cato forced to leave Rome
- 57  Cicero recalled : Pompey in charge of corn supply
- 56  Conference of Luca
- 55  Consulship of Pompey and Crassus : Caesar's Gallic command prolonged
- 54  Death of Julia
- 53  Death of Crassus
- 52  Murder of Clodius and riots : Pompey sole consul till August 1st
- 50  Various proposals concerning Caesar's resignation
- 49  Caesar crosses Rubicon : civil war : Pompey withdraws to Greece : Caesar dictator at Rome
- 49–44  Legislation of Caesar carried out
- 48  Battle of Pharsalus
- 47  Caesar crushes Alexandrine revolt : battle of Zama
- 46  Battle of Thapsus
- 45  Battle of Munda
- 44  Caesar murdered : Octavian made Caesar's heir : Mark Antony in charge of affairs : Cicero's Philippics : battle of Mutina
- 43  Conference at Bononia : Second Triumvirate : proscriptions : Cicero killed
- 42  Battle of Philippi : conspirators defeated
- 41  Antony in the East
- 40  Octavian captures Perusia : treaty of Brundisium
- 39  Treaty of Misenum
- 37  Conference at Tarentum
- 36  Battle of Naulochus : defeat of Sex. Pompeius : Lepidus' revolt crushed
- 33–27  Octavian holds extraordinary power
- 32  Antony divorces Octavia
- 31  Battle of Actium
- 30  Suicides of Antony and Cleopatra
- 29  Octavian returns to Rome
- 28  Censorship of Octavian and M. Vipsanius Agrippa

B.C.

27   Beginning of Principate : first settlement : Octavian takes name of Augustus
25   Marriage of Marcellus and Julia
23   Augustus critically ill : second settlement : Marcellus dies
22–19   Augustus visits the East
21   Marriage of Agrippa and Julia
18   Agrippa receives *tribunicia potestas* and *maius imperium*
17   Augustus adopts L. and C. Caesar
12   Deaths of Agrippa and Lepidus : Augustus becomes *pontifex maximus*
11   Marriage of Tiberius and Julia
6   Tiberius receives *tribunicia potestas* : retires to Rhodes
2   Banishment of Julia

A.D.

2   Tiberius returns to Rome : death of L. Caesar
4   Death of C. Caesar : Augustus adopts Tiberius
6   *Aerarium militare* started
9   Lex Papia Poppaea
14   Death of Augustus

## 2. RELATIONS WITH ITALY

### (*Traditional or uncertain dates*)

B.C.

753–509   Kings of Rome continually at war with neighbours : Rome becomes most powerful city in Latium
496   Battle of Lake Regillus
493   Alliance with Latins : *foedus Cassium*
489–431   War against Sabines, Aequi and Volsci
486   Hernici join alliance of Rome and Latins
480   Veii defeats Rome, wiping out the Fabian *gens*
430   Aequi driven back from Mt. Algidus : Volsci also defeated
396   Conquest of Veii
390   Disaster of the Allia : Gauls bribed to leave Rome

### (*Probable or certain dates*)

389–380   Final struggle with Aequi and Volsci
367   Land assignations of Licinius Stolo and L. Sextius
360   Reorganisation of Latin League
356–351   Etruscan War
354   First alliance with Samnites

B.C.

349 Invasion of Gauls checked

343–341 First Samnite War

340–338 Great Latin War

338 Latin League dissolved : new settlement of Latium

331 Senones make peace with Rome

328 Colony of Fregellae established

327–304 Second Samnite War

321 Disaster of Caudine Forks

315 Disaster of Lautulae

314 Colony of Luceria established

312 Via Appia built

311 Etruscans make war on Rome : defeated : individual cities make
    terms, and armistice made between Rome and Etruscan League

298–290 Third Samnite War

295 Battle of Sentinum

283 Rome crushes the Senones

281–275 War with Pyrrhus

280 Battle of Heraclea

279 Battle of Asculum

275 Battle of Beneventum

272 Surrender of Tarentum

264 Roman supremacy recognised throughout peninsular Italy by this
    date

225 Gauls defeated at battle of Telamon

223 Lex Flaminia Agraria

220 North Italy subdued by this date : colonies of Cremona and
    Placentia established : construction of Via Flaminia and Via
    Aurelia

186–180 Campaigns in Liguria

177 Allies' share in war booty diminished

167 Land-tax in Italy abolished

133 Tib. Gracchus' land commission established

125 Fulvius Flaccus proposes to give citizenship to Italians, but fails

123–122 Citizen colonies founded by C. Gracchus : Ligurians subdued

c. 120 Land allotments allowed to be sold

c. 118 Land allotments discontinued

111 Existing tenure of landholders confirmed

100 Saturninus proposes citizen colonies

91 Laws of Livius Drusus for enfranchisement of Italians rejected

91–88 Social War

## 3. RELATIONS WITH STATES OUTSIDE ITALY

B.C.

348   Treaty of Rome with Carthage

302   Second treaty with Carthage

279   Alliance of Rome and Carthage against Pyrrhus

273   Egypt recognises Rome as a major power

264–241   First Punic War

263   Hiero becomes Rome's ally

262   Romans capture Agrigentum

260   Naval battle of Mylae

257   Naval battle at Tyndaris

256   Regulus defeats Punic fleet at Ecnomus and lands in Africa

255   Xanthippus routs Romans in Africa, and returning Roman fleet
        wrecked after victory off Cape Hermaeum

254   Romans capture Panormus

250   Battle of Panormus : siege of Lilybaeum

249   Naval battle at Drepanum

247–242   Hamilcar Barca operating in Sicily

242   Battle of Aegates

241   Carthage makes peace with Rome

238   Romans occupy Sardinia and Corsica

236   Hamilcar founds Punic dominion in Spain

230   Roman fleet sent against Queen Teuta

228   Hasdrubal succeeds Hamilcar in Spain

227   Beginning of organised provincial government : two new praetors
        govern (a) Sicily, (b) Sardinia and Corsica

226   River Ebro in Spain fixed as boundary between Rome and
        Carthage

221   Hannibal succeeds Hasdrubal in Spain

219   Roman fleet defeats Demetrius

218–201   Second Punic War

218   Hannibal takes Saguntum : battle of the Trebia

217   Battle of Lake Trasimene : Scipios operate in Spain

216   Battle of Cannae

215–205   First Macedonian War : death of Hiero

212   Hannibal seizes Tarentum

211   Scipios defeated in Spain : territory south of Ebro lost : Syracuse
        taken by Carthage : Capua retaken by Rome

210   Scipio the younger made commander of a new army in Spain:
        Agrigentum and rest of Sicily submit to Rome

B.C.

209   Scipio captures New Carthage
208   Battle of Baecula
207   Battle of River Metaurus
206   Battle of Ilipa : Spain soon lost by Carthage
204   Scipio lands in Africa
203   Scipio destroys camps and armies of Hasdrubal and Syphax
202   Battle of Zama
201   Carthage makes peace with Rome
200–196   Second Macedonian War
197   Battle of Cynoscephalae : Spain organised as two provinces : warfare in Spain continuous till 133
196   Macedonia remains independent : Greece declared free
195   M. Porcius Cato subdues Hither Spain : Hannibal arrives at the court of Antiochus III of Syria
192   Antiochus lands in Greece
191–190   War with Antiochus : battles of Myonnesus and Magnesia : Syria becomes a client kingdom : Romans evacuate the East
179   Tib. Gracchus pro-praetor in Spain : death of Philip of Macedon, succeeded by Perseus
171–168   Third Macedonian War
168   Battle of Pydna : Macedonia becomes four separate republics : Pergamum and Rhodes lose favour with Rome : C. Popilius Laenas forces Antiochus to withdraw from Egypt
165   Many Achaeans depart and go to Rome
150–148   Revolt of Andriscus : fourth Macedonian War
150   Embassy sent from Rome to Carthage
149–146   Third Punic War
148   Macedonia annexed as a province
146   Destruction of Carthage and Corinth : Africa becomes a province
146–141   Viriathus in Spain victorious against the Romans
133   Scipio Aemilianus captures Numantia : Spanish wars end : kingdom of Pergamum bequeathed to Rome
129   Province of Asia formed
123   Balearic Islands subdued
120   Gallia Narbonensis annexed as a province
112–105   War with Jugurtha
105   Defeat of Caepio at battle of Arausio
102   Battle of Aquae Sextiae : Teutones defeated
101   Battle of Vercellae : Cimbri defeated
96   Cyrene bequeathed to Rome

B.C.

88 Mithridates VI of Pontus gains control of Asia Minor

86 Sulla expels Mithridates' Greek expedition : Athens captured : battles of Chaeronea and Orchomenus

85 Sulla negotiates peace with Mithridates

83-82 Mithridates pushes Murena out of Cappadodia and Pontus

77-72 Pompey operating against Sertorius in Spain

74-67 Campaigns of Lucullus against Mithridates

67 Pompey subdues the pirates

66 Pompey replaces Lucullus in the East : battle of Nicopolis

66-63 Pompey's settlement of the East

58-49 Julius Caesar conquers Gaul

53 Battle of Carrhae : loss of Roman standards

49-45 Civil War fought out in the provinces

40 Parthia overruns Asia Minor and Syria

39-38 Parthians expelled by Ventidius, Antony's lieutenant

37 Capture of Jerusalem : Herod made king of Judaea

36-33 Antony's campaigns against Parthia unsuccessful

35-34 Campaigns of Octavian in Illyricum

34 Donations of Alexandria

30 Egypt made a province by Octavian

29-28 Operations against the Moesians and Thracians

27-26 Augustus visits Gaul and Spain

26-19 Final pacification of Spain

25-24 Arabian expedition

25 Galatia made a province

23-21 Agrippa appointed inspector-general of eastern provinces

22-19 Augustus visits East

20 Recovery of Crassus' lost standards by diplomacy

17-13 Agrippa against appointed inspector-general in East

16 Sugambri defeat a Roman legion on the Rhine

15 Conquest of Rhaetia by Drusus and Tiberius

12-9 Drusus reaches the Elbe : Tiberius subdues Pannonia

A.D.

4-6 Tiberius commander on the Rhine

6 Pannonian revolt : Judaea becomes a province

c. 6 Province of Moesia formed

9 Loss of legions in Germany under Varus

14 Death of Augustus : mutiny of German legions

## (B) A.D. 14–A.D. 235

### 1. INTERNAL HISTORY

A.D.

19   Death of Germanicus

23   Death of Tiberius' son Drusus

27   Tiberius retires to Capri : Sejanus in control

29   Death of Livia : Agrippina and her children imprisoned

31   Fall of Sejanus

48   Messalina forced to suicide

49   Claudius marries Agrippina

55   Nero dismisses Pallas, poisons Britannicus

61   Nero kills Agrippina

64   Great fire at Rome : persecution of Christians

65   Conspiracy of Piso : death of Seneca

68   Galba enters Rome

69 (Jan.)   Galba murdered by Praetorians : Otho proclaimed emperor in Rome, Vitellius by Rhine legions

69 (April)   Vitellius enters Rome

69 (July)   Vespasian proclaimed emperor in the East

69 (Oct.)   Danube legions support Vespasian, defeat Vitellians

70 (Oct.)   Vespasian arrives in Rome

79   Eruption of Vesuvius

88–89   Conspiracies against Domitian

106–113   Trajan in Rome

136   Hadrian adopts Aelius Verus

193   Pertinax, Julianus and Septimius Severus struggle for throne

212   Caracalla extends citizenship to all free-born provincials

222   Alexander Severus only thirteen : government by committee of senators

235   Death of Alexander Severus

### 2. THE FRONTIERS

*(a) The German Frontier*

A.D. 14   Germanicus invades Germany :

    *(a)* March up R. Lippe

    *(b)* 15   By sea to R. Ems : reaches Teutoberg : damaged by storm on return

    *(c)* 16   By sea to R. Ems : penetrates to R. Weser : defeats Arminius at Idistaviso

A.D.

17   Frontier divided into upper and lower Germany

47   Corbulo's campaigns against Frisii and Chauci

73   Vespasian annexes and fortifies Black Forest district, connecting Rhine and Danube

83–84   Domitian's expedition against Chatti : annexation of Mt. Taunus district ; more advanced line fortified between Rhine and Danube

Peace until *c.* 250

(*b*)  *The Danube Frontier*

A.D. 85   Daci, organised by Decebalus, defeat Sabinus and overrun Moesia

87   Fuscus, after invading Dacia, is conquered

89   Julianus restores the position : Domitian makes peace

101–106   Trajan decides on invasion

First campaign : 101, advancing towards Iron Gates Pass, fights near Tapae, but retires : 102, entering Dacia by Red Tower Pass from east, compels Decebalus to make peace. Roman garrison in Sarmizegethusa

Second campaign : 105, Decebalus having recovered Sarmizegethusa and crossed Danube, Trajan (106) closes on Sarmizegethusa from east and west : Decebalus killed

Dacia annexed : Sarmizegethusa renamed Ulpia Traiana

166–180   Marcus Aurelius' campaigns. Expeditions against : Quadi and Marcomanni in the north-west, Iazyges and Sarmatians in the north-east : plan to annexe new provinces of Marcomannia and Sarmatia, but abandoned by Commodus

*c.* 250   New wave of invasion begun by Goths

*c.* 273   Dacia abandoned by Aurelian

(*c*)  *Eastern Frontier*

A.D. 53   Vologeses of Parthia invades Armenia and installs Tiridates

57   Corbulo sent East ; captures Artaxata and Tigranocerta : installs Tigranes, who is soon driven out again by Parthians

62   Paetus' surrender at Randeia : leads to compromise

69–79   Annexation of Commagene and Lesser Armenia accompanied by advance of frontier posts

113   Chosroes of Parthia places Exedares on Armenian throne, Trajan invades Armenia and makes it a province

114   Trajan invades northern Mesopotamia : winters army at Nisibis

115   Moves down R. Tigris : occupies Ctesiphon

A.D.

116  Visits Persian Gulf and Babylon : revolts in northern Meso-
        potamia and Cyprus crushed : northern Mesopotamia and
        Assyria made provinces, but abandoned by Hadrian

163  Statius Priscus captures Artaxata

165  Ctesiphon captured ; Media invaded ; withdrawal from all except
        northern Mesopotamia

227  Asia Minor threatened by Sassanids

231  Alexander Severus defeated by Ardashir

241  Gordianus III's campaign against Persians

258  Valerian captured by Shapur : Asia Minor and Syria overrun :
        Odonethes of Palmyra rallies eastern forces against Persia

273  Independence of Palmyra ended by Aurelian


(d) *Britain*

A.D. 43  Under Aulus Plautius Romans cross Thames : capture Camulo-
        dunum : E. Anglia, Midlands and southern districts conquered

47–52  Ostorius Scapula defines western frontier by Fosse Way from
        Lincoln to Exeter : advanced posts at Deva, Uriconium,
        Glevum : attack on Ordovices (N. Wales) and Silures (S.
        Wales) : Caractacus' last stand

58–61  Suetonius Paulinus attacks Mona, druid stronghold

61  Iceni under Boudicca sack Camulodunum, Londinium and
        Verulamium : defeat Cerealis : overcome by Suetonius on
        Watling Street

71–74  Cerealis advances frontier to Eboracum

74–77  Frontinus overcomes Silures

78–84  Agricola subdues Ordovices and Mona (78) : Brigantes (79).
        Invades Caledonia : fortifies Clyde–Forth isthmus (80) : in-
        vades Highlands : battle at Mons Graupius (83) : recalled by
        Domitian (84)

c. 122  Hadrian visits Britain : withdraws frontier to Tyne–Solway
        isthmus : building of the Wall

143  Lollius Urbicus re-establishes Clyde–Forth frontier

180  Frontier overrun and legions defeated : Albinus (governor)
        makes bid for throne : defeated by Septimius Severus (196) :
        Septimius' campaigns into Highlands, rebuilds Hadrian's Wall :
        dies at York (211)

287  German sea-raids begin

287–297  Independent empire in Britain under Carausius and Alexander

407.  Legions withdrawn

## (C) FROM A.D. 235 ONWARDS

A.D.

235–284  General anarchy : emperors include Maximinus, Gordianus I and II, Pupienus, Balbinus, Gordianus III, Philip Arabs, Decius, Trebonianus, Valerian, Gallienus : and during the period of recovery, Claudius, Aurelian, Claudius Tacitus, Probus, Carus, Carinus and Numerianus

286  Diocletian rules the East from Nicomedia : appoints Maximian as fellow-Augustus to rule the West

293  Redistribution of empire : Diocletian rules East : Maximian rules Italy, Africa and Spain : Galerius rules Balkans : Constantius rules Gaul and Britain

305  Maximian replaced by Constantius, Diocletian replaced by Galerius. Constantine goes to Britain : is proclaimed Augustus of the West

314  Constantine divides empire with Licinius

323  Battle of Chrysopolis makes Constantine sole emperor

325  Council of Nicaea

337  Death of Constantine

364  Partition of empire by Valerius and Valens

378  Valens killed fighting Goths

409–419  North and east of Gaul conquered by Franks and Burgundians : Spain conquered by Suebi and Vandals

410  Alaric sacks Rome

429  Vandals occupy Africa

451  Aetius with the help of Goths defeats Attila

455  Vandals sack Rome

476  Son of last Roman emperor deposed : end of western empire

1453  Capture of Constantinople by Turks ends eastern empire

# B: LEGIONS AND PROVINCES

## Distribution of the Legions at the Death of Augustus (A.D. 14)

Spain:
   3 legions—IV. Macedonica, VI. Victrix, X. Gemina
Lower Germany:
   4 legions—I., V. Alauda, XX. Valeria Victrix, XXI. Rapax
Upper Germany:
   4 legions—II. Augusta, XIII. Gemina, XIV. Gemina, XVI.
Pannonia:
   3 legions—VIII. Augusta, IX., XV. Apollinaris
Dalmatia:
   2 legions—VII., XI.
Moesia:
   2 legions—IV. Scythica, V. Macedonica
Syria:
   3 legions—III. Gallica, VI. Ferrata, X. Fretensis
Egypt:
   3 legions—III. Cyrenaica, XII. Fulminata, XXII.
Africa:
   1 legion—III. Augusta

Total number 25

## List of Provinces at the Death of Augustus

1. Senatorial:

   (a) Governed by consular proconsuls

   | Asia | Africa |

   (b) Governed by praetorian proconsuls

   | Sicily | Achaia |
   | Baetica | Bithynia and Pontus |
   | Narbonensis | Cyprus |
   | Macedonia | Crete and Cyrene |

2. Imperial:

(a) Governed by legati Augusti propraetore

| | |
|---|---|
| Tarraconensis | Lusitania |
| Pannonia | Aquitania |
| Dalmatia | Lugdunensis |
| Moesia | Belgica |
| Syria | Galatia |

(b) Governed by prefects or procurators

| | |
|---|---|
| Egypt | Alpes Maritimae |
| Sardinia and Corsica | Alpes Cottiae |
| Raetia | Judaea |
| Noricum | |

## LIST OF PROVINCES IN A.D. 117

### SENATORIAL

#### Consular

Asia, 133 B.C.
Africa, 146 B.C.

#### Praetorian

Baetica, conquered 197 B.C. separate prov. in 25 B.C.
Narbonensis, 120 B.C.
Sicily, 241 B.C.
Macedonia, 146 B.C.; Imp. A.D. 15–44
Achaia, 146 B.C.; Imp. A.D. 15–44
Crete and Cyrene. Joined as a prov. in 27 B.C.
Cyprus, 27 B.C.
Bithynia, 74 B.C. Imp. after A.D. 135
Armenia, A.D. 114. Praet (?)
Mesopotamia, A.D. 115, abandoned 117, reconquered 165. Praet (?)
Assyria, A.D. 115. Praet (?)
Commagene, absorbed in Syria, A.D. 72

### IMPERIAL

#### Consular

Tarraconensis, organised as prov. 25 B.C.
Germania Superior, A.D. 17 Inferior, A.D. 17
Britain, A.D. 43
Pannonia, A.D. 10. Divided by Trajan
Moesia, A.D. 6. Divided by Domitian
Dacia, A.D. 107
Dalmatia (formerly Illyricum)
Cappadocia, A.D. 17
Syria, 64 B.C.

#### Praetorian

Lusitania, separated from Hispania Ulterior in 27 or 25 B.C.
Lugdunensis
Belgica } Became separate
Aquitania } prov. in A.D. 17
Galatia, 25 B.C.
Cilicia, 64 B.C.
Arabia, A.D. 105
Pamphylia, 25 B.C.
Lycia, A.D. 43.

*Dates denote the creation of the province*

IMPERIAL

*Procuratorial*

Raetia, 15 B.C., procur. up to
   A.D. 169 : then praet.
Noricum, 15 B.C., procur. up to
   A.D. 169 : then praet.
Thrace, A.D. 46
Mauretania Tingitana, A.D. 40
Mauretania Caesariensis, A.D. 40
Sardinia and Corsica, 231 B.C.
   Sen. till A.D. 6, then Imp.,
   Sen. under Nero.   Imp.
   under Vespasian and after
Alpes Maritimae, A.D. 14
Alpes Cottiae, under Nero

---

Egypt, 30 B.C., governed by a
   praefectus of equestrian rank

---

Judaea, procuratorial A.D. 6–41
   and A.D. 44–70.   After 70
   became a separate prov.,
   distinct from Syria under a
   praetorian legatus.   Consular from Hadrian's time
   under name of Syria Palaes-
   tina

*Dates denote the creation of the province*

# C: THE ROMAN EMPERORS, FROM AUGUSTUS TO CONSTANTINE

| | | | |
|---|---|---|---|
| Augustus | 27 B.C.–A.D. 14 | Maximinus | A.D. 238 |
| Tiberius | A.D. 14–37 | Gordian I | 238 |
| Caligula | 37–41 | Gordian II | 238 |
| Claudius | 41–54 | Balbinus | 238 |
| Nero | 54–68 | Pupienus | 238 |
| Galba | 68–69 | Gordian III | 238–244 |
| Otho | 69 | Philip | 244–249 |
| Vitellius | 69 | Decius | 249–251 |
| Vespasian | 69–79 | Trebonianus | 251–253 |
| Titus | 79–81 | Aemilianus | 253 |
| Domitian | 81–96 | Valerianus | 253–260 |
| Nerva | 96–98 | Gallienus | 253–268 |
| Trajan | 98–117 | Claudius Gothicus | 268–270 |
| Hadrian | 117–138 | Aurelian | 270–275 |
| Antoninus Pius | 138–161 | Tacitus | 275–276 |
| M. Aurelius | 161–180 | Florianus | 276 |
| L. Verus | 161–169 | Probus | 276–282 |
| Commodus | 180–192 | Carus | 282–283 |
| Pertinax | 193 | Carinus | 283–285 |
| Didius Iulianus | 193 | Numerianus | 283–284 |
| Septimius Severus | 193–211 | Diocletian | 284–305 |
| Caracalla | 211–217 | Maximian | 286–305 |
| Geta | 211–212 | Constantius | 292–306 |
| Macrinus | 217–218 | Galerius | 293–311 |
| Elagabalus | 218–222 | Licinius | 311–323 |
| Severus Alexander | 222–235 | Constantine | 306–337 |

FAMILY TREE OF THE JULIO-CLAUDIANS

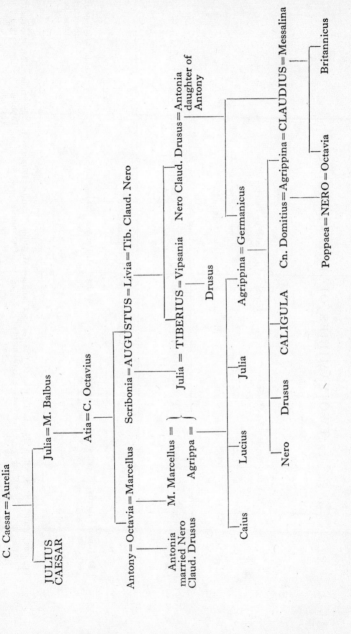

# TWO FAMILIES OF THE REPUBLIC

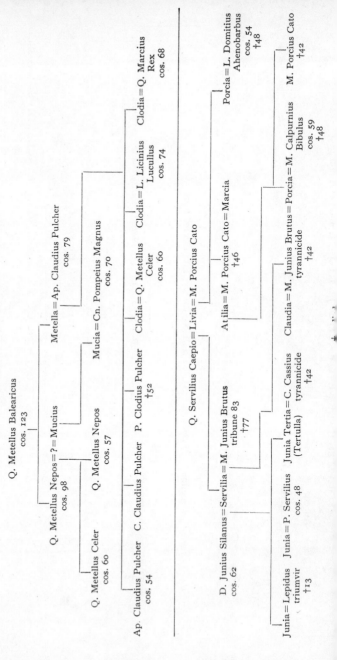

# INDEX

Achaean League, 102-3, 104-5

M'. Acilius Glabrio (consul 191 B.C.), 101

Actium, 218

Adherbal (Carthaginian), 74

Adherbal (Numidian), 147-8

Adige R., 151

Adriatic Sea, 98

aediles, curule, 63, 205, 340

aediles, plebeian, 56, 63, 340

Aedui, 186-7

Aegean Sea, 97, 182

Aelia Capitolina, 299

C. Aelius Gallus, 238

P. Aelius Hadrianus — Hadrian

L. Aelius Seianus, 251-2

M. Aemilius Aemilianus, 325

Q. Aemilius Laetus, 316

M. Aemilius Lepidus (praetor 49), 197

M. Aemilius Lepidus (triumvir), 164, 165 (leads rising), 204, 207 (after death of Caesar), 210 (in Gaul), 211 (second triumvirate), 213-14 (dismissed)

L. Aemilius Paullus, 78, 89, 103, 132

M. Aemilius Scaurus, 142

Aeneas, 17

Aequi, 31-2

aerarium, 54, 247, 267-8, 340

aerarium militare, 248, 267

Aesernia, 44

Aetolia, Aetolian League, 98, 100, 101-2

L. Afranius, 198

Sex. Afranius Burrus, 254-5

Africa, 94 (Roman province), 198 (during civil war), 238 (under

Augustus), 297 (under Hadrian), 343-4 (decline)

Ager Falernus, 59, 220

Agrigentum, 72, 81

Agrippa — Vipsanius

Agrippina (the Elder), 251-2

Agrippina (the Younger), 253, 254, 255

Alba Fucens, Fucentia, 39, 156

Alba Longa, 17, 18, 21

Alban Hills, 5

Alesia, 190

Alexander of Epirus, 41-2

Alexander of Macedon, 97

Alexander Balas, 109

Alexander Severus (M. Aurelius Severus Alexander), 323-4

Alexandria, 97, 109, 199, 271, 283, 366

Alfenius Senecio, 317

Algidus, Mount, 31

A. Alienus Caecina, 276-7, 278, 281

Allia R., 33

Allobroges, 92-3

Alps, 4

Alps, Carnic, 4, 89

Alps, Julian, 89

Ambiorix, 189

ambitus, 120

Ancus Marcius, 20

Andriscus, 104

Anicetus, 255

Anio R., 6

Anio Vetus, 367

L. Annaeus Seneca (minister of Nero), 256, 266

C. Annius, 161

T. Annius Milo, 192, 194

391

M. Annius Verus — M. Aurelius
Annius Vinicianus, 254
Antioch (Syria), 97
Antiochus III, 98, 101, 105-8
Antiochus IV, 109
Antium, 36
Antonia, 252
Antoninus (T. Aurelius Antoninus), 290-1
P. Antoninus Geta, 321
C. Antonius (consul 63), 171
L. Antonius (tribune 44), 213
M. Antonius (triumvir), 205, 207
    (after death of Caesar), 208-10
    (struggle with Octavian), 211
    (second triumvirate), 213-18
    (defeat by Octavian), 214-16
    (war with S. Pompeius)
M. Antonius (admiral), 181-2
M. Antonius Gordianus, 324
M. Antonius Primus, 278
L. Antonius Saturninus, 281
Aous R., 98, 100
Apennines, 3, 4, 5
Apollonia, 98, 100
Appius Claudius, 367
L. Appius Norbanus, 281
L. Appuleius Saturninus, 143-145
Apsus R., 98
Apulia, 11
Aqua Appia, 367
Aqua Marcia, 368
Aquae Sextiae (Aix), 92, 151
Aquileia, 89, 185, 271
M'. Aquilius (consul 129), 109
M'. Aquilius (consul 101), 153, 176
Arabia, 298
Arae Flaviae, 287
Arausio, 143, 151
Arcadius, 336
Archelaus, 176-7
Archidamus, 41
Arelate, 203
Ariminum, 78
Ariobarzanes, 239
Ariovistus, 186, 187

Aristion, 176
Aristonicus of Pergamum, 109
Armenia, 176-80, 215-17, 238-9, 260-2, 297-9
Arpinum, 126
Arretium, 78
Arsacids, 193
Artabanus III, 260
Artabanus V, 322
Artaxata, 179, 299
Artaxias II, 238
Arverni, 92-3, 186, 189-90
Asander, 204
Asculum, 43, 147
Asia (Roman province), 109, 176
Asia Minor, 105-8 (war against
    Antiochus), 176-80 (Mithridatic war), 200 (civil war), 212-
    213 (Antony's war against
    triumvirate), 238-9 (under
    Augustus)
C. Asinius Pollio, 210
Ateste, 232
Athenion, 153
Athens, 99
Atilius Regulus, 73, 74
C. Atinius, 137
Atintania, 98
Attalus I of Pergamum, 98-9
Attalus III of Pergamum, 109
Attila, 337
P. Attius Varus, 198
augures, 27, 162
Augusta Praetoria, 232, 241
Augusta Taurinorum, 232
Augustus: As Octavian: 205
    (named in Caesar's will), 208
    (change of name), 211 (second
    triumvirate), 213-18 (victory
    over Antony), 214-15 (war
    with S. Pompeius), 227 (assumes name of Augustus). As
    Augustus: 224-6 (methods of
    government), 235-43 (frontiers
    of empire), 243-5 (military reforms), 245-7 (provincial administration), 248-9 (succession)

Aurelian (I. Domitius Aurelianus), 328-9
M. Aurelius (M. Aurelius Antoninus, formerly M. Annius Verus), 291, 296, 303, 361
M. Aurelius Antoninus — Caracalla
M. Aurelius Antoninus — Elagabalus
T. Aurelius Antoninus — Antoninus
M. Aurelius Carausius, 331
M. Aurelius Carus, 330, 341
M. Aurelius Claudius — Claudius
M. Aurelius Severus Alexander — Alexander Severus
C. Aurelius Cotta (consul 75), 165
L. Aurelius Cotta (praetor 70), 167
C. Aurelius Diocletianus — Diocletian
M. Aurelius Probus, 329-30
M. Aurelius Valerius Maximianus — Maximian
Avaricum, 190
Aventine Hill, 8, 56, 141
Avidius Cassius, 291, 299

Babylonia, 109
Baecula, 83
Baetis R., 269
Bagradas R., 74
Balearic Isles, 92
Baltic Sea, 272
Bar-Coceba, 299
Basilica Portia, 368
Batavi, 240
Bato, 242
Belgae, 185, 188
Beneventum, 44
Bibracte, 187
Bithynia, 176-8
Bituitus, 93
Black Sea, 97
Bocchus I, 149, 150
Boii, 41, 88

Bononia, 88
Boudicca, 265
Bovianum Vitus, 157-61
Brigantes, 285
Britain, 188-90 (Caesar's invasions), 264-5 (conquest), 272 (trade before conquest), 285 (under Flavian emperors), 303-305 (under Hadrian), 307, 308 (trade and industry), 317-18 (under Severus), 336 (detached from empire)
Brundisium, 173, 197
Bruttium, 80, 85
Brutus — Iunius
Byzantium, 333

Q. Caecilius Metellus Celer, 172
Q. Caecilius Metellus Macedonicus, 91, 104, 137, 143
Q. Caecilius Metellus Numidicus, 144, 149
Q. Caecilius Metellus Pius, 180, 181
Q. Caecilius Metellus Scipio, 219
Caecilius Secundus, 295
Caecina — Alienus
Caelian Hill, 7
D. Caelius Balbinus, 324
Caere, 21
C. Caesar — Caligula
L. Caesar, 249
Caligula (C. Caesar), 239, 249, 252-3
Callistus, 254
Calpurnia, 207
L. Calpurnius Bestia, 148
L. Calpurnius Bibulus, 175
C. Calpurnius Piso (consul A.D. 48), 256
Cn. Calpurnius Piso (quaestor 65 B.C.), 170
L. Calpurnius Piso (tribune 149), 118, 124
M. Calpurnius Piso Licinianus, 276

Camillus — Furius
Campania, 11, 34-6, 130, 269, 271
Campus Martius, 8, 60, 368
Camulodunum, 264-5
Cannae, 78-9
Capitoline Hill, 8, 17, 145, 368
Cappadocia, 176-80
Capri, 252
Capsa, 149
Capua, 34, 36, 37, 38, 79 (revolts), 80, 85, 130 (industries), 165 (slave rising)
Caracalla (M. Aurelius Antoninus), 321-2
Caratacus, 264
Caria, 108
Carrhae, 193
Carseoli, 39
Carteia, 92
Carthage, 35, 51, 67-71 (extent of empire), 71-5 (first war with Rome), 75-6 (conquests in Spain), 83-4 (peace terms with Rome), 93-5 (third Punic war), 139 (Roman public land), 203 (colony under Caesar)
L. Cassius (censor 125), 138
C. Cassius Chaerea, 253
L. Cassius Longinus (praetor 44), 206, 208-9 (quarrel with Antony), 212-13 (war against triumvirate)
Cassivelaunus, 189
Catiline — Sergius
Cato — Porcius
Caudine Forks, 37
L. Ceionius Commodus Verus, 290
Celtiberians, 90-1
Celts (see also Gauls), 185
Cenis, Mount, 77, 241
Cenomani, 88
censor, 63, 64, 65-6
centuria (military), 59-60
centuria (political), 60
centuria prerogativa, 61, 119
centuriones, 45

Chaeroneia, 177
China, 313, 343
Chosroes (Parthia), 298, 299
Christianity, 333, 361, 363-6
Cilicia, 181
Cimbri, 150
Cineas, 43
Cirta, 148, 149, 203
civitates foederatae, 113
civitates liberae et immunes, 113
classis, 59
Claudius (M. Aurelius Claudius), 328
Ti. Claudius Britannicus, 254, 255
Ti. Claudius Drusus Nero Germanicus, 253-5
C. Claudius Marcellus (consul 50), 195-6
C. Claudius Marcellus (son-in-law of Augustus), 248
M. Claudius Marcellus, 81, 88
M. Claudius Marcellus (consul 155), 91
M. Claudius Marcellus (consul 51), 195-6
C. Claudius Nero, 80
Ti. Claudius Nero — Tiberius
Ti. Claudius Nero, 214
Claudius Pulcher, 74
A. Claudius Pulcher, 135, 136, 138
Cleopatra, 199, 200, 212, 215-18 (and Antony)
Clodia, 212
D. Clodius Albinus, 316, 319
Clodius Macer, 275
P. Clodius Pulcher, 191, 194
M. Clodius Pupienus, 324
Cniva, 325
M. Cocceius Nerva — Nerva
cohortes praetoriae, 232
cohortes urbanae, 232
coinage, 50, 51, 79, 125, 245-6, 267
Colline Gate, 161

coloni, 219, 294
colonies, 47, 59, 71, 88 (Northern Italy), 92 (Spain), 92-3 (Gaul), 139, 142 (plans of C. Gracchus), 144-5 (proposals by Marius), 203 (Caesar's foundations in Spain, Gaul, Africa), 232, 246 (under Augustus), 266 (early emperors), 295 (second century)
comitia centuriata, 59-62, 119
comitia curiata, 26, 53, 58
comitia tributa (see also Tribal Assembly), 62-3
commercium, 48
Commodus (L. Aurelius), 315-316
Comum, 162
concilium plebis tributum (see also Tribal Assembly), 56, 59, 124
Concordia Ordinum, 173
conductores, 294, 315
'Conflict of Orders', 55
connubium, 48
consilium principis, 232, 258, 293, 320, 341
consistorium, 341
Constantine I (Flavius Valerius), 332-3, 366
Constantine XIII, 337
Constantinople, 335, 336, 337
Constantius, 336
consuls, 53, 65, 340
contio, 63
Corduba, 32
Corfinium, 155
Corinth, 105
Cornelia (daughter of Africanus), 133
C. Cornelius Balbus, 205
L. Cornelius Cinna, 158-161
A. Cornelius Cossus, 32
P. Cornelius Dolabella (consul 44), 212
P. Cornelius Dolabella (proconsul in Africa), 259
Cornelius Fuscus, 287

Cornelius Laco, 275
Cn. Cornelius Lentulus (consul 72), 169
L. Cornelius Lentulus (consul 49), 196
Cn. Cornelius Lentulus Gaetulicus, 253
Cornelius Palma, 291
Cn. Cornelius Scipio (consul 222), 81-2
L. Cornelius Scipio (consul 83), 160
L. Cornelius Scipio (consul 190), 101, 107, 122
P. Cornelius Scipio (consul 218), 77, 81-2
P. Cornelius Scipio Aemilianus, 91 (captures Numantia), 95 (destroys Carthage), 110 (in Egypt), 137 (opposes Gracchan land reforms)
P. Cornelius Scipio Africanus, 82-3 (campaigns in Spain), 83-84 (in Africa), 92 (settles veterans in Spain), 107 (in Greece), 108, 122 (feud with Cato)
L. Cornelius Scipio Barbatus, 39
P. Cornelius Scipio Nasica (consul 191), 88, 90
P. Cornelius Scipio Nasica (consul 162), 136-7
L. Cornelius Sulla Felix, 150 (captures Jugurtha), 152, 157-161 (enemies in Rome), 161-5 (rule in Rome), 176-9 (in Asia Minor)
Cornelius Tacitus, 329
Cornwall, 67
Corsica, 67, 73, 75, 81, 112
Corycus, Cape, 107
Cos, 271
Cottius, 242
Crassus — Licinius
Cremona, 85, 88, 277
Critolaus, 105
Cunobelinus, 264
curatores viarum, 233

curiae, 25
M'. Curius Dentatus, 40, 41, 43
Cybele, 357
Cynics, 361
Cynoscephalae, 100-1
Cyprus, 97, 110
Cyrene, 97, 110, 181
Cyzicus, 178

Dacia, 302-3
Dalmatia, 104, 242
Danube, 204, 241-3, 262-3, 287-288, 302-3
Dardanelles, 177
Dardanus, 177
Decebalus, 287, 303
L. Decidius Saxa, 204
Decius, 365
P. Decius Mus, 40
Delos, 131, 182
Delphi, 362
Demetrias, 101
Demetrius I, 109
Dertosa, 82
T. Didius, 154
Didius Iulianus, 316
Diocletian (C. Aurelius Diocletianus), 330-2
Diviaticus, 187
Dolabella — Cornelius
Domitia, 282
Domitian (T. Flavius Domitianus), 281, 287-8
Cn. Domitius Afer, 271
Cn. Domitius Ahenobarbus (consul 122), 92, 108
Cn. Domitius Ahenobarbus (c. 80), 161
L. Domitius Ahenobarbus (consul 54), 194, 196
L. Domitius Ahenobarbus (consul 16), 240, 247
L. Domitius Ahenobarbus — Nero
I. Domitius Aurelianus — Aurelian
Cn. Domitius Corbulo, 262
'Donations of Alexandria', 217

Drepana, 74
Druids, 186
Drusus (Nero Claudius Drusus, stepson of Augustus), 240, 242, 249
Drusus (son of Tiberius), 250-1, 252
Drusus (son of Germanicus), 251
Dura-Europus, 299
Dyrrachium, 198

Ebro R., 76, 82, 181
Eburacum (York), 285, 319
Eburones, 189
Ecnomus, Cape, 73
edicta, 65
Gellius Egnatius, 40
Egypt, 97-8 (alliance with Rome), 109-10 (invaded by Antiochus IV), 170 (Crassus' designs on), 199 (during civil war), 218 (becomes Roman province), 359-60 (religious influence)
Elagabalus (M. Aurelius Antoninus), 322-3
Elba, 3
Enipeus R., 100
Ephesus, 105
Epictetus, 361
Epirus, 102, 103
equites, Equester Ordo, 60, 61, 119, 132, 140, 143, 146 (unite with Senate against Drusus), 162-3 (Sulla's reforms), 227 (under Augustus), 319-20 (under Severus)
Eryx, Mount, 75
Esquiline Hill, 7, 17
Etruscans, 12-16, 32-3 (Etruscan League), 39 (Roman inroads), 40 (peace with Rome), 50, 130, 355-6 (religious influence)
Eudamus, 107
Eumenes II, 106-7, 108, 109

Q. Fabius Maximus (consul 121), 93

Q. Fabius Maximus (Cunctator), 78
Q. Fabius Maximus Servilianus, 91
Q. Fabius Rullianus, 38, 39, 40
Fabius Valens, 275-7, 278
C. Fabricius, 43
Faenius Rufus, 256
C. Fannius, 141
fasces, 27, 53
fiscus, 247, 267-8, 293-4, 320-1
flamines, 27, 54
C. Flaminius (consul 187), 78, 85
C. Flaminius (consul 223, 217), 135
C. Flavius Clemens, 283
T. Flavius Domitianus — Domitian
C. Flavius Fimbria, 177
Flavius Sabinus (cousin of Domitian), 283
C. Flavius Valerus Constantius, 330-2
T. Flavius Vespasianus — Titus
T. Flavius Vespasianus — Vespasian
Florentia, 89
Fonteius Capito, 275, 277
Formiae, 126
Forum, 369
Fregellae, 36, 37, 138
Frentani, 154
Frisii, 240
Fulvia, 213, 214
M. Fulvius Flaccus (consul 125), 138, 141-2
Q. Fulvius Flaccus (consul 212), 80
M. Fulvius Nobilior (consul 189), 102
Q. Fulvius Nobilior (consul 153), 90-1
C. Fulvius Plautianus, 320-1
Fundi, 126
M. Furius Camillus, 32
M. Furius Camillus Scribonianus, 254

C. Furius Timesitheus, 325
Fuscus, 291

A. Gabinius (consul 58), 169, 204
Gades, 83, 203
Galatia, 176-80, 239
Galba — Sulpicius
Galerius Valerius Maximianus, 330-3
Gallianus (P. Licinius Gallianus), 326-8
Gallipoli, 106, 108
Gaul, 92-3 (beginning of Roman conquest), 185-6 (background history), 189-90 (Caesar's campaigns), 212 (division between Antony and Lepidus), 213 (Cisalpine Gaul part of Italy), 239-40 (under Augustus), 336-7 (overrun by Goths)
Gauls, 33 (attack on Rome), 41 (renewed invasion of Italy), 78, 84-5 (last Gallic invasion)
L. Gellius (consul 72), 169
Geneva, 92
Genèvre, Mount, 77
gentes, 25, 53, 54, 57
Genthius, 102-3
Genua, 85, 88
Germanicus (Nero Claudius Drusus), 250-1, 264
Germany, 240-1 (under Augustus), 263-4 (early emperors), 285-7 (Flavian emperors), 337 (overrun by barbarians)
Greece, 97-105 (Roman conquests), 176-8 (Mithridatic war)
Greeks, 11-12, 50, 349-50, 356-7

Hadrian (P. Aelius Hadrianus), 289-90, 296 (tours provinces), 299-302 (Jews)
Hadrian's Wall, 305
Halys R., 179
Hamilcar, 74-5, 76
Hannibal, 76 (takes command in Spain), 77 (invasion of Italy),

81, 83-4 (in Africa), 93-4 (after-effect on Roman nerves), 106 (at Ephesus), 108 (death)

haruspices, 14

Hasdrubal (son-in-law of Hamilcar), 76

Hasdrubal (brother of Hannibal), 80, 82-3

Hasdrubal (son of Gisgo), 83

hastati, 45, 152

Helvetii, 187-8

Helvidius Priscus, 282

P. Helvius Pertinax, 315

Heraclea, 42-3

Hercte, Mount, 75

Herculaneum, 284

Hermaeum, Cape, 74

Herod, 215, 245

Hiempsal, 147

Hiero, 71, 81

Hirpini, 154

A. Hirtius, 209-10

Hispalis, 203

Hispania, Citerior, Ulterior, Tarraconensis — Spain

Homonadeis, 239

Honorius, 336-7

Horace (Q. Horatius Flaccus), 235

Hordeonius Flaccus, 276

Hyrcanus, 216

Iapygians, 9

Iazyges, 303

Ilerda, 198

Illyria, 9, 98, 100, 185, 242

imperator, 27, 65, 229

imperium, 26, 28, 46, 54, 58

imperium consulare, 228, 229

imperium proconsulare, 228

India, 271, 272, 313-14, 343

Insubres, 88

interrex, 26

Isère R., 92

Istria, 89

Italica, 92

Italy, 1-5 (geography), 9-11 (early inhabitants), 47-50 political organisation by Rome), 50-1 (economic conditions), 77-80 (Hannibal's invasion), 85-9 (after second Punic war), 125-6 (political status), 128-9 (economic conditions), 137-8 (grievances over Gracchan land reforms), 154-7 (war with Rome), 196-7 (during civil war), 218-20 (economic conditions at end of republic), 268-270 (economic conditions under early emperors), 307, 309 (economic conditions in second century)

Iulia Maesa, 322

Iulia Mamaea, 323

Cn. Iulius Agricola, 285

C. Iulius Caesar, 170 (agent of Crassus), 171 (origins), 174-5 (first triumvirate), 187-8 (conquest of Gaul), 188-90 (invades Britain), 192-3 (conference of Luca), 194-5 (drifts into war with Pompey), 196-201 (civil war), 201-2 (reforms on return to Rome), 204 (dictator), 205 (death), 368-9 (public works in Rome)

L. Iulius Caesar (consul 90), 155-157

Iulius Civilis, 279

Iulius Classicus, 279

Sex. Iulius Frontinus, 285

C. Iulius Maximinus, 324

M. Iulius Philippus, 325

C. Iulius Severus, 299

Iulius Tutor, 279

C. Iulius Vindex, 256

D. Iunius Brutus, 356

D. Iunius Brutus Albinus, 188, 206, 209-10

L. Iunius Brutus (the Liberator), 22

M. Iunius Brutus (praetor 44), 206, 208-9, 212-13

M. Iunius Brutus (supporter of Lepidus), 165

M. Iunius Pennus, 138
Iunius Pullus, 74
M. Iunius Silanus, 150
Iunonia, 139, 141, 142
ius auxilii, 56, 66
ius civile, 124
ius divinum, 27, 358
ius gentium, 124
Iuvenalia, 255

Janiculan Hill, 7, 165
Jerusalem, 285, 299
Jews, 109 (rebel against Seleucids), 201 (banned under Caesar), 259 (opposition to Rome), 285 (Roman war), 299-302 (rebel under Hadrian), 358 (banished from Rome), 360-1 (religious influence)
Juba (of Mauretania), 245
Juba (of Numidia), 198
Judaea, 245, 259, 299-302
Jugurtha, 147-50
Julia (daughter of Caesar), 175, 194
Julia (daughter of Augustus), 248
Julia (sister of Caligula), 253
Jupiter, 355
Jupiter Capitolinus, 283
Justinian, 336

T. Labienus, 171, 190, 200
C. Laelius (consul 140), 135
Lampsacus, 106
Laodicea, 212
Lares and Penates, 355
Larissa, 102
latifundia, 128, 219, 268, 345
Latin status (ius Latii, nomen Latinum), 48 (definition), 156 (grants outside Latium), 203 (Caesar's grants to provincials), 284 (Vespasian's grant to Spain), 296 (further grants in second century)
C. Latinius Postumus, 327
Latins, 29-31, 35-6, 48

Latium, 5, 12, 29-31 (Latin League), 126 (political status), 154 (loyal to Rome)
Lauro, 180
Lautulae, 38
legati (provincial), 114
legions, 28, 45-6, 60 (see also Roman Army)
Lemnus, 178
Lentulus — Cornelius
Lepidus — Aemilius
Lex Aebutia, 124
Lex Aurelia, 168
Lex Gabinia, 169, 170
Lex Licinia, 128
Lex Licinia Pompeia, 192-3
Lex Manilia, 169, 170
Lex Plautia Papiria, 156-7
Lex Poetilia, 59
Lex provinciae, 112-13
Lex Rubria, 141
Lex Villia Annalis, 123, 136, 143
M. Licinius Crassus (consul 70, 55), 160-1, 166 (against Spartacus), 167 (rivals Pompey), 168-169 (consul with Pompey), 170-1 (attempt to gain control), 175, 192 (first triumvirate), 192-3 (conference of Luca), 221 (wealth)
M. Licinius Crassus (consul 30), 242
P. Licinius Crassus (consul 171), 102
P. Licinius Crassus (consul 131), 132, 135, 137, 155
P. Licinius Crassus (son of M.), 188
P. Licinius Gallianus — Gallianus
L. Licinius Lucullus (consul 74), 169, 173, 178-80
C. Licinius Macer, 166
C. Licinius Mucianus, 278-9
L. Licinius Murena, 177
C. Licinius Stolo, 59, 63
P. Licinius Valerianus — Valerian

lictors, 27, 53
Liguria, 9, 88-9
Ligurians, 9, 92-3, 185
Lilybaeum, 74
Lindum (Lincoln), 319
Liris R., 37, 38
Livia, 214, 250
C. Livius (consul 188), 107
M. Livius (consul 207), 80
M. Livius Drusus (tribune 122), 141
M. Livius Drusus (tribune 91), 146-7
Q. Lollius Urbicus, 305
Lucania, 34, 39, 154
Luceria, 38
Lucilla, 316
Q. Lucretius Ofella, 164
Lucullus — Licinius
ludi Apollinares, 120
ludi Cereales, 120
ludi Florales, 120
ludi Megalenses, 120
ludi Plebeii, 120
Ludi Romani, 120
ludi saeculares, 235, 283
ludi Tarentini, 357
Luna, 85
Lusitania, 228
Lusitanians, 90, 91, 180
Lusius Quietus, 291, 298, 303
C. Lutatius Catulus (consul 242), 75
Q. Lutatius Catulus (consul 101), 151-2
Q. Lutatius Catulus (consul 78), 165, 169
Lutetia, 269-70
Lycia, 108, 181
Lyncestis, 100

Macedonia, 97-105
Machares, 178
Maeander R., 108
magister equitum, 45, 205
Magnesia-ad-Sipylum, 108
maiestas, 144
Malaca, 90

Mamertines, 71
C. Manilius, 169
manipuli, 45
Cn. Manlius Maximus (consul 105), 143, 150
Manlius Vulso, 73
A. Manlius Vulso (consul 178), 89
Cn. Manlius Vulso (consul 189), 123
Marcia, 315
L. Marcius Philippus (consul 91), 147
Q. Marcius Philippus (consul 169), 103
Q. Marcius Rex (praetor 144), 368
C. Marcius Rutilus, 63
Marcomanni, 240-1, 303
Marcomannia, 303
Cn. Marcus Coriolanus, 31
C. Marius, 143 (leader of populares), 143-5 (and Saturninus), 149 (in Africa), 151 (victory at Aix), 152 (army reforms), 154 (Italian war), 157-9
Maroboduus, 240-1
Marrucini, 153
Mars, 355
Marsi, 37, 154
Massilia, 92-3, 186
Massinissa, 83-4, 93-4
Mauretania, 111, 149, 245, 259
Maxentius, 332-3
Maximinian (M. Aurelius Valerius Maximianus), 330-2, 333
Mediolanum, 271
Mediterranean Sea, 1
C. Memmius, 145, 148
Mesopotamia, 109, 307
Messana, 71-2
Metaurus R., 80
Metellus — Caecilius
Micipsa, 95, 147
Milvian Bridge, 333
Mincio R., 88
M. Minucius Rufus, 141
Mithras, 362

Mithridates (king of Armenia), 260

Mithridates VI (of Pontus), 176-180

Mithridates of Pergamum, 199, 204

Mohammed II, 337

Mons Massicus, 220

P. Mucius Scaevola (consul 133), 135

L. Mummius, 105

L. Munatius Plancus, 210, 219

Munda, 200-1

Mutina, 88, 210, 271

Mylae, 73

Myonnesus, 107

Narbo, 93

Narcissus, 254

Narnia, 39

Neapolis, 37

Nemausus, 203

Nero (Claudius Caesar), 254, 255-257, 275

Neronia, 255

Nerva (M. Cocceius Nerva), 288-9

Nervii, 188

New Carthage, 82

Nicomedes II, 176

Nicomedes III, 176, 178

Nicopolis, 180

nobiles, 120-3

C. Norbanus, 160

Noricum, 242

Numantia, 90, 91

Numa Pompilius, 20

Numidia, 70, 83-4 (second Punic war), 93-5 (third Punic war), 147-50 (Jugurthan war)

Nymphidius Sabinus, 256, 275

Octavia (wife of Nero), 255

Octavia (daughter of Claudius), 254

Octavia (sister of Octavius), 214, 217, 249

Octavian (C. Iulius Caesar Octavianus), see Augustus

M. Octavius (consul 133), 135

Ofonius Tigellinus, 256, 275

Q. and Cn. Ogulnius, 63

Olisipo, 203

Olympus, Mount, 103

M. Opellius Macrinus, 322

L. Opimius (consul 122), 142

L. Oppius, 205

optimates, 143

Orchomenus, 177

Orodes, 204, 216

Oscans, 34

Ostia, 131, 202, 294, 314

P. Ostorius Scapula, 264

Pacorus, 216

Paeligni, 37, 154

Paestum, 44

pagi, 10

Palatine Hill, 8, 17

Palestine, 105

Pallas, 254

Pamphylia, 181

Pannonia, 242

Panormus, 74

Panticapaeum, 180

C. Papirius Carbo (tribune 131), 137, 138

C. Papirius Carbo (tribune 89), 156

Cn. Papirius Carbo (consul 113), 150

Cn. Papirius Carbo (consul 86), 159-61

L. Papirius Cursor, 40

C. Papius Mutilus, 156

Parma, 88, 271

Parthamaspates, 298

Parthia, 193, 204, 215-17, 238-9, 260-2, 297-9, 324

Patavium, 271

paterfamilias, 25, 58

patricians, 25

Pergamum, 98, 106-10 (wars with Rome), 109 (becomes Roman province), 140-1 (rights withdrawn), 177 (Mithridatic war)

M. Perperna (consul 130), 109
M. Perperna (lieutenant of Sertorius), 181
Perseus, 102-3
Perusia, 213
C. Pescennius Niger, 316
Q. Petilius (tribunes), 122
Q. Petilius Cerealis, 265, 279, 285
Petra (Illyria), 198
M. Petreius, 172, 198
C. Petronius (governor of Egypt), 238
P. Petronius, 259
Petronius Secundus, 288
Pharnaces II, 180, 182, 200, 204
Pharsalus, 199
Philip II of Macedon, 97
Philip V of Macedon, 98-100
Philippi, 212-13
Phoenicians, 11, 94
Phraaspa, 216
Phraates IV, 238
Piceni, Picentes, 39, 154
Pinarius Clemens, 287
Piso — Calpurnius
Pistoria, 172
Placentia, 77, 85, 88
A. Platorius Nepos, 305
A. Plautius, 264
M. Plautius, 156
Ti. Plautius Silvanus, 263
plebeians, plebs, 25, 54-7, 63-4, 348
plebiscita, 62
Po R., 77
Polyxenidas, 107
Pomerium, 13, 17
Q. Pompaedius Silo, 146-7, 156, 157
Pompeii, 130 (textiles), 271 (woollens), 284 (obliterated)
Cn. Pompeius Magnus, 161 (lieutenant of Sulla), 164 (defies Sulla), 165 (co-operates against Lepidus), 166 (return from Spain), 168-9 (as consul), 173 (return in 63), 174-5 (first triumvirate), 178-80 (in Asia Minor), 180-1 (in Spain), 182 (war against pirates), 182-3 (settlement of East), 192 (regains ascendancy), 192-3 (conference of Luca), 194-5 (drifts into war with Caesar), 196-201 (civil war)
Cn. Pompeius Magnus (son of Pompey), 200
Cn. Pompeius Strabo, 156, 157, 159, 166
Q. Pompeius Rufus, 158, 159
Sex. Pompeius, 200-1, 214-16
Pontifex Maximus, 54, 340
pontifices, 27, 163
Pontus, 176-80
C. Popilius Laenas (consul 172), 109
P. Popilius Laenas (consul 132), 137
Poppaea Sabina, 255
C. Poppaeus Sabinus, 263
populares, 143
L. Porcius Cato (consul 89), 157
M. Porcius Cato ('the Censor'), 90 (campaign in Spain), 94 (hostility to Carthage), 117 (champions provincials), 122 (opposition to Africanus), 124 (law of appeal), 368 (public works)
M. Porcius Cato ('Cato of Utica'), 172, 173, 191, 200
P. Porcius Laeca, 117, 124
L. Porcius Licinus (consul 184), 124
Porsenna, 22
Sp. Postumius Albinus (praetor 180), 90
Sp. Postumius Albinus (consul 110), 148
Postumius Aulus, 148
praefectus annonae, 292
praefectus castrorum, 244
praefectus fabrum, 244
praefectus praetorio, 231, 320
praefectus urbi, 232, 320

Praeneste, 213
praetors, 53 (original name of consuls), 60, 64 (number increased), 65 (duties), 123 (appointed for provinces), 124 (praetor peregrinus : praetor urbanus), 163 (number increased by Sulla)
principes (in legion), 45, 152
proconsul, 114, 123
procuratores, 231, 246, 258, 292
propraetor, 114, 123
prorogatio, 113-14
provinciae, 111-18 (Roman government), 112 (annexation), 162-3 (under Sulla), 182-183 (Pompey's settlement of East), 202-4 (under Caesar), 219 (at end of republic), 227-8, 245-7 (under Augustus), 265-6 (under early emperors), 269-72 (trade and industry), 284-8 (under Flavian emperors), 285-305 (second century), 307-14 (trade and industry), 318-19 (under Severus), 341-2 (under Diocletian)
Ptolemaic dynasty, 97
Ptolemy II, 44
Ptolemy V, 98
Ptolemy VI, 109
Ptolemy VII, 109-10
Ptolemy XI (Auletes), 170, 192
Ptolemy XII, 199-200
Ptolemy XIII, 200, 216
Ptolemy Caesarion, 216, 218
publicani, 117, 146, 294
Q. Publilius Philo, 62, 63
Puteoli, 88, 130
Pydna, 103
Pyrrhus, 42-4

Quadi, 303
quaestio de rebus repetundis, 118, 140, 143, 164
quaestiones perpetuae, 124, 164, 168-9

quaestores, 114 (provincial), 123
quaestores (classici, Italici), 71
quaestores consulis, 45, 54, 205
quaestores urbani, 45
L. Quinctius Cincinnatus, 31
T. Quinctius Flamininus, 100-1, 106
Quintilius Maximus, 295
P. Quintilius Varus, 241
Quirinal Hill, 7, 17

Radamistos, 262
Raetia, 242
Ravenna, 196
Regillus, Lake, 29
Remi, 187
Remus, 16
Rhine R., 269
Rhodes, 98-9, 108, 109
Rhône R., 92-3, 186
Rhyndacus R., 177
Roma et Augustus, 247
Roman Army, 37, 44-7, 59-60, 126-7, 152, 243-5, 305-7, 339-340
Rome, city, 7-8 (site), 16-19 (origins), 23-8 (conditions and organisation of early city), 33 (capture by Gauls), 50-1 (economic conditions), 76-8 (threatened by Hannibal), 130-132 (trade and industry), 139-140 (corn supply), 201-2 (under Caesar), 232 (under Augustus), 283 (under Flavian emperors), 333 (Constantine transfers capital to Byzantium), 355 (public worship), 367-71 (public works)
Romulus, 16, 20
Rubicon R., 196
Rubrius (tribune 122), 139
P. Rutilius Rufus, 146, 155, 156

Sabines, 16, 31-2
Saguntum, 76-7
St. Bernard (passes), 241
Salo R., 90

Q. Salvidianus, 213
Salvius, 152
Salvius Iulianus, 293
M. Salvius Otho, 276-7
Sambre R., 188
Samnites, 34-41, 154, 161-2
Sanhedrin, 285
Sardinia, 67, 73, 75, 81, 112-13
Sarmatia, 303
Sarmizegethusa, 302
C. Scribonius Curio, 195, 198
Segovia, 180
Seleucid dynasty, 97, 109
C. Sempronius Gracchus, 136,
    139-42
Ti. Sempronius Gracchus (tri-
    bune 133), 133-6
Ti. Sempronius Gracchus (con-
    sul 177), 90, 133
Sempronius Longus, 77
Senate, 26, 53, 54, 63-4 (ple-
    beians in), 121 (power of
    nobles), 135-6 (resists Ti.
    Gracchus), 139-43 (and C.
    Gracchus), 143 (and Marius),
    146-7 (and Drusus), 162-3
    (Sulla's reforms), 168-9 (Pom-
    pey and Crassus), 206 (death
    of Caesar), 227 (under Augus-
    tus), 257-8 (early emperors),
    282-3 (under Flavians), 291-2
    (after Nerva), 319 (under
    Severus), 340 (second century)
senatus consultum ultimum, 142
seniores, 60
Senones, 40, 41
L. Septimius Severus — Severus
Septimontium, 17
Sequani, 186
L. Sergius Catilina, 170-2
Q. Sertorius, 160, 180-1
Servianus, 291
C. Servilius (Roman commis-
    sioner), 147
Cn. Servilius Caepio (censor 125),
    138
Q. Servilius Caepio (consul 140),
    91

Q. Servilius Caepio (consul 106),
    143
Cn. Servilius Glaucia (praetor
    103), 143, 145
P. Servilius Isauricus (consul 79),
    181
P. Servilius Rullus, 171
Servius Tullius, 20, 22
Severus (L. Septimius Severus),
    316-21
Seviri Augustales, 235
L. Sextius, 59, 63
C. Sextius Calvinus, 92
Shapur, 325, 326
Sibylline Books, 356
Sicily, 12 (early settlements), 43
    (invaded by Pyrrhus), 67, 71-5
    (first Punic war), 81 (second
    Punic war), 112-13 (Roman
    administration), 130 (grain ex-
    ports), 133, 152-3 (slave rising),
    198 (civil war)
Sicoris R., 198
Side, 107
C. Silius, 254
slaves, 128-30, 152-3, 268, 274
Smyrna, 106
socii, 48-9
socii et amici, 112
Sohaemus, 299
Sosigenes, 202
C. Sosius, 216
Spain, 11 (Phoenician colonies),
    75-6 (Carthaginian conquests),
    81-3 (Scipios' campaigns), 89-
    92 (Roman conquest), 112-13
    (Roman administration), 130
    (silver), 180-1 (Sertorius' re-
    bellion), 196-7 (during civil
    war), 239 (under Augustus),
    271 (minerals), 284 (Latin
    status), 337 (overrun by bar-
    barians)
Spartacus, 165-6
Stabiae, 284
Statius Priscus, 299
Stephanus, 282
Stesichorus, 17

Stoics, 361
Sucro, 181
Suebi, 186, 187
C. Suetonius Paulinus, 265
Sulpicianus, 316
P. Sulpicius Galba, 99, 100, 118
S. Sulpicius Galba, 256, 275-7
P. Sulpicius Quirinius, 239
P. Sulpicius Rufus, 157-8
Suthul, 148
Syphax, 83
Syracuse, 70, 81
Syria, 97, 105, 182, 193, 366

Tacfarinas, 259
Tanaquil, 20
Tarentum, 35, 36, 41-4 (war with Rome), 70 (naval base), 80, 85, 98, 130, 215
Tarpeian Rock, 27
Tarquinius Priscus, 20
Tarquinius Superbus, 20
Tarracina, 38
Tarraco, 203
Telamon, 84-5
Tempe, 100
Tencteri, 188-9
M. Terentius Varro, 78
A. Terentius Varro Murena, 241
Tettius Iulianus, 287
Teuta, 98
Teutones, 150
Thapsus, 200-1
Theodosius I, 336
Theodosius II, 336
Thermopylae, 101
Thessaly, 97, 99, 101, 199
Thurii, 42
Tiber R., 5, 8, 24
Tiberius (Ti. Claudius Nero), 214, 288-9 (mission to Armenia), 240 (in Germany), 242 (on Danube), 249 (succession to Augustus), 250-2 (rule), 275 (late absence from active service)
Tiberius Alexander, 278-9
Tiberius Gemellus, 253

Ticinus R., 77
Tigellinus — Ofonius
Tigranes I, 176-80, 182
Tigranes II, 238-9
Tigranes V, 262
Tigranocerta, 179
Tigurini, 151
Tiridates I of Armenia, 262
Tities, 20
Titus (T. Flavius Vespasianus), 281, 285 (captures Jerusalem)
Titus Tatius, 20
Tolumnius, 32
C. Traianus Decius, 325
Trajan (M. Ulpius Traianus), 288, 289, 298 (Armenia)
Trasimene L., 78
L. Trebellius, 169
Trebia R., 78
C. Trebonianus Gallus, 325
C. Trebonius, 193, 206, 212
triarii, 45, 152
Tribal Assembly, 62, 119 (constitution), 162-3 (Sulla's reforms)
tribuni aerarii, 167, 168
tribuni celerum, 28
tribuni militum, 28, 56
tribuni plebis, 56, 66, 163, 340
tribunicia potestas, 228, 340
tribus, 25
tribus rustica, 55
tribus urbana, 55
tributum, 115
Trinovantes, 189
triumvirate, first, 175, 191-2
triumvirate, second, 211
M. Tullius Cicero, 167-8 (origins), 169 (supports Lex Manilia), 170 (against Crassus' designs on Egypt), 170-1 (elected consul), 172 (Catiline conspiracy), 174-5 (and Caesar), 192 (assault on triumvirate), 196 (negotiates between Caesar and Pompey), 201 (pardoned by Caesar), 206 (and death of Caesar), 207, 209 (after death

of Caesar), 209 (attack on Antony)
Q. Tullius Cicero, 189
Tullius Hostilius, 20
Turdetani, 89
Tuscany, 11, 12-16
Twelve Tables, 56, 57-8, 124

Ulpius Marcellus, 315
M. Ulpius Traianus — Trajan
Usipetes, 188-9
Utica, 94, 95

Valens, 336
Valentia, 92
Valentinian, 336
Valeria Messalina, 254
Valerian (P. Licinius Valerianus), 325-6
M. Valerius, 60
L. Valerius Flaccus (consul 86), 162, 177
M. Valerius Laevinus, 98
Valerius Licianus Licinius, 333
Valerius Maximinus Daia, 333
M'. Valerius Messala (consul 263), 72
M. Valerius Messala (consul 31), 239, 241
Q. Varius, 147
Varro, 17
Vatican Hill, 7
P. Vatinius, 175, 191, 204
Veii, 32
Velia, 8
Veneti (of Italy), 9
Veneti (of Gaul), 188
P. Ventidius, 210, 216
Venusia, 40
Vercellae, 151
Vercingetorix, 189-90
P. Vergilius Maro, 17
L. Verginius Rufus, 276
C. Verres, 167
Vesontio, 187

Vespasian (T. Flavius Vespasianus), 260 (campaigns against Jews), 264 (in Britain), 278-9 (rivalry with Mucianus), 280-1 (succession), 281-2 (opposition), 282-3 (rule), 287 (in Germany)
Vesta, 355
Vestal Virgins, 27, 54
Vestini, 154
Vesuvius, Mount, 284
Vetera, 279
Via Appia, 38, 168, 367
Via Aurelia, 85
Via Egnatia, 104
Via Flaminia, 78, 85, 233
Via Latina, 47
Via Valeria, 155
C. Vibius Pansa, 209-10
vicomagistri, 235
Viminal Hill, 7
Vindelici, 242
M. Vipsanius Agrippa, 213 (in Perusine war), 215 (defeats S. Pompeius), 232, 239 (in Spain and Gaul), 245 (tours provinces), 248-9 (proposed succession to Augustus), 367-70 (public works in Rome)
Vipsanius Agrippa Postumus, 249
Virgil — Vergilius
Viriathus, 91
Virius Lupus, 317
A. Vitellius, 277-8
Vologeses I, 262, 288
Vologeses III, 299
Volsci, 31-2
Volturnus R., 37, 38

Xanthippus, 74

Zama Regis, 84
Zela, 179
Zenobia, 327-9
Zuyda, Lake, 240